The World of the Theatre

The World

Robert W. Corrigan
The University of Wisconsin—Milwaukee

Scott, Foresman and Company
Glenview, Illinois
Dallas, Tex.
Oakland, N.J.
Palo Alto, Cal.
Tucker, Ga.
London, England

of the Theatre

Nothing, in fact, more truly portrays us
as we are and as we could be
than the play and the players.

Miguel de Cervantes, **Don Quixote**

With love to JoAnn

Library of Congress Cataloging in Publication Data

Corrigan, Robert Willoughby, 1927–
    The world of the theatre.

    Bibliography
    Index
    1. Theater. 2. Drama. I. Title.
PN1655.C63   792   78-10426
ISBN 0-673-15107-7

1 2 3 4 5 6 7-MUR-84 83 82 81 80 79 78

Cover: *King Lear*, directed by Ed Sherin at the Delacorte Theatre in New York City's Central Park. Presented by the New York Shakespeare Festival, the production was designed by Santo Loquasto and starred James Earl Jones. Photo by Fredda Slavin.

Acknowledgments

Chapter 1 Atkinson—Brooks Atkinson. *Broadway*. New York: Macmillan Co., 1970, p. 418.   Jones—Robert Edmond Jones. *The Dramatic Imagination*. New York: Theatre Arts Books, 1941, pp. 72, 83.   Langer—Excerpt from *Feeling and Form* by Susanne K. Langer. Copyright © 1953 by Charles Scribner's Sons. Reprinted by permission of Charles Scribner's Sons, p. 307.   Schechner—Richard Schechner. *Environmental Theater*. New York: Hawthorn Books, Inc., 1973, p. 319.   Serban—From "Chekhov Without Tears" by Jack Kroll, from *Newsweek* Magazine (February 1977). Copyright 1977 by Newsweek, Inc. All rights reserved. Reprinted by permission.   Wilder—From "Some Thoughts on Playwrighting" by Thornton Wilder in *The Intent of the Artist*, edited by Augusto Centeno. Copyright 1941 by Princeton University Press. Copyright renewed 1969 by Thornton Wilder.
Chapter 2 Barrault—Jean-Louis Barrault. *The Theatre of Jean-Louis Barrault*. London: Barrie and Rockliff, 1961, pp. 3, 4, 76–77.   Eliade—Mircea Eliade. *No Souvenirs*. New York: Harper and Row Publishers, Inc., 1977, p. 16.   Mircea Eliade. *Patterns in Comparative Religion*. New York: Sheed and Ward, Inc., 1958, p. 392.   Mircea Eliade. *Shamanism*. New York: Bollingen Foundation, 1964, pp. 179–80.   Goldman—Michael Goldman. *The Actor's Freedom*. New York: Viking Press, 1975, pp. 47, 154.   Sendak—"Caldecott Award Acceptance" by Maurice Sendak. Reprinted from *The Horn Book Magazine*, August 1964. Copyright © 1964 by The Horn Book, Inc.   Spitz—René A. Spitz. "Life and the Dialogue." Herbert S. Gaskill, ed. *Counterpoint: Libidinal Object and Subject*. New York: International Universities Press, Inc., 1963, pp. 170–71.
Chapter 3 Butcher, Fergusson—Francis Fergusson. "Introduction" to Aristotle's *Poetics*, translated by S. H. Butcher. New York: Hill and Wang, 1961, pp. 8, 9.   Farrington—Conor A. Farrington. "The Language of Drama." *The Tulane Drama Review*, 1960.   Magarshack—

David Magarshack. *Stanislavsky on the Art of the Stage*. New York: Hill and Wang, 1961, pp. 25–26.   Rahner—Hugo Rahner. *Man at Play*. New York: Herder and Herder, 1965, p. 65.   Trilling—Lionel Trilling. *The Experience of Literature*. New York: Doubleday & Co., 1967.   Vilar—Jean Vilar. *The Tradition of the Theatre*. Paris: L'Arch, 1955.

Chapter 4 Bentley—From *The Life of the Drama* by Eric Bentley. © 1964 by Eric Bentley. Reprinted by permission of Atheneum Publishers and Laurence Pollinger Ltd., pp. 200–201, 229, 309, 353.   Birenbaum—Harvey Birenbaum. *Tragedy and Innocence*. San Jose: San Jose State University Press, 1977, p. 1.   de Montherlant—Henri de Montherlant. Cited by J. L. Styan. *Drama, Stage and Audience*. New York: Cambridge University Press, 1975, p. 71.   Fitzgerald—F. Scott Fitzgerald. Letter to his daughter cited in *The New York Times Book Review* by Robert Clurman, August 5, 1956.   Fry—From "A Playwright Speaks" by Christopher Fry. Copyright 1952 by Christopher Fry. Reprinted by permission of ACTAC (Theatrical & Cinematic) Ltd.   Goldman—Michael Goldman. *The Actor's Freedom*. New York: Viking Press, 1975, p. 19.   Heilman—"Tragedy and Melodrama: Versions of Experience" by Robert B. Heilman, from *Texas Quarterly* (Summer 1960). Copyright © 1960 by Robert B. Heilman. Reprinted by permission of Robert B. Heilman.   Langer—Excerpt from *Feeling and Form* by Susanne K. Langer. Copyright © 1953 by Charles Scribner's Sons. Reprinted by permission of Charles Scribner's Sons, p. 331.   Mann—Thomas Mann. *Last Essays*. New York: Alfred A. Knopf, Inc., 1958, p. 197.   Santayana—George Santayana. "The Comic Mask" and "Carnival" in *Comedy: Meaning and Form*, ed. by Robert W. Corrigan. San Francisco: Chandler Publishing Company, 1965, p. 78.   Stevenson—Robert Louis Stevenson. Cited in *The English Stage: 1850–1950* by Lynton Hudson. London: George G. Harrap & Co., Ltd., 1951, p. 110.   Webster—*The Duchess of Malfi* by John Webster in *John Webster and Cyril Tourneur*, Eric Bentley, editor. New York: Hill & Wang, 1956, p. 213.

Chapter 5 Ashley—Quote by Elizabeth Ashley from "People" section of *Time* Magazine, September 22, 1975. Reprinted by permission from *Time, The Weekly Newsmagazine*; Copyright Time Inc. 1975 and Elizabeth Ashley.   Barrault—Jean-Louis Barrault. *Reflections on the Theatre*. London: Rockliff Publishing Corporation, 1951, p. 124.   Burton—Hal Burton, editor. Interview with Richard Burton by Kenneth Tynan in *Acting in the Sixties*. London: British Broadcasting Corporation, 1970, p. 18.   Carnovsky, Cornell, Poitier—Lewis Funke and John E. Booth, editors. *Actors Talk About Acting*. New York: Avon Book Division, 1973, pp. 112, 132, 217.   Evans, Gielgud, Redgrave, Richardson—Hal Burton, editor. *Great Acting*. New York: Hill & Wang by arrangement with the British Broadcasting Corporation, 1967, pp. 133, 136, 143, 105–6, 64, 71–2.   Grotowski—Jerzy Grotowski. *Towards a Poor Theatre*. New York: Simon and Schuster, 1968, pp. 16, 209.   Kerr—Excerpt from "Her Magic Transforms an Unmagical Play" by Walter Kerr, from the *New York Times* (March 1976). © 1976 by the New York Times Company. Reprinted by permission.   Marowitz—Charles Marowitz. *The Method as Means*. London: Herbert Jenkins, Ltd., 1961, pp. 17, 42.   Olivier—Excerpt from an interview of Sir Laurence Olivier by Richard Meryman for *Life*. Copyright 1964 Time Inc. Used with permission.   Rosenberg—Harold Rosenberg. *Act and the Actor*. New York: The World Publishing Co., 1970, p. 4.   Scofield—From "The Player" by Lillian Ross and Helen Ross from *Actors on Acting*, New Revised Edition, edited by Toby Cole and Helen Krich Chinoy. Copyright © 1961 by Lillian Ross, copyright © 1962 by Lillian Ross and Helen Ross. Reprinted by permission of Simon & Schuster, a Division of Gulf & Western Corporation.   Southern—Richard Southern. *The Seven Ages of the Theatre*. New York: Hill & Wang, 1961, p. 23.   Worth—From "Irene Worth Talks About Art, Energy—Even Acting," by John Russell in the *New York Times*, February 5, 1976, p. 26. © 1976 by the New York Times Company. Reprinted by permission.

Chapter 6 Blackmur—R. P. Blackmur. *Language as Gesture*. New York: Harcourt Brace Jovanovich, Inc., 1952, p. 3.   Bolt—From the introduction to *Vivat! Vivat Regina!* by Robert Bolt. Copyright © 1971 by Robert Bolt. Reprinted by permission of Heinemann Educational Books Ltd. and Random House, Inc., pp. vii, viii.   Brecht—Bertolt Brecht. *Brecht on Theatre: 1933–1947*, edited and translated by John Willett. New York: Hill and Wang, 1964, pp. 116–17.   Eliot—From "Sweeney Agonistes" by T. S. Eliot from *Collected Poems (1909–1932)* by T. S. Eliot. Copyright 1930 by T. S. Eliot, Copyright 1934, 1936 by Harcourt, Brace and Company, Inc. Reprinted by permission of Harcourt Brace Jovanovich, Inc. and Faber and Faber, Ltd., Publishers.   Sartre—From *Sartre on Theatre* by Jean-Paul Sartre, translated from the French by Frank Jellinek, edited by Michel Contat and Michel Rybalka. Copyright © 1976 by Random House, Inc. Reprinted by permission of Pantheon Books, a division of Random House, Inc.   Shaffer—From "The Cannibal Theatre" by Peter Shaffer, from *The Atlantic Monthly* (October 1960). Copyright © 1960, by The Atlantic Monthly Company, Boston, Mass. Reprinted with permission of *The Atlantic Monthly* and The Lantz Office, Inc.

Chapter 7 Magarshack—David Magarshack. *Chekhov the Dramatist*. New York: Auvergne Publishers, 1952, p. 84.   Meyerhold—Vsevolod Meyerhold. *Meyerhold on Theatre*. New

York: Hill and Wang, 1969, p. 62.   Sontag—A selection from "Against Interpretation" from *Against Interpretation* by Susan Sontag. Copyright © 1964, 1966 by Susan Sontag. Reprinted with the permission of Farrar, Straus & Giroux, Inc.   Vilar—From "Murder of the Director" by Jean Vilar. First published in *The Drama Review*, Vol. 3, no. 2, December 1958. © 1958 by *The Drama Review*. Reprinted by permission. All Rights Reserved, p. 6.

Chapter 8   Clurman—From *Lies Like Truth* by Harold Clurman. © 1958 by Harold Clurman. Reprinted by permission of Macmillan Publishing Co., Inc., p. 278.   Duvignaud—Jean Duvignaud. "The Theatre in Society: Society in the Theatre" in *Sociology of Literature and Drama*, ed. by Elizabeth and Tom Burns. Middlesex: Penguin Books Ltd., 1973, p. 89. Eliade—Mircea Eliade. *The Sacred and the Profane*. New York: Harcourt Brace Jovanovich, Inc., 1959, p. 29.   Giedion—Siegfried Giedion. *Space, Time and Architecture*. Cambridge, Mass.: Harvard University Press, 1967, p. 31.   Jones—Robert Edmond Jones. *The Dramatic Imagination*. New York: Theatre Arts Books, 1941, pp. 69-70.   Mielziner—Jo Mielziner. *Designing for the Theatre*. New York: Bramhall House, 1965, pp. 18-19.   Schechner—Richard Schechner. "Towards a Poetics of Performance" as it appeared in *Alcheringa: Ethnopoetics*, edited by Michel Benamou and Jerome Rothenberg. Boston: Alcheringa/Boston University, 1976, p. 49.   Yates—Frances A. Yates. *Theatre of the World*. Chicago: The University of Chicago Press, 1969, p. 189.

Chapter 9   Carnovsky—Lewis Funke and John E. Booth, editors. Interview with Morris Carnovsky as it appeared in *Actors Talk About Acting*. New York: Avon Book Division, 1961, p. 127.   Clurman—From *Lies Like Truth* by Harold Clurman. © 1958 by Harold Clurman. Reprinted by permission of Macmillan Publishing Co., Inc.   Guthrie—Tyrone Guthrie. *A Life in the Theatre*. New York: McGraw-Hill Book Company, Inc., 1959, p. 350.   Jellicoe—Ann Jellicoe. *Some Unconscious Influences in the Theatre*. Cambridge: Cambridge University Press, 1967.   Schechner—Richard Schechner. "Towards a Poetics of Performance" as it appeared in *Alcheringa: Ethnopoetics*, edited by Michel Benamou and Jerome Rothenberg. Boston: Alcheringa/Boston University, 1976.   Trilling—Lionel Trilling. "All Aboard the Seesaw" as it appeared in *The Tulane Drama Review*, 1960.   Vilar—From "Secrets" by Jean Vilar, translated by Christopher Kotsching. First published in *The Drama Review*, Vol. 3, No. 3, March 1959. © 1959 by *The Drama Review*. Reprinted by permission. All Rights Reserved.   Jean Vilar. *The Tradition of the Theatre*. Paris: L'Arch, 1955.

Preface

The origins of this book date back to the fall of 1975 when I taught the Introduction to Theatre class at the University of Wisconsin—Milwaukee. In looking through the introductory textbooks that were available, I discovered that many were first-rate but were somehow lacking a governing idea of the theatre. Most of them did not deal with the many diverse elements of theatre from a clearly defined point of view, and the majority of them had an essentially literary/historical organization. They tended to approach theatre as performed works of literature within the context of theatre history. This is certainly a valid and time-honored approach to the subject. But too often it is an approach that does not capture the immediacy and excitement of going to the theatre. It does not adequately express the dynamic interaction that always exists between performers and audiences. In short, it cannot—or so it seems to me—capture the vital and tangible reality of our experience of the theatrical event.

Then there were the students. Who were they? What were their expectations? The students were a mixed bag. Some were theatre majors; most were majors in other fields who were satisfying distribution requirements; still others were there because they needed a class at that hour and theatre sounded interesting; some were there to meet women, some to meet men. But underlying all those reasons was a single expectation: All the members of the class were attracted to the idea of taking a theatre course which they hoped would be an exciting experience, one which would enhance what they knew or imagined theatre to be. So, I have written this book to introduce theatre as the exciting experience it is. I have written out of the conviction that the introductory course is the most important one in any theatre curriculum. It is here that the future practitioners of theatre are touched at an early point, and it is here that future audiences are formed. The course and text must, therefore, capture the liveliness of theatre as we actually experience it.

My concern has been to explore the nature of theatre as a direct and immediate experience. To this end, the chapters seek to answer in some detail these four basic questions:

1. What are the human impulses that lead to the creation of the theatrical event and what are the human needs fulfilled by our experience of that event?
2. What is the unique nature of the dramatic form and in what ways is that form made manifest in performance?
3. What is the nature of each of the elements that make up the theatre and how are they combined to create the theatrical event?
4. What is the nature of the audience's expectations and what relationship does the theatre have to the society of which it is a part?

I hope that in discovering why and how theatre takes place, each person who uses this book will be able to experience more fully and more deeply the central fact of every theatrical event—its vitality: the vitality of one's spirit being awakened; the vitality of the mind being forced to come to grips with alien aspects of experience; the vitality of the imagination as it seeks to encompass mystery; the vitality of the body that inevitably springs from the interaction of actors and audience.

The book is structured in the following way: The first three chapters deal with the nature of the theatrical event, the human impulses and needs that prompt the creation of theatre and are fulfilled by it, and the general ways in which plays are made or composed. Chapter 4 discusses the characteristics and view of life that govern each of the five major forms of drama in the Western theatre. The last five chapters deal with the role and contribution of each of the major participants in theatre—the actor, the playwright, the director, the designer, and the audience. The book has an annotated bibliography of readily available books pertinent to a general understanding of theatre. Two other editorial features are important to note. First, throughout the book you will find set off on the page numerous quotations by noted theatre artists, scholars, and critics. These passages sometimes support the ideas in the text, at times amplify them, and at still other times almost contradict them. They are included because I believe they are an interesting extension of the text. Second, the illustrations are occasionally grouped as photographic essays. These supply important visual information that words alone could not provide.

Finally, I have the pleasant task of acknowledging with thanks the many people who have played a role in bringing the book into being. First, the people who advised on the manuscript at some stage of its development: Vincent Angotti (Auburn University), Milly Barranger (Tulane University), Randall L. Edwards (Los Angeles City College), Earle R. Gister (City College of New York), Douglas Kerr (Fort Steilacoom Community College), Richard France (Lawrence University), Doyle McKinney (Saddleback Community College), and especially Hugh Dickinson (University of Illinois—Chicago Circle Campus) whose help with the manuscript throughout the whole process was invaluable. I must also mention Richard Huett, my good friend and now semi-retired former editor at Dell, who read the first draft and reacted with his usual stimulating and helpful comments.

My colleagues in the theatre department at the University of Wisconsin—Milwaukee have been most encouraging and supportive. Sanford Robbins not only read the manuscript, but also used a draft of the book as a text in one of his classes. This test run was a big help in shaping the final manuscript. Al Tucci, Maura Smolover, and E. J. Dennis were of great assistance in locating picture sources, and I am pleased to include examples of their work. Corliss Phillabaum was always generous in sharing his encyclopedic knowledge as well as his magnificent library. And of course there were the many students in my "Introduction" classes who were indirectly responsible for the whole project. I must also thank Chancellor Werner A. Baum and Vice-Chancellor William L. Walters, who made it possible for me to arrange my schedule so there was time to write.

I happily acknowledge my debt to Richard Schechner, Eric Bentley, David Cole, Michael Goldman, and—as always—my dear friend Herbert Blau. Their important explorations into the nature of theatre have significantly influenced my own and the mark of each of them will be found in what I have written.

I also want to thank the publishers of some of my earlier books—Dell, Houghton Mifflin, and Macmillan—who gave me permission to revise a few passages in those books for inclusion in this one. Thanks, too, to the many people who let me use their photographs. Without their generous and gracious assistance, an essential part of the book could not have been realized.

There is always a small core of people who are indispensable. My students, Jan Gaetano, who helped with picture research, and Sandy Hays, who handled the arduous job of text permissions, worked many long hours and their efforts have contributed much to the final form of the book. But without a doubt the most important person in the whole enterprise was my wonderful secretary, Margaret Rotter, who typed the manuscript. She had to decipher my illegible handwriting from my first rough notes to the final version of the manuscript—a task that makes all words of gratitude insufficient.

Finally, my thanks to the staff of Scott, Foresman, and especially to Richard Welna and Joanne Trestrail, who made the writing of this book a pleasurable and exciting adventure, and to JoAnn Johnson, who originally conceived the project and then guided it from start to finish.

Robert W. Corrigan
Milwaukee

Contents

The World of the Theatre

The theatre is . . . a bright enigma.

What it produces is not a "product."

    It produces moods, dreams, ideas, beauty, imagined characters.

    It is a form of incantation.

If the dialogue in a play, if the movement of the actors,

if the personalities of the actors, if the scenery and sound

    do not lay a spell on the audience, they have no value,

    no matter how admirable they may be in themselves.

A successful production has to beguile several hundred strangers every performance

    into becoming a community of believers.

Although the theatre is not life, it is composed of fragments or imitations of life,

    and people on both sides of the footlights have to unite

    in making the fragments whole and the imitations genuine . . .

because every production begins with a vision of something that never existed before.

Brooks Atkinson, **Broadway**

Chapter 1
The Theatrical Event

THAT'S ENTERTAINMENT

Yaou and a friend are going to the theatre. You've had a good
dinner together and are rushing down the crowded street to
get to the box office to pick up your tickets. As you enter the
theatre's lobby, you are conscious of people milling about, chatting,
waiting—there is an atmosphere of expectancy and a special kind
of excitement. You get your tickets, turn them in at the door, and
enter at the back of the brightly lit auditorium and wait for the usher
to take you to your seats. Program in hand, you gradually settle
down and begin to look about to see who else is in the theatre. There
is talking and more milling as people take their seats. Soon—the
theatre now nearly filled—you begin to read the program; the
theatre becomes quieter and people look up at the stage in anticipation. An undifferentiated crowd of people has become an audience with special appetites and expectations it is ready to have
fulfilled by the actors who have the task of satisfying them. The
houselights dim. The curtain is dazzlingly bright and the theatre is
hushed. The curtain rises. It is that special moment in the theatre
referred to as "magic time." It is a time of transformation when
"something that never existed before" comes to life, each time as if
for the first time. At that moment entertainment begins, that
dynamic interaction between the world of the audience and the
world of the stage which must exist if the theatrical event is to take
place.

As the performance starts, you realize you are experiencing
something quite different from anything you experience in your
everyday life. In fact, the world unfolding on the stage is unlike any
world you know. No matter how realistic the setting may appear to
be, it has an aura of unreality about it (no living room ever *really*
looked that way) and the details of the decor almost pop out at you
with a special kind of potency. The actors are certainly recognizable
as human beings, yet there is something uncanny and inhuman
about them, too. They are people being *other* people, and they are
playing other people with the consciousness they do it for people
watching. Even the dialogue, no matter how natural it sounds, is
unlike any conversation you've ever heard outside the theatre;
people just don't talk that way. In short, there is something strange
about the whole experience and this uncanny strangeness is a central fact of all theatre.

You probably have had a limited experience of "live" theatre.
Perhaps you've been to the senior-class play at high school, attended a few college productions, been to a nearby summer or
dinner theatre, or seen a few professional companies. No matter
what your experience of the theatre has been, it is important to
realize that the desire to participate in theatre seems to spring from
certain basic human impulses and to fulfill other equally basic
needs. Theatre has existed in some form since the beginning of

recorded history, and while it may appear in many different guises, it is always recognizable as theatre. There is something remarkably stable about the nature of the theatrical event.

If, for instance, you were to go back through time to the theatre festivals in Greece in the fifth century B.C., what would you discover? On the plains of Epidaurus there is a huge outdoor amphitheatre seating nearly 20,000 people surrounding a large circular playing space or performance area called an *orchestra*. It was both a religious and civic duty for every free citizen to attend the performances presented there in honor of the gods. The plays, based on ancient legends, were performed in daylight by actors wearing masks and elaborate, larger-than-life costumes. Most of the actors sang and danced as members of the chorus. The principal actors—never more than three—spoke the lines of dialogue in a formal, almost operatic, fashion. There was little or no scenery and very few stage effects. The performance was quite unlike what we associate with the theatre today. Yet this event would be immediately recognizable as theatre—as anyone knows who has ever attended a contemporary re-creation of the Greek tragedies in one of those ancient theatres. Whenever actors and an audience come together to interact, the theatrical event comes into being.

We would discover the same thing if we were to attend a performance of a Shakespearean play at the Globe Theatre outside London at the end of the sixteenth century. This theatre was no longer religious in nature, but was a form of popular entertainment. The plays were based on historical accounts and legends of the monarchs and heroes of British history and on well-known stories. The theatre building was smaller, without a roof, open to the sky, and the boisterous audience—made up of everyone from noble lords to commoners selling oranges—moved inside for the afternoon performance. Compared to the simple playing floor of the Greek theatre, the Elizabethan stage was complex. The action took place on many different levels, often simultaneously. The masks of the Greek theatre were gone, the costumes were much closer to the clothes worn in daily life, and there were realistic stage effects. But this kind of theatre would be strange to us, too. The actors moved in

When the curtain rises we feel a frenzy of excitement focused like a burning-glass upon the actors. Everything on the stage becomes a part of the life of the instant.... The terrible and wonderful **dynamis** of the theatre pours over the footlights.

Robert Edmond Jones, **The Dramatic Imagination**

measured ways and often spoke in verse; the women's roles were played by boys; and performances went on for hours with numerous interruptions and a great deal of socializing in the audience. But again, we would have no trouble recognizing this experience as theatre: actors coming together to enact a story for an audience.

Theatre has assumed varied shapes throughout history, from performances at the Royal Court of Versailles in seventeenth-century France to the popular melodramas of nineteenth-century London to the jazzy cabaret theatres in Berlin in the 1920s. Each variety is very different from the others, yet much the same. The theatre has had many faces and taken on different forms. Like a chameleon it is always changing. This is true because the theatre reflects the society in which it takes place. As customs and manners, life-styles and fashions, values and public attitudes have changed throughout history, the theatre has mirrored those changes. But its continuing power and appeal reside in the constant of every theatrical event: actors playing to an audience.

The same is true today. We have a bewildering mix of theatrical forms from the bright, large-scale, and frankly commercial Broadway musical to the far-out, seemingly incomprehensible experimental production in some out-of-the-way loft. As in the past, this broad range reflects the diverse nature of our society. But for all their differences, these theatrical forms have certain similarities, as do our experiences of them as members of an audience. A performance of *Hair* on a college campus may seem far removed from the citizens of Athens participating in a production at the Festival of Dionysus, but those experiences are inseparably linked by elements that are a part of all theatre, no matter what its time or place.

WHAT IS THE THEATRICAL EVENT?

The opening lines of Shakespeare's *Hamlet* are:

Who's there?
Nay, answer me. Stand and unfold yourself.

Who really is up there on the stage? And who is out there in the auditorium, that crowd transformed into an audience? What is being unfolded on the stage? Already we know it is unlike the world as we usually experience it, but just what kind of "world" is revealed to us each time a theatrical performance takes place? It is a realm of spirits and demons, of wild fantasy and soaring aspiration. It is a place of foreboding darkness and brightest light. It is a world of fear and loss and also one of triumph and joyous fulfillment. To enter this world is to enter a realm of mystery, and the moment at which we do so is truly a "magic time" of the most profound kind.

This experience—the theatrical event itself and our experience of the other world it creates—is the subject of this book. Our purpose will be to explore what Brooks Atkinson, long-time drama critic of the *New York Times*, referred to as "a bright enigma," to seek out answers to those basic questions the theatre presents us with every time it takes place, whether it involves a chic New York audience attending the opening of a new play on Broadway; a group of students at a college production; a handful of people working improvisationally in some out-of-the-way theatre in London or Minneapolis; or a crowd of thousands sitting on the plains of Epidaurus in Greece watching a performance of a Sophoclean tragedy first produced in the same theatre more than 2,500 years ago. These questions are evoked by every theatrical event, whether it be a production of a Shakespearean tragedy or an extravagant Broadway musical, an aristocratic Japanese Nōh drama or Neil Simon's latest comedy. Considering these questions will help us understand our experience of both the "bright enigma" and the dark heart of mystery presented every time the lights dim and the curtain opens.

We have used the term "theatrical event" several times in these opening pages. Just what do we mean by it? The first thing we are conscious of when we think about the nature of any theatrical event is how many dissimilar elements are combined to create it. Living actors interact with each other. There is usually a script—although there need not be one—that has been written for the actors by a playwright. Words are spoken and sounds uttered with varying degrees of tone, pitch, and intensity. There are broad, decisive movements and gestures as subtle as the flutter of an eyelid. There may be mime or, occasionally, dance. And there are variations on each of these from one performance to another, making each performance unique. All this activity takes place in a special environment created by a scene designer, and that environment includes everything from the simplest stage props to the most elaborate settings. Special lighting not only illuminates the playing area, but creates meaning and mood as well. There may be sound effects and special music. Costumes give characters their identities and disguise them at the same time. All these elements are shaped, coordinated, and given focus by a director. The environment and the atmosphere of the theatre building itself (a small, intimate room or a vast auditorium) influence the quality of the theatrical occasion. Finally, and most important, there is the phenomenon of people coming together to perform in the presence of other people who have come to watch that performance.

All of these elements, involving a rather large group of people, are combined to create what we mean by a theatrical event. Clearly, theatre is a highly complex art form. But in spite of the complexity, people of all ages, social classes, and levels of sophistication have always found the theatre accessible and important to their lives.

We tend to associate the theatrical event with the great dramas written throughout history—Sophocles' *Oedipus the King*, Shakespeare's *Hamlet*, Ibsen's *Hedda Gabler*, and Chekhov's *The Cherry Orchard*, for example. But the idea of theatre is much broader than this. It has also been associated with religious ritual, primitive exorcism, circuses, communal celebrations, courtly masques and processions, political and social ceremonies, seasonal festivals, popular entertainments, impersonation, and pageantry. The list could go on and on. All these occasions have one thing in common: one or more performers and an audience come together.

Consider the importance of theatre to every culture in history: the entire free population of Athens attended the performances of the Dionysian festivals in the fifth century B.C.; in the Middle Ages players regularly performed interludes (indoor entertainments that sometimes included singing and dancing) for the nobles in their castles and less formal entertainments for the common folk in the streets; in Asia theatrical performance has always played an important role in community life; during Elizabethan times Shakespeare and his contemporaries were as popular with the members of the lower class (known as the "groundlings") as they were with the aristocracy; King Louis XIV may have been Molière's patron in seventeenth-century France, but Molière appealed every bit as much to the audiences in the provinces as he did to those at the palace of Versailles; in Victorian England theatre was the major form of popular entertainment and in the 1880s there were more than 150 theatres in London alone.

In our own time, thousands of people attend performances of Shakespeare's plays in New York City's Central Park (not to mention the many other Shakespeare festivals) throughout the summer. Large audiences of migrant farm workers regularly attend the performances of the *Teatro Campesino* as it travels up and down the state of California. Theatre festivals of all kinds take place in many cities and towns throughout the world. Countless people are excited by the transformation of their friends and neighbors in community and school theatres. Theatre in all its many forms continues to be a flourishing institution.

The fact is, the theatre has been a major form of human expression in every culture and society throughout all of human history, and no matter how the world changes, the nature of the theatrical event and our response to it remain fundamentally the same. Theatre thrives in times of peace and also in times of tyranny, war, and military occupation; it flourishes in periods of economic collapse as well as in eras of prosperity; it takes place in prisons, concentration camps, and mental hospitals at the same time that it prospers on the boulevards of the great cities of the world; it survives periods of extreme repression and rigorous censorship, times of apathy and indifference, and outbursts of revolution and social upheaval. In short, there have always been strong and persisting impulses prompting the theatrical event and equally strongly felt human needs that are fulfilled by it.

Why is this? If every theatrical performance presents another world and if a central fact of our experience of the theatrical event is its uncanny strangeness, why do we have such a persistent need to be in contact with that strangeness?

It is precisely because the theatre does make manifest the other world of mystery that it has always had a powerful hold upon our imaginations. Ultimately, a central concern of all human beings has been to deal with the mysteries of life. Why are we here? Where did we come from? How to be? The nature and definition of mystery may differ from culture to culture and may change from age to age because our experience proves that what was once considered mysterious need not be so. While the relationship of our planet to the sun is no longer much of a mystery, for example, there are certain abiding questions in human life which we can never totally understand or explain in rational terms no matter how hard we might try.

This may make theatre sound remote and mysterious and difficult to understand, but in our daily lives most of us have experiences that have much in common with the experience of theatre.

THE THEATRICAL IN EVERYDAY LIFE

The strange, the unexpected, the unplanned makes us uncomfortable when we meet it in daily life. One remarkable characteristic of the human imagination is the fact that when we confront an unfamiliar situation, we invariably perceive it as having a theatrical quality and we tend to react to it in theatrical terms. When we travel in foreign countries and observe what is, to us, alien behavior, it is almost like watching a play. For example, the wailing and keening of women in mourning in Sicily or Greece would strike most of us as unbelievably excessive—as if no one would put on such an intense display of grief for so long. If we were to witness a tribal ceremony in Africa, New Guinea, or the jungles of South America, we would experience it as theatre and not as the religious rite it actually is. Even in societies with customs more like our own, we experience the same thing. To people visiting a London court for the first time, the special robes, wigs, and ceremonial behavior may seem as much a theatrical performance as the play they saw the night before in the Shakespearean Theatre in Stratford-on-Avon. We don't have to go to foreign lands to have this experience. For most non-Roman Catholics, the celebration of a High Mass (particularly if it is said in Latin) is a kind of pageant. The same thing could be true of a Polish polka festival, a jet-set discothèque, a Greek Orthodox wedding, an Amish community, a Quaker meeting, a political convention, a congressional hearing, or even an ethnic bar. The fact is, as long as we are outsiders, all unfamiliar customs and behavior will appear theatrical to us. We are like spectators at a play. But it is equally clear that all these strange goings-on seem perfectly natural to those who believe, practice, and participate in them.

What happens when circumstances make it impossible for us to remain outside the action? Sometimes, whether we like it or not, we have to give up our spectator role and become a participant. Again, we perceive both ourselves and our behavior in theatrical terms. We become actors; we imitate what we believe is expected behavior in order to fit in. Think of how children "act" as they must increasingly participate in a grown-up world. What do freshmen do when they get to college and discover that all those clothes they got with their parents are horribly wrong and conspicuous? They put them away, go down to a campus clothing store, and get the kind of clothes worn by upperclassmen. We put on costumes as a way of mastering an unfamiliar world. A similar pattern of behavior occurs whenever we must enter a new world as a participant, whether it be a new job, a new social milieu, or the learning of a new dance or game. Acting is a means of mastering a new and unknown reality.

There is yet another way in which we perceive ourselves theatrically. Some experiences overwhelm us or are too difficult for us to handle directly. As a result we step out of ourselves and behave somewhat as if we were actors in a play. There are accounts of people whose grief was so great at the death of a loved one that the only way they could get through the funeral was to transform the occasion into a play in which they were the central actors performing grief for the attending "audience." Something similar occurs to many people when they serve on a jury—particularly in murder trials. The responsibility of passing judgment on a fellow human being becomes too much for them so they create a role that will help them to get through the experience.

Or to take one more example, relatively few people are ever arrested or put in jail; the closest most of us come to that experience is to be stopped for speeding. But even that experience is so unnerving that often in the few moments before we must confront the police officer, we prepare a little play, complete with dialogue,

1

1. Queen Elizabeth II's coronation in 1953. The Archbishop of Canterbury is about to place the crown on the queen's head, she having been invested with the royal robes and scepters. To most Americans, a coronation is a lavish ceremonial drama—it was watched by millions on TV as a theatrical event—but to her loyal British subjects, the new queen has symbolically taken on the sacred power of the monarchy.

2. Former President Nixon standing on top of his car greeting the crowd after his meeting with Pope Paul VI at the Vatican in 1970. Not having the ceremonies of monarchy, leaders of democratic countries sometimes invent their own. Because they are invented, there is something inauthentic about them: they lack the validating power of inherited ritual. Hence, we also view such behavior as theatrical.

2

3

3. Convicts being led back to their prison cells. The photographer, Danny Lyon, has captured the essentially dramatic nature of parades and processions. Like theatre, they are celebratory. They give significance to an occasion, an accomplishment, an event, social status, or political power. While returning to their cells is only a daily routine for the prisoners, and far from theatrical, the photograph has a theatrical quality to it because we view it as a procession.

4. The march to Montgomery, Alabama, during a voter registration drive in 1965. The late Dr. Martin Luther King had a deep understanding of theatricality and its power to move people. Here the innately theatrical nature of the procession is consciously used to dramatize American blacks' struggle for equal civil rights. Participants in such processions were aware of themselves as actors in one of the nation's most significant dramas.

4

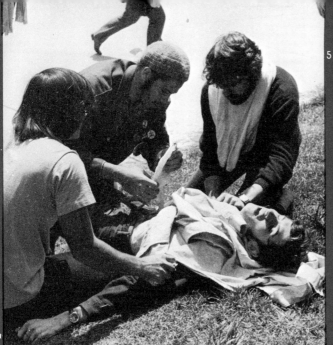

5

TAGE ALL THE WORLD'S A S

5. Shooting at Kent State University, 1970. In the late 1960s and early 1970s there were countless demonstrations on college campuses protesting United States military involvement in Southeast Asia. These were essentially theatrical forms of activity. But the lines between life and art often broke down. In theatre we experience protest, violence, and struggle without threat. Conflict on stage is only an illusion. That is the source of its meaning and power. However, when we theatricalize everyday life, there is always the danger that violence will become actual, resulting in death and suffering.

6. A brawl on ice. Many sports are a form of ritualized violence. They are based on conflict within a context of clearly defined rules. In this respect, all games are like theatre. However, the lines between the real and the theatrical are often and easily blurred. The violence becomes actual, the rules are broken, and suffering and injuries regularly occur. Many spectators are attracted to those sporting events where the line between ritual and actual violence hardly exists. Under these conditions, athletes are often referred to as gladiators.

6

7

7. Kiss performs. One of the reasons for the popularity of many rock groups is that their performance embodies some of our most bizarre fantasies. The outlandish costumes, surreal makeup, and wild antics (usually sexual) on stage are theatricalized expressions of our desire to flout the codes of socially accepted behavior. The very nature of the performance—blinding lights, overpowering sound, bright colors—assures us that we can get caught up in the rhythmic spirit of anarchic revolt without risk of consequence.

8. Kids made up like Kiss. The very perversity of many rock groups has long been a lure to their largely teen-age audience. The fact that parents don't understand or relate to these acts makes them all the more important to their faithful followers. In making up like their heroes on the stage, the audience expresses its desire to identify with them. They put on an act to become one with the actors.

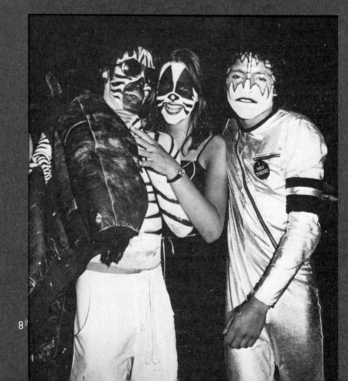

8

gestures, and facial expressions. Unfortunately, the officer is usually an experienced audience of this kind of play, so our performance fails.

Finally, we are aware of the many roles—roles not necessarily related to each other or to the person we think we are—that we play as an actor plays roles. We know how important "make believe" and "play" are to our lives, not just as children but in our adult behavior and fantasies as well. We realize that our lives are frequently judged in such theatrical terms as "good show," "great performance," "get your act together," "you were really on tonight," etc. The point is, the more you think about it, the more aware you become of how much of life is perceived, experienced, and judged in theatrical terms. There is a theatricality in all human action.

This is more true today than ever before in history. In fact, given the pervasive presence of television, almost everything about our lives is instantly theatricalized. Television has made us very sophisticated in the ways of watching and being watched. The planning of presidential and other political campaigns is largely directed by media advisors who turn the political process into a carefully composed dramatic scenario. We experience war, landings on the moon, sporting events, and natural disasters as theatrical events that have been channeled into our living rooms. Most of us see more "drama" on the tube in a week than people of earlier generations would go to in a lifetime.

Yet television has been an alienating force as well. It lacks a sense of occasion and festival (even the "specials" are not so special any more), and it fails to provide the experience of relished joy and community, or the powerful confrontation of ourselves we have when we are presented by others. Our society may have been "dramatized" by television but our lives nonetheless seem to lack real drama. Those shadows on the screen are disturbingly unreal. Think of how unreal it is for the President of the United States to explain his plans and policies to us in the privacy of our own homes. Perhaps more important, because television distorts reality by accommodating human behavior to the demands of the medium, the world that it presents tends to estrange us from our own experience. The more the world is made present via television, the more complicated and strange the world becomes. As a result, today we have a greater need to organize and master strangeness than ever before and this probably accounts for the increasing theatricality of our everyday lives. Our clothes have become costumes; both sexes wear carefully applied makeup; our homes—direct from the pages of *House Beautiful*—are stage sets; our conversations are little dialogues, and much of our public behavior is a well-calculated performance. If we think about it, we come to recognize that much of everyday life has theatrical qualities—we are all like people acting in a play.

ALL THE WORLD'S A STAGE

However, this is not something unique to life today. Human beings have always thought of their lives in theatrical terms and images. One of the oldest metaphors to express the fundamental nature of human experience is voiced by the melancholy Jaques in Shakespeare's *As You Like It:*

> All the world's a stage,
> And all the men and women merely players.

From the beginnings of history and in almost every known culture, a dominant image of humanity's view of itself is that we play our lives out as if on stage following a script not of our own making before an audience of our fellow human beings. No matter how boldly each of us may assert that "I am the master of my fate; I am the captain of my soul," we are nonetheless haunted by a nagging sense that there are unseen, undefined, or unknowable forces that shape our lives; that there is a script of someone else's making which directs what happens to us; that no matter how deeply involved we may be in our ordinary, everyday lives, our experience is unreal, or at least it could be more real; that no matter how close to other people we may be, we really do not know them; that, in fact, we can never really know ourselves.

While we can acknowledge the unreal and theatrical nature of much of our everyday lives, the idea still makes us uncomfortable and sometimes downright hostile. People tend to describe, and often judge, everyday experience in terms of the arts, and it is revealing to compare the positive tone inspired by most of the arts with the negative tone inspired by theatre. We refer to landscapes as "poetic," an individual's struggle with adversity as "epic," a beautiful body as "statuesque," graceful movements as "balletic," a woman's beauty as "lyric," a powerful image as "graphic," any kind of happy blending together of diverse elements as "symphonic," and so on. Invariably metaphors from the arts tend to have positive and flattering connotations. But just think of those that come from the theatre-related arts! When life experience is described as "theatrical," "operatic," "melodramatic," or "stagey," the connotation is usually hostile and reveals our feelings that somehow the experience is insincere or phony and therefore not to be trusted. Certainly, when we use such expressions as "he's not for real—he's just playing a part," "putting on an act," "playing up to," "making a scene," "making a spectacle of oneself," or "playing to the gallery," we are usually indicating disapproval or implying some personal shortcoming. The negative tone of these expressions reveals a deep-seated prejudice against the theatre. Why is this?

On the conscious level it is probably due to the fact that while we may experience life in theatrical terms, we abhor the thought that we are helpless puppets performing in a play over which we have no control. We believe or want to believe that we make choices that control our lives. We know that we do have an effect on the lives of other people that cannot be predetermined. While we acknowledge the fact that we play many different roles in life (a person may be a father, son, husband, brother, student, and employee at the same time), we believe that role-playing in life is not the same thing as what actors do in the theatre. In short, no matter how apt the idea that "all the world's a stage" may seem, we feel it does not express how our life really is. But this does not fully explain our negative feelings toward the theatre.

There is probably a deeper and largely unconscious reason for our strongly held prejudice, and it has the same roots as those impulses that make the theatre attractive to us. Most of us, most of the time, have to go about the business of living without giving too much thought to life's mysteries. There's homework to do, a job to think about, obligations to meet, bills to pay. We haven't time for mysteries. But our private fears have a way of creeping into our consciousness no matter how busy we are with our mundane daily tasks. They keep coming back to haunt us. We may attempt to escape or to be distracted from their disturbing presence—with work, drugs, alcohol, shopping, indiscriminate sex, food—and we sometimes try to deal with them in more creative and constructive ways such as entering into some form of psychiatric therapy or sincerely embracing a religious belief. Because these mysteries haunt us, we have always used our imaginations in an effort to find some way of dealing with them. We create imaginative constructs to explain the mysterious in the hopes that we may thus be able to control it. Art, religion, philosophy, and science are some of these imaginative constructs. So is the theatre. But it is one of a very special kind.

THE NATURE OF THE THEATRICAL METAPHOR

We have suggested that everything about the theatre implies another world—a world related to our everyday life as we live it, but different from that life in many significant ways. We do not need to be experienced and sophisticated playgoers to know this. What we witness on the stage is an imaginative, invented reality that is recognizable but unlike what we experience outside the theatre.

Our need for imaginative worlds to sustain, enrich, and explain our lives is underscored by the fact that we are metaphor-making creatures. A metaphor suggests a similarity or common power between two dissimilar aspects of our experience. For example, when Creon says in his opening speech in Sophocles' *Antigone:*

> I have the honor to inform you that our Ship of State, which recent storms have threatened to destroy, has come safely to harbor at last. . .

he is comparing the navigation of a ship to the process of governing, and the trials and tribulations that the City of Thebes has gone through with the stormy weather of the seas. The two worlds—politics and the seas—are not necessarily directly related to each other, but in this metaphor they are transformed into a new image with great communicative powers. Every time we forge a metaphor we create an imaginative reality which is, in fact, another world. To paraphrase the Spanish playwright Federico García Lorca, the poet links two antagonistic worlds with a metaphor, and by a leap of imagination creates a new universe. No one, for instance, would confuse an apple with the sea; but Lorca said that for the poet

> the apple and the sea evoke the same response; for he knows that the world of the apple is as infinite as the world of the sea. The span of the apple, from the time of its flowering till it falls from the tree to the grass in a burnish, is as great and mysterious as the measured rhythms of the tides.[1]

The theatre is such a metaphoric form of expression.

Of course, this is true of all the arts. Artists—poets and painters, filmmakers and composers, sculptors and dancers—are "makers" of other worlds. No matter how much these created worlds may resemble the "real" world, they are not the same. They are the products of the artist's imagination. They are metaphors. An artist takes the chaos, complexity, contradiction, and inconclusiveness of actual experience and creates a work in which the inconsistencies of life are made whole and coherent. The created realm of imaginative truth is different from the seeable and graspable present reality that we experience every day. The artist's combination of temperament, imagination, and the capacity to create form enables him or her to impose a meaning and order on the fragments of our lives so we can experience them as whole.

Artists are dedicated explorers who cross the frontiers of our common life and enter into the uncharted areas of human experience. They make maps for us which celebrate the best and the worst, the most beautiful and the most painful experiences men and women have thought and felt. But maps are abstractions. While they may guide us, they are far different from what we actually experience when we ourselves enter the terrain. A map of the city or town we live in is composed of grids, street names, colors, and irregular shapes designating parks, lakes, and so forth. But our experience of this environment is a combination of specific places and spaces, memories of events, what we see as we drive in our car or ride the bus, the trees and gardens of certain streets, the smells of nearby factories, views of the lake, the special character of our neighborhood. The map is not the town; it is a metaphor for the town. In comparison to the town it is like a work of art, it is another world, one that organizes and gives form to the apparent disconnectedness of our actual experience.

The Theatrical Event

Above: Initiation ritual, Upper Volta (West Africa). The masked dancers, impersonating mythological figures, reenact the child's drama of coming to maturity in the presence of the other adult members of the tribe. While not theatre, this rite has all the characteristics of the theatrical event.

Below: The final scene of the Royal Shakespeare Company's 1967 production of **Macbeth.** Paul Scofield and Vivian Merchant played Macbeth and Lady Macbeth, Peter Hall directed, and the designs were by John Barry and Ann Curtis. The production was performed in several major theatre centers throughout Europe.

Above: A performance of the rock-musical **Jesus Christ Superstar**, directed by Tom O'Horgan. The musical is the best known and most popular form of theatre in the world today. It incorporates lavish costumes, dazzling spectacle, virtuoso dance, and music into the theatrical event.

Below: A nineteenth-century Punch-and-Judy show. These popular puppet shows were performed in streets, parks, and town squares. Characterized by violence and bawdy humor, they appealed to the "let's pretend" instincts of people of all ages.

Above: A performance of the aristocratic Japanese Nōh play **Momiji-gari**. In the play the hero is entertained by a demon disguised as a princess, played in this production by the famous actor, Umewaka Masatoshi. All of the roles in Nōh drama are played by male actors.

Below: A Mardi Gras parade in New Orleans. Parades and processions are one of the prototypes of the theatrical event. At carnival time, the Lord of Misrule reigns supreme. People can dress up, play other roles, and behave in ways that are not normally acceptable.

Members of the Alwin Nikolais dance company
in their 1975 production of **Tribe.** Nikolais's
performances are brilliant examples of experimental multimedia theatre. Neither dance nor
theatre, yet vividly theatrical, they have greatly
expanded our sense of what theatre can be.

Theater exists in a place that is inside and outside, here and there, now and then, mine and yours, actual and fantasy. A place where performers are themselves and others, where deeds are real and symbolic, where the dead come back to life, the old grow young; where audiences are seated yet carried away, touched yet left alone, still yet moved. Where stories are immediate and distant, where space is concrete and abstract, time accelerated, distorted, and slowed. From where do theatrical events come? They are not the purely personal actions or fantasies of the performers; they are not objective events taken from everyday life; they are not fiction; they are not embodiments of the director's wishes; they are not realizations or interpretations of a text; they are not recreations of earlier events. There is something of all these in a performance: a precarious arrangement of unstable elements, a juggling act. **Theater is situated between all the contending forces that give it life; and theater is itself a life-giver.**

Richard Schechner, **Environmental Theater**

Like all the arts, theatre bridges the gap between our need for the coherence of an imaginative world and our experience of the chaotic real world. It is "another reality" that attracts us because it transcends the limitations of everyday experience. It allows us to perceive the world as stable and comprehensible rather than as constantly changing through history. At the same time, theatre differs from the other arts in several significant ways and these differences are a source of its unique power. The special qualities that distinguish theatre from other art forms are these:

1. The theatre's primary means of expression is the living presence of the actor.
2. The theatre exists in the perpetual present tense.
3. The theatre is conceived in the "mode of destiny."

The Living Presence of the Actor

Earlier we said that every theatrical performance is a combination of many elements—script, settings, lighting, actors, etc. While this is generally true, finally the single irreducible element of all theatre is the living presence of the actor acting before an audience. It is possible to have theatre without a written script produced without costumes or stage properties in natural light without the guiding services of a director. But there can be no theatre without actor and audience.

One reason our experience of the theatre differs from the other arts is that we experience the actor both as a real human being and also as a fictional character. The actor on the stage does not present any real person but, rather, a fiction—a character in a play. The actor is the primary means by which we experience the theatrical metaphor. The presence we experience in the theatre is the presence of imaginary persons who are the product of a playwright's imagination. As such, they have no life of their own and can exist only within the context of the play. The character Hamlet does not exist except in the play *Hamlet*. It is not any real Hamlet we see there on the stage. If there ever was a real Hamlet, he died long ago and is buried somewhere in Denmark. Any references we make about the character Hamlet to our real life outside the theatre will have meaning only insofar as they relate to the context of the play.

Yet the actor playing Hamlet is also a living, real person and we are always aware of his presence. We are conscious of the fact that the Hamlet on the stage is not only Shakespeare's character but is also Laurence Olivier and that if Lord Olivier were suddenly to have a heart attack and die, the performance (and the performed character of Hamlet) would end at that moment. On one hand, the character Hamlet exists and has meaning only in terms of the world of the play, but he also exists in fully realized form only when embodied by a living actor. The theatre does, in fact, make present a world of fictions, but it does so through the medium of living actors. And the presence of living actors creates the illusion of a real world in which the events of the drama are actually happening at the very moment we experience them. This fact sets theatre apart from the other arts.

The Perpetual Present Tense

Of all the arts, theatre alone makes a special kind of presence. This is a two-fold process. On one hand, in every performance imaginary characters and events take on the concrete *presentness* of actual people and actions. At the same time, these actual people and actions are *presented* to us with all the completeness and coherence of an imaginative form—a form in which all the unpredictabilities of everyday life have been removed. For this reason we say all theatre is about presence, presentness, and presenting. Everything that takes place on the stage occurs, as Thornton Wilder put it, "in a perpetual present tense." It is happening *now*, right before our eyes. Unlike a novel in which the past is reported in the present, or a painting which is fixed forever and has already been seen in its finished form (if only by the painter), or a movie which has been completed prior to our seeing it, our experience of Oedipus or Hamlet in the theatre always takes place in the present tense. As the

Novels are written in the past tense. The characters in them, it is true, are represented as living moment by moment their present time, but the constant running commentary of the novelist ("Tess slowly descended into the valley"; "Anna Karenina laughed") inevitably conveys to the reader the fact that these events are long since past and over.

The novel is a past reported in the present. On the stage it is always now. This confers upon the action an increased vitality which the novelist longs in vain to incorporate into his work.

This condition in the theatre brings with it another important element:

In the theatre we are not aware of the intervening story teller. The speeches arise from the characters in an apparently pure spontaneity.

A play is what takes place.

A novel is what one person tells us took place.

A play visibly represents pure existing. A novel is what one mind, claiming to omniscience, asserts to have existed.

Thornton Wilder, "Some Thoughts on Playwrighting"

actor moves and speaks, it is as if for the first time. The theatre has immediacy.

The immediacy of the theatre is a very special kind of present and quite different from the way we usually experience presentness outside the theatre. When we watch a play unfold before us on the stage, we are almost immediately conscious of the play's past—a specific past built into the play that shapes the present moment. For example, in Henrik Ibsen's *Ghosts*, at the same time that the present situation of the play's protagonist, Mrs. Alving, is being directly presented to us, we are also discovering just what events in the past created this situation. As the play moves forward in the perpetual present, the playwright reveals to us those elements from the past that have created it. The play opens with Mrs. Alving preparing to dedicate a new orphanage which she has had built in honor of her deceased husband. We soon learn that she had been married to a dissolute old captain who had made her life unbearable. Because she and the man she loved (Pastor Manders) feared the scandal it would cause if their relationship were fully revealed, she put up with her husband's drunkenness, took his illegitimate daughter into her household, and sent their son away to France so he would not discover the kind of person his father was. The building of the orphanage is, in fact, Mrs. Alving's attempt to exorcise the ghosts of the past that haunt her. She fails in this because the real ghosts reside within her. As she says to Manders:

> I am half inclined to think we are all ghosts, Mr. Manders. It is not only what we have inherited from our fathers and mothers that exists again in us, but all sorts of old dead ideas and all kinds of old dead beliefs and things of that kind. They are not actually alive in us; but there they are dormant, all the same, and we can never be rid of them. . . . There must be ghosts all over the world. . . . And we are so miserably afraid of the light, all of us . . . and I am here, fighting with ghosts both without and within me.[2]

Throughout the play Ibsen reveals that the present moment shown on the stage is laden with its own shaping past. Mrs. Alving's present struggle is always defined by the past from which she wants to escape.

In every play we experience both the present *and* the past that has created it. This making present of the past is what we refer to as the play's exposition. To construct a play so that past action is communicated without impeding forward movement is one of the playwright's most difficult tasks. No matter what devices are used to accomplish this—a messenger, the chorus of Greek tragedy, a Shakespearean soliloquy, an actor's aside to the audience, a scene between two minor characters—exposition makes the audience conscious of how specific events in the past continue to live on in the present events taking place on the stage.

The Mode of Destiny

In addition to the present and its shaping past, we are also aware that the present moment of the theatre is moving toward a preordained although still unknown (to us) conclusion. We sense consequence. The present tense of the theatrical event has its future as well as its past built into it. We sense this in the form of the play itself and also because we know the actors *know* where the play is going. The actors are creating the play's future.

This is so unlike what we experience in our daily lives. In life, we observe an action and know it will have consequences, but we can only guess what those consequences will be. We can never be sure. There are always unforeseen elements that affect what happens. In the theatre this is not the case. Even though we may not know what a play's conclusion will be, we know that the consequences have been fixed. Every action in the play will be fulfilled in a predetermined, unchanging way. Each actor knows what the future of his or her character is going to be even if we do not know it. When King Lear chooses to divide his kingdom among his three daughters or Antigone decides to disobey Creon's decree, we may not know what the actual consequences of these acts will be, but we do know that they have been determined and that they will be revealed to us.

This sense of definiteness, this knowing that the movement of a play cannot be changed, is a source of pleasure in going to the theatre. It also explains why we can enjoy the production of a play more than once. Relatively experienced theatregoers have probably seen *Twelfth Night*, *Macbeth*, *Death of a Salesman*, or *The Importance of Being Earnest* several times, just as many of us may have heard Beethoven's "Eroica" symphony or a Brahms piano concerto many times. Why don't we say, "I've already seen that play (or heard that symphony) and I know how it all turns out, so I won't see it (or hear it) again"? Because one of the chief sources of our pleasure is experiencing the play or symphony as it is being fulfilled. We know it will be resolved in the same way every time it is performed. Like children hearing a favorite story over and over, we don't want it changed.

The theatre, unlike the other arts, presents not an illusion of finished realities and events but the immediate, visible responses of human beings. "On the stage," said Thornton Wilder, "it is always now." But it is a special kind of now: it is a present that has its origins in clearly defined past actions and moves toward an equally well-defined, even if still unknown, future. Thus it is a perpetual present defined by both its past and its future. This union of present, past, and future creates the tension that gives a play its dramatic quality. Think of it this way: we are watching Brutus in Shakespeare's *Julius Caesar* and we learn of his decision to participate in the assassination of Caesar. As Brutus stabs him and Caesar utters his last words ("*Et tu Brute!*"), the moment on stage carries with it much more than just the murder. We are conscious of Brutus's own pride and ambition combined with his fear of Caesar's power. This scene is given added dimension by warm yet tortured encounters between Brutus and his wife, Portia, and it prefigures Brutus's own lonely death on the battlefield of Philippi as Caesar's ghost returns. Even though we may not consciously link all these things together, we sense that the whole play is contained in any single moment of it in the same way that a drop of water contains the sea. Each moment of a play contains *all* of the play. We always know that every event taking place on stage has its origins in specific causes already made known to us that will eventually reach predetermined consequences.

The awareness that this combination energizes the theatrical event prompted philosopher Susanne Langer to assert that the theatre differs from all other arts in that it alone is conceived in what she called "the mode of destiny." What does she mean by this? We all know our actions will have consequences, but we usually do not think of the future as a total experience coming out of our past and present acts. When people reach a very old age, they can look back and see that everything that has happened to them is connected

It has been said repeatedly that the theatre creates a perpetual present moment; but it is only a present filled with its own future that is really dramatic. A sheer immediacy, an imperishable direct experience without the ominous forward movement of consequential action, would not be so. As literature creates a virtual past, drama creates a virtual future. The literary mode is the mode of Memory; the dramatic is the mode of Destiny.

Susanne Langer, **Feeling and Form**

and is all of one piece. Then they can say—sometimes with satisfaction, sometimes with dismay—"This is my life!" But most of us, most of the time, do not live with the consciousness that each moment carries within it both its past and its future. For the most part we experience life in fragments, or as novelist Thomas Pynchon put it: "Life is what happens to us while we are planning other things." This is probably just as well. If we had to live with a sense of destiny all the time it might be more than we could stand.

Because a character in a play is whole in ways that we are not, there is a direct and inevitable relationship between a character and his or her fate. Dramatic characters are makers of their own destinies (whether or not they actually choose them)—destinies that will be fulfilled by the action of the play. We are conscious of this because on the stage every idea expressed in conversation, every gesture and movement, every change in tone of voice, every feeling betrayed by a look is determined by the total action of which it is a part.

These, then, are the characteristics of the theatrical metaphor. In the following two chapters we will discuss why it has always had such a powerful hold on our imaginations and consider some of the fundamental ideas related to its composition. But before we do so, we will briefly consider how theatre differs from the performing arts with which it has most in common—film, television, and dance. (One could also include the various forms of musical theatre here, but we shall discuss them in Chapter 9.)

HOW THE THEATRE DIFFERS FROM MOVIES, TELEVISION, AND DANCE

While your experience with live theatre may be limited, you probably have had a great deal of experience with movies and television. Movies especially seem to have much in common with theatre—at least we often experience them in a similar way. There are actors acting in both cases, there are the elements of costume, lighting, and scenic design, there is a director who coordinated the artistic process, there is a script. We sit in a theatrelike building to watch a movie; we are part of an audience. We may even get the same "message" from a filmed version of *One Flew Over the Cuckoo's Nest* as from a live stage version of the same play. Yet the two experiences are quite different, both in how they are created and in how they are perceived.

The *living* presence of actors playing characters who resemble actual human beings distinguishes the theatre from the other performing arts. Certainly, most films use actors to represent actual people. But what do we actually see up there on the screen? A shadow. We are there with a film, not with Jane Fonda or Robert De Niro. Yes, sometimes the people on the screen can seem very real, very believable, but in fact the only other living element involved with an audience's experience of a film is the projectionist. When the projectionist turns off the projector, the performance stops. Think of how distorted our experience of the actors on the screen actually is. Who ever saw people in real life with faces twenty feet high, moving in slow motion, or performing any of the other feats permitted by film technology?

The unreality of the medium becomes even more apparent when we realize how films are made. Scenes in movies are rarely filmed sequentially; it is not unusual for the last scenes to be shot first. They are filmed in short segments, usually with far more film shot than could possibly be used, and the scenes are cut and edited later to make a coherent whole. Actors who forget a line or miss a cue get another chance; the scene can always be reshot. This is one of the essential differences between movies and theatre: a movie never really "happens" until all the people who made it happen have come together and then dispersed. There is never a moment or hour when the movie happens (as theatre happens) until the finished print of the film exists. This being the case, film actors do not create sustained roles so much as they develop a series of loosely related vignettes that are later given coherence by the director in the editing room. Each scene is usually shot several times and the director selects the best "take" long after it was actually shot. A common complaint of film actors is that their best work ended up "on the cutting-room floor." Unlike theatre, film is a directors'/editors' medium, not an actors' medium.

Television is very similar to movies, particularly if—as it usually is—the performance has been filmed before the showing on our TV screen. Once again we have a medium of edited shadows. This is true even of so-called "live" television. Everything is edited by the director, who determines which of the several camera shots is to be actually used and whether we will see it close up or from a great distance. Unlike the theatre, where we in the audience are free to watch whatever it is on the stage that interests us or compels our attention, in television, even in a "live" show, our vision is controlled from the "control" booth.

In theatre, unlike movies and television, it is always now. One of the most beautiful and painful facts of human existence is its transitoriness. Once a moment has passed it is gone forever. There are no "instant replays" in life as we live it. This same transitory quality characterizes the theatrical event. Once a performance (even a moment in a performance) in the theatre has finished, it can never occur again in quite the same way. Each performance is a unique event because each one is a new combination of the actors' energy and an ever changing audience. There are no instant replays in the theatre, either.

But what about the dance? Here we have living human beings actually performing before an audience. Yet it is not the same as theatre. First, with very rare exceptions, we experience dance only in terms of movement and even then it is as an abstraction. We marvel at the leaps of Baryshnikov or Nureyev because they appear to transcend human limitations. That is not how real people move, behave, or act. Second, as human beings we communicate with both our physical movements and our voices, and this interaction between voice and movement is present in the theatre but not in dance. Finally, in a very real way music plays a controlling role in much of dance. Dance is choreographed in ways that the most stylized theatre never is. The meaning of dance is in large measure shaped by the music. Today in the dance world there are many experiments taking place that attempt to break down these distinctions. When they succeed, dance gives up many unique properties of its form, and we correctly call such experimental performances "theatre dance" or "dance theatre." But even in these performances we do not experience the quality of the actor's doubleness. Only in the theatre do we have actors who create total presence—living actors embodying fictional characters so as to create an illusion of being in a real world.

We said at the beginning of this chapter that all theatre manifests another world. The theatrical event is a metaphoric form which lets us confront some of the never-resolved mysteries of our being by making them present for us through the medium of living actors. Throughout history there have always been certain strong and persisting impulses that prompt the theatrical event and equally strongly felt human needs that are fulfilled by it. Put as simply as possible (and the next chapter will develop this fully): I believe there is a basic human need met by theatre in all times and all places. In theatre we confront the mystery at the root of human experience by making it present through the medium of actors.

NOTES

[1]Federico García Lorca, trans., Ben Belitt. "The Poetic Image in Don Luis de Gongora." *Quarterly Review of Literature*, Vol. VI, #1, 1950.

[2]From *Ghosts, An Enemy of the People, The Warriors at Jelgeland* by Henrik Ibsen, translated by R. Farquharson Sharp. An Everyman's Library Edition. Published in the United States by E. P. Dutton, and reprinted with their permission and the permission of J. M. Dent & Sons Ltd., Publishers.

Chapter 2

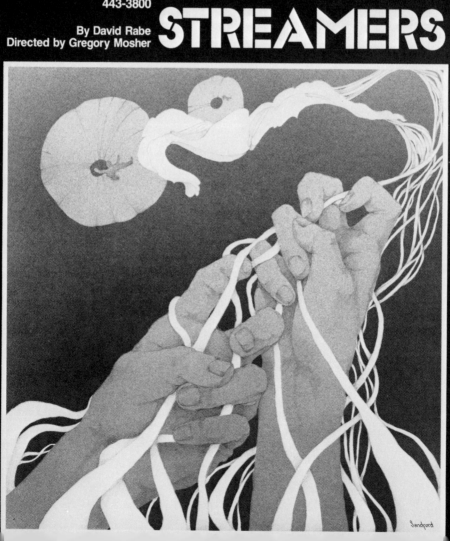

Best American Play 1976
N.Y. Drama Critics Award

March 31-May 1
Goodman Theatre
Entrance to Theatre on Monroe, one block east of Michigan
443-3800

By David Rabe
Directed by Gregory Mosher

STREAMERS

Man in his struggle for life began with dances, shouts, songs, incantations, and warlike mimes
　meant to bring to him the strength of his ancestors and power over his enemies.
These manifestations were part of a profound,
　mysterious, and metaphysical reality which was at one with life.
When man began to trace graffiti of animals on walls,
　it was in order to protect themselves from animals,
　to master them in order to eat them or to make use of them.
　It was therefore a form of magic.
When men sculpted their first masks,
　they aimed at giving form to their inner face or to the traits of their assumed role;
　they were trying to bring to light the appearances of their most mysterious instincts. . . .
The origin of the theatre lies in the attempt to imitate and to recreate these forms of human behavior.

Jean-Louis Barrault, **The Theatre of Jean-Louis Barrault**

The "Other" World
of the Theatre

In Chapter 1 we explored the special nature of the theatrical event, referring several times to the idea that the theatre presents another world, a world of mystery. In later chapters we will discuss what goes on in a theatrical event—how a play is put together and who creates it. But here we will consider something else: What are the impulses that lead to the creation of the theatrical event and what are the human needs that are fulfilled by our experience of that event?

There are many reasons why we go to the theatre and because it takes place inside us as much as it does on the stage, every theatrical performance produces a wide range of feelings and responses within each member of an audience. The theatre is exciting. It stimulates the mind and stirs the emotions. It can be beautiful or shocking. Sometimes it provokes wonder and joy, sometimes sadness. It is sexual. It is spiritual. Yet within this rich variety there is a single governing power which not only gives definition to the basic dynamic of the theatrical event but shapes our experience of it as well.

Put briefly, the theatre presents us with another world, a world of mystery that confronts all the difficult, unanswerable questions humanity has always pondered—the mysteries we can never explain. As we said in the last chapter, the fact that theatre does present such a world accounts for its powerful hold on our imaginations. Mystery both attracts and repels us, and we experience these conflicting responses in some form whenever we attend a performance.

THE MASK AS THEATRICAL EMBLEM

To begin, let us consider the implications of the mask as a theatrical emblem. The masks of comedy and tragedy used as a symbol of the theatre are much more than a simple decorative motif. They symbolize some of the mysteries at the heart of the theatrical event, mysteries of otherness and of the inanimate.

We all know how strange it is to wear a mask. There is something exciting about it and something eerie, too. In a sense we hide our identity behind the mask, but in doing so we liberate many hidden aspects of our secret selves. Our voices change; we tend to move and gesture differently; we become somebody else, yet we are still ourselves. Perhaps the mask gives us the freedom to be even more ourselves than usual. The appearance of someone else points to another self within us. A mask can reveal as much as it hides. Wearing a mask also gives us a sense of power; it makes us both invisible and invulnerable. We can see without being seen. In a mask we are both actor and audience.

A **tovil** performer from Sri Lanka (Ceylon). The shaman assumes the appearance and role of a demon, which he will exorcise after dancing into trance.

But there is something dehumanizing about masks. They enlarge our humanity and liberate our spirit by imposing a rigid, fixed expression upon us. They are also scary. They evoke strange sounds from us and they frighten children. They remind us of all the life-giving ecstasy of carnivals (think of Mardi Gras!) and yet we associate their inanimate nature with death. They evoke images of voodoo, evil spirits, and primitive demons.

Masks are not just a disguise, but are in fact personifications of a power or spirit. They express psychic forces which are activated and then released through the medium of the mask. For primitive people, masks were usually thought of as embodiments of deified ancestors, demons, or spiritual beings, and they were worn as a means of bringing these spirits back to life. The mask was the medium through which the members of the tribe made contact with the other world of the gods and the tribal ancestors who inhabited the land of the dead. As such it was endowed with the powers of both the living and the dead—it was highly animate and disturbingly inanimate at the same time.

ON MASKS

Sculpture of a comic mask used in the classical Greek theatre.

We have forgotten entirely that the primary symbol of the theatre is the mask. . . . In the mask lies a law, and this is the law of the drama. Non-reality becomes a fact.

Yvan Goll

The human face reflects the human soul and the mysterious links which might connect a human being with the supernatural world. From his earliest childhood man likes to impersonate parts, and to impersonate somebody is to change face; it is to adopt somebody else's face. The attempt to wear another man's face aims at trying to get out of oneself, and in that line of thought, the action of placing on one's face the mask of another face is something far more striking and stimulating than the act of making up to play a given part. A mask confers upon a given expression the maximum of intensity together with an impression of absence. A mask expresses at the same time the maximum of life and the maximum of death; it partakes of the visible and of the invisible, of the apparent and absolute. The mask exteriorizes a deep aspect of life, and in so doing, it helps to rediscover instinct.

Jean-Louis Barrault, **The Theatre of Jean-Louis Barrault**

One becomes what one displays. The wearers of masks **are** really the mythical ancestors portrayed by their masks. But the same results—that is, total transformation of the individual into something **other**—are to be expected from the various signs and symbols that are sometimes merely indicated on the costume or directly on the body: one assumes the power of magical flight by wearing an eagle feather, or even a highly stylized drawing of such a feather; and so on.

Mircea Eliade, **Shamanism**

The mask in all its forms retains a magical cruelty, a ghostliness, a sense of flaying—a face beside itself, austere with the fact of its separation from the body.

Michael Goldman, **The Actor's Freedom**

Today many of us might reject all this as mere superstition. In fact, the strange experience we have whenever we put on a mask or costume has its roots in these primitive practices and beliefs which still have a profound psychic validity whether we consciously acknowledge them or not. The mask is the emblem of our condition of otherness. It symbolizes the fact that we always feel separated from others, no matter how we may try to become close or "one" with them. In its mysterious way it embodies and gives life to all the ghosts that haunt us. In wearing the mask, we conquer the ghost by becoming it. We become strange to master strangeness.

This is what happens in the theatre. Like children hiding behind their hands playing now-you-see-me-now-you-don't, the theatre is a masking and unmasking of another world—one that is more and less than real, more liberating and more frightening, more powerful and more vulnerable than the realm of our ordinary daily existence.

The mask, then, symbolizes both the nature of the theatrical event and also our response to that event. It embodies the power of the other world of mystery which the theatre makes present for us and also the excitement, awe, and fear we feel when we experience that presence. The experience of otherness and the experience of the inanimate are part of our response to the mask, and both are at the root of our response to theatre.

THE MYSTERY OF OTHERNESS

The concept of otherness may seem like a new one to you, but it is a thought or feeling most of us have had at one time or another. Put simply, it is your realizing that no matter how long or well you have known someone, there is always something unknown between you, something that separates the two of you.

A significant distinction between a child and a relatively mature adult is that the adult can perceive and accept another person as an other, as a person separate from oneself. But each of us knows—no matter what our age or stage of development—that the uneasy fact of our otherness is difficult to understand and even more difficult to live with. Real intimacy and the love we associate with it can exist only when each person accepts the other as separate and not merely as an extension of the self, which is the way children conceive of and wish to experience relationships. The capacity for love and intimacy characterizes people capable of dealing with otherness.

But otherness is also threatening. For primitive people, everything that existed outside the immediate precincts of the tribe was a threat. The world outside *was* the world of the other—of other

Ocean shell death mask. Found in the Brakebill Mound in Tennessee, shell masks like these were placed in the grave to give the dead a permanent face.

ON OTHERNESS

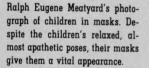

Ralph Eugene Meatyard's photograph of children in masks. Despite the children's relaxed, almost apathetic poses, their masks give them a vital appearance.

T he self discovers its identity in fear and deprivation. It is through our relationship with the ghosts who arise at that discovery—with unstable, inexorable, haunting presences disturbingly like our parents, as disturbing in their sorrow as in their anger, arousing fear and urgency and guilt—that we begin to learn, like Hamlet, about the dangerous forces lying within us and around us. What these ghosts are, psychology still struggles to learn. . . . For our purposes, it is only necessary to acknowledge that, whatever they are, they haunt us, and begin to haunt us as we begin to discover that we are separate, beleaguered selves.

Michael Goldman, **The Actor's Freedom**

people, of demons and aggressive spirits, and especially of the ghosts of the dead who represented the greatest threat of all. Today we have internalized that primitive fear, for the most part, but it still exists within us and all the security blankets in the world do not seem to weaken its grip on our imaginations.

As long as I am I and you are you, there will always be a gulf between us. There can never be perfect communication, total participation, or real oneness between any two (not to mention more) people. Even when we are most involved with another—say, in

L ast fall, soon after finishing **Where the Wild Things Are,** I sat on the front porch of my parents' house in Brooklyn and witnessed a scene that could have been a page from one of those early notebooks. I might have titled it "Arnold the Monster."

Arnold was a tubby, pleasant-faced little boy who could instantly turn himself into a howling, groaning, hunched horror—a composite of Frankenstein's monster, the Werewolf, and Godzilla. His willing victims were four giggling little girls, whom he chased frantically around parked automobiles and up and down front steps. The girls would flee, hiccuping and shrieking, "Oh, help! Save me! The monster will eat me!" And Arnold would lumber after them, rolling his eyes and bellowing. The noise was ear-splitting, the proceedings were fascinating.

At one point Arnold, carried away by his frenzy, broke an unwritten rule of such games. He actually caught one of his victims. She was furious. "You're not supposed to catch me, dope," she said, and smacked Arnold. He meekly apologized, and a moment later this same little girl dashed away screaming the game song: "Oh, help! Save me!" etc. The children became hot and mussed-looking. They had the glittery look of primitive creatures going through a ritual dance.

The game ended in a collapse of exhaustion. Arnold dragged himself away, and the girls went off with a look of sweet peace on their faces. A mysterious inner battle had been played out, and their minds and bodies were at rest, for the moment.

I have watched children play many variations of this game. They are the necessary games children must conjure up to combat an awful fact of childhood: the fact of their vulnerability to fear, anger, hate, frustration—all the emotions that are an ordinary part of their lives and that they can perceive only as ungovernable and dangerous forces. To master these forces, children turn to fantasy: that imagined world where disturbing emotional situations are solved to their satisfaction.

Maurice Sendak, in **The Horn Book Magazine**

making love—we are always conscious of otherness. We depend on that person's otherness at the same time that the otherness threatens us. Unless we can accept a person as an other, we can never really touch that person; and without such contact we can never touch the world of all human beings. Yet since we can never really know an other, the other will always be a threat, the source of our greatest fears. This ambiguous combination of need and fear is also central to our experience of the theatrical event.

Sources of Otherness

What is the source of otherness we all live with? How does it enter our lives? And what does it have to do with our experience of the theatre?

Psychologists tell us the infant's first major experience of anxiety is that moment—usually somewhere between the sixth and eighth month of life—when it first becomes conscious of the mother as the mother; that is, as someone other than itself, not just an extension of itself. This is the first significant step in the infant's emotional development, and it is mixed with conflict and fear. In distinguishing between the I and the non-I, the child must both recognize and confront the stranger or the "other" for the first time. As the infant becomes conscious of itself as a separate being, it also experiences a sense of loss—it becomes aware of a gulf between the self and the source of life.

Something must bridge this new gulf between the infant and the mother if life is to continue, and certainly if it is to continue with a more or less normal pattern of development. That bridge is what psychologists refer to as "primal dialogue." By primal dialogue they don't mean just talking, but touching, fondling, kissing, cooing, listening, observing; in short, a pattern of action and response that involves all the senses. Its essential quality is give-and-take; the child must experience real interaction—first with the mother and then with others—if it is to deal with the anxieties of separateness. Indeed, if that connection is not established and maintained, it is questionable if life can continue.

North American eagle mask, wood. Courtesy of the Denver Art Museum, Denver, Colorado.

The mask of mime. Marcel Marceau in his immortal role of Bip.

Entire books are written on this subject. It is not possible or appropriate to explore this idea in depth in an introduction to theatre. But the point to understand here is that a ghost haunts each of us from our infancy to our grave and it comes from our first awareness of separateness or otherness. We try to bridge this experience of separation with primal dialogue. At first this primal dialogue is established and maintained by the mother, but as we grow older we enter into it with other people and other agents. But as each of us discovers, the dialogue is never perfect and never removes our fear of the ghost.

THE ANIMATE AND THE INANIMATE

Before we discuss how otherness relates to our experience of the theatre, let us consider another idea related to human development. Psychologists have observed that at exactly the same time (between the ages of six and eight months) that the infant first experiences separation and loss, it also comes to recognize the difference between the animate and the inanimate. This major achievement causes great anxiety. A number of studies of this aspect of child development have concluded that this anxiety stems from the elements of strangeness or unfamiliarity that the child associates with inanimate objects. They are unreal, alien to its experience, and therefore potentially dangerous. The infant's consciousness of the inanimate and its new awareness of otherness are directly related. The anxiety of otherness is heightened by the strangeness of inanimate objects. These two psychic shocks combine to form a "ghost reaction," the term psychologists use to describe the effect these two experiences have on the child at this stage.

As the child develops, his or her attitude toward inanimate objects begins to change. The more the child deals with fears of otherness, the more attractive the inanimate becomes. Unlike people, objects are safe and controllable; they can be experienced as extensions of the self. So the teddy bear, the Raggedy Ann doll, or the security blanket becomes the child's constant companion. The child loves it, takes out aggressions on it, and cannot go to sleep without it. The toy becomes the means by which the child begins to achieve separation from the mother; it assists the child in moving from total dependence to the first stages of selfhood. Through the inanimate, the child becomes animate in his or her own right and begins to experience the terrible freedom of having an identity of one's own. The inanimate becomes attractive to us as children and as adults because the fears of otherness that *it* provokes can be mastered. Because we can conquer the inanimate, we are assured in our relationship with the other. Yet we are repulsed by it at the same time because its very existence makes us more aware of our condition of separateness.

These two phenomena—the recognition of the other and the recognition of the inanimate—are inextricably related. They account for the fear of strangeness we carry with us all of our lives, and they create a need in us that we can never totally fulfill. For this reason, our response to them is ambivalent: we resent the strangeness but we need to be in touch with it if we are ever to master the anxieties it produces.

This need provokes deep angers. Primal dialogue, while absolutely necessary for normal growth and development, is finally an inadequate substitute for the perfect oneness we experienced before becoming aware of otherness. Similarly, inanimate objects, while also necessary, are never a completely satisfactory means of mastering our fear of strangeness. Our consciousness of the boundaries between self and other and animate and inanimate is always blurred. The "ghost reaction" can never be totally dispelled and it resides within us always. It fascinates us and at the same time it scares us silly.

You are all aware that this uncertainty of boundaries provides the devices used in ghost and horror stories, in myth and legend, since time immemorial, including the myth of Oedipus. It cannot be accidental that we have gone to such length to prove in our so-called "age of reason" that the supernatural, that the ghost stories, are untrue, a pack of lies, that they cannot and must not be. Are we by any chance whistling in the dark?

René Spitz, "Life and the Dialogue"

THE THEATRE AND PRIMAL DIALOGUE

Now what does this discussion of psychological development have to do with the theatre and our experience of it? The governing impulse of all primal dialogue is to restore that oneness we experienced as infants. Each of us yearns to return to a condition without tension where all the conflicts of otherness have been removed. We want a world where otherness doesn't exist. Our sense of separation and loss sends us to forms that will fulfill our longings. And this is one of the theatre's basic appeals.

In large measure, the theatre is able to meet these needs. In theatre we experience anxiety, aggression, conflict, and fantasy without fearing the consequences of such experiences. Theatre is a place where that cycle of action and response called primal dialogue can be fulfilled. Our relationship to the actors in a performance is a carefully orchestrated, socially acceptable, and emotionally satisfying public form of the same patterns of behavior that we first experienced with our parents as infants. Moreover, theatre is satisfying in a way that other forms of primal dialogue are not: the audience knows there is a fixed period of time when the primal dialogue of the theatrical event will take place. A performance of *Hamlet* will begin at eight o'clock and end at eleven; we come to the theatre fully aware of that fact. We can depend on it, and that is reassuring. We know that when we go to the theatre we can count on our union with the figures on the stage for a certain agreed-upon period of time. This is satisfying—life itself is not so predictable. Every performance structures an opportunity for primal dialogue between the actors and the audience. In fact, some people insist that the theatre's essential purpose is to provide an occasion for primal dialogue to take place.

While we seek this experience in the theatre, our pleasure in this

Ansky's **The Dybbuk**. The rabbi's mask in Eugene Vakhtangov's 1922 production in Moscow.

dialogue is often mixed with some hostility. This may be because our experience of the theatre is founded on the conflicting emotions generated by our sense of loss and our need to do something about it. It can also be explained by the fact that no matter how safe we may feel sitting in the darkened auditorium surrounded by our fellow audience members, any performance implies a kind of threat, and the fear that threat engenders can never be totally neutralized. The very strangeness of the theatrical event cannot help but disturb us at some deep level of our being and hence provoke hostile feelings within us. But the main reason for our negative response is that no matter how realistic a performance may be, we are always conscious of the fact that it is not real. Think how we react when we feel the actors on the stage are actually being threatened or really are in danger. We jump whenever a gun is shot on the stage. Even though we know it is loaded with blanks and therefore not dangerous, when it is fired there's always an instant of shock when the distinctions between illusion and reality are blurred. Losing touch with reality is always unsettling. Theatre specializes in pulling us away from reality and putting us back again—never back to quite the same spot as before. Is it any wonder the experience makes us a little uneasy?

You might be thinking all this makes theatre sound like an activity that is, at best, rather unpleasant. If our experience of the theatre is so disturbing, why do we spend our money and time going to it? What attracts people to representations of conflict, unhappiness, fear, confusion, death, and crisis? If going to the theatre involves the confrontation of some of our deepest anxieties, why is it so exciting? One answer to these questions is suggested by the very fact that you are reading this book. Why do so many students who have no intention of pursuing a career in theatre take Introduction to Theatre courses? Why do so many students who would never think seriously of being professional actors want to take a course in acting? Many students are attracted to theatre courses because they believe that by studying and participating in theatre they will discover more about themselves. They are right in feeling this. The "other" world made present in the theatre is directly related to that otherness so central to the experience of each one of us. The world of mystery unfolded in every performance has its origins in those mysteries which haunt us all of our lives.

MYTH, RITUAL, AND THEATRE

Our fear of the other and our need to confront it, our recognition of the inanimate and our need to deal with it are part of our experience of the theatrical event. Throughout history people have dealt with the same mysteries in different ways. We spoke in the last chapter of

Masks used in Jean-Louis Bar-
rault's production of Aeschylus'
The Oresteia at Théâtre de France,
Paris, 1961.

WHAT OUR LANGUAGE TELLS US ABOUT THEATRE

We define our experience with the words we use. This being the case, some of these words—both ancient and modern—associated with the theatrical experience will provide us with clues as to how people have thought about that experience.

"theatre" from **theatron** (Greek, a seeing place where one comes to possess a new knowledge) Our words "theatre" and "theory" are derived from the same source.

"orchestra" from **ornynai** (Greek, to rise, as from the dead) and **rghayati** (Sanskrit, the ravings, rages, and tremblings of one in a trance) The orchestra was the performers' area in the outdoor theatres of ancient Greece. Those who danced in the orchestra in the tragedies (which evolved out of ritual dances) were called **korybantes** (dancers in a state of ecstasy or divine madness) or **maenads** (madwomen who participated in the ritual mysteries). Dionysus was the demonic god the Greeks associated with the theatrical muse. The theatre activity dedicated to Dionysus was concerned with sacrifice and rebirth, limitation and transcendence; the performances grew out of almost abandoned madness; in it they expressed the darkest mysteries of human nature.

"thespian" from **Thespis** (Greek, the legendary first actor in the ancient Greek theatre) Thespians were those singer-dancers thought to be possessed by the gods during performance.

"histrionic" from **hister** (Latin, of or pertaining to actors, derived from the Greek **hyster,** the womb) An actor was one who journeyed to another world by getting out of himself through some form of trance.

"hypocrite" from **hypokrites** (Greek, actor, one who answers) In the fifth century B.C., the Greek actor's function was to answer questions about the world of the gods. As the envoy from this other world he was set apart, someone different; yet he was also a member of the community (as represented by the chorus of singers and dancers) pretending to be someone else. Hence the modern connotations of dissembling and insincerity associated with the word "hypocrite."

"rehearsal" from **rehercier** (French, to harrow again) Originally, "to harrow" meant to descend to the underworld in order to bring back the souls that reside there.

our need to create imaginative worlds or constructs in order to explain and deal with the unknown. A scientific theory is such a construct, as are art, philosophy, and religion. What these constructs have in common is that they are organized systems of perception. Each of them sorts out the random stimuli of a chaotic world, finding answers to questions it phrases in its own terms. Our need to confront the mystery of existence is deeply rooted in human nature and can be seen in the earliest recorded myths and rituals of the most primitive people. Confronting mystery has always been the chief function of myth and ritual. We make myths and participate in rituals in the hope that we will be able to control the mysterious.

The similarities between ritual and theatre have led to the idea that theatre has its origins in religious ritual. Ritual and theatre have much in common and unquestionably their development in primitive cultures was closely related. But there are so many fundamental differences between the two forms of expression that it is probably more accurate to say only that ritual and theatre spring from the same impulse: our need to create imaginative constructs as a way of dealing with mystery. We may be tempted to imagine theatre developing out of ritual since in their earliest manifestations both forms used the subject matter of myths and as a result their structures had striking similarities. For example, we know that the structure of the classical Greek comedies of Aristophanes and the fertility rituals of earlier Attic societies had much in common. In both we will find the battle between winter and spring, a ritual marriage, and a celebratory feast followed by a triumphal procession. Similarly, the theme, characters, and plot of Euripides' *The Bacchae* appear to be very much like what we know of the ancient Dionysian myths and rituals. These similarities are interesting; however, their differences underline theatre's unique qualities.

Kwakiutl four-headed mask. Courtesy of the Denver Art Museum, Denver, Colorado.

Myths are imaginative constructs meant to explain cosmic mysteries. How did we get here and where did we come from? How was the world created? No person can really live easily with the idea that the world just *happened*. Hence, every culture has its creation myths to explain how the world came into being. Who would create a world as imperfect as the one we live in? To answer this question, most cultures have myths of a fall from grace, the Garden of Eden, or a loss of an earlier perfect world. Even as we experience the fall from a perfect state, we are given a chance for rebirth and regeneration through a savior or culture hero (for example, the many legends of Theseus in Greece or Osiris in Egypt). These myths are linked to our awareness that not only does nature regenerate itself, but that human nature does as well.

However, myths have never, in themselves, been able to ease all of humanity's fears. People have also developed patterns of action based on myths in an attempt to control the mysterious. These patterns are called rituals. In performing rituals we insure that the myths that explain life's mysteries will continue to be true. The Indians of the American Southwest, for example, performed rain rituals as a way of insuring that the tribal gods would send rain at the appropriate time.

The myth-making impulse involves the imaginative processes we usually associate with the creation of works of art—painting, drama, poetry. But myth comes from an essentially religious or spiritual impulse and not an aesthetic one. Myth, as we said, is concerned with cosmic mysteries: What is the source of human life? Why do the powerful forces of nature operate as they do? Why do things grow? Why do we die?

Although myth is a mode of symbolic expression, it is not a metaphor that stands for something else. Unlike art, a myth is not a conscious, individual composition. A person doesn't meditate on life's mysteries and sit down and create a myth. Myth is a collective form of expression that grows out of the experience of a community and is directly participated in by its members. A myth cannot be true or false. As long as it satisfactorily answers our questions about how the universe works, we will continue to believe it and it will be true for us. The mythic imagination is a believing imagination; it

Myth is, before everything else, a tale, that . . . has no other function than to reveal how **something came into being**. Modern man's attraction to myths betrays his latent desire to be told stories, to learn how worlds were born and what happened afterward.

Mircea Eliade, **No Souvenirs**

Naturalistic wooden headdress of the Tlingit people of the northwest coast of North America.

imagines its objects as actually existing. Perhaps most important, myths are expressions of the mysteries of the self and the universe. As long as the myth is believed in, the mystery is resolved and we can live with it. Anyone who literally and truly believes in the Adam and Eve account of creation as told in the book of Genesis, for example, has no problem with the mysteries of creation or the fall from grace. The story tells us how and why it happened.

Rituals related to myth are similarly believed in—not imitations of events, but events themselves. They are representations of life that have a practical end. As Jane Harrison points out in *Ancient Art and Ritual*, in actual life primitive people hunt and fish, plow and sow for the practical purpose of growing food; their rituals of the seasons—while composed of such impractical acts as singing, dancing, and mimicry—also have a practical purpose: to induce the return of the food supply. Rituals reiterate the events of myth and cannot be used for something else. G. S. Kirk states it very simply: "Ritual . . . implies a closely controlled set of actions performed in an established sequence for a specific supernatural end."[1]

Rituals are enacted on behalf of the whole community—they both express and enforce what the community believes and values. All ritual is intended to produce results that extend beyond the performance of the ritual itself. Because ritual involves belief, everyone who partakes of it, whether as an enactor or as a watcher, is a participant. (The priest celebrating the Christian Eucharist is not an actor playing Christ, and those in the congregation are not members of an audience.) To participate in a ritual requires initiation. Everyone participating must learn the ritual for it to be effective—for it *to be*. In ritual there are neither actors nor spectators, for in ritual there is no distinction between art and life.

"The Milkmaids," larger-than-life costumes worn in a parade at the annual carnival in Nice, France, in 1932. These carnivals had political themes. Masked troupes such as the one shown here were the predecessors of groups like the Bread and Puppet Theatre in the United States.

How Theatre Differs from Ritual

While theatre springs from the same impulse as ritual (to confront mystery), has much in common with them, and fulfills many of the same needs, it is profoundly different in nature from ritual and functions in a completely different way. Theatre is not religious in nature (even when it uses religious themes), and it does not have any practical purpose. While ritual is intended to produce specific results beyond itself—insure a good crop, produce rain—a theatrical performance is not. Unlike the participants in a ritual, the performers in a play are actors acting. They are not the characters they represent and we in the audience know this, just as we know we are spectators and are clearly meant to be spectators. In theatre, the distinction between actor and spectator is well-defined. If, as spectators, we did begin to actually participate in the performance the performance would stop immediately. A person in the audience at a performance of *Oedipus the King* who suddenly jumped up on the stage and grabbed Oedipus to prevent him from putting out his eyes would be grabbing not Oedipus but the actor playing the role. (At that point the performance of the play would in all probability come to an end.) Furthermore, theatre requires no special initiation for us to be a spectator. We need not have anything in common with the actors in a play but our humanity and a willingness to share in the theatrical event.

There are two even more crucial distinctions to make between theatre and ritual. First, while ritual recreates the events of myth so that the mystery is explained and resolved, in theatre the mystery is never completely explained or resolved. In theatre, mystery is presented to us, or, to put it more accurately, it is made present for us. Theatre raises questions for which there are no easy answers—indeed, for which there are no answers at all. There is no final explanation for the mystery at the heart of such plays as *Hamlet*, *Macbeth*, or *Oedipus the King* (the countless books and scholarly articles attempting to provide one just prove the fact). No one has ever completely understood Hamlet, just as no one has fully explained to everyone's satisfaction why he acts as he does. Great dramatic characters tend to evoke so many conflicting impulses and contradictory responses that they can never be completely understood. Great plays are often referred to as moral puzzles for this reason. Theatre presents and makes present the most joyful, the most painful, and the most puzzling mysteries of human nature so that we can come to a larger understanding of them. In short, we *experience* the mystery, which is far different than fully comprehending it.

Second, the theatre, unlike myth, is not primarily concerned with cosmic mysteries. Its chief concern is with the mysteries of *self*—of being, identity, and personal relationships, especially those of the family. These mysteries are all connected to our sense of otherness. The theatre is not likely to consider how humanity came to be on this planet but, rather, how people live and interact with each other—what we *are* to each other. This difference is crucial to our understanding theatre's special hold on our imagination.

Perhaps now we can begin to understand why our experience of the theatre is both exciting and strangely frightening at the same time. The theatre is like life and yet is both more and less than life; it is powerfully alive yet strangely inanimate; the actor is both real (a living human being) and not real (a character in a play). The theatre has always celebrated these contradictions.

The mask of Oedipus in Tyrone Guthrie's 1955 production of Sophocles' **Oedipus the King** at Stratford, Ontario.

E very ritual has the character of happening **now**, at this very moment. The time of the event that the ritual commemorates or re-
enacts is made **present**, "re-presented" so to speak, however far back it
may have been in ordinary reckoning. Christ's passion, death and resurrection are not simply **remembered** during the services of Holy Week;
they really happen **then** before the eyes of the faithful.

Mircea Eliade, **Patterns in Comparative Religion**

To some of you, these preliminary discussions may seem alien
to what your experience of the theatre has been, or at least quite
different from the ways you usually think about this popular art
form. After all, what does all this talk about mystery and ghosts and
hostility and need have to do with what happens when we attend a
performance of *Fiddler on the Roof*, *The Odd Couple*, *A Chorus
Line*, or even a classic such as Molière's *School for Wives* or Jonson's
Volpone? But think about it! The poignancy, joy, and sense of affirmation we experience when seeing a production of *Fiddler on the
Roof* derive from our recognition that all these life-enhancing feelings are rooted in the persecution, exile, and death which make up
the ground of that play's being. Even the haunting music (and
haunting is just the right word) is composed, for the most part, in
dark, minor keys. Similarly, a Neil Simon comedy can provoke a
laugh a minute, but his plays are invariably based on some form of
sexual unhappiness or conflict, the failure of people to communicate, and the awkwardness of being in compromising situations.
Simon may eventually resolve these conflicts, but never to such a
degree that we can really understand why most human relationships are entwined as much with suffering, humiliation, and blindness as they are with love, understanding, and acceptance. And we
cannot easily explain the fact that we in the audience have taken
great pleasure in watching the representation of other people's unhappiness. Finally, there are no satisfactory answers to all the
questions a production of a Simon play raises. A certain element of
mystery always remains.

We have been discussing the very personal and individual experience of the play in production—the theatrical moment. There is
another important dimension of going to theatre, and that is the
communal sharing of the experience as a member of the audience.
That aspect of theatre will be discussed in Chapter 9. The next step
in our exploration of the world of the theatre is to discover just how
the theatre goes about making the world of mystery present for us.

Modern Iroquois False Face mask. Such masks were worn by shamans and portrayed the faces of legendary heroes whose exploits were recounted in Iroquois mythology.

We have said theatre, like myth and ritual, is an imaginative construct created out of our need to find ways of dealing with the mystery in our lives. This idea of something created or constructed imaginatively is significant. The theatre, like all works of art, is something constructed or made. In the next chapter we will turn our attention to *what is constructed* in that imaginary world we call the theatre and *how* it is made.

NOTE

[1]G. S. Kirk. *Myth: Its Meaning and Functions in Ancient and Other Cultures.* University of California Press, 1970, p. 29.

Chapter 3

BY ARRANGEMENT WITH DONALD ALBERY THE YOUNG VIC CO LTD PRESENTS
THE YOUNG VIC IN

ROSENCRANTZ
& GUILDENSTERN
ARE DEAD
BY TOM STOPPARD

CRITERION THEATRE
PICCADILLY CIRCUS W1 BOX OFFICE 01-930 3216
EVENINGS 8.15/MATINEES THURSDAY & SATURDAY 5.00

LESSEES: WYNDHAM THEATRES LTD/LICENSEE & MANAGING DIRECTOR: DONALD ALBERY

In the theatre you have to make the unreal believable.

Jean Vilar, **The Tradition of the Theatre**

The theatre sets out to induce in an audience
the belief that the things and events it presents
are not what they are known to be.

Lionel Trilling, **The Experience of Literature**

The Making
of the World of the Play

You have just been to a performance of a brand new play by an unknown playwright. You and the people around you applaud as the actors bow. The curtain closes for the last time and the houselights come on. The sound of applause eventually gives way to the noise of people finding their coats and car keys and exchanging opinions of the performance. "What did you think of it?" "The acting was excellent." "I liked it." "I was bored." "Wasn't it good?" "What an ending!" "How pretentious can you get?" "Marvelous!" Many of these responses are reactions to the whole performance experience rather than, strictly, to the play. But what of the play? What can you say about what you just saw? Did the play hold together? What was it in the interaction of theme, character, and events that made the experience interesting? How did the playwright achieve the effects that moved you? In short, did the play work and, if so, why did it work? What are basic principles underlying the construction of theatrical reality and the unique nature of the dramatic form?

THE THEATRICAL EVENT IS COMPOSED

Because the world of the play is a "made" or created world, and not real life, its elements are put together purposefully. That is what we mean when we say the theatrical event is composed. In the theatre we witness a segment of human experience as something complete and total. We see more consequences of action than we usually perceive in everyday life. In real life we may have a conversation with a friend. We know its effect upon us but we are not certain how our friend felt. A playwright might show us the friend telling his brother about that conversation. In doing so, the playwright tells us all we need to know. This is a source of the theatre's power and attractiveness, and it also explains why we experience theatre as a fiction. In terms of our lives, its wholeness is unreal. We never see cause and effect so regularly in life as in a play. Action in life is always ambiguous, vague, and obscure; even our understanding of the tones of speech is ambiguous. (Think of the anxiety revealed when we say, "Just what did he mean by that?") This ambiguity is unsettling. But action in the theatre is never ambiguous. Even if we cannot see its meaning at first, we know that eventually all of its meanings will be revealed to us.[1] We know this because every element of the world of the play has been composed—the world itself is a *created* work of art. The playwright and all the other artists involved in presenting a play are creators.

As with any art form, the theatre is governed by certain principles of composition. For example, a poet setting out to write a sonnet knows he or she will write fourteen lines, no more and no less.

The playwright makes artistic choices within the context of the traditional conventions and forms unique to theatre. These are important in understanding how the world of the play is created and how the playwright can "make the unreal believable."

What Situations, Characters, and Themes Are Chosen?

Any situation is potentially dramatic. Certain situations—political turmoil, a family feud, a broken promise, a sudden death, unrequited love—seem ideally suited to drama, but less obvious dramatic circumstances—the unexpected arrival of guests, waiting for news, an accidental insult—lend themselves to theatre equally well. The playwright chooses a situation in which he or she senses dramatic possibilities that can be developed in interesting ways. The situation must be compatible with the themes and ideas he or she wishes to explore.

In *Miss Julie*, for example, Swedish playwright August Strindberg was interested in dealing dramatically with the battle of the sexes, class conflicts in nineteenth-century Sweden, self-

Strindberg's **Miss Julie** at the British National Theatre, 1965. The skeletal setting creates a sense of reality because of its openly theatrical character.

punishment, the desire for power, and the irreconcilability and instability of human feelings. The situation and characters he chose enabled him to focus on these themes. The events of the play take place during the festivities of Midsummer Eve. It is an occasion of drinking, dancing, and wild abandon. Emotions are high, the atmosphere is charged with sex, and anything can happen. The play's two major characters are Miss Julie, the neurotic daughter of a count who is not at home, and Jean, the count's ambitious valet. In a state of intoxication, Julie willfully dances with Jean and then follows him to the servants' quarters. Strindberg has now created a situation in which he can dramatize the play's central conflicts. The characters reveal themselves, taunt and flirt with each other, continue to drink, and this eventually leads to the valet's seduction of his master's daughter. Her honor besmirched, Julie is at a loss as to what to do. She can't remain in the house, nor can she bring herself to run away with Jean as he suggests. With no way out, she sees no choice but the suicide which ends the play. Strindberg chose a situation and characters that enabled him to develop his themes in the most powerful and theatrically effective ways. As he put it in his preface to the play:

> When I took this theme from real life—I heard about it a few years ago and it made a deep impression on me—I thought it would be a suitable subject for a tragedy, for it still strikes us as tragic to see a happily favored individual go down in defeat, and even more so to see an entire family line die out. . . .
>
> I have motivated the tragic fate of Miss Julie with an abundance of circumstances: her mother's basic instincts, her father's improper bringing-up of the girl, her own inborn nature and her fiancé's sway over her weak and degenerate mind. Further and more immediately: the festive atmosphere of Midsummer Eve, her father's absence, her monthly illness, her preoccupation with animals, the erotic excitement of the dance, the long summer twilight, the highly aphrodisiac influence of flowers, and finally chance itself, which drives two people together in an out-of-the-way room, plus the boldness of the aroused man.[2]

What Is the Setting in Which Events Take Place?

The world of the play must have a physical world. That is, every play is set in an environment that expresses the play's meaning. By this we do not mean the environment of the stage space (although this is a significant factor in the theatre), but rather the world in which the play itself takes place.

The world in *Miss Julie* was carefully chosen by Strindberg. Samuel Beckett's *Waiting for Godot* depicts the "no man's land" of the human spirit and is appropriately set in a nearly empty space. The barrenness of the play's environment expresses the psychic and philosophical emptiness of the play's world. Strindberg's Norwegian

contemporary, Henrik Ibsen, was very interested in his characters' inner lives, and he was also extremely conscious of how the physical environment shaped his characters' behavior. He took great pains to describe the stage settings of his plays in precise detail. He thought of the stage set as another character. In *Hedda Gabler*, Ibsen deliberately chose to have a portrait of Hedda's father dominate the living room in which the action takes place. This living room is consciously designed to show that General Gabler dominates not only Hedda's home, but her spiritual and psychic life as well.

Josef Svoboda's production of Sophocles' **Antigone** in Prague, 1971.

What Type of Language Do the Characters Use?

In Sophocles' *Antigone*, Antigone disobeys Creon's edict not to bury her brother. In doing so, she asserts the principle of love and nearly destroys her own humanity (and her own capacity for love) in the process. Her greatness lies in her capacity to push principle beyond self-denial to the rediscovery of love and her own humanity. Throughout the play, Antigone speaks in passionate and ever more expressive verse:

> O tomb, vaulted bride-bed in eternal rock,
> Soon I shall be with my own again
> Where Persephone welcomes the thin ghosts underground:
> And I shall see my father again, and you, mother,
> And dearest Polyneices—
> dearest indeed
> To me, since it was my hand
> That washed him clean and poured the ritual wine:
> And my reward is death before my time![3]

Antigone's character contrasts sharply with that of Creon, her uncle, who never reaches Antigone's stage of self-discovery. Creon is a man of intelligence, shrewdness, and strong resolve, but he lacks the humanity necessary to understand his fate. Until the final scenes of the play, Creon speaks in the prose of a public political figure:

> I am aware, of course, that no Ruler can expect complete loyalty from his subjects until he has been tested in office. Nevertheless, I say to you at the very outset that I have nothing but contempt for the kind of Governor who is afraid, for whatever reason, to follow the course that he knows is best for the State; and as for the man who sets private friendship above the public welfare, —I have no use for him, either. [3]

The difference between the two characters is revealed to us in many ways, but chief among them is the kind of language each character uses. Their language reveals not only the nature of their values, but also their capacity to know themselves and understand their situations.

The original production of Tennessee Williams's **A Streetcar Named Desire** in 1947. Directed by Elia Kazan, it featured Marlon Brando and Jessica Tandy.

Similarly, in a modern play, the basic conflict in Tennessee Williams's *A Streetcar Named Desire* is between the brutish Stanley Kowalski and his sister-in-law, Blanche DuBois, who has pretensions to the refinements of a bygone era. The differences between the two protagonists are expressed in many ways, but the language of each is appropriate to the character and defines their opposing natures. This can be seen in one of their first confrontations:

BLANCHE: I was fishing for a compliment, Stanley.

STANLEY: I don't go in for that stuff.

BLANCHE: What—stuff?

STANLEY: Compliments to women about their looks. I never met a woman that didn't know if she was good-looking or not without being told, and some of them give themselves credit for more than they've got. I once went out with a doll who said to me, "I am the glamorous type, I am the glamorous type!" I said, "So what?"

BLANCHE: And what did she say then?

STANLEY: She didn't say nothing. That shut her up like a clam.

BLANCHE: Did it end the romance?

STANLEY: It ended the conversation—that was all. Some men are took in by this Hollywood glamor stuff and some men are not.

BLANCHE: I'm sure you belong in the second category.

STANLEY: That's right.

BLANCHE: You're simple, straightforward and honest, a little bit on the primitive side I should think. To interest you a woman would have to—*(She pauses with an indefinite gesture.)*

STANLEY *(slowly)*: Lay . . . her cards on the table.

BLANCHE *(smiling)*: Well, I never cared for wishy-washy people. That was why, when you walked in here last night, I said to myself—"My sister has married a man!"—Of course that was all that I could tell about you.

STANLEY *(booming)*: Now let's cut the re-bop![4]

Again, we see how the play's meaning is revealed to us by the qualities of language the playwright chooses for his characters.

In What Sequence Are the Episodes Arranged?

Probably nothing makes us more aware of a play's composed nature than the way the playwright chooses to order the sequence of events. Much of a play's meaning is revealed by its structure. To see this, let us consider the structure of the first part of Shakespeare's *Othello.*

The situation is established in the first scene where we discover that Othello has made two important decisions: the black general has secretly married Desdemona, daughter of a Venetian nobleman, and he has appointed as his lieutenant his friend Michael Cassio instead of the veteran soldier Iago. These decisions have dramatic consequence. They trigger a chain of events that becomes the play's plot and determines its tragic outcome. In the first act of the play, we see Othello as a great general who is both needed and honored by the state because Venice is at war with the Turks and there is a job for him to do. As the first act ends, with Othello departing for Cyprus to fight the Turks, he is the master of himself and the situation. The play's opening scenes reveal that Othello's self-confidence, self-knowledge, and psychic security are inseparably linked to his role as a warrior.

But between act 1 and act 2 there is a great storm and the Turkish fleet is destroyed. Othello arrives in Cyprus only to discover that his "occupation's gone." There is no one to fight, he is cut off from the court that supports him; in short, all of the things that have supported him heretofore have been removed. Here is where the matter of sequence becomes openly significant. By removing the war, Shakespeare moves Othello into a position of vulnerability. The play is not to be about the "pomp and circumstance of glorious war" but, as it soon becomes apparent, it is a domestic drama of marital jealousy which the hero is poorly equipped to handle. This change in direction (and the play's meaning) is achieved by the playwright's ordering of events.

By the middle of the second act Othello is beginning to lose his vaunted self-control. It is against this background, with Othello shaken, disillusioned, bewildered, and perplexed, with no war available in which to exhibit his prowess and rebuild his sagging ego, that the villainous Iago goes to work on Othello's imagination, which is no better or no worse than anyone's in a time of insecurity. Because of that insecurity, Iago can convince Othello that his wife has been unfaithful to him with Cassio. Overwhelmed by seething jealousy, Othello is eventually driven to murdering his wife and then committing suicide when he realizes the horror and wrongness of his actions. Shakespeare prepares us for Othello's downfall by the way he orders the sequence of the scenes.

Laurence Olivier as Othello and Frank Finlay as Iago in the British National Theatre's 1964 production of **Othello**, directed by John Dexter.

These are just a few brief examples of what we mean when we say that the theatrical form is composed. The playwright makes choices about the play's situation, characters, themes, setting, language, and sequence of events, and these choices determine the nature, meaning, and shape of the play created. It is important to note that everything about the playwright's process of selection is moving toward a completion of an "other," created world and it does so beginning with the opening scene. Every play has an ending that makes everything that happens within it comprehensible and meaningful; it connects everything; it gives events an order that we do not experience in everyday life.

While the elements of this fictive other world may be drawn by the playwright from the ordinary real world we live in, he or she does not mirror these elements, but rather selects and arranges them—composes them. To be sure, the resemblance to the real world makes these events recognizable to us, but it does not make them real or meaningful in themselves. Their composition creates meaning.

WHAT MAKES A PLAY AUTHENTIC?

If all these choices are made, if in creating the other world of the play the playwright has been governed by principles of selection, construction, and organization, why does our experience of the play in performance seem so directly related to our own lives? What makes the performance authentic?

This can be a difficult issue. While a play's meaning is communicated by a composed form which is not lifelike, that form must make sense to us in terms of our own life experience. What takes place on the stage must strike us as authentic. This does not mean we must believe what happens on the stage has real-life consequences that extend beyond the performance; but rather that we believe what happens *while* it is happening. When Oedipus tears out his eyes we never for a moment believe the actor is actually blinding himself, no matter how realistically the scene is played. Rather, the play has been so composed that when the character of Oedipus finally comes to recognize how spiritually blind he has been, we believe his decision to blind himself is the only appropriate one for him to make. Let us think about what this distinction implies. Why is it that when we see composed behavior in life we tend to reject it as artificial, but when we see it on the stage we accept it as natural? We would think it very odd if someone argued passionately with us in metered verse, yet it strikes us as valid in a Shakespearean play. In plays, unbelievable things happen and we still believe them. Why?

The late John Barrymore as the diabolic king in his production of Shakespeare's **Richard III** in 1920.

In just about every play ever written you will discover that the most outlandish things occur. In Shakespeare's *Richard III*, a prince murders his brother, the king, and then woos the king's daughter-in-law during the funeral procession. In Ben Jonson's *Volpone*, a greedy and extremely jealous man is duped into pandering his wife in the hopes of receiving Volpone's fortune. In Jean Giraudoux's *The Madwoman of Chaillot*, three eccentric old women lure all the power brokers of Paris into the underground sewers of the city and do away with them. In Luigi Pirandello's *Six Characters in Search of an Author*, ghostly characters suddenly pop out of nowhere during a rehearsal and demand to be put in a play. In *Othello*, the noble and articulate Moor becomes so jealous he is not only reduced to speaking incomprehensible gibberish, but is also persuaded that he must murder his innocent wife, and having done so can still insist that he was "one not easily jealous." The list is almost endless. Clearly such situations are far removed from life as we live it every day, yet we believe these events as they happen on stage. We respond to them *as if* they were real.

To say that in life equally unbelievable things happen—that truth is stranger than fiction—may be true, but it is really ducking the question. Why do we willingly believe what is so obviously unbelievable? Why do we do this so regularly and so successfully even when we go to plays totally alien to our sensibilities, our history, our values, or our life experience?[5] The clue to resolving this problem resides in those ever present but always changing conventions which govern our participation in the theatrical event.

Ben Jonson's **Volpone** as produced in 1951 by the Hollywood Actor's Laboratory. Morris Carnovsky played the title role in this bitter comedy on human greed.

Conventions in Life and Theatre

Conventions are mutual agreements about the meanings of actions, gestures, and words that let us interpret and understand the social behavior of others almost spontaneously. They are based on commonly accepted norms of how people should act. Because conventions express values and standards of behavior shared by the people who participate in them, they make us feel secure and trusting in our dealings with others. From the "Good morning, how are you?" as we meet a neighbor to the kiss of a loved one at night, our lives are largely governed by that common social shorthand, those rules of the game called conventions. To be sure, conventions differ from place to place and from country to country, they can have variations even within a culture, they evolve and change through time, and they often continue to be practiced even after they have lost their original meaning. Still they always operate in some form because without them it would be next to impossible for us to carry on social communication.

Conventions Are the Rules of the Game

What is true about convention in our daily lives applies equally to theatre. It, too, has its rules of the game that are meant to provide an immediately recognizable means of communication between all who participate in the theatrical event. Like conventions in life, conventions in theatre differ, evolve, and become obsolete, but they always exist in some form. Without them it would be impossible for the audience always to know what is happening on the stage.

One of the few unbreakable laws of the theatre is that the audience must at all times *know* what is going on even if it does not understand the meaning of these events until the end of the performance. Conventions are an important means of passing on to the members of the audience the information they must have if they are to know what is going on. For example, in *Othello*, Iago is a master manipulator who is both an accomplished villain and a complete hypocrite. As such, if he were true to his nature he would never reveal his manipulations or just how villainous and false he was. This would be hidden from the audience as it is hidden from the other characters in the play. But we in the audience have to know what Iago is really like and what he's up to if we are to understand the play. If we were as blind about Iago as the other characters, the play would be incomprehensible. Shakespeare used the convention of the aside—a device commonly agreed upon by the playwright, actors, and audience whereby an actor seems to step out of the play to tell the audience what is going on—as a way for Iago to inform us of his real intentions.

Only that convention can be said to be good and scenic on the stage which helps the actors and the performance to recreate **the life of the human spirit** in the play itself and in its different parts. This life must be convincing. It cannot possibly take place in conditions of barefaced lies and deceptions. A lie must become, or at any rate must seem to become, truth on the stage before it can be convincing. And truth on the stage is what the actor, the artist, and the spectator believe to be true. Therefore stage conventions, too, must bear a resemblance to truth, that is to say, be credible, and the actor himself and the spectators must believe in them.

David Magarshack, Stanislavsky on the Art of the Stage

Dramatic conventions are not a limiting but a liberating factor in the drama. They liberate because they permit selection of manner and matter to suit the characters and issues of the play.

Conor A. Farrington, "The Language of Drama"

DESDEMONA: The heavens forbid
  But that our loves and comforts should increase,
  Even as our days do grow!
OTHELLO: Amen to that, sweet powers!
  I cannot speak enough of this content;
  It stops me here; it is too much of joy:
  And this, and this, the greatest discords be *(Kissing her.)*
  That e'er our hearts shall make!
IAGO: *(Aside)* O, you are well tun'd now!
  But I'll set down the pegs that make this music,
  As honest as I am.

Similarly, in *Hamlet*, the troubled prince decides to feign madness in an attempt to discover the truth about his father's murder. We in the audience must know this prior to the time he puts his "antic disposition on" if we are to understand what is happening. So Hamlet tells us of his decision in a soliloquy—a dramatic monologue Elizabethan playwrights used to express a character's inner thoughts. Both the aside and the soliloquy are conventions we accept. The first is a means whereby the character can pass on secret but necessary information to the audience, and the second reveals how a character communicates with himself or herself.

  Conventions are the grammar of the theatre. They are the rules that govern a play's composition. One might even go so far as to say that in a very real way, the history of the theatre is a history of its conventions. There are conventions of language and movement; conventional character types; conventions of theme; conventions of form; conventions of staging, design, and costume; even conventions regarding the relationship of the audience to the stage. We will be discussing many of these conventions in later chapters. For now it is important to understand that each of these conventions communicates something we need to know if we are to believe what is taking place on the stage. They make us feel at home in the world of the play.

Besides supplying us with needed information, conventions serve another important function. They give a performance a quality of authenticity. Like social conventions, they are not as artificial as they might first appear to be. In fact, theatrical conventions are very much related to our actual life experience. The soliloquy is similar to those conversations we have with ourselves as we walk the dog or drive the car or shave or put on makeup before a mirror. These real-life soliloquies are ways we communicate with ourselves. They help us stay in touch with ourselves. They authenticate our existence and when used in the theatre they authenticate our experience there as well. The same is true of the aside. Think of all the ways we pass on secret but necessary information in everyday life. The confidential report, the conference between lawyer and client in the courtroom, the whisper at a party, the background information given to guests before a newcomer arrives are all forms of the aside.

This is not to say theatrical and social conventions are the same. But they are related to each other and function in a similar way. Social conventions make life manageable because when we agree on them and observe them we don't have to think about certain mechanical aspects of life—who should speak first, who should thank whom, etc.—they free us from having to cope anew with many of the small but necessary situations of life every time they occur. Likewise, conventions in the theatre are rules of etiquette. They ease the passing on of information the audience needs. They also say: *This is theatre. It is not real life. It is theatre much like it has always been and always will be.* Conventions are the simplest way of making the events happening onstage lifelike because they free us from the distraction of having to rethink and reinvent the experience every time we go to the theatre. Conventions ensure that certain things are already established between play and audience. They authenticate the performance for us in the sense of making us feel at home in the world of the play not because we are used to asides and soliloquies and choruses in real life (we are not, or at least not in the same way) but because they let us experience the performance as if it were an actual series of events. As long as we accept this contrivance (the convention) as a substitute for its real-life counterpart, it will add up to an authentic, lifelike event. Conventions help us to experience dramatic action as true to life.

When Conventions Change

Nothing underscores the function and importance of conventions more clearly than to observe an audience's responses when, for any number of reasons, a production introduces a new convention or uses an established one in a new way. One discovers audiences don't like it when the rules of the game have been changed. Some people feel lost and confused ("Just what's going on?"); others believe the production has failed and feel cheated; still others are downright angry. No matter what the response, whenever conventions change in the theatre, the changes inevitably provoke hostility because the common grammar that governs communication in the theatre is not operating in its customary way.

The same thing happens with social conventions. As attitudes and customs change, there are corresponding changes in the behavioral shorthand of our conventions. It used to be, for instance, that when a man and a woman walked down the street, the man automatically walked on the curb-side of the sidewalk. This was a convention of male courtesy and protectiveness. As the nature of traffic, our behavioral patterns, and our views regarding women's role in society changed, this convention has gradually disappeared. Many older people still observe it; others are disturbed that its disappearance is yet another symptom of bad manners in our youth; but the majority of people probably don't even give it a thought. The point is, for most of us this particular social rule of the game is no longer operative. There is a direct relationship between changes in social conventions and those of the theatre. When attitudes change

John Osborne's **Look Back in Anger**, starring Alan Bates, Mary Ure, and Kenneth Haigh, flouted theatrical conventions and shocked London audiences in 1956.

to such an extent that social conventions are altered, this change is likely to be reflected in some way by changes in the conventions of the theatre.

For example, when John Osborne's *Look Back in Anger* opened in London in 1956 it caused a tremendous uproar among regular theatregoers. It is a play about the conflicts and tensions in the lives of lower-middle-class people whose vocabulary is liberally sprinkled with four-letter words. It shocked audiences. Why? After all, everyone knew that the majority of the British population was of this class and certainly that was the way they spoke. But up until that time, the governing conventions of the English theatre dictated that you did not use people from the lower classes as the central characters of plays, and characters on stage were not permitted to use four-letter words. Osborne had broken the rules of the game and in so doing had disturbed a large segment of his audience. Interestingly enough, his play created a whole new audience of people who had previously felt the theatre was too far removed from their experience to be interesting to them. The play's success with this new kind of theatregoer produced a new breed of playwrights. Osborne was, in fact, mirroring the changes that had taken place in British society as a result of the Second World War—and particularly the collapse of the rigid class structure which had dominated the country for centuries. In a very short time these shattering new theatrical conventions became commonplace because they corresponded to the social conventions at work in post-war England. What had originally been confusing soon became accepted and authenticating.

Similarly, in the United States in the late 1960s, productions of the Living Theatre's *Paradise Now* and the Performance Group's *Dionysus in 69* shocked audiences not just because there was so much nudity on stage, but because the performance required people in the audience to become involved with the actors in the production. These companies broke the long-established rule that there be a gulf between the active participants on the stage and the passive spectators seated in the auditorium. We know, looking back, that these performance groups were actually responding to and expressing the new participatory mood of America at that time. Like Woodstock, protest marches, and campus revolts, the participatory theatres of the sixties reflected changes in social attitudes and conventions. It was not long before actor-audience participation became as conventional as those conventions it originally violated.[6]

When conventions change, as they did in these examples, most audiences are confused. Conventions are truly the rules of the game in theatre. They are its grammar. They provide a structure of meaning in which the playwright can create a fictional world we experience as coherent and believable. As long as the conventions are followed, we feel at home in that other world and can receive the play with a minimum of confusion.

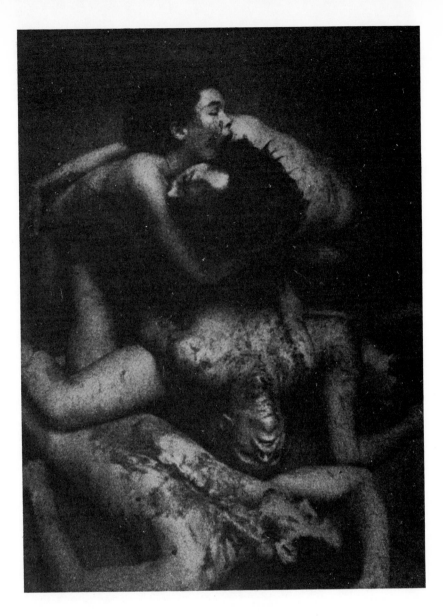

Dionysus in 69 brought international attention to the Performance Group, founded by Richard Schechner with a group of New York University students. This production, based on Euripides' The Bacchae, not only featured nudity but, more important, experimented with new performer/audience relationships.

DRAMA IS AN IMITATION OF AN ACTION

We have seen that every play is composed and that its meaning is communicated and authenticated by conventions. This combination of composition and convention gives coherence and intelligibility to the theatrical event. Now we must ask about the nature of that form which we actually experience in the theatre. A novelist must, like the playwright, choose characters, themes, situations, settings, language, and sequence. Still, a novel is not a play. We would not mistake one for the other. What is the unique nature of that coherent world we call a play?

When people begin to investigate the nature of the theatre, before long they invariably refer to the Greek theatre of the fifth century B.C. We have already done so several times. We do this because the Greeks were the first to study the nature of the theatre and their investigations are still applicable today. They provided our first critics, and foremost among them was the fourth-century philosopher Aristotle (384–322 B.C.). His well-known treatise on the theatre, the *Poetics*, ranks as one of the landmarks in the history of dramatic criticism. It is important not only because it provides a terminology for the understanding and criticism of drama which is still useful, but also because his description of what happens in drama and what constitutes the structure of a play is still extremely helpful to us and can be meaningfully applied to most plays. Let us look at some of the pertinent passages from the *Poetics:*[7]

> Drama, then, is an imitation of an action that is serious, complete, and of a certain magnitude; in language embellished with each kind of artistic ornament; the several kinds being found in separate parts of the play; in the form of action, not narrative; through pity and fear affecting the proper purgation of these emotions.

* * * * *

> In every drama there are six constitutive elements or forms by means of which the action is expressed and realized: Plot, Moral Disposition, Intellect, Language, Spectacle, and Melody.

* * * * *

> Drama in its essence is an imitation, not of men as such, but of action and life, of happiness and misery. And happiness and misery are not states of being, but forms of activity; the end for which we live is some form of activity, not the realization of a moral quality. Men are better or worse, according to their moral bent; but they become happy or miserable in their actual deeds. In a play, consequently, the agents do not perform for the sake of representing their individual dispositions; rather the display of moral character is included as incidents of the plot, and the structural ordering of these incidents constitutes the first principle or form of the action.

It will be useful for us to closely examine three key concepts in these passages from the *Poetics*. They are:
1. Drama is an *imitation*.
2. It is an imitation of an *action*.
3. The action of a play is expressed and realized by the *forms* of action.

These are difficult ideas, but they are important to our understanding of the structure of a play. Let us examine each of them briefly here.

We have been considering the idea that the theatre is a place where the ghosts we carry with us all our lives are made present so that we can experience them as if directly without having to fear the consequences of that confrontation. The "as if" is important. In theatre, we are always conscious that what's going on only appears to be real. It is all an illusion. It is a representation of reality, not reality itself. It must be make-believe. Many events taking place on the stage—even in the frothiest comedy—would at best be anxiety-provoking and in most instances would be too difficult to bear if we were dealing with them directly. But in theatre we do not have to face them directly. One of the most interesting characteristics of theatre is that it continually draws our attention to its own pretense and illusion.[8] In fact, the word "illusion" is derived from the Latin word meaning "to mock." The theatre mocks itself. One reason we experience theatre without directly experiencing fear, pain, or anxiety is that it is always mocking the unreality of its own nature. The theatre can speak the unspeakable and show that which should not be shown because we are never allowed to forget we are watching a play with players playing.

What do we mean when we say the playwright *imitates* an action? Looking the word up in a dictionary would not help much since current dictionary definitions are far removed from the meaning of the word as Aristotle used it. Today, imitation connotes exact replication or likeness, reproduction or duplication. An imitation is a fake. To imitate is to copy. In Aristotle's time *mimesthai* meant something very different. For Aristotle, an imitation 1) was something derived from the imagination and was therefore a fiction which belonged to the realm of symbols and make-believe; and 2) was something consciously made or crafted. An imitation was a creation, not a copy. It is in this latter sense that we say theatre is an imitation of an action. In aesthetic terms, the idea of imitation is directly related to two main concepts we have already developed: the idea that *theatre involves the creation of imaginary other worlds* and the idea that *theatre communicates meaning through composed form*.

The concept of imitation on the psychological level is particularly pertinent to our present discussion. In his *Play, Dreams and Imitation in Childhood*, which has shaped so much of our thinking about developmental psychology in the twentieth century, French psychologist Jean Piaget presents overwhelming evidence that we tend to imitate through the imaginative ways of play those things that cause the most ambivalent emotions within us. We do this to handle the fears that those things, because of their strangeness, evoke. We imitate the unknown as a way of mastering and gaining dominance over it.[9]

I n the last analysis there is a secret, a mystery, at the heart of every
form of play.... To play is to yield oneself to a kind of magic, to enact
to oneself the absolutely other.... The mind is prepared to accept the un-
imagined and incredible, to enter a world where different laws apply, to
be relieved of all the weights that bear it down, to be free, kingly, unfet-
tered and divine.

Hugo Rahner, **Man at Play**

Imitation, as understood by both Aristotle and Piaget, is a process by which we confront and transform our fear of the strange and
unknown by becoming one with them. Every play is an imitation
that confronts mystery. It does so in human—not abstract—terms
through the living presence of the actor, who is both a real person
and at the same time a fictional character.

Defining Dramatic Action

The impulse to imitate is first observed in the play of our childhood.
While this impulse is inseparably related to our theatrical instincts,
the imitation of children's play is not the same as that form of imitation which we call "a play." Drama is a very specific kind of imitation. It is an imitation of an *action*. What does the word "action"
mean when used in the context of a dramatic composition? It should
be clear from the excerpts from the *Poetics* we just quoted that Aristotle did not use the term "action" to refer to those external deeds,
incidents, situations, and events we tend to associate with a play's
plot. Elsewhere in his writings he likens the relationship of action
and a play to that of the soul and the body. He sees action as the
source of the play's inner meaning. As such, it is an inward process
that cannot be perceived directly; it is a spirit that moves through the
play and holds all its elements together in a meaningful way as the
play works its way to a conclusion. Perhaps it can be best understood as the governing motivation that shapes the thoughts and
feelings of all the characters in the play, the choices they make, and
the deeds they both commit and react to. It includes not only the
rational elements of behavior and response, but all the emotional
and spiritual elements as well, including childhood memories,
dreams and fantasies, conscious and unconscious desires, and responses to sensuous and emotionally charged images. "Action" is,
in short, the play's all-encompassing purpose, that which is to be
fulfilled in performance.

The Forms of Action

While "dramatic action" is the play's animating force, it is not something that can be directly pointed to or recognized. We do not say about any element of a play: *this* is the dramatic action. In particular, we should not think of dramatic action as plot. Plot is the arrangement of the events and the incidents of a play's story. How do we come to know the dramatic action of a play? Like the soul or psychic life of a human being, dramatic action is revealed and expressed by external forms or what Aristotle called "the forms of action." We come to know other people by what they do, the way they think and express themselves, and by the quality of the world that surrounds them. Similarly, we come to understand what a play's central action is through the events of the plot, the nature of the characters as they interact, the language used, and the inanimate but ever present elements of the production which make up the play's environment. These are the things Aristotle is referring to when he says, "There are six constitutive elements or forms by means of which the action is expressed and realized."

Perhaps the best way to understand this simple yet complex basic idea of the theatre is to begin with an analogy. When we meet a woman for the first time—say at a party—we have little sense of who she is, what she is like, or what motivates her. We observe her appearance, her facial expressions, gestures, and voice quality and begin to draw some conclusions about her. As we talk, the subjects of conversation and her way of expressing herself reveal still other

---

Action is that compendious expression for all of those forces (in a play) working together towards a definite end.
S. H. Butcher, Introduction to his translation of Aristotle's **Poetics**

One must be clear, first of all, that **action (praxis)** does not mean deeds, events, or physical activity: it means, rather, the motivation from which deeds spring. Butcher* puts it this way: "The **praxis** that art seeks to reproduce is mainly a psychic energy working outwards." It may be described metaphorically as the focus or movement of the psyche toward what seems good to it at the moment—a "movement-of-spirit," Dante calls it. When we try to define the actions of people we know, or of characters in plays, we usually do so in terms of motive.

*Aristotle's **Theory of Poetry and Fine Arts**, by S. H. Butcher, 4th ed., London: 1932.
Francis Fergusson, Introduction to Aristotle's **Poetics**

qualities. This continues throughout the encounter. By the end of the evening, if we have enjoyed ourselves, we may agree to see each other again but we can hardly say we know that woman as a person any more than she really knows us. Over a period of time we may do things together and see her in action—making choices, acting and reacting, expressing emotion—and gradually we come to feel we know what makes her tick. Now we know what her needs are, what her responses will be, what her motivations are, what she wants out of life, and so on. We have come to know her because in the sharing of experience she has revealed her inner nature to us. Much the same thing happens to us in our experience of a play in performance: the inner "action" is revealed through the external "forms of action."

In the *Poetics*, Aristotle refers to six forms of action: plot, moral disposition, intellect, language, spectacle, and music. For our purposes these will be more easily understood if we reduce the number to four.[10]

1. Plot
2. Character
3. Language
4. The inanimate elements of production

Plot. As in life, action is first revealed by deeds. Plot consists of those deeds, events, and incidents chosen and arranged by the playwright to tell a story. When we talked about the sequence of events in *Othello*, we were really talking about a well-constructed plot: Othello is goaded to jealousy, murder, and suicide by the villainy of Iago. These are the events of the play—they are the observable things that happen. If we think of a play as a living organism, then the plot is its body and of prime importance to the life of it (just as dramatic action is the play's soul). Plots can take many forms, ranging from those that grew out of the legends of ancient Greece, to those of Shakespeare's history plays based on the chronicles of English history, to those of Neil Simon's comedies based on the behavior of modern urban people. They can be complex and confusing as in farce or uneventful as in the plays of Anton Chekhov or Samuel Beckett, where very little seems to actually *happen*. In Beckett's *Waiting for Godot*, two people wait in an unspecified place for Godot, who never comes. They don't go anywhere or do anything but wait. Whatever its form, the dramatist tells the story, creates suspense, reveals character, and brings the play to its resolution by means of the plot. It is the spine that holds the work together. Plot is the totality of deeds that make up a play, and since we first perceive experience in the form of deeds or events, Aristotle correctly refers to the plot as the "first form" or manifestation of a play's action. It is the body that makes it possible for the play's inner life and soul to be expressed.

Samuel Beckett's **Waiting for Godot**, produced in Paris in 1961 under the direction of Jean-Marie Serreau. The setting is by the sculptor Alberto Giacometti.

Character.   While the plot is the primary means by which a play's action is expressed, the events of the play obviously cannot be separated from the characters who participate in them. The play's dramatic action is also revealed to us by the characters of the play. The nature and quality of the characters give meaning to the deeds they perform. The play's themes emerge from the actions of the characters. Medea is driven by revenge to murder; so is Hamlet. The deeds are the same, but the differences in their characters make the meanings of the two murders profoundly different. When Medea murders her children, she is motivated by jealousy, frustration, and anger. Hamlet's murder of Polonius is an accident. The term "character" encompasses all aspects of the characters' lives including their intellectual and mental powers, their moral qualities and purposes, their innermost feelings and desires, their wills, their fantasies, even their passing moods. The playwright discovers, creates, and shapes these elements of character so that they will contribute to the fulfillment of the play's action.

Unlike people in actual life who are constantly changing, and whom we can finally know only intuitively, everything about the characters in a play is fixed. They can be fully known. They have a coherence and definition we seldom have and only rarely experience. We may know someone for ten years and never feel we really know that person; there are things about that person we will never know. But there are no undiscovered or unknown facts about the characters in a play. There is no unknown secret in Hamlet's life. A character may be quite simple (a butler who has only one line in the whole performance) or as complex as Hamlet, but in all cases we in the audience are informed of all we need to know about that character. Characters in drama are defined by their acts. We can't know what Stanley Kowalski is feeling in *A Streetcar Named Desire* unless he tells us or does something to show us—pushes someone or throws a radio out the window. As far as we in the audience are concerned, Stanley has no feelings unless we can observe them. The meaning of Stanley Kowalski as a character is determined by the coherence of his acts, not by his unformed thoughts and feelings. In theatre, if a thought is not expressed—shown either in words or in behavior—it does not exist. Because plot—not character—is primary in the theatre, it provides the structure of acts which defines the characters.

In this regard, the relationship of character to plot in the theatre is very much like our relationship to the law. If I am asked, "Who are you in the eyes of the law?" the answer must always be "nobody." In the eyes of the law we don't exist until we have committed—or are alleged to have committed—an offense. If our case is brought to trial, we become *characters* in a legal action; the law creates a kind of fiction in which our character is defined by the illegal deeds we are alleged to have committed.[11] If the judge and jury believe that fiction, it matters very little that we are kind to children and animals. If at the last moment in the trial incontrovertible evidence that we could not have committed the crime were to be introduced, we would once again revert to being "nobody" in the eyes of the law. Like the theatre, the law creates a fiction in which participating characters are defined by that sequence of acts we call a plot. This is the distinction Aristotle was making when he wrote: "In a play, consequently, the agents do not perform for the sake of representing their individual dispositions; rather the display of moral character is included as incidents of the plot. . . ."

Language.   The major function of dramatic language as a means whereby the action of a play is expressed and realized is related to the characters. In our daily lives we define ourselves or, perhaps more accurately, we define our consciousness of ourselves through language and we judge other people in the same way. We infer, for instance, that people who indiscriminately use four-letter words in practically every sentence have impoverished imaginations. Their vocabulary reveals something about them. The rhetoric of politicians—which tends to carry over into even the most private situations—reveals not only the public nature of their personalities, but also their sense of themselves as public figures. They always seem to be making a speech. We observe the same thing when we see people presenting themselves as *macho* or childish, preachy or sexy. They reveal their sense of themselves in a given situation through the language they use. What is true of everyday life also holds true for the characters in a play. They reveal themselves and their sense of themselves as they relate to the events of the plot through their language.

Notice, for example, how this is achieved in *Othello*. In the first act, Othello is full of self-confidence and he meets the first challenge to his marriage to Desdemona with language that reveals that confidence:

Keep up your bright swords, for the dew will rust them.
Good signior, you shall more command with years
Than with your weapons.

By the beginning of the fourth act, ravaged by jealousy and his confidence gone, Othello's language has disintegrated to near gibberish:

Lie with her! Lie on her! We say lie on her, when they belie her. Lie with her! ('Zounds,) that's fulsome!—Handkerchief—confessions—handkerchief!—To confess, and be hang'd for his labor;—first to be hang'd, and then to confess.—I tremble at it. Nature would not invest herself in such shadowing passion without some instruction. It is not words that shakes me thus. Pish! Noses, ears, and lips.—Is't possible?—Confess—handkerchief!—O devil!

The shifts in Othello's language reveal the transformation of his sense of himself.

The acts of characters in a play are based on conscious choices, and those are expressed by the language they use. All theatre is about acts. For these acts to have meaning they must grow out of decisions to act. These choices give the play a sense of organic movement which is the essential characteristic of dramatic action. Events on the stage do not happen haphazardly or at random. The scenes in a Shakespearean play must be performed in proper sequence—rearranged, they would be meaningless. An important function of language in the theatre is to express the consciousness of characters that makes their decisions to act dramatically meaningful. It is not enough for Oedipus to go dashing from the stage and put out his eyes. If his blinding is to have meaning, we must know why he does it and what the consequences of his act will be. These meanings can be expressed only in language. This can be seen, for example, in Oedipus' speech to the Theban elders after he has gouged out his eyes:

Do not counsel me any more. This punishment
That I have laid upon myself is just.
If I had eyes,
I do not know how I could bear the sight
Of my father, when I came to the house of Death,
Or my mother: for I have sinned against them both
So vilely that I could not make my peace
By strangling my own life.
                              Or do you think my children,
Born as they were born, would be sweet to my eyes?
Ah never, never! Nor this town with its high walls,
Nor the holy images of the gods. . . .
After exposing the rankness of my own guilt,
How could I look men frankly in the eyes?[12]

The growth, movement, and rhythm of consciousness that govern a play's action are rendered in the words.[13] The plot of a play is determined by the choices the characters make. We can understand the meaning of those choices only through the language they use. Through the nuances available to language—tones, imagery, syntax—we come to know and understand that ordered sequence of choices which in their totality make up the play's plot.

Inanimate elements of production. The final form of action includes all elements associated with the production of a play—stage settings, properties, costumes, lighting, sound effects and music, and even the arrangement and movements of actors on the stage. Each of these elements is a significant means of expressing a play's action.

Even a completely empty stage expresses meaning. In Beckett's *Waiting for Godot,* the stage is a kind of barren no-man's land with nothing on it but a scrawny little tree. The tree has no leaves in the first part of the play and one leaf during the second. Clearly, the set is saying a great deal about the drab yet fierce emptiness of the characters' lives as they huddle together in an apparently absurd universe, waiting for a Godot who may or may not come. The appearance of a single leaf shows some kind of growth—limited, to be sure—in the play's "waiting" action. Similarly, the picture of General Gabler in the Tesmans' living room, which we mentioned earlier, does much more than help to establish the bourgeois physical environment of *Hedda Gabler;* it is central to the action of Ibsen's play—namely, that the play is about Hedda, the daughter of General Gabler, and not Hedda, the wife of George Tesman. The setting reinforces this important aspect of the play.

Lighting illuminates the stage, but it also creates mood and atmosphere, indicates progression in time, and can reveal significant changes in both the lives of the characters and the development of the plot.

Henrik Ibsen's **Hedda Gabler**, designed by Jack Doepp and produced at the Virginia Museum Theatre in 1965. Notice how the portrait of General Gabler dominates the set.

Costumes tell us about the period in which the play takes place and the social position of the characters, but they can also reveal aspects of the characters' personalities and relationships with each other. Costumes, too, express action. For instance, the identification of King Lear with the Fool in the play's "heath" scene is powerfully expressed by the similarity of their costumes. The king's royal robes have been reduced to tattered rags like those worn by the Fool. The same holds true for all inanimate elements of a production. They serve many functions, but finally—and this relates them to plot, character, and language in a meaningful way—their chief purpose is to express the play's governing action.

A play's action, then, is its motivating purpose. It is the force that governs the play's movement through time until it is fulfilled. Since action is an internal process, it can never be directly experienced. It is made known to us through those external forms of expression (the forms of action) that we experience directly in performance—the events of the plot, the nature of the characters, the kind of language spoken, and the various production techniques employed. These are the forms of action; they are, as Aristotle observed, the means whereby an "action is expressed and realized." Since our understanding of the relationship of action to the forms of action is crucial to our experience of the theatre, let us examine this relationship in terms of a well-known American play.

THE ACTION OF *DEATH OF A SALESMAN*

Arthur Miller's drama of a little man's pursuit of a false American dream that ends in a nightmare of suicide, doomed hopes, and familial rejection touches a sensitive nerve in audiences. Although critics have been debating the significance of *Death of a Salesman* from the beginning, most people are moved by the play and tend to identify with it even though there are few external resemblances between themselves and Miller's characters. On the surface, there is little in Willy, his wife, and his two ne'er-do-well sons to which we can relate. Yet we do. The subconscious needs and desires, the hidden passions and fears, and the deep struggles expressed in this play make us heed Miller's admonition: "Attention must be paid to this man." Why? To answer this question we must understand the distinction between the action of a play and the forms of action by which it is expressed, and also the inseparable relationship that exists between these two concepts.

Death of a Salesman is not about the false American dream, although that is certainly one of its themes. It is not preeminently about an unimportant man, although it shows us ordinary people of small imagination pitted against extraordinarily big issues. While the play has its roots in family life and much of the plot concerns family conflict, the drama is finally not about the family. These are all themes and they give the play a textural richness. But we must probe more deeply to get at the action of this play. On a conscious level much of the play is about the indignities inflicted on a human being by an indifferent universe. We identify with Willy Loman (low man, everyman) because we, too, are vulnerable to indifference, to a pathetic need for attention. But this, too, is only a theme of the play. It is not that all-encompassing, motivating force that Aristotle called "action."

The action of the play is revealed in Willy's irreversible movement to suicide. Miller shows us the *death of this particular salesman*, and in so doing he expresses the potential suicidal drama that resides in everyone. Now death is not necessarily dramatic—it is a fact of life. Even suicide is not automatically dramatic in itself. The hold this play has on our imaginations is due to the fact that Miller has taken the deep-rooted fear of and attraction to suicide that exists in each one of us—if only unconsciously—as well as the suicidal impulses operative in all family life, and has shaped these impulses so that we experience suicide as Willy Loman's destiny. Willy's movement toward suicide is the source of the play's inner meaning; it is the source of dramatic action. It is the all-encompassing purpose that was there from the beginning—even if we can only dimly know it at first—and it is fulfilled at the end. Everything about the play moves toward his death and every element of the performance expresses and is related to that movement. Willy's suicidal impulses are the governing motivation that shapes the thoughts and feelings of all the characters, the choices they make, the deeds they both commit and react to, the image patterns in their language, and even the setting where they live and in which Willy dies.

While the title of the play clearly points to where it is going, the action of suicide is not an external theme but an internal process. Willy is not conscious of his movement toward suicide. He never once uses either the word "suicide" or "death" (in fact, neither word is ever used until after his death at the very end of the play), yet we become increasingly aware that this is what the play is about. We sense this because each of the forms of action—plot, language, characters, and inanimate elements of production—expresses it.

We learn of Willy's erratic driving, the accidents, his blacking out on the highway; we discover the hose attached to the gas heater in his basement. The actual suicide follows a hallucinatory conversation with his brother Ben. The themes and images of this conversation dominated previous ones woven throughout the play and foreshadow its end. (Of particular significance is the strong death wish associated with the images of "Africa," "dark jungles," "diamonds," the grave, and the journey within, never to return.) All the relationships between the characters show Willy's unflagging

Jo Mielziner's skeletal set for the original production of Arthur Miller's **Death of a Salesman** (1949). The cast included Lee J. Cobb, Mildred Dunnock, and Arthur Kennedy.

drive to regain an infantile freedom in death. Even the set, which Miller describes as "a solid vault of apartments around a small fragile-seeming home," evokes the casket that will be Willy's final home. From the haunting siren call of the flute at the opening of the play to Linda's epilogue at the grave, every element of the play in performance expresses the play's central action: Willy Loman's movement toward death by suicide.

Audiences are not moved by *Death of a Salesman* because Willy is a sad little man or because this uncomprehending salesman is the victim of a false American dream. We identify with the action of the play because Miller has given meaningful form to those intimations of escape through self-destruction that each of us carries inside us. We are moved because we share his inner terrors, because the demon of suicide is within us and our defenses against it are—like Willy's—weaker than we can consciously acknowledge. The forms of action are a complete expression of this action. The events, characters, setting, and language all consistently and coherently express the inner dramatic action. They combine to represent this dangerous inner drama—which, like Willy, most of us can never know directly—and in so doing, Miller binds us to that danger.

The playwright makes public to the audience that which in life might be unknown, and he or she does so in such a way that we believe our experience of the performance. Even in an admittedly obscure play—say one of Harold Pinter's—we know what we need to know to experience it. It is comprehensible, and by the time the play has reached its conclusion, all its meanings will have been revealed. This does not mean that we will necessarily see or totally understand them, but all the meanings *inherent* in the play are there for us to contemplate. Often we do not see all the meanings at first and it takes different productions, varied interpretations by actors and directors, the writings of sensitive and sensible critics, and even time itself to reveal more and more of the meanings not first apparent to us.

In these opening chapters we have described the nature of the world of the theatre and how that special world is constructed. Once you realize that events on stage appear there purposefully rather than haphazardly and are the result of careful choices made by the playwright, it becomes exciting and involving to discover how those choices work (or don't work). Once we actually enter into the world of the theatre we will find it is much more diverse and richly varied than our discussion here might imply. The mysteries of human life are countless and they take many forms. And these forms are constantly changing and blending into one another.

The theatres of different cultures have responded to life's mysteries in a great variety of ways. Indeed, given the infinite variety of the human condition, theoretically the forms of theatrical expression could be almost limitless. The fact is they are not. In the theatre, certain dramatic types became established very early on and have persisted pretty much unchanged throughout history. In the following chapter we will examine in some detail the five major forms of drama that have dominated the theatre of the Western world. (We do this knowing that, except for an occasional reference, the many interesting dramatic forms of the Oriental and other non-Western theatres will have to be omitted. However, since most American theatregoers have little or no occasion to experience these forms, it is probably best not to confuse the issue by discussing them.) What kind of world, then, does the playwright create when he or she writes a tragedy, a comedy, a melodrama, a farce, or a tragicomedy?—for these are the types of drama we will discuss in the next chapter and each of these types creates a different world.

NOTES

[1]This statement may seem inconsistent in light of our observation in Chapter 2 that "great dramatic characters tend to evoke so many conflicting impulses and contradictory responses that they can never be completely understood." We shall resolve this apparent contradiction later on in this chapter.

[2]August Strindberg. "The Preface to *Miss Julie*," trans. by Evert Sprinchorn. San Francisco: Chandler Publishing Co., 1961. Cited in *The Modern Theatre*, ed. by Robert W. Corrigan. New York: Macmillan and Company, 1964, pp. 420-21.

[3]Sophocles. *Antigone*. In *Greek Plays in Modern Translation*, ed. by Dudley Fitts. New York: The Dial Press, Inc., 1947, pp. 486-87 and 464.

[4]Tennessee Williams, *A Streetcar Named Desire*. Copyright 1947 by Tennessee Williams. Reprinted by permission of New Directions Publishing Corporation and International Creative Management.

[5]Nineteenth-century poet and critic Samuel Taylor Coleridge described what we do when he referred to this phenomenon as "the willing suspension of disbelief."

[6]We might add that the reason this "new" convention lasted such a short time is probably due to the fact that real participation never actually occurred in performance. It proved to be a false convention, one that failed to communicate what its use implied it would.

[7]Translations are the author's. In Aristotle's text he used the word "tragedy" rather than "drama." However, our purposes are best served by reading "drama" for "tragedy." One can make this change without disturbing Aristotle's meaning.

[8]The play within the play is a good example. Many of the conventions we mentioned earlier also serve this purpose. Certainly as Hamlet discusses the art of acting with the players who have come to the castle, we can't help but be reminded that the play's protagonist is also an actor.

[9]One of the basic premises of Bruno Bettelheim's *The Uses of Enchantment* is that the frightening figures in the fairy tales of our childhood serve a very similar function in our development to maturity.

[10]There are two reasons for doing this. First, in Aristotle's time a person's moral inclinations, emotional life, and intellectual capacity were thought of as separate and not always related aspects of human nature. We think of them as inseparable and interrelated parts of our nature. I have combined the second and third of the Aristotelian elements under the heading of character. Second, because the Greek theatre began as a choral drama, music played a much more important role in all performance than it has subsequently. I refer to both music and spectacle as inanimate elements of production.

[11]For a full discussion of this idea, see *The Tradition of the New* by Harold Rosenberg (Horizon Press, Inc., 1959) pp. 136–37.

[12]Sophocles. "Oedipus Rex." In *Dimensions in Drama: Six Plays of Crime and Punishment,* ed. by J. Kent Clark and Henry Dan Piper. New York: Charles Scribner's Sons., 1964, p. 62.

[13]This is true even in a form like mime in which the performers do not use words. For the performance of mime to have any meaning we must always sense that the mimist's actions are based upon conscious choices and these are expressed to us in the performance by what is significantly referred to as "body language."

THE CHERRY ORCHARD

BEAUMONT THEATER LINCOLN CENTER

The last word on man is very far from being spoken.
  There is always something new under the sun, because a mystery never ages.
Our difficulty is to be alive to the newness,
  to see through the windows which are so steamed over with our daily breath,
  to be able to be old and new at one and the same time.
And the theatre we should always be trying to achieve
  is one where the persons and events have the recognizable ring of an old truth,
  and yet seem to occur in a lightning spasm of discovery. . . .
It is a province of large extent;
  I see it ranging from tragedy, through comedy of action and comedy of mood,
  even down to the playground of farce;
  and each of these has its own particular conflict, tension, and shape,
  which, if we look for them, will point the way to the play's purpose.

Christopher Fry

Chapter 4
The Forms of Drama

When we use the term "forms of drama" (as we did in the title of this chapter), we are referring to the dominant dramatic forms of our theatre. These are the types of plays or genres of drama playwrights have traditionally chosen to express their vision of some aspect of experience. Throughout the history of the Western theatre there have been five major dramatic forms, and we will examine them in some detail in this chapter. They are tragedy, melodrama, comedy, farce, and tragicomedy. Obviously there have been numerous hybrids and variations on these forms—there is no such thing as an absolutely pure comedy, for example—and yet we feel it is helpful to think of plays in terms of these categories. Such labels help us define our experience of the theatre and they suggest how the materials in the play will be handled. We quickly recognize that we are watching a comedy when we attend a performance of Neil Simon's *Barefoot in the Park*. Sometimes the label or category is not so easily decided, but each of the dramatic forms represents a fundamentally different view of human experience. If we are to realize theatre's great potential for enriching our lives, it is important for us to understand these distinctions.

The writing and production of plays is more than a matter of the principles and techniques we've discussed. At the root of every performance is a governing vision; that is, each performance expresses a view of life. That point of view is inherent in the playwright's text. Presumably there could be as many visions as there are people or plays. But this is only partly true. In each culture certain ways of viewing experience tend to become dominant. As long as they are dominant, these views shape the forms of our art, our religious and social institutions, our economic, political, and judicial systems, and even the ways people think about themselves. And the theatre is certainly not exempt. There is a definite correspondence between the theatre of any given period in history and the civilization of which it is a part.[1] The issues, concerns, and uncertainties that govern a people's imagination in any given period will be expressed in their theatre. Moreover, these concerns have a large role in determining the kinds of plays written and produced.

In this chapter we will examine the several most significant ways Western people have perceived their own experience, and how those different views have shaped the forms of our drama. Notice that certain words will come up again and again in our discussion: *fate, freedom, choice, fortune, disaster, fear, love, revenge, fantasy, hope*. These ideas have always been basic concerns of Western civilization and they have been reflected in our various theatrical forms. (These concerns have either not been central or have been thought of in radically different ways in the Orient. As a result, the nature and forms of Asian theatre are totally different from those known in the West. We will not be discussing Oriental forms here.) Each of the genres of drama involves a different mode of perception and each of them presents a fundamentally different structure of experience.

While there is an almost infinite variety of subject matter available to the dramatist, including personal experience, history, and the traditions of drama itself, these materials are, in fact, neutral or without meaning in themselves. Only by the playwright's shaping of them do they take on meaning. Not to understand this is to blur the crucial distinctions between art and life. In life, the meaning we assign to any situation—an attempt at sexual seduction, for example—will be the product of our personal attitudes and experiences. But our response to a seduction scene in a play will be the product of the causes built into that play by the playwright. Our experience is shaped by the playwright's mode of perception. The dramatist asks us to consider these particular events *in this certain way*—as tragedy, for example, or as comedy or as farce or whatever. Clearly, we can go to the theatre and enjoy it without being aware of the differences among the forms. But our pleasure will be that much greater when we understand the genres and our responses to them.

E verything in nature is . . . tragic in its fate.
George Santayana

TRAGEDY

Going all the way back to Aristotle, there has been a tendency to discuss tragedy in terms of form and structure. That is, we tend to describe, define, and judge tragedy in terms of characteristics of form which we claim are common to all tragedies, just as we may define a sonnet as having fourteen lines, or a symphony four movements. We may think a tragedy must have a noble hero who suffers a downfall or that its subject matter must deal with death or that it must be written in elevated language. But tragedy cannot be pinned down so easily. A tragedy may very well have these characteristics, but that is not really what makes it a tragedy.

Any structural or formal definition of tragedy cannot begin to be a fruitful approach when dealing with the broad variety of modern theatre; it is not helpful even as a way of studying tragedy from past periods. The tragedies written by Marlowe, Jonson, and Shakespeare in Elizabethan England over 450 years ago are all quite different from each other. The approach won't work for fifth-century Greek theatre either. Sometimes we think of theatre of that period as being so homogeneous in nature that we tend to refer to all the tragedians writing in the fifth century B.C. as "the Greeks." In fact, "homogeneous" does not describe all the plays even of any one of the Greek tragedians. (Sophocles' *Antigone*, *Electra*, *Oedipus the King*, and *Oedipus at Colonus* are quite different in form.)

For the Greeks, any play based on the legends of the historical aristocracy and performed at the seasonal festivals honoring Dionysus was a tragedy (literally, "a goat song"). But this tells us very little about Greek drama and next to nothing about tragedy. If we look at the thirty-three extant plays of Aeschylus (525–456 B.C.), Sophocles (496–406 B.C.), and Euripides (485–406 B.C.), what do we find in the way of a structural common denominator? Aeschylus wrote in the trilogy form (three directly related plays performed as a single unit), while Sophocles and Euripides did not. The chorus played a central role in Aeschylean and Sophoclean drama, but in the plays of Euripides it often seems to serve no dramatic function. We tend to think of death as an obligatory event in tragedy, yet in the majority of the classical Greek plays it is not central and often it does not occur at all. None of these ingredients (the trilogy form, chorus, death) holds up as essential to tragedy. Still, all of these plays were called tragedies.

The issue of defining any drama in terms of form or structure gets even more confusing if we start comparing tragedies written in different periods of history or in different countries and cultures. There is no way we can relate the Elizabethan *Hamlet* to the Greek *Antigone*, Euripides' *Hippolytus* to Racine's seventeenth-century French classical tragedy on the same theme, or the nineteenth-century tragedies of Ibsen to any of their predecessors in terms of form. If they have something in common—and they do—it is something other than their structural elements. If we want to deal in a meaningful way with those plays called tragedies, we must resist the "formalistic fallacy" in the study of dramatic genres. That is, we must avoid the kind of thinking about drama that assumes tragedy of all ages has certain formal and structural characteristics in common.

What do they share? It is a common spirit or view of experience which has come to be known as "the tragic view of life." It is a view that centers on our fate and, more specifically, on our need to give meaning to our fate despite the fact that we are doomed to failure and defeat.

The Tragic View of Life

The tragic writer of all ages has always been chiefly *concerned with the fate of humanity*. We consider Aeschylus, Sophocles, Euripides, Shakespeare, Racine, Ibsen, and O'Neill tragedians because their plays—although greatly different in form—*give expression to the tragic nature of the human condition*. The fate of each one of us is that we are doomed to failure and defeat; we are born to die. This view has been expressed in many different ways, but the distin-

Tragedy: The witches' scene of the Old Vic production of Shakespeare's **Macbeth**, starring Michael Redgrave as Macbeth and Edith Evans as Lady Macbeth (1946).

guishing characteristic of the tragic view of life is the awareness that the central fact of the human condition is that we always fall short. It assumes that no matter how hard we try, our wills, our physical strength, our capacity to love, and our imagination will ultimately fail us. It assumes that life will defy all attempts to order and control it by rational means. It assumes that life is violent and self-defeating, unjust and unfair, and marked by compromise at every turn. Finally, it assumes that to live is to face the absurd contradiction that life is most fully affirmed by death. All writers of tragedy view life as a doomed struggle with necessity.

Necessity is seen by tragic dramatists not as some kind of social disease that those who would change the world can ignore, soften, or legislate out of existence. Necessity embodies life's smallness, absurdity, and fragility; it acknowledges the limitation and mortality of all human experience. Humanity's struggle with necessity has been expressed in many forms and in varying contexts throughout history, but it is the constant element of tragic drama and it links all those writers we call tragedians, insofar as they can be linked.

The tragic view of life begins by insisting that we accept the inevitable doom of our fate. This fact is the mainspring of all tragic drama. But our experience of tragedy will tell us it is more than this. The great tragedies of history celebrate with equally compelling force the fact that, while we may have to learn to face and accept necessity, we also have an overpowering need to give meaning to our fate.

The spirit of tragedy is not passive; it is a grappling spirit. The nature and terms of the struggle vary in direct relationship to the individual dramatist's belief in the meaning of the struggle. It may take the form of a fierce pursuit of a finite goal as it does in so many of Ibsen's plays, or it may entail an almost suicidal aspiration toward the infinite as it does in the tragedies of Christopher Marlowe

We sing that we are mortal, that life is right not merely in spite of death but because of it. Yesterday dies that today may be born. Each flash of the present lives at the expense of all time. The softness that makes us frail makes us tender. In our fear lies triumph. In our fury lies love. The grotesque and the sickening are reflexes of desire. The world of the stage—like the stage of the world—is littered with our dead surrounded by the dying. Life is impractical, unfeasible, inconceivable—yet the human animal will take more of it. So, in grim optimism, we congratulate each other: things couldn't be worse. I wish you joy of the worm.

Harvey Birenbaum, **Tragedy and Innocence**

or Pierre Corneille. In every great tragedy we sense the validity of a meaningful struggle and the real possibility of it. Tragic characters may win or lose, but the struggle itself is the source of the dramatic significance. It is out of this struggle with necessity that heroes are born.

The Tragic Hero

When we think of tragic heroes, we usually think first of their nobility of spirit. Tragic heroes may be right or wrong, they may suffer and be destroyed, but the emotional depth and intellectual capacity each of them brings to suffering stamps him or her with the mark of greatness. We admire the hero who resists the forces of fate.

Here I think Aristotle—or at least the usual interpretation of the *Poetics* —has misled us. Aristotle called that characteristic of human will which dares to stand up against the universe and struggle with necessity *hubris*, or "overweening pride." In Aristotle's view such pride was the cause of the hero's suffering and ultimate destruction. Given the Greek philosopher's admiration for moderation in all things, we can understand why he interpreted the essential quality of the hero's character in this negative way. Such an interpretation, however, is refuted not only by the long history of tragic drama but, more importantly, by the responses of audiences as they experienced that drama. For tragedy reveals that *hubris* is that quality which defies the status quo of being human; it is our protest against the limitations of the human condition. It cannot be considered a character defect; it is an integral part of human nature. It is a necessary element of every feeling and thinking being.

Throughout history people have had to come to grips with one painful contradiction: we demand freedom but we will to submit. The tragic hero refuses to make such a compromise. Antigone is doomed not because she has "a tragic flaw" (what Aristotle called *hamartia)* but because she refuses to accept a ready-made fate. She wants her own fate—not the one the gods have chosen for her, not Creon's, not even that dictated by traditional beliefs. Antigone's tragic condition is that she, like all human beings, will ultimately fail. In her determination to honor her brother Polyneices, she chooses what is fated and so accepts the responsibility for her fate. The magnificence of this declaration of responsibility makes her heroic. Her fate is hers and no one else's.

Let us take another example. Assume that you, like Oedipus, are the crown prince of the city of Corinth and while at a party you overhear people saying the king and queen are not your real parents. Understandably, this information gnaws on you and finally you go to the Oracle at Delphi (the source of all truth) to find out if this is, in fact, true. The oracle answers your question by telling you that you will murder your father and marry your mother. That is your fate. So what do you do? Go back to Corinth and say to yourself, "Isn't it too bad that I have such a horrible fate? Oh, well, what will be, will be"? No, Oedipus didn't say that. Nor would any hero. In effect, he said, "I won't have it! If that's my fate I will fight it. I will change it." Oedipus, in trying to escape his fate—something tragedy continually confirms we never can succeed in accomplishing—insured its realization. In refusing to passively accept it, he not only triggered a chain of events leading to heroism, even more significantly he made his fate *his* fate. He earned it, he made it his fate and his alone. If Antigone or Oedipus has a flaw *(hamartia)*, it should not be thought of as a sin or a prideful assertion of egotism, but as the human response to the limitation of our tragic condition.

This confrontation with fate leads the hero into what theologian Karl Jaspers has called "boundary situations," those areas of experience where human beings are shown at the limits of their capacities and powers. At this frontier, the hero with faith and that wisdom derived from experience attempts to map his or her universe. What happens finally in tragedy is a failure of maps: in the tragic situation, human beings find themselves in a primitive country they believed their forebears had tamed, civilized, and charted only to discover they had not. Or the landscape has been distorted by an earthquake, or the map is simply inaccurate, or it does not go far enough, or it has gotten worn at the edges. In tragedy, even if the maps fail, the exploration goes on. This explains why tragedy has always had such a great hold on our imagination: it brings us into direct touch with the naked landscape of the spirit.

Division, Choice, and Responsibility

To move into an area where the maps have failed is to throw us back upon ourselves, and each of us has a divided nature. To understand tragedy we must recognize that it has its roots in the basic dividedness of human nature. There is a split between our rational and emotional selves; conflicting feelings war within us; we constantly have to deal with the struggle between what we want to do and what we believe we should do. Tragedy is about the failure that results because we can never be consistently whole. It is about the fact that the source of our failures resides within us and is not due to the operation of some external force.

All drama is built on catastrophe (literally, "a shift in direction")—any event that overturns or reverses the previously existing order or system of things. As such, catastrophe itself lacks moral meanings; it is equally capable of producing joy and happiness or

Tragedy: A highly stylized version of Racine's **Berenice** directed by Roger Planchon in Paris (1969).

sadness and grief, depending on the context in which it occurs. Catastrophe is not unique to tragedy. *The most important characteristic of tragedy—the one distinguishing it from all other dramatic forms, especially melodrama—is that all significant "catastrophic" events are caused by the inner dividedness of the protagonist and not by some external force.*

Shakespeare's *King Lear* and John Webster's *The Duchess of Malfi* have many things in common, but Lear is clearly defeated by the dividedness of his own nature while the duchess, in spite of her inner conflicts, is ultimately destroyed by forces not of her own making (her brothers, the social system, the pattern of revenge) and over which she has never had any control. We therefore consider Shakespeare's play a tragedy and Webster's a melodrama. A similar distinction can be found in classical Greek drama: certainly there is as much suffering in *The Trojan Women* as in *Oedipus the King*—probably more. But because the victimized women of Troy are not responsible for their suffering and Oedipus so clearly is, the difference between the two dramas is the difference between

Tragedy: Eugene O'Neill's dark, autobiographical tragedy of the family, **A Long Day's Journey into Night**. The cast was composed of Florence Eldridge, Frederic March, Jason Robards, Jr., and Bradford Dillman.

melodrama and tragedy. This is an important distinction. If the catastrophes of experience are considered the result of an external force—whether it be a divinity, a power of nature, or society—then the character is ultimately not responsible for them no matter how much he or she might suffer because of them. Tragedy, however, cannot exist if the hero does not eventually come to accept responsibility for his deeds and recognize that his fate is the result of choices he has made.

Tragedy begins by moving the hero into those "boundary" areas of experience where humanity is confronted with the limits of its knowledge and power. In this boundary situation, what happens? What qualities does a person reveal? Through suffering, what does she learn about herself? The tragic dramatist carries the action to the uttermost limits, exploring the furthest reaches of human possibility. The affirmation of tragedy is that it celebrates a kind of victory of the human spirit over fate.

Oedipus the King as Tragedy

Since the time it was used by Aristotle in the *Poetics* as the model of classical Greek tragedy, Sophocles' *Oedipus the King* has always been considered one of the great achievements of the tragedian's art. Sophocles took the legends of the cursed house of Laius and forged a powerful drama on the limitations of the human mind in solving riddles of the self and the universe.

Oedipus was the son of Laius and Jocasta, the rulers of Thebes. Because a curse foretold that Laius would be killed by his son, the king ordered that the infant Oedipus be taken to Mount Cithaeron, chained at the feet ("Oedipus" literally means "club footed"), and left to die of exposure. Having pity on the child, the shepherd who was to carry out the king's charge released Oedipus and gave him to a shepherd from Corinth. Taken to the palace of the king and queen of Corinth, Oedipus was brought up as their son. Many years later, the young prince overhears people saying that he is not their son. Disturbed by this, Oedipus goes to the oracle at Delphi to find out the truth. While he learns nothing about his past, he is told by the oracle that he is fated to kill his father and marry his mother.[2]

Tragedy: Sophocles' **Oedipus the King** directed and designed by Josef Svoboda at the Prague National Theatre (1963).

Horrified, Oedipus flees from Corinth and hastens to Thebes. On his way he meets a small company of men. An argument ensues, and Oedipus unknowingly kills a man who turns out to be his father. One servant escapes and returns to Thebes to report the murder of Laius. When Oedipus arrives in Thebes, the city is being devastated by the mythological monster, the Sphinx. The only way this devastation can be stopped is for someone to answer the Sphinx's riddle successfully.[3] (To fail means death.) Oedipus solves the riddle and the city is saved. In admiration and gratitude, the Thebans ask Oedipus to succeed the murdered Laius as their king and to marry his widow, Jocasta. Oedipus does, thus fulfilling his cursed fate. He reigns with wisdom, has four children—Antigone, Ismene, Eteocles, and Polyneices—and the kingdom thrives. After many years, the city is beset with a deadly plague which the oracle says will be stopped only when the murderer of Laius is found. This is where the play begins. The elders of Thebes come to Oedipus asking him to use his intelligence to discover who killed Laius.

It is interesting to note that nowhere in the play does Sophocles make a moral judgment about murder or incest. The central concern of tragedy is not guilt or innocence, but rather our struggle with fate. *Oedipus the King* dramatizes the tragic insufficiency of human intelligence in its confrontations with the riddles of existence. The action of the play really begins with Oedipus' attempt to escape the oracle's prophecy. There is no way one can deal rationally with a prophecy. It is either true or false. If it is true, what is foretold will happen. If it is false, it is irrelevant. As we said earlier, Oedipus' refusal to accept his fate is admirable. It is a mark of his grappling heroic spirit. It also sets in motion the wheel of fate, for, ironically, in attempting to escape his fate, Oedipus insures that it will happen. Oedipus cannot escape his fate—although he tries—he can only earn it. This is the tragic action of Sophocles' play.

On the face of it, Oedipus' fate is not of his own making. He had nothing to do with the original crime of his grandfather (Cadmus) that doomed the family. He did not ask to be born and he did not ask to be spared as an infant. He is fated to a suffering he did not deserve. If this is true, he is only a helpless victim, but this is not the case. We may pity Oedipus, but we also feel he is personally responsible for his doom. Why is this? Everything that happens to Oedipus is the result of conscious choices he has made. He may be fated, but he makes his fate.

Oedipus is a hero of intelligence. He is confident that his rational powers will enable him to resolve all of life's problems. When in doubt about his origins, he goes to the oracle. When informed of his horrible fate, he logically determines that the best way to avoid that fate is to leave Corinth. When confronted with the Sphinx, he uses his intelligence to solve its riddle. As king of Thebes, he will use that same intelligence to search out the source of the plague—the murderer of Laius. Everything about Oedipus reveals his great clarity of mind. He knows how to solve problems and he always arrives at the right answers. But he is also betrayed by his nature. He goes to the oracle to find out about his past, when she can tell him only what his future will be. He learns he is fated to kill his father, and shortly thereafter he loses his temper and rashly kills a man. He solves the riddle of the Sphinx and, as a reward, accepts the hand of the widowed Jocasta in marriage. In his search for the slayer of Laius, he insults the blind seer, Tiresias, and thereby sets in motion a chain of events that will lead to the revelation of his own guilt. Oedipus' greatest virtue becomes the source of his own undoing. He is both blessed and cursed by his pride in his own rational powers.

Oedipus always pushes on. What begins as a quest for knowledge becomes a quest for self. The play derives its greatness from Oedipus' capacity for self-knowledge, and his blinding of himself at the end of the play seems fitting because it is the ultimate act of self-knowledge. He would shut out the deceptions of the world to know himself more fully. He accepts the fact that, for all his powers to see and to understand, he has been blind to the central facts of his existence.

Oedipus the King is a success story. Oedipus succeeds! He finds and he is found. He seeks his identity in going to the oracle and discovers it in seeking out the killer of Laius. But whenever a human being discovers his or her real identity—as distinct from what others (parents, siblings, friends, colleagues, even enemies) believe or desire him or her to be—that person becomes conscious for the first time of his or her own unique and individual struggle with necessity. It is the individual's sense of identity that transforms the Fate of Humanity into the fate of a human being. There is glory in the discovery of self, but it has a price. Great tragedy has always affirmed this ambiguity.

Oedipus is a foundling story, and the foundling story is an archetypal expression of the conflicts involved in discovering who we are. The Oedipus story expresses the fundamental urge to become ourselves through the process of losing ourselves. Intelligence creates the possibility of such freedom; it dangles before us the vision of a free self, and taunts us to rebel. But such freedom can never be realized, for we can never fulfill ourselves apart from an ordered system even though our very nature demands that we try. The tragic hero makes a desperate effort to achieve autonomy and refuses to compromise. Oedipus is doomed not because he has a tragic flaw but because he refuses to accept a ready-made fate. He wants his own fate—not the gods'! His personal fate may be cut short by his doom, but Oedipus insists upon his own responsibility by blinding himself. It is his declaration of responsibility that makes him so heroic. His fate is *his*, and no one else's. If he has *hamartia*, it is not a sin or a flaw, but the ungovernable tragic ignorance of all people.

Human intelligence cannot solve, cover, foresee, or account for all that happens to us. Experience always makes a fool of the mind, for the answer to the question "Who am I?" is discovered only by living, and is therefore always unique. Oedipus attempts to understand everything, including his own identity, in a rational way. But for all his determination and intelligence there is a dark, nonsensical element in experience that escapes his understanding and thereby leads him to his destruction.

The Turbulence of the Tragic

We find tragedy exciting, in spite of the suffering it portrays, because it captures what critic William Arrowsmith referred to as "the turbulence of ideas under dramatic test."[4] Struggle is inevitable when people try to impose meaning on their own lives and on the world around them. And struggle and conflict can be dramatically stimulating. It is important to recognize that the constant element in tragedy is the tragic view of life or the tragic spirit: that sense that life is "essentially a cheat and its conditions are . . . those of defeat." This spirit takes many forms—both in drama and in life—but it is always there as a backdrop to the fate of humankind, and tragedy is that dramatic form which both celebrates and protests against this condition.

We are merely the stars' tennis-balls,
struck and bandied which way please them.
John Webster, **The Duchess of Malfi**

MELODRAMA:
The Drama of Disaster

The image that most often comes to mind when melodrama is mentioned is that of an innocent heroine tied to the railroad tracks as the hero and the mustachioed, black-caped villain battle nearby, with thunderous piano music as accompaniment to the action. This is, indeed, one kind of melodrama. But it is a narrow and distorted view of a form that has been popular throughout history and remains popular today.

There is a vast deal in life where the interest turns, not upon what a man shall choose to do, but on how he manages to do it; not on the passionate slips and hesitations of the conscience, but on the problems of the body and of the practical intelligence, in clean open-air adventure, the shock of arms or the diplomacy of life. [This is the realm of] melodrama.

Robert Louis Stevenson

Serious critics of the theatre often dismiss melodrama. It is a form, they say, that deals with externals, is simplistic in its attitudes, is sensational and sentimental in its effects, and—worst of all—appeals to the lowest level of public taste. In particular, melodrama has been unfavorably compared to tragedy and, because it lacks tragedy's broader moral dimensions, has been pronounced inferior. Hence, the less said about it by serious-minded people the better. Fortunately, during the past few years this negative view has been changing. We have rediscovered why melodrama has always been the most popular form of theatre. After all, more melodramas have been written and produced throughout history than all the other dramatic forms combined.

If we dismiss melodrama as shallow and insignificant, we are failing to appreciate the view of experience or mode of perception unique to this form. The melodramatic mode of perception clearly speaks to audiences and satisfies some of our most basic needs. It not only gives form to our deepest fears, it also seems to resolve them. Melodrama underscores a basic truth of the human condition: the majority of the crises and conflicts in our daily lives lack tragedy's broader moral dimensions.

The Melody of Melodrama

Before we talk about the special characteristics of this form, we should say something about the word *melodrama* itself. The word is Greek in origin (literally, "music drama" or "song drama") and it referred to those parts of the ancient Greek festivals that included choral songs and dances. The word was first used in modern times in connection with the theatre in the second half of the eighteenth century. As Michael Booth tells us in *Hiss the Villain*, "Rousseau applied it *(le mélodrame)* to his *Pygmalion* (1775), a *scène lyrique*, in which a character expresses action through speech and dumb show

to music."[5] The form was introduced to the British theatre by Guil-
bert de Pixerécourt (1773–1844), the leading French melodramatist,
and it was the most popular form of theatre during the nineteenth
century. In this early melodrama, music was used to heighten the
emotion and the sense of impending disaster present in the scripts
themselves. We can best understand this function if we think of the
music of a typical Hollywood film score. The popular movie *Jaws* of
the mid 1970s is an excellent example. The "shark music" played a
central role in the film and was largely responsible for the effective
building of suspense. Every time we heard that churning music our
hands went to our mouths in nervous excitement. Danger was lurk-
ing in the deep and as the music built to a crescendo we knew the
killer shark was near. In all probability the music did more to create
the effect than the actual representation of the shark itself. Certainly
without the music the shark would not have been as horrifying.

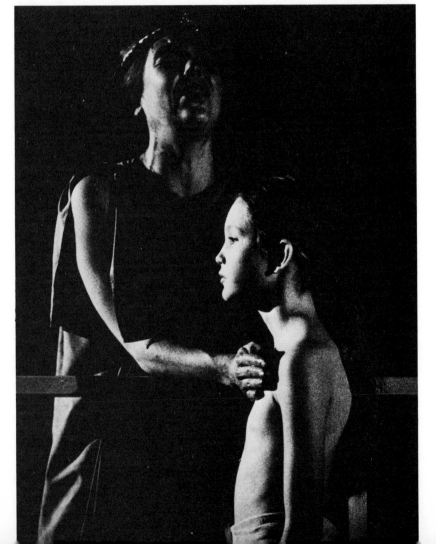

Melodrama: Andrei Serban's production of Euripides' **The Trojan
Women** at Ellen Stewart's La
Mama Theatre in New York
(1974).

Melodrama: German actress Elizabeth Bergner as the Duchess in John Webster's **The Duchess of Malfi** produced in New York (1946). Canada Lee also starred as Bosola.

What is true of this movie is also true of the melodramas of the nineteenth- and early twentieth-century stage. Booth points out:

> The stage directions of Thomas Holcroft's *The Tale of Mystery* (1802), one of the first important melodramas, contain such instructions as "music to express the discontent and alarm . . . threatening music . . . violent distracted music . . . music of painful remorse." A single striking chord may be employed; for instance, in C. P. Thompson's *The Shade* (1829), the spectre of the murdered Laurent calls on his friend for vengeance:

> SHADE *(points to the ruined Cloister).* Blondel—there thy friend was foully murdered! *(Music in a terrific chord)* Blood for blood! *(chord more terrific)* . . . Revenge! *(chord—thunder)*[6]

As we read such passages, they seem laughable; but such stage music was very effective in the last century. While music has gradually disappeared from the melodramas of the modern theatre, movies and television continue to rely on musical scores much as the nineteenth-century melodramas did. All melodrama depends upon visceral effects, and the use of music is one of the chief ways of achieving them. But as important as music has been to the successful production of melodrama, it is finally only a device to achieve effects and it is not central to the life of this popular dramatic form.

What is the source of melodrama's strong hold on our imaginations? Why has it always been such a popular form? What are its characteristics? And what view of experience does it express?

The first important characteristic of melodrama (and this distinguishes it from all other dramatic forms) is that all the significant events of the plot are caused by forces outside the protagonists. ("Protagonist" literally means "first actor" and refers to the leading characters in a play.) This is just the reverse of tragedy, where the source of conflict is within the protagonist and results from the dividedness of his or her nature. Making this distinction is not just academic nit-picking or an exercise in pedantic labeling. Tragedy and melodrama are two fundamentally different structures of experience, and each must be considered on its own terms.

Perhaps we can make the distinction even clearer by temporarily dropping the term "melodrama" (which has acquired so many negative connotations) and using in its place "drama of disaster." "Disaster" literally means "that which happens because of the stars," and it identifies the unhappiness and suffering that come to us from without; that is, from nature, society, or other individuals. Disastrous events can be just as painful and moving as the events of tragedy, but they are profoundly different. Unhappiness due to the stars, after all, is not our responsibility. Unlike tragedy, in the drama of disaster the protagonist is a victim who is acted upon, whose moral character is not essential to the event, and whose suffering does not imply related guilt or responsibility—in fact, there need not be any meaningful relationship between the suffering of the protagonist and the cause and nature of the disastrous event. You might say the unhappiness happens to the protagonist in melodrama while the protagonist in tragedy chooses it or causes it.

Let us deal with this distinction by coming at it in another way. Suppose a close friend is driving along the highway when suddenly a truck coming from the other direction goes out of control, crosses over the guard rails, colliding with his car, and he is killed. Inevitably the newspapers, your friends, and even you yourself would refer to the event as a tragedy. But in terms of the discussion here, what happened was, in fact, a disastrous accident. That truck could have been a defective airplane, an armed robber, or a bolt of lightning. What happened was an unplanned death. There is no direct and inevitable relationship between the choices your friend made and his fate; in fact, nothing was chosen. There is no sense of moral consequence in the event. It brings no larger understanding. It just happened. That doesn't mean we do not feel great pain, a deep sense of loss, and any number of other powerful emotions. It does not resolve the mystery of why it happened to that particular person at just that moment in time. But it is not tragic. It is a disaster, and our response to the event is similar to the one we experience with melodrama.

"Woe Is Me!"

Disaster is a powerful and mysterious reality, and this fact probably accounts for the overriding tone of paranoia in melodrama. (Why me? Why does the universe have it in for me?) When catastrophic events occur for which we are not responsible and over which we have no control, we cannot help but feel persecuted by a blind, meaningless, and hence absurd fate. Try as we may to come up with rational explanations for such catastrophes, there is always the hovering shadow of the bogeyman, something or someone out to get us. This attitude does much to account for melodrama's strong hold on the imagination, and it also explains the overpowering sense of reality we sense in melodrama even when, on the surface, it seems so unreal.

One of melodrama's greatest achievements is its capacity to give direct, objective form to our irrational fears. Why else the compelling appeal of Dracula or Frankenstein's monster? Because these characters have been endowed with the power and energy of our irrational fears. Why else the great popularity of horror movies at midnight? Because our most savage superstitions, our most neurotic fantasies, our most grotesque childhood imaginings are given uninhibited, yet harmless, expression. Even the wild and threatening landscape (the windswept moor, the haunted house, the thunder and lightning of a night storm) in which so many melodramatic actions are set enhances this paranoiac effect.

The paranoiac aspect of the melodramatic view of life is related to a quality of melodrama almost unique to this form and equally important to our understanding of it: its tone of self-pity. All literature of disaster, from Homer to a James Bond thriller, deals with people alive in a universe of danger. The realm of disaster, as we just said, is dominated by irrational fears; this, in turn, encourages self-pity. As Aristotle pointed out in the *Poetics*, whenever we shift from feeling sorry for a character who suffers pain to fear that we could be responsible for causing pain, we move from the sense of disaster toward the tragic sense. In melodrama neither the characters nor the audience make such a shift, with the result that its dominant style is one of exaggerated self-pity.

From the wailing women of Troy in Euripides' *The Trojan Women* to poor Eliza or Nell tied to the railroad tracks, the characters of melodrama feel sorry for themselves. They may live every moment at a high pitch of stress (the energy and visceral strength of melodrama are amazing), but ultimately they react to their unhappy condition with a plaintive "Woe is me!" We shouldn't feel superior in observing this truth. Self-pity is a powerful force in our lives. We often feel it is as a response to our sense of helplessness. In a world where so many things happen which we either do not comprehend or over which we have no control, it is not surprising that we feel sorry for ourselves. In giving form to this condition, melodrama is

W e pity the hero of a melodrama because he is in a fearsome situation; we share his fears; and, pitying ourselves, we pretend that we pity him. To rehearse these facts is to put together the dramatic situation of the characteristic popular melodrama: goodness beset by badness, a hero beset by a villain, heroes and heroines beset by a wicked world.

Pity represents the weaker side of melodrama, fear the stronger. Perhaps the success of a melodramatist will always depend primarily upon his power to feel and project fear. Feeling it should be easy, for fear is the element we live in. "We have nothing to fear but fear itself" is . . . the most indestructible of obstacles. Therein lies the potential universality of melodrama.

Eric Bentley, **The Life of the Drama**

---

deeply satisfying because it offers clear-cut resolutions to human problems. In giving answers, and not just more questions, as in tragedy, it tends to ease our own feelings of self-pity.

Melodrama might best be defined as a world of "if only." It expresses our yearning for a world that is simple, unambiguous, and coherent. Self-pity is the purest expression of "if only." If only life were fair! If only the punishment always fit the crime! If only people loved me as I loved them! Alas, life is not that way. In melodrama it is. Melodrama combines our paranoiac fears and our self-pitying responses to those fears and resolves them. This resolution is at the core of every successful melodrama. The absence of ambiguity is satisfying.

One always knows where one is in melodrama. Moral principles are clearly established, and so, too, are the rules of proper conduct—factors which help explain the stereotyped characters and rigid moral distinctions so characteristic of the form. Motives and psychological explanations tend to be simple or nonexistent because the actions taking place on stage usually speak for themselves and are readily understood and easily judged. Only in melodrama does the punishment always fit the crime. The plot may be full of violence, but we accept these terrible catastrophes because we know virtue will triumph eventually. Our pleasure in melodrama is largely due to the knowledge that no matter how dire the circumstances, all will turn out right. (In this regard, the conventional nineteenth-century melodrama is much like our TV soap operas of today. Critics of contemporary culture have observed that the reason for soap opera's great popularity is that many people actually experience their lives as soap opera. In a sense, soap opera is a natural extension of the earlier popular melodramas of the stage.)

The melodramatic organization of experience has a psychological structure.... In most general terms, what it affords is the pleasure of experiencing wholeness ... the sensation of wholeness that is created when one responds with a single impulse or potential and lets this function as a surrogate for the whole personality. In this quasi wholeness he is freed from the anguish of choice and from the pain of struggling with counter impulses that inhibit and distort his single direct "action." If there is danger he is courageous; he is not distracted by fear, expediency, or the profit motive. Or he can be serene in adversity, unhampered by self-seeking, by impatience with the frailties of others, or by doubt about ends.... One is untroubled by psychic or physical fumbling, by indecisiveness, by weak muscles or strong counterimperatives.

Melodrama, in sum, includes the whole range of conflicts undergone by characters who are presented as undivided or at least without divisions of such magnitude that they **must** be at the dramatic center; hence melodrama includes a range of actions that extend from disaster to success, from defeat to victory, and a range of effects from the strongest conviction of frustration and failure that serious art can dramatize to the most frivolous assurance of triumph that a mass-circulation writer can confect.... There is a continuous spectrum of possibilities from the popular play in which the hostile force is always beatable to the drama of disaster in which the hostile force is unbeatable; at one extreme we view man in his strength, at the other, in his weakness.

Robert B. Heilman, "Tragedy and Melodrama: Versions of Experience"

The Good Guys vs. the Bad Guys

Melodrama's view of the world as simple and rational explains why the basic melodramatic plot form has always been the good guys versus the bad guys. However, it is a more sophisticated structure than such a simple statement may suggest, and it has been consciously used by dramatists usually classified as "tragic," such as Euripides, Shakespeare, Webster, Ibsen, Tolstoy, Synge, and O'Neill, to name a few.

An important characteristic of melodrama, as critic-scholar Robert B. Heilman has described so persuasively, is that in it, people are essentially "whole." By this he means the characters of melodrama are not caught up in moral dilemmas or contradictory and conflicting feelings and impulses. The protagonist of melodrama usually is incomplete in real-life human terms, but that incompleteness is not the issue of the drama.

Wholeness, then, is the essential quality of the characters in melodrama. And win or lose, the action of melodrama is basically that of an undivided protagonist facing an outer conflict. The issue, as Heilman points out, is not self-knowledge and the reordering of one's relationship to the universe (as it is in tragedy), but rather the maintenance of self in a hostile world and the reordering of one's relations with others. For this reason, resolution of melodramatic conflict is clear-cut and simple: the protagonist is engaged in a conflict which finally is either won or lost. The resolution of tragedy, on the other hand, is always complex and ambiguous.

Melodrama as Popular Entertainment

At the beginning of this discussion I said melodrama has always been the most popular form of drama. Certainly, if we apply the broad definition of "drama of disaster" developed in this chapter, the majority of the plays ever written have been in this form. A brief look at theatre history confirms this observation. Many of the extant classical Greek plays are, in fact, dramas of disaster even though they are referred to as tragedies for historical reasons. The dominant form of the Elizabethan (1558–1603) and Jacobean (1603–25) theatres in England was the melodrama of blood and revenge. (One of Shakespeare's most interesting achievements was the way he transformed the popular "revenge" play into tragedy, as with *Hamlet, Macbeth,* and *Othello.*) The lines between tragedy and melodrama are very much blurred in most of the seventeenth-century French plays of Pierre Corneille and Jean Racine. The English Restoration drama (1660–85) is essentially melodramatic. And since the second half of the eighteenth century, some form of what we have called the drama of disaster has been the basic staple of both the European and American theatres. Why is this? Why has melodrama always been the most popular form of theatrical entertainment?

The beginnings of an explanation will be found in a statement by Henry Irving, a distinguished and well-known British actor of the nineteenth century. In describing melodrama and its great appeal to audiences, he wrote:

> To the common, indifferent man, immersed as a rule in the business and socialities of daily life, it [melodrama] brings visions of glory and adventure, of emotion, of broad human interest. To all it uncurtains a world, not that in which they live and yet not other than it, a world in which interest is heightened and yet the conditions of truth are observed, in which the capabilities of men and women are seen developed without losing their consistency to nature, and developed with a curious and wholesome fidelity to simple and universal instincts of clear right and wrong.[7]

The special appeal of melodrama is that it both simplifies and idealizes human experience. In melodrama the issues are clear-cut: good and evil, justice and injustice, truth and falsehood, the faithful and faithless are readily identified. This is in marked contrast to the dramas of our everyday lives.

How many times have you heard someone say (including, pos-

Melodrama: **Dracula** (1977), with Frank Langella in the title role, sets and costumes by Edward Gorey.

sibly, yourself), "I've got enough troubles of my own. I don't have to pay good money to see more of them in the theatre!" or "The last thing I need after a hard day is to spend the evening watching someone else's problems!"? We turn to entertainment (the theatre, movies, TV) to escape from our troubles. But do we? Take the most escapist play, movie, or TV show you can think of and you will find it is filled with troubles, problems, and complications—more of them, by far, than we ever encounter in our own lives. We don't want to escape from problems, we want them resolved! And we want them resolved the way they "ought" to be; that is, the way we wish they could be but seldom are in real life.

That's the nice thing about melodrama: all issues are resolved in a well-defined way, without the ambiguous shadows and doubts that always remain in the resolution of tragedy. This resolution is possible—and this is another reason we find melodrama so attractive—because the melodramatic vision of experience locates the sources of evil, pain, and suffering outside us. Disaster may strike, but we are not responsible for it. Melodrama allows us to feel outrage at life's troubles—and to enjoy the emotional release of those feelings—without questioning our responsibility for them.

The average person is still very much like the one described by Henry Irving. We want things to come out right. We tend to draw rigid moral distinctions. We want to empathize with heroes directly associated with values we aspire to. When Irving wrote about melodrama, the theatre was to Victorian England what television is to us today—the major form of popular entertainment—and the majority of the works produced were melodramas. Today, melodrama is every bit as popular in the theatre as it was then, but it is not as visible. In the past fifty years movies and television have replaced the theatre as the dominant forms of popular entertainment, but they attract audiences for the same reasons. These media are superbly suited to melodrama since they can provide the combination of effective sound and music and the rapid series of short scenes and quick, radical changes characteristic of the form. So the next time we turn on the television set to watch our favorite melodrama, we should remember that our counterparts of a hundred years ago would be going to the theatre in cities and towns throughout the country to see the latest "hit" melodrama, and they would be doing it for the same reasons and to satisfy the same longings.

However, it would be very misleading to allow our discussion of melodrama to rest here. One of the reasons the form has come to have a bad name is the fact that its popularization in the nineteenth and twentieth centuries has tended to narrow its scope and diminish its vitality. By reducing melodrama to a neat formula, in which the good guys *always* win and right *always* triumphs, the popular melodramatists of the past 150 years have denied to disaster the great power we know it has. Of all dramatic forms, melodrama has the capacity to express the idea that our lives are shaped, for good *and* for ill, by forces outside of us which we neither fully understand nor ever totally control. This is a source of its abiding appeal to audiences and the reason so many great playwrights have chosen to write in this theatrical form.

Riders to the Sea as Melodrama

Let us bring all these ideas about the vision of melodrama together by discussing one of the major dramas of disaster written in the twentieth century—John Millington Synge's *Riders to the Sea* (1904). This Irish one-act play is a particularly good example for us to use since it is not only considered one of the masterpieces of the modern repertoire, but it is almost invariably referred to as a tragedy rather than as a melodrama. Our discussion, then, can sharpen our understanding of the distinction between these two forms.

Briefly, the plot of *Riders to the Sea* concerns an old mother, Maurya (a name meant to be identified with the *Moira* or Fate of classical Greek mythology), who lives in a fishing village in the

Melodrama: One of the many productions of J. M. Synge's **Riders to the Sea** at Dublin's Abbey Theatre.

Aran Islands of western Ireland. She has lost a husband, a father-in-law, and four of her six sons to the sea. The play opens with the discovery that her fifth son has also been lost at sea, and it ends with the drowning of her last remaining son, Bartley, as he attempts to take the family's gray pony to Connemara to be sold.

The sea is the active force in the play and, in a sense, is its main character. It has destroyed all the men in a single family, and we witness the suffering of the remaining women who are helpless before its overwhelming power. Certainly the characters do not choose their fate, and we are not conscious of any divisions within them. What happens to them just happens, and there is no larger meaning in it. The reasons of the sea are as unfathomable as its depths. When old Maurya cries out softly at the end of the play, "They're all gone now, and there isn't anything else the sea can do to me," we do not have the arrogant yet humble challenge of the tragic hero who affirms human possibility in her suffering and despair. Rather, there is a spirit of resignation within a context of lamentation. As other women surround her "with crying and lamenting" while white boards are prepared for the making of the last coffin, Maurya speaks her final words for the dead. Her speech concludes, in quiet and resigned grief, with "What more can we want than that? [A deep grave.] No man at all can be living forever, and we must be satisfied."[8]

The play is a lament—a mood piece—in which Synge evokes the ever-present reality of death in the lives of the Irish peasants by developing variations on the theme of grief. To be sure, we experience the sadness of death, but the dominant emotion the play expresses is one of deep compassion and pity. Such pathos is not characteristic of tragedy, but it manifests that gloomy world of disaster in which we attempt to live as fearful victims in the midst of great external forces we can never control.

E verything in nature is ... comic in its existence.
George Santayana

COMEDY

Nearly twenty years ago an article appeared in a New Orleans newspaper which in no way dealt with the subject of comedy, and yet in a way it points to some of the significant elements of this complex dramatic form. The article read as follows:

MAN'S CORK LEG CHEATS DEATH
Keeps Him Afloat After Leap into River

A carpenter's cork leg kept him afloat and prevented him from taking his life by jumping into the Mississippi River from a Canal St. ferry, Fourth District police reported Monday.

Taken to Charity Hospital after his rescue was Jacob Lewis. . . . Suffering from possible skull fracture and internal injuries, he was placed in a psychiatric ward for examination.

Police said that after his release from the hospital he would be booked for disturbing the peace by attempting to commit suicide.

The incident occurred about 11:25 P.M. Sunday while the ferry M. P. Crescent was tied up on the Algiers side of the river.

Police quoted a ferry passenger as saying he saw the man leap from a rest-room window into the water. When the call was sounded, two employees . . . lowered a boat and rescued Lewis.

He was brought into the boat about 100 yards from the ferry after he refused to grab life preservers the men threw him.

Ferry employees said he told them he had no desire to live. His attempt on his life might have succeeded if his cork leg had not kept him afloat, police said.

(New Orleans *Times Picayune*)[9]

We cannot help laughing at this report of a thwarted suicide. The situation is ludicrous, if not downright absurd; death and utter despair are cheated in such a preposterous fashion that we laugh at the irony. Even the man's physical injuries seem secondary to the insult of being booked for disturbing the peace. In its own grim way the story underscores the common idea that comedy and laughter are serious business.

When beginning to consider the subject of comedy, there is always a temptation to get so caught up in related but side is-sues—the psychology or physiology of laughter, the politics of humor, conventions of comic acting, etc.—that we forget the main subject altogether. We should remember the lesson to be learned from the first recorded attempt to take comedy seriously. In Plato's *Symposium*, Socrates is carrying on a long dialogue with several of his colleagues after a sumptuous banquet. They discuss aesthetics well into the night, and finally it is early morning and Socrates is still rambling on. He then begins talking about comedy and proposes his theory that tragedy and comedy spring from the same roots. "To this [his colleagues] were constrained to assent, being drowsy, and not quite following the argument. And first of all Aristophanes dropped off to sleep." As Henry Myers has pointed out in "The Analysis of Laughter," "Such was the charm of the first theory of comedy! We leave the symposium with an unforgettable picture of an eminent philosopher putting an eminent comic poet to sleep with a lecture on the Comic Spirit."[10]

In our discussion of comedy we will want to resist what we referred to earlier as the "formalistic fallacy" in the study of dramatic genres. The essential qualities of comedy are not structural, and its

Comedy: Aristophanes' **The Frogs** as produced at the Berliner Ensemble under the direction of Brecht's former colleague Benno Besson (1964).

nature cannot be defined in terms of form. The structure of each play is unique to that play and even within the works of an individual playwright there are growth and change which make it impossible to consider his or her plays in terms of consistent structural patterns. Aristophanes' *Lysistrata* and Shakespeare's *The Taming of the Shrew* have very few structural characteristics in common, yet they are both comedies. Similarly, Molière's comedies *School for Wives* and *Tartuffe* differ greatly in structure and form. We know what comedies are, but they cannot be linked in terms of structure.

Neither can they be linked in terms of subject matter. There are no themes, situations, or character types which are the sole and special province of comedy, or even more compatible with comedy than with other dramatic forms. If one tries to set rigid guidelines about the proper subject matter of comedy, one finds more exceptions than there are rules. *Oedipus the King*, for example, is a story of "the lost one found." As such, like the comedy *The Importance of Being Earnest*, it is a "success" story, a story type which traditionally has been well suited to comedy. There is no doubt that *Oedipus the King* is a success story, but it is not a comedy. The reverse is equally true: seemingly dark and tragic subject matter doesn't need to be treated in a dark and tragic way. J. M. Synge's *The Playboy of the Western World* is a story of first a reported and then an attempted murder of a father by his son, but it is considered a comedy. There is no question that we invariably associate fools and jesters with comedy, yet one of the most moving tragic scenes in all of theatre occurs between King Lear and the Fool when they meet on the heath in act 3 of *King Lear*.

Clearly, no one plot or character or theme can be said to be unique to comedy. The playwright's view of a situation and the value he or she assigns to it will determine whether we, the audience, consider a situation serious or comic or remain completely indifferent to it. For example, the "battle of the sexes" is usually mentioned as a typical comic plot. While it is true that the struggle for power in the home has provided a comic base for many plays, from Aristophanes' *Lysistrata* right up to Neil Simon's latest hit, this same struggle is also at the heart of such serious works as *Macbeth* and Strindberg's *The Father*. Or again, a woman surrounded by a host of suitors has been used as the basic predicament of countless comic plots, but this is also the situation of such non-comic plays as Ibsen's *Hedda Gabler* and O'Neill's *Strange Interlude*.

In short, for every comic use made of a given situation, one can find examples of a serious use of the same situation. In each case, the way the playwright views the experience and the value he or she assigns to it determine whether the situations in a play will be comic or serious. In this way the playwright shapes the audience's response to his or her creation. The common denominator from comedy to comedy is not a certain kind of plot or character or structure but the playwright's comic view of life.

> omedy is an art form that arises naturally wherever people are
> gathered to celebrate life, in spring festivals, triumphs, birthdays,
> weddings, or initiations. For it expresses the elementary strains and res-
> olutions of animate nature, the animal drives that persist even in human
> nature, the delight man takes in his special mental gifts that make
> him the lord of creation; it is an image of human vitality holding its
> own in the world amid the surprises of unplanned coincidence.
>
> Susanne Langer, **Feeling and Form**

The Comic View of Life

The quality common to all comedy from the time of Aristophanes in
fourth-century Greece to the present is the comic view of life. This
view of experience celebrates humankind's capacity to endure.
Comedy dramatizes the fact that no matter how many times we may
get knocked down or fall short, we will somehow manage to pull
ourselves up and keep on going. There is something physical and
instinctive about the comic—and this is a source of comedy's energy
as well as its appeal to audiences. It reveals the unquenchable will
to survive. This is the spirit that governs characters as diverse as
Shakespeare's Falstaff, Molière's Scapin, and Shaw's Candida. All
great comic characters celebrate the forces of life.

At the center of comedy is an instinctive and deeply felt trust in
life. The comic spirit expresses elation over the way life not only
survives, but pushes on, of the many ways life continually asserts
and regenerates itself. The spirit of comedy is the spirit of resurrection. Our joy in comedy comes from the realization that despite all
our individual defeats, life does nonetheless continue.

That all comedy celebrates life's capacity to renew itself is underscored by the frequent central presence of lovers in comedies.
Despite the invariable obstacles they must overcome—parents who
separate them, mistaken identities, petty jealousies or temporary
rivals, enforced absences, money problems—by the end of the play
they are happily united and the closing note is always bright with
hope for the future. Lovers embody the energy and joy of life that is
always pushing on.

But when we think about any of the comedies we may have
seen or read, we realize that for all our talk about energy and joy, at
the heart of comedy is a condition of discord, confusion, or threat.
Comedies may end happily, but along the way there is nothing but
trouble. Parents thwart the wishes of their children; children rebel

against their parents; people lie, cheat, steal, insult, and behave in countless petty ways; the social system is often corrupt or breaking down. The essential fact of the comic world is disturbance. It is a world of lost fortunes, separated lovers, mistaken and threatened identities, tyrannical or threatening imposters, knavishness, blind and willful authority figures, exile, and melancholy. Yet we laugh at and enjoy all these unpleasant people and unhappy goings-on! Why do we have such a joyous response to events and situations which are so clearly painful, unhappy, or uncomfortable? To answer this question we must discover the special world in which comedy takes place and the boundaries that define it.

The Protected World of Comedy

The world of comedy is characterized by the absence of real pain. If the play is to ring true, the characters in comedy must experience the same kinds of social pressures and restraints that we in the audience experience in our daily lives. Yet in a comedy we always feel the characters exist in a protected realm. We know that if their well-being is threatened, those threats will eventually be cut off or removed. Repressive authority (usually in the form of a parental figure or an imposter) is there, but it is always overcome by some form of wild and antic daring. Life has its shortcomings, but in comedy we always feel the possibility of change. The phony is seen for what it is. In comedy, good sense always triumphs and because it does, discord is dissolved and social order restored. At the end of every comedy we have a condition of momentary stability—there is equilibrium. The world that comedy presents on the stage is quite different from the world of tragedy.

The mysterious freedom that characterizes comedy's protected world is probably most fully embodied by the figure of the fool or trickster who appears in some form in most comic plays. From Greek and Roman comedy through Shakespeare and Molière to Charlie Chaplin and the Marx Brothers, the fool has had a primitive and magical power to strip us naked as he exposes the folly of all human effort. He can act free of law and order, free of the constraints of space and time, and always untouched by the terrors of reality. Like the heroes of the fairy tales of our childhood, the fool moves through the play as if protected by a shining halo of bright and joyous light. His presence assures us that the discord at the heart of the comic situation will eventually be made right.

Fools and tricksters express the wisdom of the comic world. They have what Susanne Langer described as a quality of "brainy opportunism in the face of an essentially dreadful universe." Through a kind of logical luck, which does not seem like luck while we experience the play in performance, the fool convinces us that

Comedy: **A Midsummer Night's Dream**, presented by the American Shakespeare Festival in Stratford, Connecticut (1967). Cyril Ritchard directed and also starred.

somehow we, too, are capable of triumphing over our tragic fate. This explains why we take such pleasure in comic predicaments. We know that at all times the world of the play does not permit painful consequences. We know morally offensive possibilities may be suggested but will never be permitted to happen.

The Boundaries of the Comic

What are the boundaries of this protected world of comedy? Although Aristotle said very little about comedy, he did provide us with some clues that will help us deal with this question. At the beginning of the fifth chapter of the *Poetics* he defines comedy as follows:

> Comedy is, as we have said, an imitation of characters of a lower type—not, however, in the full sense of the word bad, the Ludicrous being merely a subdivision of the ugly. It consists in some defect or ugliness which is not painful or destructive. To take an obvious example, the comic mask is ugly and distorted, but does not imply pain.[11]

The two key ideas in this definition are *the ludicrous* and *the absence of pain;* and although it is clear from what follows in the *Poetics* that Aristotle is more concerned with their contrasts— the serious and the painful—he does establish two fundamental boundaries of the comic. Let us examine them briefly.

One boundary of the comic is that line where the ludicrous and the serious meet. By "ludicrous" we mean obviously absurd, incongruous, exaggerated, or eccentric. An audience will not laugh at a serious presentation of what it believes to be true, good, or beautiful. The serious becomes funny to us when our serious expectations are undercut by some ludicrous, incongruous element, some falling short. We laugh at an absentminded professor because absentmindedness is inconsistent with the learning and seriousness we expect of professors. When Trofimov falls down the stairs in *The Cherry Orchard* it is a comic event not because falling down stairs is funny—it obviously is not—but because it undercuts his pompous behavior which preceded his fall. We can never be induced to laugh at the beautiful *as* beautiful. A beautiful woman is not funny; a beautiful woman who speaks in a high, squeaking voice is very funny because she fails to measure up to the standard her appearance had previously established. Such a standard may not always be logically defensible—more often than not it is not—but it holds in the theatre as long as the audience accepts it.

We laugh in these cases not simply because of the incongruous or unexpected. For incongruity, no matter how it is conceived, does not, as many theorists have maintained, necessarily evoke a comic response, and it is not the sole property of comedy. Incongruity has

Comedy: The screen scene in Richard Brinsley Sheridan's **The School for Scandal** as produced at the Old Vic Theatre in London (1948).

been effectively used in all dramatic forms, serious and comic. It can produce fear or pain as well as side-splitting laughter. The coming of Birnam Wood to Dunsinane in *Macbeth* is unquestionably incongruous, but no one in the play or the audience thinks it is funny. Indeed, as Aristotle pointed out in the *Poetics*, to show a terrible act committed by a character from whom we expect love (hence, an incongruous act) is the most effective way of producing a tragic effect. In fact, a good case could be made for the idea that incongruity is the cause of horror in the theatre as well as laughter.

When we refer to the ludicrous as a boundary or limit of comedy's protected world, we are talking about more than incongruity. We mean a perceptible falling short of an already agreed-upon standard of seriousness which we have set for the object (beautiful people talk with beautiful voices), or which is set by the object for itself (self-proclaimed serious people, like Trofimov in *The Cherry Orchard*, don't talk pretentious nonsense in serious situations). Two examples will make this point clear. To abandon an infant is a serious matter; but in *The Importance of Being Earnest*, when Oscar Wilde has Ernest/Jack Worthing abandoned in a handbag in Victoria Station by such an obviously dotty character as Miss Prism, he pushes the potentially serious situation to such a ludicrous extreme that we cannot possibly take it seriously, and it provokes our laughter. In Shakespeare's *Twelfth Night*, Malvolio is treated by almost all the other characters in the play in such humiliating ways that we should feel sorry for him. But we don't. In fact, Malvolio becomes the comic butt because he is such a self-righteous prig that we actually enjoy his humiliations. Malvolio's sense of self-importance so far exceeds his position in the world and his relations to the other characters in the play that he is ludicrous.

One boundary of the comic's realm, then, is that line where the ludicrous and the serious meet. We turn now to its other boundary, the absence of pain. Pain is never funny in itself. Painful circumstances that turn out to have no serious consequences do provoke laughter. In comedy, action has definite consequences, but these consequences have had all elements of pain and permanent defeat removed. The pratfall is a fitting symbol of the comic. Even death is never taken seriously or considered a serious threat in comedy. Aristotle perceived that the ludicrous is the proper subject matter for comedy (whether it takes the form of the grotesque, or exaggeration, or of physical deformity), and that the ludicrous must be made painless before it can become comic. The writhings of a cartoon character who has just received a blow on the head, the violent events in some of Molière's plays, and the mayhem committed by slapstick clowns remain funny only as long as it is quite clear no real pain is involved. One reason the violence of slapstick is so effective in films (one thinks of the pies and boppings of the Three Stooges or the Ritz Brothers) is that it is virtually impossible to feel afraid for the characters since the actors have no physical reality. If, on the other hand, a fight on the stage—even one intended to be funny—appears to be an actual fight, the audience may well begin to fear for the actors, to take seriously the possibility of pain.

Whenever a serious deed or event is allowed to enter the field of comedy (as frequently happens), the serious effect must be cut off in some way. In Ben Jonson's *Volpone*, the possibility of the rape of Corvino's wife by Volpone is never seriously considered because the circumstances of the play insure that it will not happen. In Synge's *The Playboy of the Western World*, we never take Christy

Mahon's threat to murder his father seriously because all Christy's earlier fantasizing about the murder assures us that the dreadful threat will never be carried out. Conversely, one of the reasons Chekhov's *The Cherry Orchard* is so difficult to interpret is that the line is so thin between actual pain and the characters' self-dramatizing about suffering. The same kind of ambiguity exists in *Twelfth Night* with Malvolio. Shakespeare pushes the cruelty almost too far, and if we begin to feel sorry for Malvolio, the comic effect of the rest of the play is jeopardized.

Comedy, then, operates in that middle zone between the serious and the absurd which Aristotle called the ludicrous. It is an area which excludes nobility of character, painful consequences, and the consummation of any events likely to offend our moral sensibilities.

The Tricks of Scapin as Comedy

Let us now see how these ideas about comedy and the comic spirit work when applied to a specific play. A play by Molière (1622–73) is a fitting example not only because this seventeenth-century French dramatist was one of the great masters of comedy, but also because his plays contain so many of the features we usually associate with comedy. This is particularly true of *The Tricks of Scapin*, a play that vibrates with the energy and life of the comic spirit.

The plot of the play is quite simple. While their fathers are traveling in a foreign country, two young men, Octave and Leandre, have met and fallen in love with Hyacinthe and Zerbinette (indeed, Octave has been married to Hyacinthe for three days). The play opens with the disturbing news that both fathers are returning with the intention of marrying the sons to young women the fathers have chosen for them. Understandably, the young couples are very upset and they go to the famous trickster Scapin and ask him for help. The rest of the play is largely concerned with the many ways Scapin outwits and humiliates the mean and miserly fathers who, angered at what their sons have done, would thwart the course of true love. Everything turns out right in the end when it is discovered that Hyacinthe and Zerbinette are actually the old men's lost daughters and the very girls the fathers intended their sons to marry in the first place.

While this may sound both simple and farfetched, it is a comic plot frequently encountered in the theatre. Many elements often found in comedy are in this play: the central position of the lovers, the woes of thwarted love and the angry carryings-on of tyrannical and small-minded fathers, the son's fear of the father that gradually gives way to mastery over him, lost children and mistaken iden-

Comedy: Oscar Wilde's **The Importance of Being Earnest.** This production featured John Gielgud and Edith Evans.

tities, the young person needing cash and threatened with disinheritance, humiliation of the parental figure, exposure of corruption in society (in this case, the gouging practices of the legal system), beatings that are humorous rather than painful, threats that are never taken seriously, bizarre scenes and events, improbable adventures, the triumph of fortune through the workings of blind luck ("So sheer chance has brought about what the fathers had carefully planned"), and a resolution in which everyone is forgiven and happily reconciled.

Finally, however, the character of Scapin holds our attention. His scheming antics and inventive spirit are the driving forces of the play. He steps into the turmoil of the troubled situation and by means of tricks and double-dealing, lying and stealing, and logic and common sense he contrives to set matters right. He succeeds, but not without being revealed as a charlatan and being temporarily banished as an imposter. He has one more trick up his sleeve, though. At the end of the play he feigns dying, is forgiven by the fathers he has duped, and is allowed to join the wedding celebration which concludes the action.

The theme of the play may be the triumph of true love, but we see very little of love—in fact, the lovers' scenes are the dullest ones in the play. Rather, the events of the play deal with overcoming obstacles to love. An important part of the triumph is the maturation of the two young men, thanks to the wily trickster, who loves to live dangerously and has a marvelous heroic spirit within a comic context. Indeed, some of Scapin's speeches actually read like those of traditional tragic heroes, but we laugh at and with him because we know there is no element of danger in his situation. The absence of threat and pain does not mean the play is without consequence. There is a powerful truth to its nature. Scapin's tricks—outlandish though they may be—underscore the fact that common sense can triumph over blindness, inauthentic behavior, and the forces of re-

The art of comedy is an undeceiving, an emancipation from error, an unmasking, an art, if you will, of denouement or "untying." But a knot cannot be untied without first having been tied. A denouement comes at the end: through most of the play we have in fact been fooled. Thus, by a truly comic paradox, the playwright who exposes our trickery does so by outtricking us. In that respect, he is his own chief knave, and has made of us, his audience, his principal fool. The bag of tricks of this prince of knaves is—the art of comedy.

Eric Bentley, **The Life of the Drama**

pression. The lovers' naiveté is balanced by an innate trust in their own feelings. The old men are shown to be capable of arriving at a new spirit of generosity. As the well-known interpreter of Molière, Ramon Fernandez, said, "Molière teaches us the unspeakably difficult art of seeing ourselves in spite of ourselves."[12]

So life pushes on! The spirit of comedy celebrates our capacity not only to endure our tragic fate, but to overcome it with energy and exuberance. Comedy insists that our good fortune is every bit as active a force in our lives as our limitations. Our fate may be tragic, but comedy, in all its forms, asserts the joy of survival in an acceptable and accepting world.

Farce is the logic of the absurd.
Theodore Gautier

FARCE

We have said the different forms of drama express different basic views of experience. One form is not better or more significant than another, and they do not cancel each other out. Each of them embodies a clearly defined perspective on the human condition and reveals that perspective in terms of dramatic form. When we come to farce, it is not so easy to see what the controlling vision is. Everything seems to be in a state of chaos.

Farce is often dismissed by critics and scholars as essentially cotton-candy fluff, little more than the work of delightful pranksters—entertaining but shallow. In the world of farce, characters are seldom complex; we do not worry about their fates, there is little psychological development, and motivations seldom seem plausible. The resolution of the plot is without significance. Compared to the other forms of drama, everything about farce seems superficial.

The world of farce is filled with madcap situations and characters. Farce has a cartoon quality. We do not experience it as a continuing narrative, but as a series of apparently unrelated lightning flashes. The plot seems to have no logical sequence, yet there is a zany logic to what happens. (In one film, Charlie Chaplin comes upon a pathetic old man suffering from a severe case of palsy. He wants to help but doesn't know what to do. Suddenly, an idea: he gets a drum and puts it underneath the old man's shaking fingers.) People get caught unexpectedly in the wrong bedrooms and hastily hide under tables or put on outlandish disguises. They get drunk

Farce: An updated version of Plautus's **The Merchant** as designed by Donald Oenslager for a production at the Yale Drama School.

and say or do preposterous things. They go into harangues only to discover that they are carrying on with the wrong person. They hatch outrageous schemes that somehow, as if by magic, succeed. Or elaborate plans come to nothing. In short, in farce everything that happens is usually unexpected and always slightly screwy from the beginning.

The Spirit of Farce

Since the laws of logical cause and effect do not apply in the world of farce, the facts of our daily existence are presented in what seems to be a distorted fashion. Yet farce is always faithful to our inner experience. The spirit of farce is one of violence and rebellion. It is an anarchic vision directed at strong, publicly approved values and standards of behavior.

Farce is the expression of repressed wishes. As Eric Bentley points out in *The Life of the Drama*, farces are much like dreams in that they are the disguised fulfillment of repressed wishes. It's probably fair to say they fulfill our conscious fantasies and wishes as well. Our pleasure in witnessing farce is that our wildest fantasies can be acted out without our having to suffer the consequences. In technique it is like psychiatric therapy: the doctor urges patients to talk about their fantasies within the safe confines of the office so they will not feel so compelled to act them out in perhaps destructive ways elsewhere. In watching farce, we participate in the action vicariously, with presumably the same therapeutic effect.

This relationship often leads to a misunderstanding. The literature on farce is invariably concerned with farce as an expression of sexual fantasies. "Bedroom farce" is the term commonly applied to all plays in this form of drama. There is some justification for this, but when we see the plays of any of the great writers of farce, or farceurs, as they are called, we notice that, although sex is present, so are many other subjects. In Molière's one-act farces, we have portrayals of class struggles, the debunking of the educational system, and hypocrites of all kinds. In Chekhov's riotous early plays we find everything from long monologues on the harmfulness of tobacco to amusing spoofs of the theatre itself. Or think of the best known of our modern farceurs: Charlie Chaplin, Buster Keaton, the Marx Brothers, Abbott and Costello, Laurel and Hardy. Sex and slapstick have often been combined, but never exclusively, except in the old-time burlesque routines. Farce's spirit of violence and rebellion is directed to other situations and standards of value such as wealth, social class, urban or rural life, and even the arts.

The creation of farce depends on strong, publicly shared values and standards. If, for instance, a society in any given period in history holds adultery to be wrong both in principle and practice, then some people may refrain from committing adultery out of feelings of fear and guilt. This does not mean that they do not have adulterous feelings but that those feelings are usually repressed. This social condition is ideal for farce. What has been repressed in the lives of the audience can live with open abandon on the stage.

Perhaps we can understand farce's dynamic of fantasy and repression as it relates to commonly shared standards of value when we realize that the last really big-hit bedroom farce on Broadway was *The Seven-Year Itch*, first produced in 1952. The date is significant. Sexual taboos and rigid standards of sexual behavior have been dissolving (or at least are changing profoundly) so rapidly in the past couple of decades that the old-fashioned bedroom farce has just about disappeared.

The classical French farces of the nineteenth-century—particularly those of George Feydeau—are still regularly revived, but

Farce: Carlo Goldoni's **The Servant of Two Masters**, directed by Giorgio Strehler at the Piccolo Theatre in Milan (1947).

Farce: Molière's **The Miser**, directed by Douglas Campbell with designs by Tanya Moiseiwitsch at the Tyrone Guthrie Theatre in Minneapolis (1963). This production starred Hume Cronyn and Zoe Caldwell.

F arce in general offers a special opportunity: shielded by delicious darkness and seated in warm security, we enjoy the privilege of being totally passive while on stage our most treasured unmentionable wishes are fulfilled before our eyes by the most violently active human beings that ever sprang from the human imagination. In that application of the formula which is bedroom farce, we savor the adventure of adultery, ingeniously exaggerated in the highest degree, and all without taking the responsibility or suffering the guilt.

Eric Bentley, **The Life of the Drama**

most audiences consider them delightful museum pieces rather than as representations of anything relevant to their own lives. *Up in Mabel's Room* and *Getting Gertie's Garter*, popular American farces of the 1920s, are absurd but not funny today.[13]

As more liberal sexual attitudes develop (people talk openly about subjects they used to feel comfortable only snickering at), farce has tended to move to other realms such as the family, money and social caste, accomplishment and pride, bureaucratic power and the system. The real point, however, is that farce has always had the ability to lampoon subjects other than sexual mores. It can and does have many targets.

The Tempo of Farce

Obviously, the rebellious and violent energy of farce would be lost if played at a slow and leisurely pace. Too often, however, farce is played at breakneck speed. This results, more often than not, in confusion rather than art.

If we are most fully to experience farce in performance, we need to know something of its inner dynamics. The rapid pace is not applied to the play as compensation for the frivolity of the script (as if the play had to move so fast that the audience would never have time to question its implausibility). The pace is inherent in the form itself. Perhaps the best way to think of the tempo of farce is in terms of our dreams. Like a dream, farce is made up of images and these images shift constantly and move rapidly one into another. First one image appears, then the focus quickly shifts to something else. At times characters seem to split, then they merge into each other. Something strange suddenly becomes clear and the inconsequential becomes important. A whole series of apparently unrelated episodes turns out to be a part of an organic whole. And so on. Like our dreams and like fairy tales, farce is essentially a surrealistic art.

Farce: Maggie Smith in Noel Coward's **Private Lives** (1973). This London production also featured Robert Stephens.

Farce is an art of images. Like a giant collage, it is composed of violent juxtapositions, short, bright flashes, and scattered patterns having no apparent continuity. But through all the external hilarity, we become aware of the childlike truth of its nature and the logic of its means. Both in its techniques and in our responses to them, the dynamics of farce are much like those of a Punch-and-Judy show.

Farce and the Actor

Farce is the actor's medium *par excellence*. When we look at the origins of most theatres throughout history—for example, the earliest known plays of Greece (the satyr plays) and the earliest plays of the Roman Republic, or the first secular plays in medieval Europe—we find that farce is usually the first clearly developed theatrical form. Many scholars have called farce the root form of all drama. More than any other dramatic form, farce depends completely on the quality of the actor's performance to communicate both its nature and its meanings. In fact, most of the great farceurs in history—Plautus, Molière, Feydeau, and Chaplin, to name some of the best, were actors.

Farce should always be acted. Farce is not easy to *read*. Its most important qualities cannot be found inside the covers of a book. Farce relies on the actor's facial expressions, mimicries, physical gestures, timing, and delivery of lines for its effects. Indeed, they are achieved more often by visual than by verbal means. The language of farce is a special combination of the verbal and non-verbal, sound and movement. (The silent film was an ideal medium for farce.) To capture the dynamic of farce is next to impossible except through performance itself.

The fact that farce really exists only in performance probably accounts for the great difference between the audience's enthusiastic response to it and the scholar's general lack of regard for it. There is very little we can say about the literary texts of farce. The influential nineteenth-century French critic Francisque Sarcey observed that "all farces congeal when they are transformed from the stage to a cold description of them." What do you say, for example, about the text of a play like Ann Jellicoe's farce *The Knack* in which two characters say "Ping" for several pages to the tune of "The Blue Danube" waltz, and whose main character does little more than shout "Rape!" throughout the last act? Farce is not primarily a literary form. More so than most plays, farces must be visualized rather than read. They are written for actors, not readers.

This being the case, we shall not describe the workings of a specific example of farce as we have done with the other forms. But before we move on to our discussion of the last of the major forms of the Western theatre, we should remind ourselves that farce is not simply the work of delightful pranksters. It is one of the undervalued riches of the theatre. To experience farce requires the open spirit of a child and the child's eager response to the acting impulse. Farce is not simply weak comedy played very quickly. It is the acting out of wishes and dreams and its tempo and logical chaos are like something out of a dream. To experience the plays of any farceur properly, we must first willingly and wholeheartedly enter into fantasy's magic realm.

I t all comes to the same thing anyway; comic and tragic are merely two aspects of the same situation, and I have now reached the stage where I find it hard to distinguish one from the other.
Eugene Ionesco

TRAGICOMEDY

So far we have discussed four major forms of drama. We have discovered that at the heart of each of them is the experience of some kind of pain or discord within a context of conflict. Yet each of the forms is markedly different and we have no trouble distinguishing among them.

The final form we will consider is tragicomedy. As the term suggests, it combines some of the qualities of tragedy and some of those of comedy. In tragicomedy, the serious merges with the ridiculous; helplessness is cast in a humorous vein; pain and despair are transcended or are miraculously overcome; joy and sadness become indistinguishable from one another. It is an interesting hybrid form that has dominated American and European drama since the second half of the last century.

At certain times in history, the more or less clear distinctions between the forms of drama seem to break down or to become blurred. Tragicomedy flourishes at these times. This breakdown is not due to anything that happens in the theatre but is caused by shifts in values that take place in the larger society of which the theatre is a part. In fact, we can generalize that whenever social values are in a state of radical change, distinctions between the forms of drama tend to become blurred.[14] The most striking example of this phenomenon has been in Europe and America in the past 125 years. Tragicomedy seems to thrive in a society in a state of flux.

Tragicomedy and Changing Values

The meaning and significance of the traditional forms of drama in any period of history depend on the existence of generally accepted standards of value within a society. Such norms make it possible to get wide agreement on what is serious and what is funny. All the forms of drama we have discussed thus far are based on this agreement. This publicly shared view of what is true provides the artist with a basis for communication. It enables the playwright to communicate emotion and attitude by simply describing incidents; it provides a storehouse of symbols with guaranteed responses; above all, it enables the playwright to construct a plot by selecting and organizing events that, because of this community of belief, are significant to the audience. The dramatist is bound more by plot than other writers are (novelists, for instance) because a play's action is first perceived by the audience through the events of the plot. The very existence of plot depends on agreement between writer and audience on what is significant in experience. All drama, if it is to communicate to an audience, depends on a shared view of what is significant in experience. Issues must really matter before we can consider any outcome tragic or comic.

Once this shared public truth is shattered and replaced with our individual private truths, all experience tends to be equally serious or equally ludicrous. This is what has happened in the last century. There is no publicly shared view of what is significant. This is the meaning of the contemporary French playwright Eugène Ionesco's statement with which we opened this discussion of tragicomedy.

Let us look at an example that illustrates what this means. The subject is the sexual seduction of a young woman. In the English theatre of the Restoration (the late seventeenth and eighteenth cen-

Tragicomedy: A stunning East German production of Shakespeare's **The Tempest** (1970).

Tragicomedy: Andrei Serban's unconventional version of Chekhov's **The Cherry Orchard** as presented at the Vivian Beaumont Theatre of New York's Lincoln Center (1977). Irene Worth starred as Madame Ranevsky.

turies), seduction was comic in both theme and situation. Its use as subject matter in the theatre—which was very common—reflected the commitment to dalliance, infidelity, and sexual conquest which characterized the lives of the court nobility who made up the audience of that theatre. A playwright like William Congreve (1670–1729) or William Wycherley (1640–1715) could introduce a seduction scene into one of his plays and know exactly how his audience would respond to it. They would laugh and enjoy it. His only task (no small one, to be sure) would be to do it with wit. To achieve any response other than laughter would require an elaborate manipulation of the plot and characters, since the audience's attitude toward seduction was so firmly fixed. But by the end of the eighteenth century and all through the nineteenth century, the public attitude toward seduction changed radically. The seduction of the innocent during that period was seen as a horrible catastrophe ("Poor Nell!") and as the source of personal tragedy, family dishonor, abandonment, and any number of other soul-wracking, handwringing results. Once again the public attitude, although completely different, was clearly defined and known, and a playwright could use a seduction scene (or plot) with the certainty that it would evoke a guaranteed response—shock and disapproval.

Now, what about our own times? What is the commonly shared public attitude toward seduction? Although each of us might have his or her own view on the subject—including seduction of whom by whom and what sex by what sex—we would all probably have to admit that if there is any widespread public view on the subject at all, it is "Who cares?" A playwright using this theme today has to build into the play not only the event but the ways the audience is supposed to respond to it. Even this will at best create only ambiguity, for since there is no commonly held public attitude, neither the playwright nor the members of the audience can know for certain how they will respond. We know that seduction can be harmless and even joyful. We also know that it can be the occasion of sadness, pain, outrage, and a deep sense of loss. Which one is it? Both? Neither? We can never be sure, and a world of ambiguous values is the miasma from whence tragicomedy emerges.

Tragicomedy and the Modern Theatre

Tragicomedy has thrived at various times throughout the history of the Western theatre, but without question the most significant period has been the past hundred years. Indeed, it is becoming increasingly difficult to use the terms *tragedy* and *comedy* with any precision at all. A striking characteristic of the modern drama is the way the old distinctions between the tragic and the comic (the serious and the ludicrous, the painful and the painless) have been erased. Ours has been a time of mongrel moods, and there are a number of reasons for this.

The drama's general pattern of development during this time can best be described as a gradual but steady shift away from publicly shared philosophical and social concerns toward the crises and conflicts of an individual's inner and private life. This very major change in the concerns of the theatre grew out of and reflected profound social changes in the period.

One of the dominant ideas of the modern period is the conviction that it is impossible to know what the world is really like. Before Martin Luther (1483–1546), society generally believed that there is a direct and recognizable relationship between our external actions and our innermost motivations and feelings. In rejecting a direct relationship between the outer and inner worlds, Luther began a revolution in thought that gradually made it impossible for humanity to attach any objective value to the world of experience. This insistence on such a clear-cut division between the physical and the spiritual aspects of reality had a profound effect on modern dramatists, who grew increasingly distrustful of sensory responses to the "outside" world. At the same time they tended to lose whatever belief they might have had in the truth of their own feelings and sensations. Playwrights could no longer hold a mirror up to nature, at least not with any confidence. They could only reflect their own feelings and responses to the world, knowing that these feelings and responses are inconsistent, often contradictory, and deeply personal.

One force in the nineteenth century that did much to destroy belief in an established norm of human nature and to begin this process of internalization in the theatre was the development of psychology as a field of study. Psychology has demonstrated that the distinction between rational and irrational behavior is not clear-cut, and that labelling any behavior as abnormal or inappropriate is a tremendously complicated task. Psychology has made it difficult, if not impossible, for the dramatist to present characters in a direct way. In earlier times, when it was believed there was a sharp distinction between the sane and the insane, irrational be-

Tragicomedy: Samuel Beckett's **Endgame** as directed by Jack Witikka in Helsinki, Finland (1957).

havior was dramatically significant because it could be defined in terms of a commonly accepted standard of sane conduct. It seems clear, for instance, that in Shakespeare's presentation of them, Lear on the heath is insane while Macbeth at the witches' cauldron is not. But for the modern dramatist, deeds do not necessarily mean what they appear to mean, and in themselves they are not directly related to the characters. For example, we can never be sure why Hedda Gabler or Miss Julie acts as she does. Once a playwright believes that the meaning of every human action is relative, the dramatic events of the plot cease to have meaning in themselves. The playwright cannot count on a commonly shared view of truth to give meaning to events in a play. They take on significance only as the individual motivations of the characters are revealed. (The technique of earlier drama was just the reverse: the motivations of the characters were revealed by the events of the plot.)

While the development of psychology was a very powerful force in shaping the modern theatre, there were other factors at work as well. The industrial revolution and developing industrial technology brought incredible change to working and family life, and the speed of change made the future increasingly unpredictable. People were forced to live with uncertainty and growing isolation.

At the same time, discoveries made by nineteenth-century archeologists and the resulting interest in anthropology tended to break down existing attitudes toward human nature. Early anthropologists made it clear that human nature is not something fixed and unchanging but only a kind of behavior learned in each culture. Furthermore, by the middle of the century, democracy was finally beginning to be established both as a way of life and as a form of government. Today we tend to forget what a revolutionary idea democracy is and the shattering effects it had on the values of eighteenth- and nineteenth-century Europe. In 1835 Alexis de Tocqueville had observed in *Democracy in America:*

> Not only does democracy make every man forget his ancestors, but
> it hides his descendants and separates his contemporaries from
> him, it throws him back forever upon himself and threatens in the
> end to confine him entirely within the solitude of his own heart.

By the second half of the nineteenth century, every established view of God, human nature, social organization, and the physical universe was beginning to be seriously challenged, if not rejected outright.

These profound changes in values and attitudes had a tremendous influence on the nature of dramatic form. As beliefs and values crumbled and changed, the clear-cut distinctions between the established forms of drama became fuzzy. This was particularly true of the forms of tragedy and comedy. When you can't be sure what actions really mean, and when the relationship between actions and results is unclear, the serious tends to be inseparable from the ludicrous. Or you can turn this idea around, and it still comes out much the same way: the trivial can become the most effective way of communicating the serious. Either way, it is the best way to describe the vision dominant in the theatre during the past one hundred years. It is certainly the controlling vision of most of the plays of Ibsen, Strindberg, Chekhov, Pirandello, Giraudoux, Brecht, Duerrenmatt, Beckett, Ionesco, Pinter, and Albee. Even Eugene O'Neill—who had a tragic sense of life, if anyone ever did—remarked as far back as 1939 that:

> It's struck me as time goes on, how something funny, even farcical, can suddenly without apparent reason, break up into something gloomy and tragic. . . . A sort of unfair *non sequitur*, as though events, as though life, were to be manipulated just to confuse us. I think I'm aware of comedy more than I ever was before—a big kind of comedy that doesn't stay funny very long.[15]

In the modern theatre the lines of the comic mask have become indistinguishable from those of the tragic. This is the realm of tragicomedy. Probably no one embodies the spirit of this realm more fully than Gogo and Didi, the central characters of Samuel Beckett's *Waiting for Godot*. We don't know who Godot is, or why Gogo and Didi are waiting for him. By the end of the play Godot has still not come and they decide to go.

VLADIMIR: Well? Shall we go?
ESTRAGON: Yes, let's go.

But the last line of the play is a stage direction: *"They do not move."*[16] Gogo and Didi are two irreducible specimens of a humanity whose only capacity is to remain comically, tragically, ambiguously alive with the courage of their hallucinations as they wait for a Godot who may or may not ever come.

"Hope Springs Eternal . . ."

The vision of tragicomedy is one of almost unrelieved despair. It lacks the heroism, the sense of accomplishment, and the spirit of fulfillment we discovered in tragedy. Tragedy may be painful and at times even sad, but there is something glorious and affirming in the hero's capacity to become one with his or her own fate. Tragicomedy also lacks the life-enhancing energy and the sense of triumph we associate with comedy. All the qualities of the comic world—reconciliation, change, the restoration of social order, and the celebration of new possibility—are either absent or not working.

If the vision of tragicomedy is despairing to the point of horror, why would playwrights feel compelled to choose this form? More important, why would audiences want to experience it? What healthy need could this kind of theatre fulfill? Clearly, we do not go to the theatre to witness representations of our own happiness and despair. We do not need theatre for that. Actually, the explanation is quite the reverse. Of the dramatic forms, tragicomedy is most like life itself as we live it day by day. Think about it: How often do we achieve a clear resolution to anything? We fall in love, but how often does true love last? How often is suffering ennobling or the source of wisdom? Why does success so often prove to be hollow and empty? How capable are we of really changing things? Our experience tells us that all we can do is to "grin and bear it." That is the perfect motto for tragicomedy. It expresses the way life really is with an unsparing honesty.

That brings us back to the original question: Why do we pay our hard-earned cash to spend two or three hours of our leisure time watching unhappiness and frustration when we have our fill of that in our everyday lives outside the theatre? The answer is—and this is

Tragicomedy: Helene Weigel in a powerful performance of **Mother Courage.** The play, written by Weigel's husband, Bertolt Brecht, was also directed by the playwright at the Berliner Ensemble in 1949.

one of the mysteries of human life—most of us never give up hope. "Hope springs eternal in the human breast!" Going to the heart of tragicomedy—beyond the despair—we find hope. Why do Beckett's Gogo and Didi keep on waiting for Godot rather than hang themselves? Why do Chekhov's three sisters go on living even as their dream of Moscow is shattered? Why does Brecht's Mother Courage, all her children dead, go trudging on? Because though their lives may be meaningless and empty, broken and sad, they never give up the hope that maybe tomorrow things will change for the better. For most of us, hope is the miracle of existence, and tragicomedy insists that we need never give up hoping. Tragicomedy may bring us pictures of despair about the meaning of existence, but it does not stop there. It celebrates the fact that despair can be transcended because of our undying capacity for hope.

Chekhov and the Tragicomic Vision

One dramatist whose work fully embodies the vision of tragicomedy was the Russian playwright Anton Chekhov (1860–1904). In all his work he tried to present life as it is, with the result that in each of his plays the comic and the tragic, the ludicrous and the painful, are inextricably linked. Each of them reflects the mood of spiritual discouragement of the modern world. All his life Chekhov despaired of the fact that he was unable to answer life's important questions. "Life," he said, "is an insoluble problem." At the end of the first act of *The Sea Gull*, Dorn—one of the many doctors in Chekhov's plays—is trying to comfort the distraught and unhappy Masha, but all he can find to say is, "But what can I do, my child? Tell me, what can I do? What?" This question—"What can I do?"—runs through all Chekhov's works. He was conscious of humanity's helplessness before the overpowering forces of circumstance; he was aware of our littleness, our insignificance in a gigantic and impersonal universe;

R eal hope can be found only through real despair. . . . The appeal of that comedy which is infused with gloom and ends badly, that tragedy which is shot through with a comedy that only makes the outlook still bleaker, is that it holds out to us the only kind of hope we are in a position to accept. And if this is not the hope of a Heaven in which we would live forever, it is not the less precious, perhaps, being the hope without which we cannot live from day to day.

Eric Bentley, **The Life of the Drama**

One has to face the fact that man is a failure. His conscience, which belongs to the spirit, will probably never be brought into harmony with his nature, his reality, his social condition, and there will always be "honorable sleeplessness" for those who for some unfathomable reason feel responsible for human fate and life. If anyone ever suffered from this, it was Chekhov the artist. All his work was honorable sleeplessness, a search for the right, redeeming word in answer to the question: "What are we to do?" The word was difficult, if not impossible, to find.

Thomas Mann, **Last Essays**

he knew that no matter how closely we huddle together, we can never really communicate. In short, he was aware of the fact that the very conditions of life doom us to failure and that there is nothing anyone can do about it. He knew the utter impossibility of finding an answer to the question, "What can I do?" There is no continuity upon which his characters can depend; everything seems absurd, painful, and hopeless. In short, there is nothing one can do, and we notice increasingly, in Chekhov's later plays, that nothing is even attempted.

But this is not the whole story. If it were, Chekhov's plays would be little more than unrelieved pictures of gloom, and they are not. Chekhov, in spite of his realization that we are essentially alone and doomed to failure in all our attempts to find meaningful relationships and meaningful action, never abdicated his sense of responsibility for human life—he never gave up hope. Even though Chekhov knew there were no solutions, all his life he tried to find an answer, and his plays are a record of that quest. The central and creative tension in Chekhov's life and work was his recognition that for all of us there is a great disparity between the facts of our animal existence and the ideals we aspire to live by. Chekhov accepted both, and he saw the life of each human being as the meaningful yet pathetic, ludicrous, and tragic attempt to bridge this gap.

The Three Sisters as Tragicomedy

The Three Sisters, first produced by Konstantin Stanislavski at the Moscow Art Theatre in 1901, is a drama of dispossession and failed hopes. It is the story of three sisters and their brother who live in the old family house in a provincial Russian town. Their lives are monotonous and dull and the sisters yearn to go back to Moscow, where they had lived as children, and which they associate with life and excitement. In the meantime, the only diversion in their lives is provided by frequent visits from the army officers stationed at the barracks in this remote town. The oldest sister, Olga, is a teacher at the local girls' school. She dislikes teaching, would like to be married (if anyone would ask her), and more or less runs the household. The next sister, Masha, is unhappily married to a boring and unimaginative—albeit well-meaning—schoolmaster. And the youngest sister, Irina, is looking for some meaningful occupation until Prince Charming comes along and sweeps her off her feet. The girls' older brother, Andrey, is sitting and getting fat while he waits for an invitation to teach at the university at Moscow.

The action of the play covers a span of more than three years. It begins with the arrival of a new battery commander, the talkative, philosophizing Colonel Vershinin, and it ends with the departure of the battery, which has been transferred to another town. Throughout the play the recurring theme is, "If only we could go to Moscow!" Moscow is the symbol of a new life, new beginnings, happiness, meaningful relationships, and so on. We sense from the outset that they will never go, and we learn as the play progresses that it really wouldn't make any difference if they did. Still they hope, and that blind and deluded hope seems to sustain them.

In the meantime, we see everything the family doesn't want to happen come to pass. Andrey marries the grasping, bourgeois Natasha, and takes a job as clerk to the county board. Natasha, meanwhile, takes over the house, has an affair with Andrey's boss, and by the end of the play has succeeded in driving the sisters out of their house completely. Olga, as unmarried as ever, has become the one thing she dreaded most—headmistress of the school. Masha fell in love with and had an affair with Vershinin; now he is leaving and she faces the unpleasant prospect of spending the rest of her life with her dull husband. Irina tries her hand at several jobs but finds them all disappointing because they lack "poetry" and soul. She decides to marry one of the officers, Baron Tusenbach, even though she does not love him, but he is killed in a duel just before the play ends.

Even from this abbreviated and much simplified account, it should be clear that everything this family dreams of comes to naught. Yet we care for these characters and their pathetic destinies, and we admire the nobility of spirit that marks their futile attempts to change or overcome that destiny. We care because in spite of everything, they never give up hope. They have a resilience of spirit in the face of disappointment and despair. As the play draws to a close, Tusenbach has been killed, Vershinin has said good-by, and the soldiers are leaving to the lively strains of band music. The three sisters stand together outside the house that was once theirs, but their spirits are not broken. Here are their final speeches:

The three sisters stand huddled together.

MASHA: Oh, listen to the music! They're leaving us . . . one has already gone, gone for good . . . forever! And now we're left alone . . . to start our lives all over again. We must go on living . . . we must go on living . . .

IRINA (*puts her head on* OLGA's *breast*): Some day people will know why such things happen, and what the purpose of all this suffering is . . . Then there won't be any more mysteries . . . Tomorrow I'll go away alone and teach in a school somewhere; I'll give my life to people who need it . . . It's autumn now, it will be winter soon, and everything will be covered with snow . . . But I'll go on working . . . I will work . . .

OLGA (*puts her arms round both her sisters*): How happy the music is . . . I almost feel as if I wanted to live! Oh, God! The years will pass, and we shall all be gone. We shall be forgotten . . . Our faces, our voices will be forgotten and people will even forget that there were once three of us here . . . But our sufferings will mean happiness for those who come after us . . . Then peace and happiness will reign on earth, and we shall be remembered kindly and blessed. No, my dear sisters, our lives aren't finished yet. We shall live! The band is playing and soon we shall know why we live, why we suffer . . . Oh, if we only knew, if only we knew![17]

Anton Chekhov was aware that the fragmented life that each of us lives is a tragicomedy. His plays suggest that human beings live in the midst of so many irreconcilable forces, both within and without, that the only way our lives can be given form in art is in this hybrid genre.

We have seen in this chapter that each dramatic form embodies a clearly defined perspective on the mysteries of the human condition and that this perspective, in turn, determines not only how the dramatist shapes every element of the play's action but also how we in the audience respond to that action. The writer of tragedy is supremely conscious of humanity's fate—namely, that the central fact of experience is that ultimately we fail because of the dividedness of our nature. The comic writer, on the other hand, celebrates the equally indisputable fact that, in spite of our fate, life somehow keeps going on; that in an almost miraculous way our fortune is capable of triumphing over our fate. The melodramatist is fundamentally concerned with the disasters of experience and the effects they have on our lives. The farceur deals with the violent and exuberant realm of our fantasy life to demonstrate the joyous triumph of the human spirit over the forces of fear and repression. The writer of tragicomedy recognizes that the tragic and comic visions of life cannot be separated: we may be doomed by fate, yet we keep pushing on. Tragicomedy celebrates our capacity to start life anew because we never cease to hope.

Making these distinctions does not imply a hierarchy of dramatic forms or any kind of value judgment. One dramatic form is not better or more significant than any other. Because tragedy is so serious, it is often treated as the highest form of theatre and clearly superior to "cheap" melodrama or "mere" farce. Each form of drama, however, is an equally valid way of looking at experience and there have been many playwrights—Shakespeare is the most obvious example—whose vision of life was so broad and varied that they have moved from one form to another throughout their careers as writers. They are not mutually exclusive visions. One need not be a playwright to view any aspect of human experience from more than one perspective at the same time. In each successful play we discover what the playwright intended and what our response should be.

Each of the forms of drama involves a different mode of perception and each of them presents a fundamentally different structure of experience. Obviously one can go to theatre and enjoy it without being aware of these differences. But getting to know the various dramatic forms is really discovering the different ways theatre presents human experience to us. And the forms are as varied and rich as life itself.

NOTES

[1]The theatre of classical Greece, for instance, is very much related in theme, form, and subject matter to the religious beliefs, the mode of government, the basic philosophies, the legal system, the forms of architecture, and the patterns of public life dominant in the fifth century B.C. The same is true of the theatre of Elizabethan and Restoration England, of France under Louis XIV in the seventeenth century, and of Europe and America after the Second World War.

[2]It is important to understand the Greek belief that while oracles knew the future, they did not create it.

[3]The riddle of the Sphinx: What walks with four legs in the morning, two legs at noon, and three legs in the evening? The answer: Man, who crawls on all fours as an infant, walks on two legs when grown, and uses a staff or cane in old age.

[4]"The Criticism of Greek Tragedy." *Tulane Drama Review*, Vol. III, No. 3, Spring, 1959.

[5]Michael Booth. Introduction to *Hiss the Villain*. New York: Benjamin Blom, Inc., 1964, p. 13.

[6]Ibid., p. 12.

[7]Henry Irving. Cited in *The English Stage: 1850–1950* by Lynton Hudson. London: George G. Harrap & Co., Ltd., 1951, p. 74.

[8]John M. Synge. *Riders to the Sea* in *The Complete Works of John M. Synge*. New York: Random House, Inc., 1935, p. 931.

[9]From "Man's Cork Leg Cheats Death" as it appeared in *The New Orleans Times-Picayune*. Reprinted by permission of the publishers.

[10]Henry Alonzo Myers. "The Analysis of Laughter." *The Sewanee Review*, 1935.

[11]Translation is the author's.

[12]Ramon Fernandez. *Molière, the Man Seen Through the Plays*. New York: Hill and Wang, 1958.

[13]Even such a blatantly lewd piece as *Pajama Tops* (first produced in the early 1960s) was most successful with less sophisticated audiences and was never brought into New York. It is interesting that many so-called bedroom farces can do very badly on Broadway and still be counted on to make money in community theatres around the country. Conversely, *Oh, Calcutta!*—one of the harbingers of the sexual revolution—was a great success with New York audiences in the 1960s, but it would have been closed down in almost every other city in the country if it had played in them at that time. Interestingly, in the 1970s it toured rather successfully in those cities that would have banned it originally.

[14]This was certainly the case in the second half of the fifth century B.C. in Greece and is reflected in the plays of Euripides. (*Alcestis* is a good example.) The last plays of Shakespeare (*Measure for Measure, Cymbeline, The Winter's Tale,* and *The Tempest*) and several of those by the Jacobean dramatists reveal that something similar happened early in the seventeenth century in England after the death of Queen Elizabeth I. The theatre in seventeenth-century France after Louis XIV is another instance.

[15]Eugene O'Neill. Cited by Croswell Bowen. *The Curse of the Misbegotten: A Tale of the House of O'Neill.* New York: McGraw-Hill Book Co., 1959, p. 259.

[16]Samuel Beckett. *Waiting for Godot.* New York: Grove Press, 1954, p. 61.

[17]Anton Chekhov. *The Three Sisters* in *Six Plays of Chekhov,* trans. by Robert W. Corrigan. San Francisco: Rinehart Press, 1962, p. 287.

NT
NATIONAL
THEATRE

The Lyttelton
Theatre

HAMLET

by William Shakespeare

Desmond Adams
Michael Beint
Kenneth Benda
Tim Block
Andrew Byatt
Oliver Cotton
Roland Culver
J G Devlin
Robert Eddison
Ray Edwards

Albert Finney
Susan Fleetwood
Carol Frazer
John Gill
Glyn Grain
Gawn Grainger
Andrew Hilton
Barbara Jefford
Brenda Kaye
Michael Keating

Brian Kent
Philip Locke
Harry Lomax
Michael Melia
Patrick Monckton
Peter Needham
Denis Quilley
Ray Roberts
Peter Rocca
Struan Rodger

Gladys Spencer
P G Stephens
Michael Stroud
Daniel Thorndike
Dennis Tynsley
Simon Ward
Harry Webster
Pitt Wilkinson

The National Theatre receives financial
assistance from the Arts Council of Great
Britain and the Greater London Council

Director
Peter Hall
Designer
John Bury
Lighting
David Hersey
Music
Harrison Birtwistle
Fight
William Hobbs

The actor must not illustrate but accomplish an "act of soul"
by means of his own organism.

Jerzy Grotowski

Acting is the Art of Self; the supreme revealment of Self.
On stage, it is Self which feeds the actor
and Self which is fed upon.
Self, in its multifarious versions from Brubage to Olivier,
has always been the great draw in the theatre.

Charles Marowitz

Chapter 5
The Actor and the Role

In talking about the nature of the theatrical event in Chapter 1, we noted that there is something uncanny and inhuman about actors. They are people being *other* people; they play other people knowing that they do it for people watching. Most of us feel actors are attractive in a special way, but they make us a little uneasy, too. In any case, the actor and the audience are the essential elements of theatre. The exchange we feel between the actors and ourselves in the audience is the real heart of the theatrical event. Of all the people who help create that occasion, the actor is the one most visible, the one we usually are most attracted to and interested in.

For us to understand how the theatre works and how all the elements of the world of the play are brought together and expressed through the actor, we must consider some specific questions. What does the actor do? What is involved in the acting process? What must the actor know and have mastered to fulfill this process successfully? What kind of people become actors? Why do they act? What is their role, if any, in society? These are the basic questions that define both the actor's art and the actor's craft.

THE FOUR PERSONS OF THE ACTOR

Acting is a complex and difficult art. This is due in part to the fact that at all times the actor must be four persons in one:
1. A person in the real world;
2. A presenter of a fictional character;
3. A presented character interacting with other presented characters; and
4. A surrogate and/or model for members of the audience.
Laurence Olivier, for example, is (1) former director of the British National Theatre, a lord of the English realm, and the husband of Joan Plowright; (2) in his production of *Othello*, he was the presenter of the title role of Shakespeare's play; (3) while presenting the character of Othello he had to interact with the character of Iago as presented by Frank Finlay; and (4) in performing the role, he was conscious of the fact that he was experiencing the play for the members of the audience. Let us examine briefly each of these four persons who, when combined, make up the actor.

. . . A Person in the Real World

Actors are human like those of us in the audience. They look and behave like us. They participate in events, demonstrate feelings, and give speech to thoughts just as we do. This is important. The theatre appeals to us because we are always conscious of the fact that the actors are fellow human beings. They share our humanity.

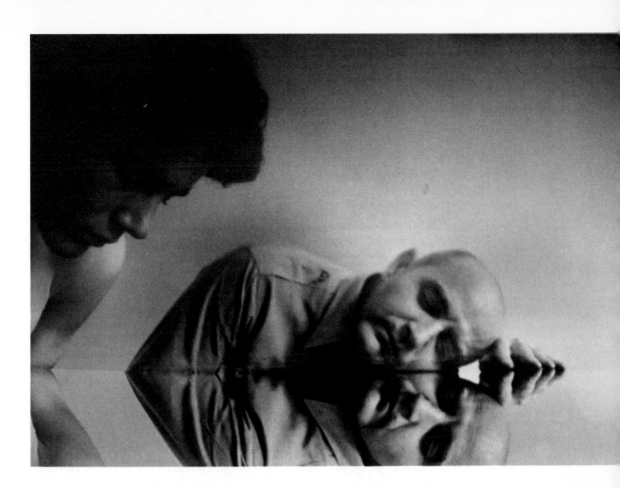

They eat, breathe, and sleep. They experience joy, anxiety, and sadness. They have headaches, trouble paying their bills, and lovers' quarrels. They come to the theatre, put on their costumes and makeup, and after the performance they have dinner and go home. Actors are people whose occupation is acting. But our consciousness of the first person of the actor—as important as it is—is almost subliminal. If we (or the actors) are too aware of them as real people, it intrudes on our experience of the theatrical event—the making present of performed characters. Actors must transform themselves into the lives of the characters that exist in the script.

. . . A Presenter of a Fictional Character

The second person of the actor is somewhat more difficult to describe and understand. The actor inhabits and becomes a creation of the unreal and fictional world of the play. His task is to give life to figures of pure fantasy. How does the actor play Hamlet? Hamlet exists only as a fiction within the words of Shakespeare's script. In the theatre, we in the audience will never know Hamlet except as the actor embodies the character in himself and presents Hamlet to us. This involves a double transformation: the actor is transformed into Hamlet (while yet remaining himself) and the fictional character of Hamlet who exists in the script is transformed into the living being of the actor. To achieve these transformations the actor must combine his own experience with the experiences contained in the script. In so doing he creates a character on stage which approximates a person in real life and at the same time is true to the imaginative world the playwright created. (We realize how significant this process is when we think of the performance of a new play or one we've never seen or read before. Under such circumstances, we can *only* know the characters as they are presented by the actors.) Finally, the actor is neither from the script nor from real life. He represents a kind of "third" world, a world derived from both life and the script, but ultimately independent of them.

An actor playing Hamlet is neither himself nor the character revealed in the words of Shakespeare's text. He is part himself and part the script, but in the end he is the performed character. He is a unique combination. And the character of Hamlet as he performs him will be different from a Hamlet played by any other actor.

The theatre has built a whole art round the actor, based on "the man and his double"— the actor and his Character.

Jean-Louis Barrault

... A Presented Character Interacting with Other Presented Characters

The actor's third person is obviously the most important one during the actual performance. A performed play is first and foremost the dramatic interaction of fictional characters. If the characters do not act and react with each other, the performance will collapse. Thus, if the Hamlet an actor performs does not interact with Polonius and Laertes as they are performed, the entire performance will collapse. Indeed, performances often do because the actors, for any number of reasons, have failed to maintain their third persons. That is, they revert to their behavior as persons in the real world rather than presenting their fictional characters. Since the interaction of fictional characters is the basis of all theatrical performance, one might think that this third person would be the easiest of the actor's four roles to sustain. After all, without a successful performance, the other three don't mean very much. This is true, but in some ways the actor's third person is the most difficult of all to achieve because it depends so much on the interaction of the actor's first two persons; that is, as a person in the real world and as a presenter of a fictional character.

Just what do we mean by this? Suppose you were a big-time producer and you wanted to do a production of *Othello* on Broadway. Today, such a production would—alas—cost hundreds of thousands of dollars. So you will have to do well at the box office. This means stars, big-name box-office draws, actors who will pack in the audiences. Now, we will grant that you are a serious producer (why else would you do *Othello*?) but you still need the stars to draw the audience. The key is how you cast Othello and Iago. So for Othello you choose Sidney Poitier, and for Iago, Dustin Hoffman— both big names, established actors, and well suited for their respective parts. But such casting will not necessarily guarantee a successful production for it does not take into account the personalities of Poitier and Hoffman (person one of the actor) or how they go about working up or creating a part (person two). They may not want to be playing in *Othello*; they may not like each other as human beings; each of them might approach the creation of his role in a radically different way. Many things could happen to make the presented roles of the performance incompatible. If this were the case, chances are the production would be a disaster because the actors' performances together as characters (person three) would be shaped by their conflicting nature as human beings (person one) and the incompatibility of the acting techniques they use to develop their characters (person two). It would be a miracle if, as actors, they could succeed as fictional characters interacting with each other. The four persons of the actor are always inseparable.

I **don't** want to play Shakespeare, essentially. First, because I am not trained sufficiently to play Shakespeare. Most of Shakespeare's stuff bores me to tears. I enjoy infinitely more to read the words, because the man was, indeed, a genius—just to read the structure of his sentences. I lie in bed with a Shakespeare book and have a ball! To play it, I'm not interested. It's that simple.

Sidney Poitier

. . . A Surrogate and/or Model for the Audience

While the fourth person of the actor may have the least to do with the craft of acting itself, it is still an important function of the actor. This aspect of what the actor does has a significant impact on society and explains why great actors have always been admired.

A play is an imaginative world in which the many roles, the many realizable selves, the different values and possibilities actually residing within us are presented in a coherent way. The performance plays these out. We know that in life we must make choices; and when we choose one thing, we necessarily pass up other possibilities. We know we must do this, and while perhaps we would not change much in our lives, still we know there are many possibilities within us that will go unrealized. This naturally gives us a sense that life is not all we dreamt it could or would be. And this sense of limitation increases as we grow older, when the opportunities for choice become more restricted.

The theatre releases us, if only temporarily, from this sense of limitation. It reaffirms the sense of almost limitless potential we all feel we have, but know we can never realize. Who doesn't want to make love with poetry like Romeo, instead of with the monosyllabic clichés most of us use? In our daydreams, who among us isn't a noble Saint Joan or gallant Cyrano? Yes, sometimes even a villain like Iago. Think of all the dramas we play out as we walk down the street. (Have you ever noticed how most people talk to themselves? They make up the dialogue they are going to use, or should have used but, in fact, seldom, if ever, use. "I'll tell that so and so, such and such!" or "If only I'd said this and this!") These interior dramas are reaffirmed and played out before us in acceptable ways by actors. As we watch them in the theatre, we can become, for a little while, romantic, daring, successful, cruel, brave, or sexy. The actor reaffirms our belief in our own possibilities. In his performance he realizes all those things which the conditions of everyday life deprive us of, and he does so with a sense of purpose, a fullness, and a completeness we do not have in our own lives.

These, then, are the four persons of the actor: the human being like all of us, the presenter of the character in the play, the character interacting with other characters, and that special figure who has the power to live out on stage our unrealizable dreams. Every actor is each of these four persons simultaneously.

The Dynamics of Performance

When we watch a performance of any play, we sense—consciously or unconsciously—energy. Energy is generated in part because the actor is four persons in one and this creates a tension. However, the dynamics of performance are more complex than this. A diagram can help us understand the relationships.

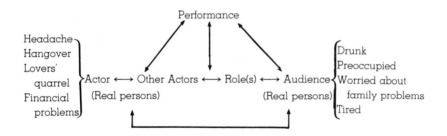

There is constant interaction between the actor's "real personality," her body as medium, the role, and the other actors. There is also interaction between the actor's performance and the living and "real" presence and response of the audience. The actor interacts not only with the role she is playing, but also with that role as it varies from performance to performance. Likewise, the audience—both individually and collectively—interacts with the individual roles as played by the actors and with the performance as a whole. This series of interactions in itself produces countless variables of response. Added to these is a factor that is totally outside the domain of the performance but which affects it profoundly; namely, the physical and psychic state of actor and audience at the time of performance. If the actor has a hangover and you, as a member of the audience, are thinking about the argument you had with your parents, the dynamics of the performance will be totally different from what they are when the actor is feeling fine and healthy and you, free of distraction, can give your full attention to the performance. This explains why the transformation of the actor into the role can never be total, and also why no two performances of the same play will ever be the same. The energy of these many interactions is always changing. Every performance will include an element of the spontaneous and improvised. Each is a unique event—as transitory as life itself.

THE NATURE OF ACTING

The basic experience of theatre is this: Actor "A" impersonates Character "B" while Audience "C" watches. This experience is realized through a three-part process. The first part involves the actor's discovery or creation of the character. This is the rehearsal process—everything from the actor's first reading of the script to the first performance for an audience. Essentially it involves the actor's taking a journey to the role; that is, finding the character that lives in the script (including all its interactions with the other characters) in herself. The second part is the transformation that takes place when the actor is possessed by the character. The third part might be called the actor's return. Having found or created the role in the text, she brings it back to present it to the audience. It is helpful to think of acting as a process of exploration and discovery by the actors, who then present what they find to us, the audience.

This process has its roots in a very human activity: the transformation we experience in play and our delight in it. We can observe it in children at play; it is the basic impulse of all primitive rituals; and it plays a significant role in our adult lives, especially when we are forced to enter into new and strange situations. Play creates a world of its own, a territory with laws of its own.

The Actor's Medium—The Body

In acting, an actor permits herself to be publicly devoured by the imaginary. The actor's aim is to make an absent or imaginary character present: the material she uses to accomplish this is her own person. The actor can only project what she has within herself. Unlike the painter who uses brush, canvas, and paint; the sculptor whose materials are a chisel, stone, or bronze; a musician who plays an instrument; a novelist or poet who uses words, pen, paper,

At the core of every part is the self of the actor who is doing it. You can say Prospero is quite different from Shylock, but at the vortex, or core, whatever you want to call it, of both parts is me. It's my Prospero, it was my Shylock.

Morris Carnovsky

or a typewriter; a filmmaker who creates with a camera; unlike even a dancer who uses the body as an abstraction and whose movements are governed by music; the actor must use her own body, mind, and spirit. What is poured into a given role springs in some sense from all she has thought and felt, read and known up to that moment and is expressed by a total human being. It is expressed first of all by a voice infinitely responsive to meaning in the text; by a body that can communicate the flow of the action without awkwardness; by a face that can reach the last row in the second balcony with the flicker of an eyelash as thought or feeling are written across it.

In short, the actor must treat her body as the means for accomplishing her art. To do this she must consider her voice, expressions, gestures, and movements as external and separate from herself. She must externalize herself. This is an unusual process that involves thinking of and using her body as an instrument. The body is to the actor what the brush is to a painter or a violin is to a violinist.

This explains, in part, our ambiguous response to her performance. Even when we are amazed and impressed by it, we are also suspicious and wary of it. It is somehow inhuman to so completely externalize oneself. The fact that the actor's body is her medium is also the clue to the demanding physical training an actor goes through, which we will discuss later in this chapter.

The Actor and the Shaman

So much of what an actor does to prepare and present a role is interior. It is fascinating to watch the results on stage but not always easy to understand the earlier process of preparation. One of the most difficult things to understand in the theatre is how the actor can become a character who dwells in the "other world" of the play and at the same time continues to be himself. An analogy may help us understand the acting process.

In recent years a number of theatre historians, theorists, and practitioners have been carrying on important explorations into the similarities that exist between theatrical performance and ritual performances in primitive societies.[1] The activities of the shaman in primitive cultures have some interesting similarities to the actor's work. Knowledge of shamanistic performance enlarges our understanding of the actor's art. In his book *Shamanism*, Mircea Eliade defines a shaman as one who

> specializes in a trance during which his soul is believed to leave his body and ascend to the sky or descend to the underworld.[2]

E. T. Kirby describes the shaman as

> a "master of spirits" who performs in trance, primarily for the purpose of curing the sick by ritualistic means.[3]

In China and Siberia, he was thought of as

> a person who is able to put himself in trance states in which he is thought to travel in heaven or the underworld or to be possessed by spirits from these places.[4]

Shamanism, as David Cole writes,

> is a religious practice found all over the world from Africa to the Arctic, from South America to Polynesia. In some cultures it is the dominant religious mode; in others it exists side by side with more conventional forms of worship.[5]

A shaman is a combination of priest, medicine man, magician, juggler, and actor with the very special power of being able, by means of trance, to go to the "other world" of the gods and/or the dead as the special envoy of his tribe. As their envoy, he takes the tribe's special wishes and prayers to the gods so that they might be fulfilled. This journey takes the form of a trance performed in the presence of the rest of the tribe.

The important things for us to notice here are that shamanistic rituals always involve an audience, and that what the shaman presents is not something symbolic, but an immediate and direct experience. His performance is a direct manifestation of a spiritual presence to an audience. While the performance is going on, the audience believes that not only has the shaman taken a journey to the "other world" of the gods, but he has, in fact, actually entered into that world. Here, significantly for our discussion, the mask is essential to shamanistic performance. When a shaman puts on a mask,

> it is believed that he becomes possessed by the spirit represented, and the utterances of the shaman are for the time being regarded as the words of the spirit [by the audience.][6]

Now we must stress that while shamans are actors of a sort, shamanistic performances are not theatre. At best, they are analogous to theatre. But studying shamanism can be very helpful to us in understanding the nature of the theatrical event, and especially how the actor goes about becoming his role. In Chapter 2 we pointed out that the ancient words for actor involved the idea of trance—that state of ecstasy in which a person gets outside of himself and takes over and is taken over by the soul of another. Obviously, one does not actually get outside of oneself during a trance, nor is one taken over by somebody else. Both trance journey and trance possession are internal psychic processes. In a state of trance we are ourselves and someone else—we are double. This is an important dimension of the shaman-actor analogy.

Shamans of Kerala, India. Although most shamans are men, the male shaman frequently assumes the dress and attributes of a woman.

The other important aspect of the shaman-actor analogy relates to the shaman's public function. Because primitive peoples believe it is both possible and necessary to be in touch with the other world of the gods if life is to continue, the shaman plays a very important role in their societies. He is a special person; his calling requires rigorous training. Because he is able to enter into this state of uncanny doubleness, he is thought to be strange, is mistrusted, and is a kind of sacred outcast. Most important, he is the tribe's special envoy to the gods on behalf of the tribe. Once again the analogy helps us understand the theatre. The actor has served a similar function and has had a similar social role throughout history.

The Actor's Journey

For our purposes, the most important thing about the link between actor and shaman is the fact that, just as the shaman's journey to the other world of the gods is a journey into himself, so it is for the actor. For the actor to become possessed by the role that exists in the imaginary other world of the play, he, too, must take a journey into himself. Or, to paraphrase David Cole, in searching for the life of the role, it is his own life that the actor searches.

One of Cole's most valuable points is the attention he draws to the similarities between shamanistic performance and the process by which the actor embodies a role. Let us look at a few descriptions of acting which sound very like shamanistic performance.

> The conscious levels of a play or part are like the levels and strata of the earth, sand, clay, rocks and so forth, which go to form the earth's crust. As the levels go deeper down into one's soul they become increasingly unconscious, and down in the very depths, in the core of the earth where you find molten lava and fire, invisible human instincts and passions are raging.
>
> Konstantin Stanislavski, *Creating a Role*[7]

> These [primitive man's efforts at acting] were the first attempts *to fly above his narrow material existence.* The possibilities inherent in him but not brought to full growth by his life thus *unfolded their shadowy wings* and *carried him far over* his knowledge and *away into the heart of a strange experience.* He discovered all the delights of transformation, all the ecstasy of passion, all the illusive life of dreams. . . .
>
> We can telegraph and telephone and wire pictures across the ocean; we can fly over it. But the way to the human being next us is still as far as to the stars. The actor takes us on this way. With the light of the poet he climbs the unexplored peaks of the human soul, his own soul, in order to transform it secretly there and to return with his hands, eyes and voice full of wonders.
>
> Max Reinhardt, *Of Actors*[8]

The idea that comes through in these passages is that the more deeply the actor penetrates the world of the play, the more the actor loses himself. This does not mean he loses consciousness. It means his consciousness, his very life, is gradually governed or taken over by the life of the role. This produces a paradoxical condition for the actor: he seeks the source of energy in himself in order to discover the role, but in the process gives up the self to the role.

This, then, is the first stage of the acting process: the actor's journey to the role. Getting there is something of a "magical mystery tour." In this stage, the rehearsal period, the actor goes to the world of the play to discover and bring back the character who lives there.

You know what a salmon does when it wants to go upstream? It feels about for the point of maximum energy in the water, the point where the water whirls round and round and generates a terrific centrifugal force. It looks for that point, and it finds it, and the water quadruples the salmon's own natural strength, and then it can jump. That's what an actor has to do with the text. The point of maximum energy is always there, but it takes finding.... [When you get] right there in the dynamic center ... [the role takes over.]

Irene Worth

What is involved in this process? How does the actor journey into himself? What does he discover? The rehearsal period is primarily a time of psychological development. To be sure, the actors must learn their lines and become comfortable with their movements on stage, but the most important function of rehearsals is for the actors to absorb the life that resides within the playwright's text. The actors take into themselves the characters they are playing—their temperament, their manner of action, the texture of their minds. This is a double discovery, for the actor must find the character that exists in the script and also find the same character as it exists within himself. An actor can play only what he contains within himself. The rehearsal period is the time when, through contemplation, emotional recall, experimentation, repetition, study, and self-discovery, he unites appropriate qualities of his own being with the unique demands of the character he is to play; that is, he must find within himself those particular characteristics that will express the role he is playing.

The rehearsal period is also the time when the actors learn to interact with each other. If an audience is going to be caught up in the life-rhythm of a play in performance, the characters on stage must establish contact with each other. This contact will be achieved only if the actors are conscious of each other. Actors aware of each other are like a couple at a party who are separated and talking animatedly to other friends or acquaintances, yet who still have their antennae out. Each is conscious of the other. They are aware of the other's gaze, they pick up the sound of the other's voice, they sense each other's movements. There is a continuous current running between them. The same thing happens in a successful performance, and the rehearsal period is the time when the human consciousness between actors is established. This, too, is part of the actor's journey.

Finally, during rehearsals the actors "fix" the dramatic action of the play. They come to know and feel comfortable with the rhythm of each scene, the emotional content demanded of it, and how one scene builds to the next. While it is impossible to control all the conditions of performance, it is possible to create an "emotional track" that will insure that the performance always stays on course, no matter what other external pressures or influences there may be. This is done in the rehearsal period. The actors come to know the play, their roles, and the interaction between the roles so well that they are usually able to overcome whatever distractions occur in any given performance.

All an actor can play is himself. Himself in the thousand-and-one variations dictated by a thousand-and-one roles. When people denounce a performer for "playing himself" what they are really condemning is his basic shallowness and lack of personal resources. A multifaceted, substantial actor **plays himself** as relentlessly as does a spare and unendowed one. The resourceful actor, because he has more to draw on, will give the appearance of variety by simply utilizing the abundance of his nature. The resourceless actor, unblessed with such abundance, can do no more than exhibit his paucity in half a dozen slightly modified versions. The crime is not acting oneself, but not having enough of oneself to act!

Charles Marowitz, **The Method as Means**

The Transformation

There is a crucial moment in the actor's search for and discovery of a character. That is the moment of transformation, the moment when the actor as seeker becomes the actor possessed by a character. This is the transformation which changes the efforts of a group of theatre persons into theatre. In Chapter 1 we observed that when we are faced with unfamiliar situations in life, we tend to imitate strange or alien behavior in order to master it, to make it our own, to become at one with it. When we do this, we suddenly and quite unexpectedly and even mysteriously discover that the role or situation becomes a part of us. We are no longer outside of it, no longer alien—we belong. This experience in life, which is so difficult to pinpoint in time (like falling in love: you know it when it has happened, but you can't know precisely when it did), is similar to the moment when the character takes over the actor. The actor searches out the role—a search that he takes through himself—and at a certain moment he is mastered by it.

This is what rehearsal is all about and it is the turning point in the process. The most difficult period in the whole rehearsal process is when this transformation begins to occur. It does not happen to all the actors at the same time. Some actors will still be searching for their characters while others have already become possessed by them. The actors are in conflict, and the result can be confusion if not downright chaos. (Unfortunately, some actors never are possessed by their roles, and this explains why we may experience unsatisfying performances in the theatre. What we are witnessing is actors in search of their characters rather than characters made present for us.) This is a crucial moment for the director. Only firm, patient, and understanding directorial guidance can lead the actors through this period of transformation.

The Actor's Return

As crucial as the journey and the transformation are, the next stage is much more important from the point of view of the audience. This step might be called "the actor's return." It is the process by which the actor, having been taken over by the role, brings it back and presents it to the audience. The actor is now possessed by the role; his life has been taken over by the character. He is ready to make the character present for the audience.

What actually happens is that the actor—like the ancient shamans—is possessed by some aspect of his own psyche, even though it may feel "other" to him. What the actor does as he searches for the role is to become available to unconscious impulses that exist within himself. We all have these impulses. They may take the form of repressed feelings, sudden flashes of inspiration, the hidden desire

Characters are like boarders. Some stay an hour; some stay weeks. I like the second way of acting. You transcend to the character, and she takes you through her journey. What you seek is to be possessed.

Elizabeth Ashley

A "personal appearance" is a condescension to the stage, a visitation of mere flesh so that onlookers can see that it is flesh, a display of presence and a parade of mannerisms, and then off, off into the night. Without having truly been there, really, without having worked, without having acted anything.... When Miss Hepburn first comes onto the stage to stir a storm of applause... we are of course attending to **her,** as a personality, as someone known in a dozen, three dozen, roles but not in this one. As she re-enters, though, and the applause does finally give up, we are gently but forcibly asked to meet someone, someone who resembles Hepburn but who is not Hepburn **solus.**... There's no doubt that Miss Hepburn has got hold of something strong, tangible, and real. Something apart from herself. And she had to find it somewhere. She found it in Enid Bagnold's play.

Walter Kerr, describing Katharine Hepburn's return to the stage in 1976 in Bagnold's **A Matter of Gravity.**

On the really big evenings of your life, when the god descends and you yourself, as an actor, feel the magic is working, does it feel as if something has taken over, or are you still in control?

Redgrave: It feels as if somebody has taken over, but in fact I think it is that you have complete control. . . . When you're working well, everything's ticking over, the glands are working right, and then, of course, it's easy, it feels as if a god were guiding you.

Michael Redgrave

to play out roles or situations we have consciously or unconsciously chosen to deny ourselves, aspects of the self that have been submerged because of social pressures and constraints, or ideas that are normally too frightening to consider. The point is, the actor finds the role in some deep substratum of his nature, and he can embody and present only those possibilities which exist within himself. During the rehearsal process the actor learns to open himself up to those possibilities.

We must stress that possession does not mean loss of consciousness or control. Rather, the actor is in a strange state of double consciousness in which he is, and is not, himself. He feels that he is "somebody else" and he is also aware that it is he who is feeling this way. No matter how deeply an actor is committed to his role, he is always aware that his character is unreal. For example, an actor is certain he is not King Lear at the very moment he is publicly appearing as King Lear and trying to convince the audience to believe in him as King Lear. He needs and gets the audience's support in this, and if he were ever to lose consciousness that he was playing the role, the character would cease to exist. There would be a gibbering idiot on the stage.

Just as there is something uncanny in our experience of actors, the actor's experience of himself is uncanny too. Sigmund Freud described uncanniness as being able "to stand outside of ourselves in order to observe ourselves in the process of acting." The actor is the observer of his own action. He has the ability to stand off from himself, from his functions and feelings, and to observe both himself and them. This kind of doubleness is not unique to actors; there are times when we experience it in our everyday lives. It is inevitably present when we participate in games or sports. We may become passionately involved with a game, but we are always conscious of the rules. If we did not have this consciousness or—as sometimes happens—if we lose consciousness of the rules, the game breaks down.

The actor is an expert in self-perception. He perceives the character as it exists within himself and he also perceives the character as it exists in the world of the play. His consciousness must be able to shift from one to the other if the role is to be successful. The performance of an actor conscious only of himself while acting would be inadequate. The actor must be conscious of himself while acting and lose himself in the role at the same time. The ability to do this is partly a matter of instinct, but it also requires special skills that can be acquired only through disciplined training.

Once you've created a character to your own satisfaction, during the course of a performance, how far are you aware of yourself in relation to the character that you've created? In other words, are you fully inhabiting the character, or are you stepping aside and having a look at him from the outside?

Richardson: Part of it is stepping aside and controlling it, that's the first thing. You're really driving four horses, as it were, first going through, in great detail, the exact movements which have been decided upon. You're also listening to the audience, as I say, keeping, if you can, very great control over them. You're also slightly creating the part, in so far as you're consciously refining the movements and, perhaps, inventing tiny other experiments with new ones. At the same time you are really living, in one part of your mind, what is happening. Acting is to some extent a controlled dream. In one part of your consciousness it really and truly is happening. But, of course, to make it true to the audience, all the time, the actor must, at any rate some of the time, believe himself that it is really true. But in my experience this layer of absolute reality is a comparatively small one. The rest of it is technique, as I say, of being very careful that the thing is completely accurate, completely clear, completely as laid down beforehand. In every performance you're trying to find a better way to do it, and what you're reshaping, the little experiments, may be very small indeed, and quite unnoticed by your fellow actors; but they are working all the time. Therefore three or four layers of consciousness are at work during the time an actor is giving a performance.

Ralph Richardson

THE ACTOR'S CRAFT

We have just mentioned disciplined training. While much of what an actor does may be mysterious, acting, like most other professions, requires long and arduous training, hard work, the knowledge and mastering of techniques, and the assimilation of the history and lore associated with the actor's art. Theatre does not just happen. It requires people who have mastered their craft. Craft may not make an actor, but no one will be an actor who has not mastered certain skills and techniques. And this is an ongoing process. The actor never completely masters her craft. It requires lifelong dedication.

To create and become a character demands an almost infinite attention to detail, a breadth of general knowledge, and that final mysterious synthesis within the imagination that can bring it all to life. The character doesn't simply take over the actor; it must be created so that it can take over. This is a conscious creative act. When the actor first confronts the character who is "hiding" in the lines of the script, she must ask herself "How can I act it, using all the resources of my own being?" Using her own self as the raw material of her creation, she must compose the character that will then possess her. To accomplish this complex process, she must have first developed and mastered all the resources of her body that she will use in the process—all the senses, the breath and voice, and the countless possibilities of physical gesture and bodily movement. In effect, the actor must totally possess herself to be possessed by the other.

Composing a character isn't building it, so much as it is creating it. "Building" implies something engineered and inanimate. As the director Peter Brook points out, one does not create a character as one builds a wall. Unfortunately, the title of the most important book on the subject, Stanislavski's *Building a Character* (published in the United States in 1949), has supported this widespread misunderstanding. Elimination is the key element in the process of creating a role. Before she can be possessed by the character she is creating, the actor must be freed of all the obstacles within her that will hinder or prevent the transformation from occurring.

To eliminate his organism's resistance to this psychic process. . . . the body vanishes, burns, and the spectator sees only a series of visible impulses.

Jerzy Grotowski

You try to simplify acting always. That seems to be the thing that you do about writing and every other branch of art in any way—a simplification. It is a process of elimination—to do it simpler, to have a straighter line.

Katharine Cornell

As you rehearse, do you find the part becomes simpler or more complicated?

Evans: I work, and other actors do too, on a thing I call a process of deletion. I like to get it clearer and simpler until it's just bare bones.

Edith Evans

These obstacles might be such things as a tendency to use clichés of feeling rather than the unique feelings of the character to be played, to communicate the intent of the play in a standardized or stereotyped manner, to refuse to plumb the depths of a character because it is disturbing to her own psyche, to substitute theatrical behavior for the felt behavior of the character, to refuse the interaction between the characters because it is uncomfortable. You know from your own experience how difficult it is to rid yourself of anxieties, fears, psychic blocks, and the ghosts of past experience. But that is exactly what an actor must do to become a character. She accomplishes this by mastering technique. The mastery of technique is the means to the actor's freedom. This mastery involves the actor's control of the essential elements of her medium: the voice, the body, the imagination, and the powers of perception.

The Voice

The voice is a special medium for expressing emotion. Each person's voice is his own, but one can express the spirit of another with the voice. In composing a character, the actor will use his own vocal flexibility, the range and the nuance of his voice to discover what seems to be the character's voice. He will experiment until he finds the voice that fits the character.

Vocal intonation is one of the primary means actors use to establish relationships between characters. We, in the audience, come to perceive the dramatic relationships between the characters through the shadings, intensity, and variations of the actors' voices. Actors do not play characters so much as they play the relationships between the characters, and these relationships are communicated in large part by intonations of the voice. Much of the meaning in theatre is communicated by a play's dialogue. Since the dialogue is made dramatic and given its particular meaning by the voice, actors know that control of the voice is the essential basis of all dialogue on the stage. The actor needs to have complete control of his breathing mechanism; he must know how to pace his speech to achieve variation and dramatic tempo; he must have superb diction (be able to be clearly heard and understood); and he must be able to project his voice to the last rows of the audience, no matter how large the theatre. He must have an accomplished command of vocal rhythms. By that we mean he must be able to reflect the changes in the character's situation with corresponding shifts in the range, intensity, and rhythm of his voice. Perhaps most important, he must be able to listen to the voices of the other characters and respond to them.

I had to start from scratch and just work on facts, making myself totally faithful to what was on the page: More was a lawyer, a man of tremendous faith, a complex and subtle character... Simply saying the lines for what they were worth would make More sound like a very pompous and noisy man. If I said the lines with all the intensity they seemed to require, he would seem an aggressive man. And he was not an aggressive man. So I had to find a way of making the man sound not pompous and not aggressive. And yet he had to sound strong. If you can see it, then you can do it. First, I had to find the way the man would feel; then I was able to find the way he should sound. Eventually, I discovered that if I used a specific range

of my voice, and characteristics of my voice that I had never used before, I might make him sound mild, even though what the lines themselves said was not mild. When I played Hamlet, I used a lot of voice. For Thomas More, I used a voice you wouldn't hear at all if I used it for Hamlet. I used an accent for More that was absolutely a bastard thing of my own. My parents are Midland people, with a very regional accent, and I drew somewhat on this accent and mixed it with some others. The way More sounded just came out of my characterization of him as a lawyer. His dryness of mind, I thought, led him to use a sort of dryness of speech. It evolved as I evolved the character. I would flatten or elongate a vowel in a certain way to get a certain effect I wanted.

Paul Scofield, on playing Sir Thomas More in Bolt's **A Man for All Seasons**

Gesture and Physical Control

Gestures reveal meaning. Behind every gesture is an inner truth which the gesture reveals. "Body language" is, in a very real way, the first language of the theatre. Like verbal language, the actor must master it if he is to communicate with it. The character speaks not only through the actor's voice but also through his body. The actor must have profound awareness of and experience with his own body to be able to put it in the service of the character. The actor finds the language of gesture in the language of the text. In other words, a character's movements and physical gestures are suggested by the script, and the actor must search for them in the language of the script. To succeed in this the actor must know the nuances and subtleties of both kinds of language and must understand how they are interrelated. Finally, he must have what French actor-director Jacques Copeau (1878–1949) referred to as the "mastery of motionlessness." Repose and silence are necessary if the actor is to open himself up to the character so it can possess him. In short, on stage the actor must be a master of time and space, and only by a control of his body comparable to that of a well-trained athlete will he be able to achieve such mastery.

Observation and Discovery

As an important part of composing her role, the actor must discover how a character would feel, sound, move, laugh, cry, or express any human emotion. The actor may never have experienced some of these emotions—the impulse to murder or commit suicide, for example—yet she must find a way to play them. We have already indicated that this is done, in part, by the actor searching within herself. Observation of others is also essential to this aspect of her work. Observation of everyday life is valuable, of course, but it can also be limiting to the actor. So much of our behavior is conditioned and clichéd; it itself has already been composed. An actor must realize that when she watches two people meet and exchange greetings at a party, she usually observes a cliché and she should be alert to any deeper meanings or intentions. Observation must lead to invention. The actor learns to choose the feelings, ideas, mannerisms, vocal and bodily gestures not only that are appropriate to the character and dramatic situation, but that will communicate them to the audience. This explains why good actors pay close attention to the performances of other good actors. They do so not in order to imitate them, but because actors learn about invention from each other.

Improvisation is another means of learning about invention. Improvisation is a free, unplanned composition of a scene based on some word, image, situation, or activity. It is experimenting. It is similar to the singer's loosening up by singing scales or the dancer's warming up at the *barre*. For the actor, improvisation is a kind of emotional limbering up that stimulates the imagination. It helps the actor discover herself, her feelings, and her reactions. And it also helps her discover (and retain) that sense of play which is the basis of all good theatre. It is questionable whether improvisation can be an end in itself, but as a rehearsal process it is a powerful way of opening the actor to discovery. If she is to be successful in her journey of discovery to the role, she must train herself to be a close observer of life.

The actor's craft, then, involves the mastery of the body and the voice (including the many ways they are interrelated), the understanding and control of one's feelings (being in touch with oneself), heightened powers of observation, a highly developed imagination capable of being attuned with the character one is playing, and an intelligence able to perceive the world of the play contained in the playwright's script. All these require some talent and a certain degree of natural ability, but they cannot operate at the professional level of craft without training.

The Actor's Training

Today everyone interested in acting is deeply concerned with the subject of the actor's training. Acting schools thrive in almost every important center of theatrical activity. Many colleges and universities have developed professional actor-training programs. And there are countless books of theories on how actors should be trained. Some people contend that in the past few decades the theatre has become so obsessed with training that it has forgotten its primary function—performance for an audience. But as in any art form, training is essential and it always has been.

Actors have learned their craft and skills in different ways throughout history. In the classical Greek theatre, the playwright —in addition to providing the script—was responsible for training the actors, singers, and dancers in the months preceding the annual festivals when the plays were presented. The commedia dell' arte companies of thirteenth- and fourteenth-century Italy and France —like the Japanese Nōh and Kabuki theatres—were often family ensembles in which the young served long apprenticeships learning the crafts of performance from their parents so they could eventually inherit their roles. The Elizabethan and French classical theatres had a highly developed program of actor training and apprenticeship that involved the learning of acting techniques and the mastery of the great roles in the repertoire. In the eighteenth and nineteenth centuries, actor-managers not only played the lead roles, directed the productions, and operated the theatres; they also trained young actors so they could play in the style prevalent in the theatre at that time. In the past, the theatre trained its young actors, and usually did so within the context of a performing company.

At the beginning of this century this method began to change. The person most responsible for the change was the Russian actor-director-teacher Konstantin Stanislavski. Stanislavski's approach to actor training was essentially psychological. He developed a system of exercises and techniques that would enable the actor to discover from his own experience the feelings and motivations of the character he was to play. Using these methods, Stanislavski believed that the actor would eventually come to identify himself with the character to such a degree that his identification with the role could be maintained throughout the performance. The most significant aspect of Stanislavski's methods is the fact that they can be practiced and applied in a context separate from the rehearsal of a specific role or play. There are, he believed, certain principles and techniques for developing a character that can be mastered by the actor and then applied to every acting situation. In short, there is a body of acting techniques—independent of a particular production—that can be learned. It was this recognition that led to the emergence of acting "schools" and the development of programs of training.

Throughout the past fifty years, there have been many different and often conflicting approaches to the training of actors. Some of the most important of them have been those of:

Vsevolod Meyerhold (1874–1942?): Stanislavski's student and one of the major influences in twentieth-century theatre, he rejected his master's psychological techniques (working from the inside out) and developed a system of training based on complete body control and acrobatics known as "bio-mechanics." Meyerhold believed in approaching a part from the outside, through mastery of physical skills and vocal techniques.

Jacques Copeau (1878–1949): This French actor-director founded the *Théâtre du Vieux Colombier* where he developed a program for training actors that combined Stanislavski's psychological approach with the training methods of the classical French theatre. This method was refined and adapted by Copeau's student, Michel Saint-Denis, who established the "Young Vic" School in England after World War II and later was instrumental in founding the Juilliard Theatre School in New York.

Bertolt Brecht (1898–1956): A German playwright-director, his theories and practice were a major challenge to those of Stanislavski, whose system Brecht thought "mystical and cultish." Brecht was not anti-psychological, but he believed this approach should not be given undue importance. He stressed the actor's need for intellectual development and social awareness.

Lee Strasberg (b. 1901): He has been the best-known acting teacher in America. Strasberg transformed Stanislavski's system of acting into an American "method." His main emphasis is on the creation of "true emotion" through improvisation and exercises in emotional recall.

Jerzy Grotowski (b. 1933): As director of the Theatre Laboratory in Wroclaw, Poland, Grotowski has been particularly influential in actor training in the last decade. Although greatly influenced by Stanislavski, Grotowski is primarily interested in the actor-audience relationship. His method of training involves arduous physical exercise as a means of giving the actor complete control of his whole being in performance.

All these approaches to actor training (as well as many others) have been effective and have achieved good results. But it is important to understand that there is no hard and fast, infallible blueprint for successful actor training. There have been many ap-

We do not look for recipes, the stereotypes that are the natural accompaniment of professionals. We do not attempt to answer questions such as: "What does one do to show irritation? How should one walk? How should Shakespeare be played?" (For in the end these are the sorts of questions usually asked.) Instead one must ask the actor: "What are the obstacles blocking you on your way toward the total act that must engage all of your psycho-physical resources, from the most instinctive to the most rational?" We must find out what it is that blocks him in the way of respiration, movement, and—most of all—human contact. What resistances are there? How can they be eliminated? I want to take away, steal from the actor all that disturbs him. That which is creative will remain with him. It is a liberation. If nothing remains, it is because he is not creative.

Jerzy Grotowski, **Towards a Poor Theatre**

proaches, but there are two constants in all the systems or theories of actor training:

1. No matter how training is approached, the many elements that are involved in the training of actors—the development of the voice and body; the mastery of diction, movement, and improvisational skills; and the learning of methods of characterization—should not be treated as separate and unrelated techniques, but must be conceived and mastered in wholeness.

2. Ultimately, the actor's work—no matter what the training—involves the ability
   . . . to project himself into the fictional world of the play;
   . . . to discover that world and its characters;
   . . . to be possessed by the characters;
   . . . to make the character and the events of the script authentic in terms of human experience; and
   . . . to present all this to an audience.

ACTING STYLES AND AUTHENTICITY

We have said the actor is human like those of us in the audience. He demonstrates our feelings and he must do so in such a way that they seem authentic—true to experience as we know it. This may seem obvious, but right off the bat we have entered into a difficult issue. There is a difference between appearing authentic and being real. The pain Laurence Olivier feels in playing Othello should seem authentic, but we know it is not real pain. That is, we should believe that Othello as presented by Olivier is truly experiencing pain, but that Olivier is not. Acting, good or bad, is never real; good acting always has the ring of authenticity to it. We believe in its humanity.

An example will help make this distinction clear. Many of you have seen Laurence Olivier's masterpiece film production of Shakespeare's *Henry V*. Most people had probably not seen or read the play before they saw the movie, and few probably knew very much about the figures of fifteenth-century England being depicted. While the text of the play was cut somewhat for the film, not one of Shakespeare's words was changed. Yet everyone who sees the movie is carried right out to the Fields of Agincourt as if actually witnessing the battle between the English and French armies. Indeed, most people's experience of that battle was probably more powerfully moving than that of watching actual scenes of war on the television news.

Why is this? Obviously, nobody speaks in verse like Shakespeare's characters (and nobody ever did—even in Shakespeare's time); the heraldic costumes bore very little resemblance to what soldiers actually wore in that period of history; at times we were conscious that the sets weren't real, but only painted scenery; indeed, sometimes the events of the play on film were shown taking place on a replication of Shakespeare's Globe Theatre to remind us that this was a representation of a play taking place on a stage. Yet we believed what was happening because Olivier and the other actors made the production seem authentic in terms of our own imaginative experience. That is, they acted in a way that seemed like natural human behavior, but that was also true to the events, people, and period of history depicted in the play. We experienced a fictitious presentation of an important time in English history as if it were an actual event.

This raises a very significant point about the nature of acting: any acting style is natural in its time and place. It is always judged by the norms of natural behavior that exist in any given society. It may be unreal—it certainly can be stylized—but it must always be recognizable as the way people behave if it is to communicate meaningfully to an audience. Every actor is first of all a human being living in the same time and place as the members of the audience watching his performance. This was certainly the central point of Shakespeare's advice to the actors in Hamlet's famous discourse in the Players' scene (*Hamlet*, act 3, scene 2):

> Suit the action to the word, the word to the action, with this special observance, that you o'erstep not the modesty of nature. For anything so overdone is from the purpose of playing, whose end, both at the first and now, was and is to hold as 't were the mirror up to Nature—to show Virtue her own feature, scorn her own image, and the very age and body of the time his form and pressure.[9]

This passage suggests there was a conception of what was natural acting in Shakespeare's time, and it was related to the way people actually behaved. Today, until you have had some experience with Shakespeare's theatre, you may think his plays are archaic, strange, difficult to comprehend, and tremendously stylized. But in his own time they were a perfectly natural form of theatre and were related to the normal patterns of behavior of Elizabethan England.[10]

In our own time, there are different but equally distinguishable patterns of natural behavior. Certain gestures or figures of speech are natural to us, but they would be nearly incomprehensible to people living in another age or culture. In the American theatre this is reflected in the "method" style of acting so popular in the 1950s and 1960s. As taught by Lee Strasberg at the Actors Studio, "method" acting was to be true to the world of the play and to appear natural in contemporary terms. For example, Marlon Brando's performance as Stanley Kowalski in Tennessee Williams's *A Streetcar Named Desire* was true to Williams's quite poetic text, yet the grunts and groans of Brando's vocal delivery and the grossness of his brutish behavior struck audiences as natural in terms of real-life behavior. (Brando is best known for his roles in *A Streetcar Named Desire* and in films like *On the Waterfront*, *Last Tango in Paris*, and *The Godfather*, but using substantially the same approach to acting, he was also moving and convincing as Mark Antony in a film version of Shakespeare's *Julius Caesar*.) Today, with the cultural diversity of American society, patterns of "natural" behavior have changed yet again and these changes are reflected in many of the plays—both new and old—produced in the past few years.

Styles of acting change only as the norms of behavior in actual life change. Natural behavior in any period is not judged on the basis of spontaneity but rather on how it conforms to norms that have been learned. What we call "naturalness" is, in fact, a convention. The "natural" actor is, in fact, imitating performances in the ordinary world that are already "composed" to appear natural. The first production of Jack Gelber's *The Connection* at the Living Theatre in 1959 is a good example of this. The play is about a group of drug addicts and much of its effectiveness depends upon the "naturalness" of the actors' presentation of people hooked on drugs. (It must be remembered that at the time of the play's original production, the drug culture was still an underground phenomenon.) The actors did not take drugs on stage and therefore they did not actually behave as drug addicts. They behaved as the audience would expect addicts to behave. They composed their behavior so it would be recognizable to the audience as addicts' behavior. The audience's belief was, in fact, a fiction. What many people thought of as natural behavior among drug addicts was a far cry from their actual behavior.

No matter how transformed, all acting must be recognizable and authentic as such. Even when one does a play from a period in history when the norms of natural behavior were significantly different from our own—in Shakespeare's England, for example—the production must always translate period styles into our own terms.[11] The actor's first task is to convince us that both he and his performance are believable and authentic in terms of our own humanity.

THE ACTOR/AUDIENCE RELATIONSHIP

While acting styles have varied throughout history, there is a basic dynamic between actor and audience that exists in every theatrical event. We have seen that the actor has a great deal in common with the shaman of primitive cultures. Like the shaman, he is society's envoy to another world that is both more and less real than our own everyday world. Like the shaman, the actor is capable of being transformed so that he is both possessed by that world and able to make it present to us. Like the shaman, his own being is the medium of the transformation. He is also like the shaman in another very important way: in the eyes of his society he holds a special—almost sacred—place, while at the same time he is so deeply mistrusted that he is treated almost as an outcast.

The actor feels the temper of the audience very swiftly, almost the moment he steps on to the stage. And, of course, it is his business to control that temper. But I don't think actors really love their audience; they are more in the nature of a lion-tamer. Perhaps the lion-tamer loves the lions, I'm not certain about that: but the actor must dominate the mood of the audience.

Ralph Richardson

This complex response to the person of the actor has very ancient roots. Actors have always been suspect because of their vocation as professional role-players. There is something uncanny—and therefore fearsome—about a person who lives inside someone else's skin, particularly when he can change that skin so readily and convincingly. But we are also tremendously attracted to actors. They command our attention; we are fascinated by them; we identify with them; they have a glamour and beauty that attracts us; and they relate deeply to our fantasy lives. They truly are stars: they "cast a spell" over us! If Laurence Olivier or Helen Hayes, Richard Burton or Katharine Hepburn, Paul Newman or Joanne Woodward were suddenly to appear nearby, the word would be out at once, we'd drop everything, and go to look at them. To speak with them? Well, that might be too much; we'd probably be speechless. There is something about actors that makes them terribly exciting public figures.

Through actors we experience our deepest fantasies and unrealizable aspects of ourselves in safe and pleasurable ways. Through actors we can play out vicariously all the dramas of our interior lives. Actors speak to our capacity for delight and wonder. They give presence to the sense of mystery which surrounds our lives. They heighten our awareness of love and beauty, pity and pain. In short, despite our innate distrust of persons who commit their lives to pretending, we go to the theatre because the presence of actors acting fulfills important needs that exist within us.

Actors have similarly ambivalent feelings and attitudes toward the audience. The actor wants and needs to be watched. Every actor, from Laurence Olivier at the British National Theatre to the teenager in the senior class play, is saying, "Watch me!" And we in the audience enjoy watching. We get pleasure not only from the role the actor plays, but also from how he plays it. This is the basic dynamic of the actor-audience relationship. If this dynamic is to work, the audience must believe in the actor and the role he is playing. If, for instance, we withdraw our belief in Richard Burton as Hamlet, then the character of Hamlet ceases to exist during his performance of the play. The audience's belief is communicated primarily through its approval of the performance. This dynamic is symbolized by the combination of the audience's applause and the actor's bows at the conclusion of the performance. The applause is the judgment, the bow is at once a gesture of triumph and submission. As director-scholar Michael Goldman put it: "Like the related tradition of applauding the audience, the bow symbolizes that combination of aggressions and reception we find everywhere in the actor-audience exchange."[12]

The actor is at the service of the audience. It is the judge and the ultimate and controlling power over any given performance. Yet the servant is also the master, because only the actor can fill the audience's abiding need for theatre which brings us to the performance

When I go out there on the stage I'm battling the world, I have to be the best as far as I can.
Richard Burton

in the first place. The box office means a great deal more than money; it reflects the audience's judgment. We come to the theatre to watch a great actor perform a role, but if the actor does not cast a spell over us so we believe him in the role, the play will probably fail. This idea was confirmed by the president of the Shubert Organization, which owns or controls the majority of professional theatres in the United States. In a panel discussion, "On Using Stars," sponsored by the *New York Theatre Review*, Bernard Jacobs observed:

> In my opinion there are only about seven or eight stars. When Richard Burton came into *Equus* to replace Tony Perkins, the box office went from $60,000 a week to $118,000 a week. That's a star. But there are very few stars of that quality, that are really going to bring a large audience in to see a performance that they would not otherwise go to see.
>
> But it is not really the star quality, but the character of the performance that makes the show what it is. When [Al] Pacino did *Pavlo Hummel*, it was the character of his performance as well as the fact that he was a star. So you must look upon whether the person who is playing the part would add a dimension to the part that would not be there if that person were not playing the role. And there are very few actors who can do that in so dramatic a way that they have a true star quality.
>
> Zero [Mostel] was a star in *Fiddler*, he would have been a star in *The Merchant*. But he was not a star in *Ulysses*. You have to equate the performer with the part, and whether or not he can effectively add that dimension to the part in order to determine whether he or she is a star.[13]

The audience can never be depended upon to approve of him; hence the actor's great distrust of it. The actor resents the fact that he needs the audience's approval if his performance is to be successful. So for the actor each performance becomes a kind of contest in which he seeks to seduce, cajole, overpower, and eventually win over his necessary antagonist—the usually friendly, always willing audience. This accounts for the phenomenon of "stage fright." Before every performance the actor has a deadly fear that the audience will not accept him; at that moment the audience is a nameless but identifiable threat which must be overcome and conquered. Yet he cannot help but resent his dependency on those who hold such arbitrary power over him.

WHY DO ACTORS ACT?

If acting provokes such ambivalent responses, one might rightly ask, "Why do actors act? What is it about the actor's art that compels some people to pursue acting as a career?" No one has asked this question more searchingly than Shakespeare did in *Hamlet:*

> Is it not monstrous that this player here,
> But in a fiction, in a dream of passion,
> Could force his soul so to his own conceit
> That from her working all his visage wann'd
> Tears in his eyes, distraction in's aspect
> A broken voice, and his whole function suiting
> With forms to his conceit? and all for nothing!
> For Hecuba!
> What's Hecuba to him, or he to Hecuba,
> That he should weep for her?

"For Hecuba!" What is this mythological figure to the actor? What kind of relationship do they have that the actor "should weep for her"?

Obviously, there is no simple answer to this question of why actors act. For some, it is dreams of money and fame, but we know this dream is realized by only a few. Most actors are out of work and the average professional actor's annual income is pathetically low. Others are attracted to the acting profession because they believe it will provide them with an opportunity to powerfully and directly communicate certain truths about life to an audience. While this sometimes happens, there are easier ways. Few forms of communication require such long and arduous work with so few guarantees of success. (Helen Hayes was once asked, "What part of acting is drudgery?" She replied, "All of it.") Psychoanalysts tell us there are deep identity needs that prompt actors to act, and while this is undoubtedly true, it is unlikely that most actors are conscious of these motivations—especially when they are acting. Others suggest it is the actor's love of applause, but—as we have just shown—why enter into a situation where the gaining of approval is such a risky business? Each of these reasons probably explains, in part, why actors act. But the testimony of most actors indicates that the desire

I'm a terrible escapist in life, and to go to a theatre, shut myself up in a dressing-room and come out as somebody else, and live a mimic life, does give me pleasure; I suppose it always has done. All children dress up and play games, but my brothers and sister and I were tremendously theatrically minded, in that way, in our nursery days, and even in our schooldays. I was always living in some sort of fantasy world.... One's got to keep the childlike thing one had when one first went into the theatre, of saying, "Oh, I'll pretend to be somebody else, and I'll try and live this part," or "I'll dress up and pretend I'm somebody else."

John Gielgud

to act has its roots in the impulse to play that each of us experiences in childhood and, to a lesser degree, all our lives. It is the love of "let's pretend" that explains why most actors act.

The attractiveness of "let's pretend" has always been that it lets us play out our fantasies and the unrealizable selves of our day-dreams. It provides an escape from the limitations and loneliness, the dullness and drabness, that each of us feels at certain times in our lives. Furthermore, the world of play can have a sense of order, sequence, and completeness that our lives usually do not have. This gives us a sense of control. In play we can master reality, and in the theatre that mastery is paid attention to by an audience.

What the actor does, in effect, is to take a normal life process—namely, the use of play as a means of mastering difficult and conflicting emotions and impulses—and makes it a way of life. What is an element in the child's gradual development to maturity is a life vocation for the actor. (It is often observed that there is something "childlike" about actors.) The actor transforms these feelings and impulses into a theatrical form by means of impersonation. Most people develop their own "character." An actor, as Michael Goldman pointed out, "develops the power to play characters."

This can be very satisfying because it gives the actor a powerful sense of being in touch with "the others" who make up the audience. When an actor plays a role, although he searches for the character in and through himself, he must also present that character in a way that seems authentic to the audience. The character must have something in common with the audience, and this "in-commonness" is always the most important quality his performance must convey. We know that in our everyday life we communicate and maintain social relationships because of this sense of "in-commonness" we share with our fellow human beings. One of the reasons human relationships—no matter how close—are never totally satisfactory is due to our awareness that commonality is not enough. There is something uniquely "me" that never comes through or is never adequately understood. We always have a sense that there is an important part of *me* that never gets dealt with in social relationships.

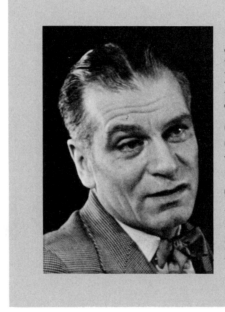

A cting is an almost childish wish, isn't it? Pretend to be somebody else.... Let's pretend—I suppose that's the original impulse of acting. That's perhaps why it does become more difficult as you get on in years. I think acting is a young enthusiasm. The childish excitement of it, the glamor disappears very early. And then comes the effort to improve yourself into different shapes, to be successful—to be famous.

Laurence Olivier

The action of a play does not leave these areas unexplored. The illusory actions of the actor belong only to what is held in common. This distinction is one of the many interesting things about Shakespeare's *Hamlet*. Everyone in the play urges Hamlet to face up to the common experience of people. "Your father died! Everybody's does—so let's get on with it." Hamlet tries to "play" this: he wears black, sighs, and looks sad. But he cannot accept this; it doesn't satisfy "that within" which is unique to Hamlet; namely, the appearance of the ghost of his father. Well, each one of us has "that within" which cannot be played out in the action of our lives, that exceeds, as it were, the stage of our life. This is not the case in the "let's pretend" world of the theatre. In a successful theatrical performance everything connects. This is what attracts audiences and what makes the experience so satisfying for actors.

Finally, the element of "let's pretend" so central to the impulse to act reminds us, in yet another way, that all theatre involves the making present of another world. As a member of both the real world in which we all live and the imaginary world of the play, the actor must create a bridge between that imaginary world and the real world of the audience. He must make the unreal believable on its own terms. Even if we cannot grasp a play's meaning at first, we know it will be made clear to us eventually. It is important that we in the audience believe this. The actor must establish the fact that he acts a lie that we, the audience, accept both as a lie and as the truth. The theatrical event is based upon the mutual trust that makes this acceptance possible. In most instances the audience comes to the theatre ready to accept (or else why be there?). The actor has the responsibility of insuring that our expectations are met. When he accepts this responsibility and succeeds, the acting process can be transforming for audience as well as actor. The other world the actors present to us in the audience was first created in the play. This being the case, we will now turn our attention to the playwright, the maker of the other world of the play.

NOTES

[1]Some of the most interesting books on the relationship of the theatre to shamanism are: *The Theatrical Event* by David Cole; *UR-Drama: The Origins of Theatre* by E. T. Kirby; *The Actor's Freedom* by Michael Goldman; *Environmental Theatre* by Richard Schechner; and *Alcheringa*, edited by Jerome Rothenberg and Michel Benamou. However, the writings on the history of religion by Mircea Eliade and especially his book *Shamanism* have probably been the most influential.

[2]Mircea Eliade. *Shamanism.* New York: Bollingen Foundation, 1964, p. 5.

[3]E. T. Kirby. *UR-Drama: The Origins of Theatre.* New York: New York University Press, 1975, p. 1.

[4]Ibid., p. 2.

[5]David Cole. *The Theatrical Event.* Middletown: Wesleyan University Press, 1975, p. 16.

[6]Kenneth M. Stewart. "Spirit Possession in Native America." *Southwestern Journal of Anthropology*, Vol. 2, No. 1, 1946, p. 327.

[7]Konstantin Stanislavski. *Creating a Role*, trans. by Elizabeth R. Hapgood. New York: Theatre Arts Books, 1961, p. 12.

[8]From "Theatre" in *Encyclopaedia Britannica*, 14th edition (1929). Reprinted by permission of Encyclopaedia Britannica.

[9]*very . . . pressure:* an exact reproduction of the age; *form:* shape; *pressure:* imprint (of a seal).

[10]As evidence of this, read this description of the Earl of Essex (a famous nobleman and reputed lover of Queen Elizabeth I) as he was executed in 1601:

Then he put off his gown and ruff, and went up before the block. He called for the executioner, who on his knees asked him pardon, to whom he said, "Thou are welcome to me; I forgive thee; thou are the minister of justice." Then he kneeled down on the straw, and, with his eyes fixed to heaven and with long and passionate pauses in his speeches he prayed unpremeditatedly, craving strength to rely to his last gasp on the promises of Christ and to have no worldly thought but only God before him. He then repeated the Lord's prayer, in which all present joined with floods of tears. (G. B. Harrison. "A Last Elizabethan Journal 1599–1603" in *The Elizabethan Journals*. Ann Arbor: The University of Michigan, 1955, p. 164.)

Shakespeare's plays were true to this performance.

[11]Throughout history there have been certain styles of acting—the Japanese Nōh (fourteenth century) and Kabuki (seventeenth and eighteenth centuries) and the French neoclassic (seventeenth century) styles, for example—which have become traditionalized. These older styles are also accepted by contemporary audiences—at least in their native lands—if the tradition still plays a vital role in the cultural life of succeeding generations.

[12]Michael Goldman. *The Actor's Freedom*. New York: Viking Press, 1975.

[13]From remarks made by Bernard Jacobs in "On Using Stars" in *New York Theatre Review*, Vol. 2, #3 (March, 1978). Copyright © 1978 by Ira Bilowit/New York Theatre Review. Reprinted by permission of Ira J. Bilowit.

Chapter 6

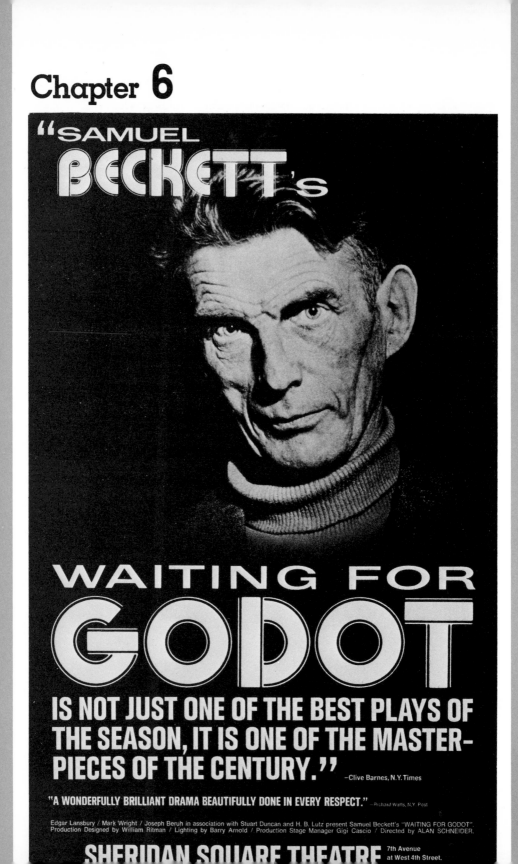

More properly it is not his subject which the playwright loves
     but the play he hopes to write about it.
More properly yet the playwright has a latent love for the play form,
     which he hopes will crystallize about his subject;
He has in his heart a play-shaped vacancy
     which he will fill now with his subject.

Robert Bolt

Words and magic were in the beginning one and the same thing,
     and even today words retain much of their magical power. . . .
Words call forth emotion and are invariably the means
     by which we influence our fellow creatures.

Sigmund Freud

The Playwright
and the Script

We experience the theatrical event primarily through the presence of the actors. We have said the actors take a journey to the other world of the play—both to find the role and to be possessed by it—and return to present the characters to us, the audience. For this to happen, the world of the play has to be there in the first place. There must be characters for the actors to find. And these characters, and the world of which they are a part, have to come from somewhere. They are created, created by the playwright.

Most theatre, with a few exceptions, begins with a script that has been written down by a playwright prior to the time that the director and the actors begin to work with it. The destination of the actors' journey has already been established as the rehearsals begin. They do not know exactly what this world is like that they are journeying to, or what they will find there. They do not know what route (more likely, routes) they will take to get to it, or even how long the journey will take. But they have some idea of where they are going, and, more important, they know that someone else—the playwright—has been there before them and has returned to give them a script, a detailed map of the world they will discover if they are talented, trained, and dedicated artists.

The playwright has related to the institution of the theatre in various ways throughout history. But no matter how his role has been defined, the playwright's first task has always been to discover the world of the play. He must find the play and the characters who exist and act within it. In doing so, he tests his discoveries against two standards:

1. his own sense of reality; and
2. what he perceives is the reality of the society of which he is a part.

Both are important. The first determines his personal vision of experience and hence the form of theatre—tragedy, comedy, or whatever—he will choose. The second is important because in searching for the play, the playwright is always conscious of his responsibility to his fellow human beings. His work must be authentic not only in his own terms, but also in terms of his audience. The playwright writes for audiences; he wants to have his play produced; he writes because he believes what he has to say will in some way be important to an audience. The playwright must pass these two tests if the experience of theatre is to take place in a meaningful way. How does the playwright do this?

WHERE DOES THE PLAY COME FROM?

This seems like a simple question, but like all creative processes, playwriting is complex. Obviously a play does not spring full-blown in the mind and imagination of the playwright, who then writes it down in script form. But if you were to read the advertising for some of the home courses in how to write plays for fun and profit, you would be surprised to discover how often they suggest a play is written this way: You start with a situation of potential conflict, from which you then evolve a story or plot, peopled with characters (some major and some minor), whose language is then shaped into dialogue. You divide this dialogue at appropriate places into acts and scenes; you provide a climax or resolution of the conflict in the final act; and, if you are really sophisticated, you make sure that each of these scenes concludes with an event of a "dramatic" nature. Finally, there must be a detailed description of the stage setting. Put this way, the whole process sounds pretty simpleminded (or the way one would write an episode for a television series), but that is the way some people think plays come about. Of course, nothing could be further from the truth. But if not this way, how?

There are probably as many approaches to writing plays as there are playwrights. It is very difficult to describe any kind of artistic creativity; for that reason, in this chapter we will concentrate less on the playwright's creative work and more on the product—the script.

Ultimately, of course, the play is the creation of the playwright's imagination. Like the actor, he searches for and finds the play within himself, though almost any thought or situation might first prompt his thinking about it. A scene on the bus, an idea while waiting for the dentist, a headline in the newspaper, a story overheard in a bar—something catches the playwright's attention. Like a hunter, he has a sense of pursuing his quarry. The idea or situation comes to dominate his imagination. He must go out and capture it in a dramatic form. At the start, he does not have an absolutely clear idea of who or what his characters are to be or what they will do or say. British playwright Harold Pinter confirms this when he says:

> I don't know what kind of characters my plays will have until they
> . . . well, until they *are*. Until they indicate to me what they are. I
> don't conceptualize in any way. Once I've got the clues I follow
> them—that's my job, really, to follow clues. . . . I think what happens is that I write in a very high state of excitement and frustration. I follow what I see on the paper in front of me—one sentence after another. That doesn't mean I don't have a dim, possible overall idea—the image that starts off doesn't just engender what happens immediately, it engenders the possibility of an overall happening, which carries me through. I've got an idea of what *might*
> happen—sometimes I'm absolutely right, but on many occasions
> I've been proved wrong by what does actually happen. Sometimes
> I'm going along and I find myself writing "C. comes in" when I
> didn't know that he was going to come in; he *had* to come in at that
> point, that's all.[1]

Most playwrights indicate that they have shared Pinter's experience. The world of the play has a life of its own. It does not just present itself; it must be found. As Pinter describes it, playwriting is

THE PLAYWRIGHT IN HISTORY

T he playwright's task has always been to create the script. He is that master of words who, through language, gives definition and cadence to the world of the play. The nature of his task and the importance of his role in the theatre have varied throughout history.

In classical Greece: The playwright was the central figure in the theatre. Playwrights wrote the plays, directed the actors, singers, and dancers, and arranged most of the details for the productions, which were presented at the festivals of Dionysus as a part of a civic and religious celebration.

In the Middle Ages: The theatre played an important part in community life, and the subject matter of the plays was church-related. Playwrights were anonymous. Plays were written by the clergy, by members of the craft guilds who presented them, and even by the actors themselves for the instruction and entertainment of largely illiterate audiences.

In Elizabethan England: The theatre had become largely secularized and once again the individual playwright was important. Troupes of actors, sponsored by the monarch or influential noblemen, performed in their own theatres. Playwrights were an integral part of these companies—some also acted—and had an honored position in the life of the court.

a process of discovery. The playwright makes certain choices, but the materials themselves dictate other choices. Sometimes the playwright's choices lead to nothing. But sometimes they lead to the discovery of a new and exciting world and the play comes to life.

We've described the playwright as a hunter. Perhaps a richer and more interesting way of describing him would be to compare him to Captain Ahab, the hero of Herman Melville's novel *Moby Dick*. Ahab had a monomaniacal compulsion to capture the giant white whale Moby Dick and he chased him all over the seven seas until he found him. The playwright is such a dedicated Ahab. Playwrights are like that driven captain of the seas in that their instincts sense the presence of the quarry in the dark depths of their own imaginations. Their skill is that of a harpooner. They throw phrase upon phrase like harpoons after the whale. Some plunge down slack and lifeless in the dark, and then at last one strikes, then another and another until the lines contain the whole strength and

In seventeenth-century France and Spain: The playwright had royal patronage. In some instances he headed his own company (Molière and Lope de Vega did this), but more often the playwright wrote for the court actors and the plays were performed for aristocratic audiences.

In Restoration England: The English theatre under Charles II was modeled on the court theatres of France. Witty comedies of manners and stately tragedies on classical themes were performed for the dandified ladies and gentlemen of the courts. The playwright, while respected, was thought of primarily as a supplier of entertainments for the idle nobility.

In the eighteenth and nineteenth centuries: While the court theatres continued, the theatre increasingly became a business. Stock companies under the leadership of actor-managers dominated, with the result that the playwright not only lost prestige but was removed from the production process. He wrote plays on assignment for the commercial system.

The modern theatre: The theatre has become democratized to the point that it is now totally eclectic; that is, there is no single dominant style or form of theatre. As a result, the playwright has varying roles. In the commercial theatre he is divorced from most aspects of the production process and is thought of primarily as a writing specialist, while in the avant-garde theatre he works very closely with the actors and directors. Today, in many experimental groups, the playwright has assumed a leadership role very similar to that of the playwright in ancient Greece.

energy of the prey. Indeed, in the theatre, the lines become the prey. It is actually by means of particular words and phrases that playwrights discover the characters. The writing of a play is a verbal process which probes, discovers, celebrates, and preserves in one action. It is the authentic excitement of discovery that makes a play, and it is the embodied reenactment of that discovery that makes theatre. Everyone in the theatre—from the playwright to the spectator—is a sharer in this experience.

The Playwright's Sources

The original inspiration for a play can be almost anything—a chance remark, an overheard joke. Whatever it is, the playwright's instincts tell her she has the germ of a play. Recall Robert Bolt's "play-shaped vacancy" which the playwright must fill with a subject.

Also recall that we have said a story is not a plot. A literal account of what you did between lunch and dinner could be a story, possibly interesting, but it is not a plot for a play or novel. For those actions to become a plot, you would have to choose to emphasize certain events and characters and to omit others. You would select and organize these to achieve a certain effect or make a certain point.

Everyday experience must undergo this kind of transformation before it can be useful to a playwright. Real life must be shaped and edited before it can be used in a play. The playwright selects characters and events and organizes her materials to create a plot. The actual life experience of most of us is so chaotic, ambiguous, implausible, and for the most part so dull, that it has to be transformed before it can become art.

Throughout history, a principal source of material for the playwright has been other writings and oral legends. Perhaps one of the reasons playwrights are attracted to legends, other plays, and stories is that they can begin with material already transformed. For example, all ancient Greek tragedy was based on the legends that grew out of the mythology of the landed aristocracy. This mythology had been passed on in Homer's epic poems *The Iliad* and *The Odyssey*. Most Roman drama was a pastiche of plots, characters, and themes drawn from the earlier Greek theatre. In his comedies, Molière plagiarized from almost any literary source he could lay his hands on—Roman plays, commedia dell'arte routines, popular stories. The sources of many of Corneille's and Racine's tragedies were biblical and classical Greek and Roman legends. Shakespeare was a prolific "borrower," and his plays can be traced back to such diverse sources as legend, Holinshed's *Chronicles* of British kings, the Roman plays of Plautus, and Italian short stories of the early Renaissance, to name a few. In this century, O'Neill, Brecht, Genet, and Beckett regularly borrowed from other playwrights, poets, and novelists. And think of some of our most popular musicals: *West Side Story* is based on Shakespeare's *Romeo and Juliet*, *My Fair Lady* on Shaw's *Pygmalion*, *The Man of La Mancha* on

CLASSICAL GREECE

Aeschylus	Sophocles	Euripides	Aristophanes
525–456 B.C.	496–406 B.C.	485–406 B.C.	450–380 B.C.

The further back in time we go the less evidence there is. The further we come forward the more evidence there is. The surviving evidence for the reign of William the Conqueror could be arranged on a kitchen table. The evidence for the year 1970 would fill a warehouse. The historian who wishes to write a readable history of 1970 will have to ignore most of the evidence available, selecting only those facts which seem to him important and making sensible connections between them. His orderly account of last year will not bear much resemblance to the confusion of last year as we lived it. But that is why we value his account. The warehouse full of old newspapers is simply so much rubbish and might as well be burned. It bears only too much likeness to last year as we lived it. It is the difference between history and life which gives history its value, and the difference is creative.

Robert Bolt, Introduction to **Vivat! Vivat Regina!**

Cervantes's *Don Quixote, Guys and Dolls* on Damon Runyon's short stories, *Fiddler on the Roof* on the tales of Sholem Aleichem. There's even *Annie*, which was based on the comic strip "Little Orphan Annie."

Fact must become fiction before it can enter into the world of the play. This is true of even the playwright's own life experiences. There is no question, for example, that many of Strindberg's and O'Neill's plays were derived from their own bitter experiences (Strindberg's tempestuous marriages and O'Neill's tortured relationship with his family). But before those experiences could become the source materials for their plays—works of art that were ordered, comprehensible, and interesting to an audience—Strindberg and O'Neill had to make a kind of fiction of their own lives.

LANGUAGE—THE PLAYWRIGHT'S MEDIUM

The play is the creation of the playwright's imagination. In Chapter 3 we said that plays are composed of acts and actions and that the playwright's first task is to create a plot that will reveal the action. But for all our talk of acts and action, the playwright must work entirely with words—language.

The language of the playwright transforms the other world of the play into reality for actors and audience. However, it cannot be just any language. Language in the theatre must have special qualities. There are many "literary" works that look like plays and are composed in dialogue form but are lifeless when brought forth in the theatre. They may even read well but, as they say in the

Plautus   254–184 B.C.

Terence   185–159 B.C.

CLASSICAL ROME

theatre, "they don't play." On the other hand, there are plays in script form that read atrociously or appear to be little more than gibberish, yet they throb with life on the stage. Eugene O'Neill, for instance, is put down by many literary people for having a "tin ear," yet most of his plays work in the theatre. He had a sense of theatre. Far greater literary talents, such as William Faulkner, Ernest Hemingway, and F. Scott Fitzgerald, did not have this sense when they tried to write drama. What makes language work in the theatre? What do we mean when we say a playwright has a sense of theatre?

We must realize at the outset that the writing of plays is not really a "literary" art and that a play is not a work of literature (although much of the time drama is taught and studied this way in our schools). A play is a medium for something else—a performance. A play does not exist in its fully realized form until it is performed on a stage by actors for an audience. That is why we say that *playwrights write only for actors*, not for silent readers. In fact, many great playwrights wrote for specific actors. Shakespeare knew that the great Elizabethan tragic actor Richard Burbage would perform his tragic heroes, just as he knew that the comic actor Will Kemp would act his major comic roles. Molière not only wrote for his own company, he knew that he himself would play many of the roles he created. From Chekhov's letters and notebooks we know how his awareness of who would be playing the roles—his wife, Olga Knipper, and Stanislavski, to name two—profoundly influenced the writing of his plays. The playwright knows that until the actor speaks his words they do not come fully alive. How does this affect his writing?

The chief function of language in the theatre is not to represent the way people actually talk in real life but to express what they experience. This is an important distinction. We said earlier in another context that we don't make love with the language of Romeo and Juliet, yet it is precisely because Romeo and Juliet speak as they do that they have great power over audiences. They express in their words the joyous but painful experience of youthful love. The experience is true to life, although the words are not. Or again, in times of great personal suffering, no one actually comes forth with bursts of poetry as King Lear and Othello do, but most people have experienced that kind of suffering and in the theatre such suffering is given a voice. If a friend were to come up to you and tell you that someone who was very close to you had been killed, you would not wax eloquent. But Horatio and Mark Antony express in long, poetic speeches the sense of loss and grief that each of us experiences at the death of a loved one. If you think about it, when we experience in real life any of those situations that so many plays deal with, we are inarticulate, if not completely silent. But the theatre must *express*—and always has expressed at its greatest moments—what human beings feel, not *represent* how they actually behave when they experience these feelings. Plays are true to human nature, but don't attempt to convince us that we are watching real life. It is not a question of how people actually use words, but rather how words in the theatre express what they experience. Words create our experience of the theatre. Nobody talks like a character in a play—not even like the most realistic character. Theatre is not lifelike—it is larger than life.

This being the case, the playwright always writes in the language of his characters and not in the language of the audience. The language must be appropriate to and expressive of the characters of the play.[2] The playwright must discover and identify with his characters and speak with their voices, rather than have them identify with him and speak in his voice. He must extract the language from the characters, not impose it upon them. (This is the discovery process Pinter described.) The language of the theatre is not that of the audience, and it is not that of the playwright. The language of the theatre is the language of the characters.

Language serves an essential function in performance. All theatre, as we said in Chapter 3, is about acts and action, but for these acts to have meaning and significance they must grow out of decisions to act. Events on the stage cannot happen haphazardly or without reason. Actor and audience alike must recognize that the acts of the characters are based upon conscious choices and that these choices give the play a sense of movement which is the essential characteristic of dramatic action. These decisions are expressed by the language. The primary function of language in the theatre is to express the consciousness of the characters which makes their decisions to act dramatically meaningful.

This explains why language is so crucial to the actor. He cannot bring to life characters who have no life and consciousness of their own. The playwright gives life and consciousness to his characters through imaginative and expressive language. A sure sign that the playwright may be having trouble doing this is the presence of countless stage directions telling the actor—or reader—what emotion the language is supposed to convey. Clearly, the playwright lacks confidence that the characters can speak for themselves. The script is the source of the actor's variety, vitality, and eloquence. It shapes and focuses the actor's energy. A good actor approaches the play's language not just as dialogue to be mastered and spoken, but as the way into the heart of the character. If language manifests consciousness, the actor must enter into and become one with the consciousness that language creates. He must be able to take words that have many meanings and connotations and empty them of meaning so as to be able to fill them with the new, unique significance created by the world of the play. The actor cannot discover this world or his character if the playwright has not provided the words in the first place. The playwright takes the initial journey to the other world of the play. The script contains that world in a condition of latency. To be fully realized it must be devoured, as it were, by the actors and re-presented in performance.

SPANISH GOLDEN AGE

Lope de Vega
1562–1635

Calderón
1600–1681

T he rehearsal of a serious play is an elaborate and quietly awful ceremony of fertilization; a ritual, despite its frequent appearance of disorganization and its very real air of friendliness, of sacrifice and rebirth. At the beginning, the playwright is accepted as God-King; he is felt to contain some truth without which the players cannot live. He is treated with deference, consulted, danced before. He speaks, or his interpreter speaks for him, and is eagerly obeyed.

For a spell the tribe, still weak and undernourished, moves at his nod; he sits enthroned in the secrets they require, assured, assuring, needed. Then, gradually the actors gain strength—his strength: they learn his words, his secrets; they cut off his hair. They take away everything he has, at first tentatively, and then boldly, with increasing assurance. They catch his quick sentences and acquire his speed; they subdue his big speeches and take away his gravity; they tear out his jokes and leave him humorless or imperceptive. They must invade him entirely and search for their nourishment in his darkness; they need his potency, and do not rest—cannot rest—until they have it. For the actor dies between roles, and comes to work seeking his spring. It is not an accident that we speak of the theatrical "season." Under that trivial word you may see primal planting, the earth wetted with life-blood, the shoots emerging, thickening, talling, harvested, and eaten: a corn of text, and words becoming flesh.

Peter Shaffer, "The Cannibal Theatre"

THE ESSENTIAL QUALITIES
OF THEATRICAL LANGUAGE

If the playwright's language is so crucial to the actor's performance, what are the essential qualities of theatrical language?
1. It reveals the consciousness of the characters at the same time that it develops the action.
2. It is eloquent.
3. It is gestural.
4. It has a quality of presence.

Some of these ideas about language may be new to you. The playwright's use of language is so important to the success of the play that we will discuss these points in detail.

It reveals consciousness while developing the action. In other words, language tells the story and moves the plot along, and while this is certainly important, by itself it is not enough. The audience must at the same time sense that the characters are aware of themselves in "dramatic" ways—that they are creating their own story.

Christopher Marlowe
1564–93

William Shakespeare
1564–1616

Ben Jonson
1573–1637

Any split in this necessarily inseparable process spells disaster. An audience will soon lose interest in what is going on no matter how clever or exciting the plot or the story may be if the characters lack self-awareness.[3] Similarly, interesting and well-developed characters will be boring to audiences if their self-awareness does not drive the plot.

The other major function of language as a means whereby the action is expressed and realized is related to the characters. As we said earlier, we know that in our daily lives we define ourselves, or perhaps more accurately we define our consciousness of ourselves through language. We are always revealing our sense of ourselves through the language we use. What is true of everyday life is also true for the characters in a play. They reveal themselves and their sense of themselves as they relate to the events of the plot and the other characters through their language. It is this sense of consciousness—which only language can create—that gives dramatic actions their significance, the significance that makes the experience of the theatre not only possible but also meaningful to the audiences.

To see how language reveals the characters' consciousness of themselves while it develops the action, let us look at an example of the two functions working together magnificently. Here is the opening of the first scene of Chekhov's *The Three Sisters:*

Act 1

A drawing room in the PROZOROVS' *house: It is separated from a large ballroom at the back by a row of columns. It is midday; there is a cheerful sunshine outside. In the ballroom the table is being laid for lunch.* OLGA, *wearing the regulation dark-blue dress of a secondary school teacher, is correcting her pupils' work, standing or walk-*

ing about as she does so. MASHA, *in a black dress, is sitting reading a book, her hat on her lap.* IRINA, *in white, stands lost in thought.*

OLGA: Father died just a year ago today, on the fifth of May—your birthday, Irina. I remember, it was very cold and it was snowing. It seemed to me I would never live through it; and you had fainted and were lying there quite still, just as if you were dead. And now—a year's gone by, and we talk about it so easily. You're dressed in white again, and your face is positively radiant . . . *The clock strikes twelve.* The clock struck twelve then, too. *A pause.* I remember, the band was playing as they carried father to the cemetery and they fired a salute. That was because he was the general in command of the brigade. And yet there weren't many people there. Of course, it was raining hard, and there was some snow, too.

IRINA: Why must we bring up all these memories?

TUSENBACH, CHEBUTYKIN, *and* SOLYONY *appear behind the columns by the table in the ballroom.*

OLGA: It's so warm today that we can keep the windows wide open, but the birches haven't any leaves yet. It was eleven years ago that father got his brigade and we left Moscow. I remember so well how everything was in bloom by now; it was warm and yet I remember everything there as though we'd left it only yesterday. Why, when I woke up this morning and saw the warm sun, saw that spring was here, my heart leapt with joy. I wanted so much to go home again. Go home to Moscow!

CHEBUTYKIN, *sarcastically to* SOLYONY: A small chance of that!

TUSENBACH, *also to* SOLYONY: Of course, it's nonsense.

MASHA, *absorbed in her book, whistles part of a song softly.*

OLGA: Stop whistling, Masha! How can you? *A pause.* I suppose being at school every day from morning till night gives me this constant headache. And my thoughts are as gloomy as those of an old woman. Honestly, I feel as if my strength and my youth were running out of me! Drop by drop; day by day; every day, for the last four years. . . . And one dream keeps growing stronger and stronger. . . .

IRINA: Go to Moscow! Sell the house, leave everything here, and go back to Moscow.

OLGA: Yes, to go back to Moscow! As soon as possible.

CHEBUTYKIN *and* TUSENBACH *laugh.*

IRINA: Andrey will probably be a professor soon, anyway he won't keep on living here. The only problem is poor Masha.

OLGA: Masha can come to Moscow every year and spend the whole summer with us.

MASHA *whistles a song softly.*

IRINA: Everything will take care of itself with God's help. *Looking out of the window.* How beautiful it is today! I don't know why I feel so joyful. I woke up this morning and remembered it was my birthday, and suddenly I felt so happy. I thought of the time when we were children and mother was still alive. And then such wonderful thoughts came to me . . . such wonderful thoughts.

OLGA: You're all aglow today—lovelier than ever. And Masha is beautiful, too. Andrey could be good-looking, too, if he hadn't put on so much weight; it doesn't suit him. As for me, I've just aged and grown

NEOCLASSIC FRANCE

Pierre Corneille
1606–84

Molière
1622–73

Jean Racine
1639–99

a lot thinner. I suppose it's because I get so angry with the girls at school. Anyway, today I'm free, I'm home, and my head doesn't ache, and I feel so much younger than I did yesterday. After all, I'm only twenty-eight, but . . . Oh well, I suppose everything that God wills must be right and good . . . and yet, it seems to me, if I had married and stayed at home it would have been better. *A pause.* I would have loved my husband, very much.

TUSENBACH, *to* SOLYONY. Really, you talk such a lot of nonsense, I'm tired of listening to you. *Comes into the drawing room.* I forgot to tell you, Vershinin, our new battery commander, is coming to call today.[4]

Notice first in the description of the setting that there are two clearly defined playing areas—the drawing room where the three sisters are and the ballroom behind them. This will prove to be important almost at once since it allows Chekhov to use a technique that reveals both character and plot. Notice also the three sisters' costumes. Although it is still too soon to know all that the costumes represent, we see that Olga is in a schoolteacher's uniform, Masha is dressed in black, and Irina in white. As the scene unfolds, we will discover that what each of them wears reflects the situation she is in and, more important, her consciousness of that situation.

John Gay
1685–1732

RESTORATION
AND
EIGHTEENTH-
CENTURY
ENGLAND

William Wycherley
1640–1715

William Congreve
1670–1729

Oliver Goldsmith
1728–74

In Olga's opening speech we learn several things: It is Irina's birthday; their father had died and not only had something gone out of their lives, but the quality of their lives has changed; it was raining then, but now it is sunny. It is a time of hope, with Irina wearing a white dress. Irina responds with: These are only memories; why bring up the past? Again the implication is that things are better now, against a backdrop of unhappiness. Just at that point, Tusenbach, Chebutykin, and Solyony appear in the ballroom. The entrance of these three male characters is a brief and hardly noticeable interruption, but Chekhov will play off their presence against

Richard Sheridan
1751–1816

Johann Goethe
1749–1832

Friedrich Schiller
1759–1805

Heinrich von Kleist
1777–1811

that of the women. Then Olga continues: Yes, things are better. The sun is shining. Then the first mention of how wonderful it was in Moscow—where everything was right, bright, and beautiful. The speech ends with the statement of one of the play's major themes: "Go home to Moscow!" Note how this dream is undercut by the speeches of the men: "A small chance of that!" "Of course, it's nonsense." The three men are carrying on a conversation completely independent of the sisters; yet by letting those lines emerge in the dialogue at just that time, Chekhov indirectly tells us something about both Olga's consciousness of her own situation and the situation as it actually exists. Already we know something important.

Then in Olga's next speech we learn that their present situation isn't so pleasant and hence the hope (illusion?) grows. This is repeated in the next two brief speeches and again we get the ironic undercut: laughter from the men. Then there is the first forward movement of the plot: mention of Andrey and Masha. Who is he? What's her problem? Again, "to Moscow," but this time the undercut comes from the Masha whose problem had just been mentioned. How does it relate to the others? What does it tell us about "poor" Masha? Irina passes it off and returns to images of her childhood and raises the question in our minds whether psychically she has never left childhood. Olga tells us more: about Andrey, the unpleasantness of her life as a teacher, her resignation to her situation, and the already idle hope for a marriage she will never have. And this is concluded with Tusenbach's moving from the ballroom to the drawing room on the line: "Really, you talk such a lot of nonsense." It clearly applies to both conversations. He then introduces the information that gets the whole play into forward gear: "Vershinin, our new battery commander, is coming to call today."

Look at what Chekhov has accomplished in less than two pages of dialogue. He has introduced most of the play's major characters (or at least prepared us for them); he has introduced the major theme—the sisters' illusory dream of going to Moscow—and has suggested its unhappy resolution; he has gotten the main mechanism of the plot started (the arrival of Vershinin, the new battery commander); and he has revealed a great deal about the three sisters (even Masha, who has not yet spoken a word). In short, Chekhov has at the same time revealed character and developed plot. The two activities must go on simultaneously to hold our interest.

It is eloquent. By this we do not mean theatrical language consists entirely of profound or beautiful or poetic words. There have been many examples of serious themes and magnificent poetry that have failed miserably as theatre. Rather, we mean that language must make the events on stage come alive with meaning and command the audience's attention.

Eloquence in the theatre is first a matter of timing or rhythm. There's a well-known theatre story about a new play in the final stages of rehearsal. It is not going well and the director, producer, some of the actors, and the playwright are huddled together trying to figure out what's wrong. Many elaborate and complex explanations are given for the trouble, when finally the playwright—who had been silent until then—pointed to the script and said, "Right here we need a 20-second speech!" The timing is critical—as much as the content of any given speech—and good playwrights have well-developed instincts about timing. Jean-Louis Barrault put it well when he said, "I think a dramatist should write with his breath, not his brain."

Notice what timing and rhythm accomplish in the final scene of Samuel Beckett's *Waiting for Godot*.

> ESTRAGON *draws* VLADIMIR *towards the tree. They stand motionless before it. Silence.*
>
> ESTRAGON: Why don't we hang ourselves?
> VLADIMIR: With what?
> ESTRAGON: You haven't got a bit of rope?
> VLADIMIR: No.
> ESTRAGON: Then we can't.
> > *Silence.*
> VLADIMIR: Let's go.
> ESTRAGON: Wait, there's my belt.
> VLADIMIR: It's too short.
> ESTRAGON: You could hang on to my legs.
> VLADIMIR: And who'd hang on to mine?
> ESTRAGON: True.
> VLADIMIR: Show all the same. (ESTRAGON *loosens the cord that holds up his trousers which, much too big for him, fall about his ankles. They look at the cord.)* It might do at a pinch. But is it strong enough?
> ESTRAGON: We'll soon see. Here.
> > *They each take an end of the cord and pull. It breaks. They almost fall.*
> VLADIMIR: Not worth a curse.
> > *Silence.*
> ESTRAGON: You say we have to come back to-morrow?
> VLADIMIR: Yes.
> ESTRAGON: Then we can bring a good bit of rope.
> VLADIMIR: Yes.
> > *Silence.*
> ESTRAGON: Didi.
> VLADIMIR: Yes.
> ESTRAGON: I can't go on like this.
> VLADIMIR: That's what you think.
> ESTRAGON: If we parted? That might be better for us.
> VLADIMIR: We'll hang ourselves to-morrow. *(Pause.)* Unless Godot comes.
> ESTRAGON: And if he comes?
> VLADIMIR: We'll be saved.[5]

Victor Hugo
1802–85

Alfred de Musset
1810–57

Eugène Labiche
1815–88

There seems to be nothing special about this dialogue. Certainly, none of the words are "poetic." Rather, it has the abrupt give-and-take of a burlesque routine or a comedy act. Its halting rhythms seem to pick up momentum only to come to a halt. Yet this rhythm—more than the meaning of the words—expresses the terror and boredom, the aimlessness and desperation, and the sense of frightening irrelevancy that are at the heart of Beckett's play.

An important source of eloquence is sound itself—the sounds of words, the sounds of movement, disembodied sound, meaningless sound, noise. Sound is a powerful means of manifesting consciousness and an effective way of expressing that consciousness to the audience. Shakespeare was a master in this regard (in almost every regard, for that matter). Notice how the seriousness and self-confidence of Othello are revealed just by the sounds of the vowels in the language he uses:

> Most potent, grave, and reverend signiors,
> My very noble and approved good masters,
> That I have ta'en away this old man's daughter,
> It is most true—true, I have married her.
> The very head and front of my offending
> Hath this extent, no more. Rude am I in my speech,
> And little blest with the soft phrase of peace.
> For since these arms of mine had seven years' pith
> Till now some nine moons wasted, they have used
> Their dearest action in the tented field.
> And little of this great world can I speak,
> More than pertains to feats of broil and battle,
> And therefore little shall I grace my cause
> In speaking of myself.

Or look at this passage from *Macbeth:*

> . . . This my hand will rather
> The multitudinous seas incarnadine,
> Making the green one red.

The sounds of "multitudinous seas incarnadine" heave like a wilderness of molten lava, in contrast with the three monosyllables, "this my hand." Macbeth expresses eloquently his awareness that his guilt has besmirched the whole universe.

Shakespeare was not unique in this. Most great playwrights have had a sense of the *sound* of language and have used it well. Much contemporary theatre has used sound (not words) to achieve eloquence. Andrei Serban's 1973 production of Euripides' *The Trojan Women*, for example, used a mixture of shrieks, groans, chants, and bits of the classical Greek, Italian, Persian, and English languages. The audience understood few of the words, but nearly everyone experienced the play in powerful ways.

There is one other important dimension of eloquence. The first law in writing for the theatre is that everything must be speakable. It is necessary at all times for the playwright to *hear* the actor speaking in his mind's ear. It is very easy when putting words on paper not to hear them being spoken. The playwright must be conscious of the voice that speaks—the rhythm, the phrasing, the pauses. He must also be conscious of the look, the feel, and the movement of the actors while they are speaking. He must, in short, render what might be called the whole gesture of each scene. To do this it is important to know what words do and mean, but it is more important to know what they cannot do at those crucial moments when the actor needs to use a vocal or physical gesture. (For example, the effectiveness of a shrug or sigh could well be diminished if it were accompanied by a too-articulate speech.) Only by listening to language can the playwright hear the words in such a way that they play upon each other in harmony, in conflict, and in pattern—and hence are dramatic. By knowing what language either cannot or need not do, by understanding pauses, stage business, movement, and what can be communicated visually by the actors' bodies, the sets, and lighting, the playwright will create theatrical eloquence.

NINETEENTH-CENTURY SCANDINAVIA

Left:
Henrik Ibsen
1828–1906

Right:
August Strindberg
1849–1912

Finally, eloquence is directly related to the character's awareness of self that we discussed earlier. Shakespeare showed the breakdowns of Othello and Lear with corresponding breakdowns in language. The gibberish they speak at the moment of collapse is a striking yet eloquent contrast to the magnificent poetry that preceded it in each case. Conversely, there are moments when the spirit of great dramatic heroes uplifts them so they can speak better than they know. In Georg Büchner's *Woyzeck*, for instance, the protagonist is a poor, victimized soldier. Driven by suffering and jealousy, he murders Marie, the woman he loves and the mother of his child. Throughout the play Woyzeck speaks in the plain and halting language of one in his lowly and unhappy condition. But as his anguish mounts, it is expressed in ever more eloquent speech. At the moment he kills Marie, Woyzeck says:

> Are you freezing, Marie? And still you're so warm. Your lips are hot as coals! Hot as coals, the hot breath of a whore! And still I'd give up heaven just to kiss them again. Are you freezing? When you're cold through, you won't freeze any more. The morning dew won't freeze you.[6]

The playwright must recognize that moment and discover the language that will express the heights of a character's emotion. Eloquence, then, is not just a matter of words; it is language that expresses a particular character. For characters to be fully alive in the world of the play, they must be given the language to express their consciousness.

NINETEENTH-CENTURY RUSSIA

Top left:
Nikolai Gogol
1809–53

Top right:
Ivan Turgenev
1818–83

Bottom left:
Anton Chekhov
1860–1904

Bottom right:
Maxim Gorki
1868–1936

Since language is an act, it cannot be dissociated from gesture; gesture finally becomes speech, just as speech becomes gesture.

Jean-Paul Sartre, **Sartre on Theatre**

It must be remembered that the bulk of my work was designed for the theatre; I was always thinking of actual delivery. And for this delivery (whether of prose or of verse) I had worked out a quite definite technique. I called it "gestic." This meant that the sentence must entirely follow the gest of the person speaking. ["Gest" can be defined as a combination of gesture and attitude.]

Bertolt Brecht, **Brecht on Theatre**

Words are made of motion, made of action or response, at whatever remove; and gesture is made of language—made of the language beneath or beyond or alongside of the language of words. When the language of words most succeeds it becomes gesture in its words.

R. P. Blackmur, **Language as Gesture**

It is gestural. The language of the theatre is an indivisible combination of the words the actors speak, all of the sounds of the production, and everything we see on the stage. But there is a problem with this: The whole process of theatre usually begins with the words of the playwright's script. How can the script suggest appropriate physical actions and gestures without including pages of stage directions? To answer this question, let's begin with a simple observation from everyday life. You are standing on the curb of the sidewalk and suddenly a car comes at you, apparently out of control. You try to get out of the way. You make a gesture of pushing it away, and you yell, "Stop!" You seem to do all these things simultaneously. But do you? Try it out for yourself. You will find that the gesture of pushing away will always precede the saying of "Stop!"—if only by a split second. Now, try to consciously make yourself say the word before the gesture. It is not only very difficult to do, it would look and feel ridiculous. Try the same thing by pointing to something falling from a building and shouting, "Watch out!" In both instances it is clear that the physical response precedes the verbal response. Indeed, the physical action in a very real way drives, shapes, and directs the verbal. The gesture is the source of the word. This is an essential quality of all dramatic language. Critic George Steiner has said that "drama is language under such high pressure of feeling that words carry a necessary and immediate connotation of gesture."[7] Gesture is not a decorative addition that accompanies language—something that the actor adds. It is part of language itself; it is the source, the cause, and the director of dramatic language.

Georg Buechner
1813–37

Friedrich Hebbel
1813–63

Richard Wagner
1813–83

Gerhart Hauptmann
1862–1931

The great French theorist-director-actor Antonin Artaud (1896–1948) was concerned with the relationship between language and theatre. He insisted that not only does gesture precede the spoken word, but that it is the true expression of what we feel, while words only describe what we feel. Artaud's basic premise, developed in his influential book *The Theatre and Its Double*, is that it is a mistake in the theatre to assume that "in the beginning was the Word." The stage, he said,

> is a concrete physical place which must speak its own language—a language that goes deeper than spoken language, a language that speaks directly to our senses rather than primarily to the mind as is the case with the language of words.[8]

There is overstatement in this passage. Obviously, he was not advocating the suppression of speech in the theatre. It is not that language is unimportant, but that its role must be clearly understood. Since the theatre is really concerned with the way feelings and passions, images and ideas, conflict with each other, the language of the theatre must be considered as something more than dialogue. It must capture the turbulence of experience. Language must "act" along with everything else on the stage. The words of the script are

THE
MODERN
THEATRE

ENGLAND AND
IRELAND

Oscar Wilde
1856–1900

George Bernard Shaw
1856–1950

William Butler Yeats
1865–1939

written to be performed. In the theatre, language and gesture are inseparable.[9]

It has a quality of presence.   Our discussion of the gestural nature of language logically leads us to consider the fourth necessary quality of theatrical language—that it have a quality of presence. The discussion of gesture suggests that there is something about language that is not immediately present. *Words come after the fact*—they are responses to physical gestures, they describe what we feel, they objectify our basic impulses, they are abstractions. If this is true, how can language be compatible with the theatre's need to be of the present? After all, on the simplest level, the words of the script have already been created before the actors begin to work with them. Sometimes the words were written hundreds or thousands of years earlier. Sometimes actors must work with a script written in a language and/or idiom quite different from their own. There is a kind of deadness to every script—a deadness that is apparent in the wooden awkwardness of early rehearsals. It comes from an earlier time; the language has a "pastness" that is opposed to the "presentness" of theatre.

In a sense, this quality of lifelessness is in the nature of language itself. Language *is* after the fact. Think about how it is in real life. We meet someone to whom we find ourselves tremendously attracted. We see each other regularly and have a great time together. It is a time of discovery—we discover each other and in the process we rediscover ourselves, the birds and the flowers, the whole world. We are falling in love and our whole being is almost bursting with emotion. At a certain point our feelings can no longer be contained and out comes "I love you!" Now, this is a natural expression, but in the very act of saying it we have ceased to *feel* love totally and directly—we have objectified, and in so doing distanced (if ever so slightly), our feelings of love into words. The words are not the feelings themselves, but descriptions of our feelings—an expression of them. This fact prompts cynics to observe that once you say "I love you," it is downhill the rest of the way. There is no question that this is true; but it is not the whole truth. "I love you" also

John Millington Synge
1871–1909

Sean O'Casey
1880–1964

John Osborne
b.1929

Harold Pinter
b.1932

sustains love, maintains love, restores love, celebrates love—in short, gives life to love.

Words, in spite of their quality of pastness, are the only means that the actor has of making present the other world of the play. Most theatre practitioners maintain that for the language of the theatre to have "presence," it must be celebratory. What does this mean? A celebration is a joyful response to a past event; it is not the event itself. A celebration—like language—is always after the fact. By means of some kind of ceremonial reenactment or occasion, we believe that the present can be endowed with the spirit of a significant event that occurred at another time. We celebrate the Fourth of July, for example, as a way of renewing the values and spirit of our nation's independence. It is a holiday (a holy day) in which the past is made present. (Of course, if we don't actually celebrate the event by entering into the spirit of the original occasion, but go to the beach instead, the holiday ceases to be one. It is only a day off.) Because celebrations have this quality of bringing back the past, the language of celebration always strikes us as something special, even when it is everyday language. It evokes memories and calls forth feelings; it inspires awe; it is important to us because the words seem to be able to do something different from what they ordinarily do—they seem transformed. It is as if they are occurring for the first time. It is just this quality—the first-timeness, which Stanislavski referred to as "the magic of the first time"—that the language of the theatre must possess. It will have it only if the playwright truly understands that he has an almost sacred mission to find the words that *belong* to the play, the words that alone can express the play. The actor can only embody and make present the genuine article. Audiences—whether they are always conscious of it or not—will not accept anything else. So if the playwright is to make present the world of the play, he must find and use the words that both express and celebrate it. This may sound like a mystical process ("Doesn't the playwright just sit down at a typewriter?"), but this is the first step by which the magic which we call theatre is created.

GERMANY AND SWITZERLAND

Frank Wedekind	Bertolt Brecht	Max Frisch	Friedrich Duerrenmatt
1864–1918	1898–1956	b.1911	b.1921

As we read some of the great plays of the past, we cannot help but compare the marvelously expressive and richly poetic language of Sophocles, Shakespeare, and Racine, for example, to the inarticulate, monosyllabic grunts of so many contemporary plays and wonder what has happened. How could the eloquence of Antigone or King Lear degenerate into the inarticulacy of Woyzeck or Stanley Kowalski? Part of the answer is that conventions change as the playwright's sense of the world changes. We may wonder why modern playwrights don't write in the poetic style of the giants of the past, but we should not forget that realistic dialogue was introduced into the theatre in the first place out of a desire for more expressive language. Ibsen, Strindberg, and Chekhov—playwrights who did much to change theatre in the nineteenth century—didn't write realistic dialogue because they had theories about language. They wrote realistic dialogue partly in reaction to the hollow rhetoric of the romantic plays of the period, but chiefly because it best expressed the characters they had created. Mrs. Alving, Miss Julie, and Uncle Vanya needed a realistic language to express themselves. Similarly, Beckett, Ionesco, and Pinter in this century have tended to reject the language of earlier realism in favor of jarring emotional speech because they believe this kind of language most fully expresses the world in which we live and the characters they wish to create. The dominant conventions of language in the theatre tell us as much about the world of which theatre is a part as they do about theatre itself. The stammering inarticulateness of the contemporary theatre is a reflection of the inarticulateness of so much of contemporary life.

Not only must the playwright have a critical and cultivated ear for language, so must the audience. In a way, the dull language of so much contemporary theatre reflects the audience's limited capacity to listen. The relationship of theatrical language to the audience's capacity to listen becomes clear if we compare our time with that of Shakespeare and his colleagues living in Elizabethan England. In Shakespeare's day the dominant means of communication was the spoken word. People needed to listen well just to live their daily lives, and this strongly established oral tradition had a deep influence on the theatre. Audiences not only knew how to listen, they could sustain their attention for long periods of time. Today we marvel at the thought of an uncut production of *Hamlet*, which would take several hours to perform. In Shakespeare's day, long afternoons in the theatre were commonplace.[10] In short, the richness of language which characterizes the Elizabethan drama was due in part to the audience's capacity to listen well.

How different it is today! We don't know how to listen. Indeed, think of the energy we expend not listening. Noise pollution requires that we block out much of what we hear just to maintain our sanity.

ITALY AND SPAIN

Luigi Pirandello
1867–1936

Ugo Betti
1892–1953

Federico Garcia Lorca
1899–1936

FRANCE

Michel de Ghelderode
1898–1962

Jean-Paul Sartre
b.1905

And television has influenced our listening abilities, as it has so much of our life. In reality the television image is nothing more than hundreds of thousands of tiny little dots of light. *We* actually create in our heads the images we see and this requires a great deal of visual concentration and effort. The sound of television is of very poor quality—it has to be, or it would make demands on us that would interfere with our "seeing" it—so this, too, does little to train our capacity to listen. Then, consider what television has done to shape our attention span. For many of us, twenty minutes at one time is about as long as we can keep our attention focused. In short, television has encouraged our visual capacities and discouraged our listening. One has the nagging fear that the awkwardness, reticence, inarticulateness, and homely language of our theatre is no longer a healthy reaction to the stuffy, inflated language of an earlier period. It is, rather, a concession to our inability to listen. Having poor ears, we may have deprived the theatre of its voice. The playwright today writes for an audience with poorer listening abilities than Shakespeare's audience.

In recent years when the subject of the breakdown of language in the theatre comes up, people usually point to the plays of Samuel Beckett, Eugène Ionesco, Harold Pinter, or Peter Handke as evidence that the collapse has already occurred. Many of these plays, they say, are unintelligible and illogical. They have little or no recognizable plot. The characters tend to speak only in meaningless clichés and stereotyped phrases. Most important, these playwrights seem to make no effort to communicate with their audiences. For example, some critics say that in *The Bald Soprano* Ionesco is dramatizing the failure of words to communicate by deliberately not communicating himself, and they quote his own discussion of the play to support this view:

> [The play] represented, for me, a kind of collapse of reality. Words had become empty, noisy shells without meaning; the characters as well, of course, had become psychologically empty. Everything ap-

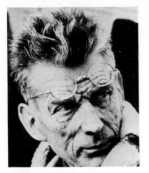
Samuel Beckett
b.1906

Jean Anouilh
b.1910

Jean Genet
b.1910

Eugène Ionesco
b.1912

peared to me in an unfamiliar light, people moving in a timeless
time, in a spaceless space. . . . The Smiths, the Martins, can no
longer talk because they can no longer think; they can no longer
think *because they can no longer be moved, can no longer feel
passions;* they can no longer be, they can "become" anybody,
anything, for, having lost their identity, they assume the identity of
others, become part of the world of the impersonal; they are inter-
changeable: you can put Martin in place of Smith and vice versa,
no one will notice.[11]

But if you look at the play—or, better still, experience a performance
of it—that is just what it expresses: the failure of communication!
Ionesco has communicated how difficult it is to communicate because of the impersonality of modern life and he has done so with
words—words that express the impersonal consciousness of the
characters.

Many people feel that Ionesco, Beckett, and Pinter are prime
examples of playwrights who have created inarticulate characters
whose language is dull. I would argue that these playwrights have
chosen to deal with the impersonality of modern life and that the
language they use eloquently expresses the impoverished spirit of
their characters. Unlike life, where the meaning of what we say can
often be tinged with uncertainty, characters in plays always say
what they mean. In the theatre there is an inseparable relationship
between consciousness and expression.

I 've gotta use words when I talk to you.
T. S. Eliot, **Sweeney Agonistes**

In 1962, Pinter published an article in the London *Sunday Times Magazine* that is worth quoting extensively because it goes to the heart of the issue we are discussing: What is the role of language in the theatre and can that role be realized today?

> Beware the writer who puts forward his concern for you to embrace. . . . This kind of writer clearly trusts words absolutely. I have mixed feelings about words myself. Moving among them, sorting them out, watching them appear on the page, from this I derive a considerable pleasure. But at the same time I have another strong feeling about words which amounts to nothing less than nausea. Such a weight of words confronts us, day in day out, . . . the bulk of it a stale dead terminology; ideas endlessly repeated and permutated, become platitudinous, trite, meaningless. Given this nausea, it's very easy to be overcome by it and step back into paralysis. . . . But if it is possible to confront this nausea, to follow it to its hilt and move through it, then it is possible to say something has occurred, that something has even been achieved.
>
> Language, under these conditions, is a highly ambiguous commerce. So often, below the words spoken, is the thing known and unspoken. . . .
>
> There are two silences. One when no word is spoken. The other when perhaps a torrent of language is being employed. This speech is speaking of a language locked beneath it. That is its continual reference. The speech we hear is an indication of that we don't hear. It is a necessary avoidance, a violent, sly, anguished or mocking smoke-screen which keeps the other in its place. When true silence falls we are still left with echo but nearer nakedness. One way of looking at speech is to say it is a constant stratagem to cover nakedness.
>
> . . . I think that we communicate only too well, in our silence, in what is unsaid, and that what takes place is continual evasion, desperate rearguard attempts to keep ourselves to ourselves. Communication is too alarming. To enter into someone else's life is too frightening. To disclose to others the poverty within us is too fearsome a possibility.
>
> I'm not suggesting that no character in a play can ever say what he in fact means. Not at all. I have found that there invariably does come a moment when this happens, where he says something, perhaps which he has never said before. And where this happens, what he says is irrevocable, and can never be taken back.[12]

These ideas about language are well illustrated in Pinter's plays. Let's look at a scene from one of his best-known works, *The Homecoming*. In the first act, Pinter establishes the situation—the return home of the oldest son and his wife for a visit with the father and two brothers. He reveals the condition of absence—the death of the mother-wife—which "the homecoming" is to fulfill. As soon as Teddy and Ruth arrive, Pinter designs the action to remove Teddy from the stage. The first forward-moving scene is between Ruth and her brother-in-law, Lenny, who have just met. It is a shocking scene precisely because the unspoken thought is spoken. After a highly charged, sexually suggestive exchange in which Ruth is clearly identified with Lenny's mother, the following dialogue concludes the scene between them:

LENNY: . . . Just give me the glass.

RUTH: No.

> *Pause.*

LENNY: I'll take it, then.

RUTH: If you take the glass . . . I'll take you.

> *Pause.*

LENNY: How about me taking the glass without you taking me?

RUTH: Why don't I just take you?

> *Pause.*

LENNY: You're joking.

> *Pause.*
>
> You're in love, anyway, with another man. You've had a secret liaison with another man. His family didn't even know. Then you come here without a word of warning and start to make trouble.
>
> *She picks up the glass and lifts it towards him.*

RUTH: Have a sip. Go on. Have a sip from my glass.

> *He is still.*
>
> Sit on my lap. Take a long cool sip.
>
> *She pats her lap. Pause.*
>
> *She stands, moves to him with the glass.*
>
> Put your head back and open your mouth.

LENNY: Take that glass away from me.

RUTH: Lie on the floor. Go on. I'll pour it down your throat.

LENNY: What are you doing, making me some kind of proposal?

> *She laughs shortly, drains the glass.*

RUTH: Oh, I was thirsty.

> *She smiles at him, puts the glass down, goes into the hall and up the stairs.*
>
> *He follows into the hall and shouts up the stairs.*

LENNY: What was that supposed to be? Some kind of proposal?

> *Silence.*[13]

AMERICA

Eugene O'Neill
1888–1954

Thornton Wilder
1897–1976

Tennessee Williams
b.1914

Arthur Miller
b.1915

Here people say what they really mean almost from the beginning. It is the truth not of facts, but of inner experience. To hear some people talk, Pinter's plays are bizarre, surreal, weird, and filled with what has been called "menace and muddle." But when we examine his plays, we discover that their language is simple, direct, and exceedingly commonplace. Like Chekhov, Pinter uses the trivial remark and the small gesture which in their apparent inconsequence seem to hide deeper meanings, but which, in fact, ultimately *reveal* the truth about people in a given situation. It is as if Pinter were saying that the great dramas of history are occurring every day in the lives of each of us—that the most ordinary people in the most ordinary situations are actually experiencing *King Lear*, *Oedipus the King*, or *Macbeth*. We feel this in Pinter's plays. The power we feel in the scene just quoted and in most of his work comes from characters who express consciousness of themselves. The action of each of the plays moves the characters to that "moment" where they say something that "is irrevocable and can never be taken back."

Discovering that moment is the playwright's most important job. To accomplish it, he or she must be a master of craft. This involves:
1. A deep understanding of the work of those individuals—actors, director, designers—who will realize the play on stage.
2. A mastery of the techniques of dramatic language.
3. A recognition of the limitations of time, space, and money which the theatre imposes on all who create for it.
4. A familiarity with the current conventions of theatre.
5. An awareness of the audience's expectations.

But playwriting requires more than mastery of craft. The playwright must bring an original view of experience or a new insight on the human condition. Like all artists, the playwright explores the unknown in searching for the world of the play. To be successful he or she needs the skills of craft, but the vision that stamps a play with greatness finally cannot be learned. It is a gift.

People will not go to the theatre to listen to representations of their own inarticulacy. We come to hear and experience what we cannot or do not express ourselves, to have crystallized for us emotions which we carry about within us, unexpressed. At times, to be sure, we come to escape out of ourselves, but there are other times when we want to discover ourselves by sharing emotionally in the life of the characters on the stage. The language of the theatre must be capable of fulfilling those needs.

Every time we go to the theatre we are performing an act of faith. We are acknowledging our belief and showing our trust that something very special will always happen there. The playwright usually takes the first step in carrying out this long and complex process.

The successful playwright—and the success of everyone in the theatrical enterprise depends on this—creates by an act of discovery a world which actors can embody and then make present to the audience.

NOTES

[1]Quote by Harold Pinter from *Theatre at Work: Playwrights and Productions in the Modern British Theatre*, ed. by Charles Marowitz and Simon Trussler. © 1967 by Charles Marowitz and Simon Trussler. Reprinted by permission of Methuen & Co., Ltd.

[2]T. S. Eliot discussed this distinction in his essay "The Three Voices of Poetry":

The first voice is the voice of the poet talking to himself—or to nobody. The second is the voice of the poet addressing an audience, whether large or small. The third is the voice of the poet when he attempts to create a dramatic character speaking in verse; when he is saying, not what he would say in his own person, but only what he can say within the limits of one imaginary character addressing another imaginary character.

(Selection from "The Three Voices of Poetry" from *On Poetry and Poets* by T. S. Eliot. Copyright 1954 by T. S. Eliot. Reprinted with the permission of Farrar, Straus & Giroux, Inc. and Faber and Faber Ltd.)

[3]This probably explains why most efforts to adapt successful works of prose fiction to the stage are usually such failures. It is not a question of bad writing or poor plots, but rather because the characters of fiction are not (and really cannot be) conceived in dramatic terms. Adaptation to film is more successful because unlike theatre, film is essentially a narrative and not a dramatic form, and therefore a more compatible medium to the other narrative forms of fiction.

[4]From *The Three Sisters* by Anton Chekhov, from *Six Plays of Chekhov*, ed. by Robert W. Corrigan. Copyright © 1962 by Robert W. Corrigan. Reprinted by permission of Rinehart Press, a division of Holt, Rinehart & Winston.

[5]From *Waiting for Godot* by Samuel Beckett. Copyright © 1954 by Grove Press, Inc. Reprinted by permission of Grove Press, Inc. and Faber & Faber Ltd.

[6]Georg Buechner. *Woyzeck*, tr. by Carl R. Mueller. Cited in *The Modern Theatre*, ed. by Robert W. Corrigan. New York: The Macmillan Company, 1964, p. 17.

[7]George Steiner, *The Death of Tragedy*. New York: Alfred Knopf, 1961.

[8]Antonin Artaud. *The Theatre and Its Double*, tr. by M. C. Richards. New York: Grove Press, 1958.

[9]No one has discussed the nature of gestural language more intelligently than the literary critic R. P. Blackmur. See his essay "Language as Gesture" in *Language as Gesture* (New York: Harcourt, Brace and Company, 1952).

[10]Furthermore, the plays probably took less time to perform than they do now because the actors could speak more rapidly and audiences—including the "groundlings"—could follow more easily.

[11]From "The Tragedy of Language" by Eugène Ionesco, tr. by Jack Undank. First published in *The Drama Review*, Vol. IV, no. 3, March 1960. © 1960 by *The Drama Review*. Reprinted by permission. All Rights Reserved.

[12]From "Writing for the Theatre" by Harold Pinter as it appeared in *The New British Drama*, ed. by Henry Popkin. Copyright © 1964 by Harold Pinter. Reprinted by permission of ACTAC (Theatrical & Cinematic) Ltd.

[13]From *The Homecoming* by Harold Pinter. Copyright © 1965, 1966 by H. Pinter, Ltd. Reprinted by permission of Grove Press, Inc. and ACTAC (Theatrical & Cinematic) Ltd.

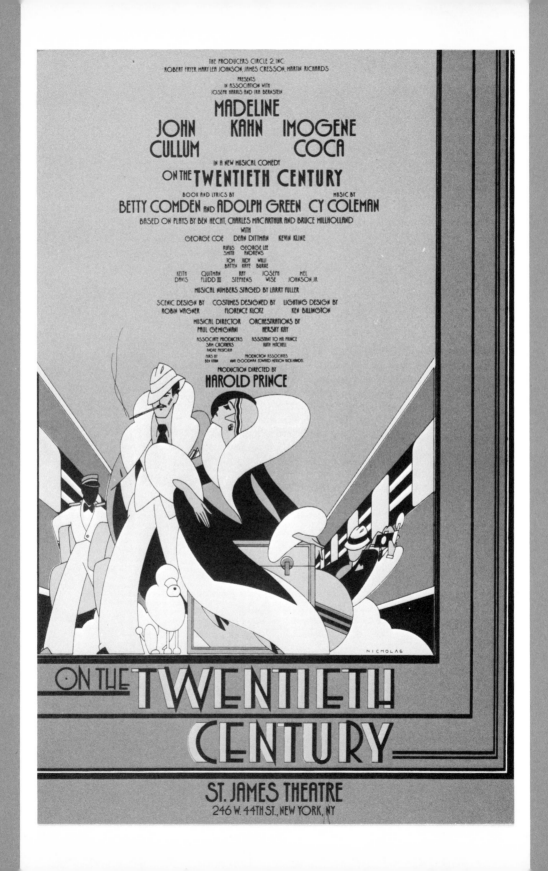

The task of the director . . .
   is to direct the actor rather than control him. . . .
He serves purely as a bridge,
   linking the soul of the author with the soul of the actor.
Having assimilated the author's creation,
   the actor is left alone, face to face with the spectator,
   and from the friction between these two unadulterated elements,
   the actor's creativity and the spectator's imagination,
   a clear flame is kindled.

Vsevolod Meyerhold, **Meyerhold on Theatre**

Chapter 7
The Director and the Play

One of the most important relationships in the theatre—and one of the most crucial for the success of a performance—is that of the director to all the other artists, especially actors. Meyerhold, whom we quoted at the beginning of this chapter, describes the director as a bridge between the playwright and the actor. Meyerhold began his theatrical career at the turn of this century as an assistant to Stanislavski at the Moscow Art Theatre and was very influential in shaping the role the director plays in the theatre. The director's function as we know it today is only a little more than a hundred years old. Meyerhold's many bold directorial experiments from the early 1900s until his death in the 1940s gave definition to this figure whom we now consider indispensable.[1]

Throughout theatre history there has always been someone who decided where actors stood for their speeches, how they spoke their lines, and which actors were best suited to which parts. Sometimes it was the playwright, sometimes a stage manager or even a patron. During the eighteenth and most of the nineteenth centuries, it was the leading actor. Not until the 1860s did the practice of a single person who guided all aspects of the production process first emerge.

In the little more than a century since Georg II, Duke of Saxe-Meiningen first "directed" a play, numerous pioneers—Meyerhold and Alexander Tairov in Russia, André Antoine and Jacques Copeau in France, Leopold Jessner and Max Reinhardt in Germany, to name but a few—developed the role of the director to so prominent a position that today such directors as the late Tyrone Guthrie, Elia Kazan, Joan Littlewood, and Peter Brook may be as well known as many actors and playwrights. The director is *the* authority figure of the theatrical process. He makes all the important preliminary decisions about casting, costumes and decor, and interpretation; he is the master of the rehearsal period; he is the final judge; he is an "audience of one."

The director is a kind of giant who incorporates into himself the playwright, the actors, the designers and technicians, the audience, and even the critics. His relationship to the actors—particularly in the early stages of rehearsal—is that of a parent. He guides and cajoles, rewards and punishes, inhibits and spurs on; in short, like a parent he provides that combination of encouragement and frustration which enables the actors to "mature" into their roles.

The director's relationship to the other artists of the theatre is that of the chief executive, if not tyrant. He is responsible for guiding each artist's interpretation of the play so the result is a unified, coherent presentation. He works with actors and technicians during rehearsals—suggesting, guiding, and correcting their work. He is like the conductor of an orchestra in rehearsal, watching for acting that is "out of tune" or rhythmically incorrect. He selects the "beat" the actors will play to. He suggests interpretations and phrasing and nuance. But unlike a conductor, a director does not appear at the performance. His job is preparing everyone for the moment when "the actor is left *alone*, face to face with the spectator," as Meyerhold said.

The playwright may have created the world of the play, but during the process of rehearsing and presenting it, he is silent in the shadows and the director is his all-powerful representative. In fact, the director is sometimes referred to as "the author of the action." Finally, the director presumes to be both a typical theatregoer and a representative of an ideal audience who will objectively view what takes place on the stage and subjectively respond to it. Through it all, the director is "the boss."

But like all parental or authoritarian power, the director's power is shaky at best. It can be undercut at any time by the producer; it depends on the craft and artistry of others for its fulfillment; it is always finally absorbed and embodied (and therefore taken away) by the actors; and it can be rejected by the audience. After a while, it becomes apparent that the seemingly all-powerful director has his power "on loan" from all the others who come together to make the theatrical event a reality. Once the play has opened, this figure whom Richard Schechner (director of the Performance Group) has referred to as "parent, enemy, outcast, savior, lover, friend, demigod" begins to disappear from view. All that remains is his name at the top of the program. Yet it is hard to imagine the theatre without him.

THE HISTORICAL EMERGENCE OF THE DIRECTOR

Given the theatre's long history, why has someone with such an apparently essential role in the·whole process become a force only in recent times? To understand the role and nature of the director's work, we must know why and how this person emerged in the last hundred years to a position of such power.

As we have said, throughout the history of theatre someone has always fulfilled, to a certain extent, many of the functions of the modern director, but that person always had a more limited role. We say "limited" because the role did not need to be more than it was. In classical Greek times, theatrical performances took place only for brief periods during three or four festivals throughout the year. The state appointed a *choragos* (a kind of producer-patron) who was responsible for raising the money to pay for the productions. From that point on, the playwright usually took over. These festival performances followed a rigid pattern—the subject matter of the plays was derived from the ancient myths, the conventions of acting were well established, and the expectations of the audience were well known. The playwright's work consisted largely of training the actors and the dancer-singers of the chorus. While this was not an insignificant task, it was a limited and relatively simple one.

The Roman theatre had two major traditions. One followed the festival pattern of the Greeks, celebrating the classical gods and heroes in Roman dress; the other was a popular tradition characterized by the comedies of Plautus. These popular comedies were based on broad character types—the braggart, the trickster, the buffoon, etc.—and were interspersed with numerous songs and dances which were written or improvised by actor-writers and performed by traveling troupes. The manager of the troupe—very often the playwright—organized the performances based on well-established conventions, but his directing function was minimal. With the decline of the Roman Empire, the theatre was largely dormant for several centuries.

It reappeared in the Middle Ages, at first under the auspices of the church, which used plays based on biblical themes as a way of instructing the largely illiterate congregation. These productions later were taken over by guilds and moved out of the churches into the town squares. The religious content of these plays gradually changed: comic characters and themes were introduced which reflected the life of the period and sensational stage effects became more and more important. (The Devil and Hell were presented in fearful ways.) Again there were managers, but they were more like organizational chairpersons who made sure everything ran smoothly, and they played an insignificant artistic role.

By the end of the sixteenth century, the theatre in most countries of Europe had become a recognized and institutionalized profession. Sponsored by the monarch or some other noble patron, companies of actors performed in permanent theatres on a more or less regular basis. These companies or troupes were under the leadership of an important actor. So began the tradition of the actor-manager which largely dominated the Western theatre until almost the end of the nineteenth century. Some famous actor-managers were the playwright Molière in France, James Burbage, David Garrick, Charles Kean, and Henry Irving in England, and Edwin Forrest and Edwin Booth in the United States. Clearly, the actor-manager was beginning to function more and more like the modern director. But while the actor-manager was increasingly concerned with the details of the production as a whole, he was still first of all an actor and viewed the whole performance from the perspective of the role he was playing.

It was not until the first half of the nineteenth century that the actor-managers began to assume a function that more closely approaches that of today's director. Between 1750 and 1850 the theatre—while immensely popular—was artistically at a low ebb throughout Europe, largely because of the debased and sloppy methods and the money-grubbing motives of the actor-managers. This condition began to concern a growing but small number of serious theatre people, and there are evidences of reform taking place during the first half of the nineteenth century.

With the formation of the company of Duke Georg II of Saxe-Meiningen in Germany in the 1860s, the director in the modern sense of the term was born. Duke Georg and his chief colleague, Ludwig Kranek, were the first real directors in history. Their influence on the theatre was incalculable. Because the Meininger Company performed throughout Europe, their revolutionary productions were seen by audiences and theatre people everywhere.[2] Before long the Meininger methods were copied in France, Russia, Germany, and England. These new directors were determined to create a "free" theatre—one free of the shoddy practices of the actor-managers of the past. Their conscious impulse was to return the theatre to a condition of purity and power as when performance was under the guidance of an Aeschylus, Shakespeare, or Molière. The first directors saw that as their mission and took steps to gain the power to achieve it.

While this account tells in a very brief form what happened up to the appearance of the director a hundred years ago, it does not explain, except in a most superficial way, *why* it happened. And this is more to the point. Actually the process that led to the emergence of the director had been going on for several centuries and can be attributed to causes both within and outside the theatre.

You will recall that in Chapter 3 we discussed how the idea of "imitation" changed in the Renaissance. Prior to that time people believed that reality could never be directly known and that they had to create symbolic representations—imitations—as the only way of expressing and experiencing it. A great revolution of thought in the Renaissance was the rejection of this traditional belief in favor of the view that we can directly comprehend reality through our senses. This shift of views had tremendous effects on all the arts. A major new idea was the belief that art should no longer be thought of so much as a symbolic form but as a direct representation of reality. This can be seen clearly in Renaissance paintings, and it was a shift that would change the theatre for centuries.

Until the end of the sixteenth century, the stage was viewed emblematically; that is, as a place that symbolized the universe the audience lived in. Shakespeare's Globe Theatre was a building where plays were put on, but the actions taking place on the stage were seen as occurring in a model of the universe. The theatre was a world—"The Globe": the trapped understage had its symbolic origins in hell, the open circle at the roof was the gateway to heaven, and the levels in between represented the hierarchies of human beings on earth—from God's representative on earth, the king, down to the humblest peasant. The theatre *symbolically* represented the world in which the Elizabethan audience lived.[3] The stage space and settings in these theatres rarely changed from play to play. There could be any number of different plays performed, but the world they took place in was the same world, and the same symbolic model was appropriate for them all.

Then, early in the seventeenth century, came a shift. The stage came to be thought of not as a symbolic world, but as a place whose reality corresponded to what people observed with their own senses. It was to be represented, therefore, as directly as possible. A street and the houses on it were to look like streets and houses outside the theatre, even though they were being represented on a stage. Theatre was to create the illusion of reality, and if this idea were carried to its logical conclusion—which it was in the nineteenth century—each stage setting needed to represent the unique reality of the world of each play. No longer could the same stage setting function for a Shakespearean tragedy and an Italianate farce.

The move toward greater realism began in Italy in the fifteenth and sixteenth centuries with the introduction into the theatre of perspective stage settings, which gave the illusion of spatial reality as our eyes actually see it. *Trompe l'oeil* ("trick-the-eye") scene painting made two-dimensional representations on canvas of such things as furniture and architectural detail look three-dimensional as in life. Elaborate machinery was developed to create realistic sound, lighting, and scenic effects. These conventions of production, by and large, dominated the theatre of the seventeenth and eighteenth centuries when the actor-managers were in control. However—and this is an all-important point—while the techniques of theatrical production became increasingly realistic, it was still believed that the world of the play was fictional and unreal. By the middle of the nineteenth century there existed the curious mixture of realistic stage settings and effects, completely artificial "ham" acting, and pretentious romantic plays. Everything was at odds, and few people cared that theatrical productions had unity as long as people came and the theatre made money. They did and it did!

It was this condition that Duke Georg of Saxe-Meiningen was rebelling against when he insisted the sets, costumes, stage movements, and acting styles correspond as closely as possible to the world portrayed by the play. Production had to have a governing unity that reflected a coherent point of view. It had to have unity based on the thorough study and research of all aspects of the play, and it was imposed by the imagination and will of Duke Georg, the director.

Of course, conditions had to be right for this to happen, and they were. The nineteenth century was one of the most revolutionary periods in the history of the West. It was a time of radical political, economic, and social change. From this period of great change, one idea emerged as dominant: *determinism*. The nature and destiny of human life came to be seen as determined by powerful external forces over which the individual had little or no control. Our fates were determined by our heredity and environment, by powerful and seemingly anonymous social and economic forces, by our unconscious emotional drives and impulses, by the unchanging laws of nature. Human life was governed by forces from without.

The Impact of Naturalism

This great revolution in thought had profound effects on the theatre that were reflected in several ways. Chief among them was the rise of naturalism as the dominant theatrical form and style. The emergence of the director corresponds in an interesting way to the rise of naturalism. A new breed of playwrights appeared in the last third of the nineteenth century whose work expressed this new aesthetic of determinism: Henrik Ibsen, August Strindberg, Anton Chekhov, Maxim Gorki, Henri Becque, Gerhart Hauptmann, and George Bernard Shaw. Their work represented a great rebirth of the playwright as a powerful force in the theatre. They produced new kinds of plays that required a new and different kind of "natural" acting style, and that required a director to make it all work. The director became indispensable to the production process. It is no accident the playwrights we have just mentioned are inseparably linked to those persons we can call the theatre's "first" directors. Indeed, the success of these playwrights depended on them almost totally. The modern theatre was created by such directors as André Antoine, Otto Brahm, Konstantin Stanislavski, Vladimir Nemirovich-Danchenko, and their numerous successors as much as it was by the new playwrights.

What was so different in the naturalist playwright's work that it led to the development of the director? The theatre that emerged in Europe at the end of the nineteenth century consciously attempted to repudiate the traditional view of the theatre. In the traditional view, *Hamlet* is about life; it may be *true* to life as we experience it, but it is not *like* life itself and Shakespeare doesn't ever pretend that it is. The naturalists were revolutionary because they aimed to show life as it actually is. Art, the naturalists maintained, should not be about life, or true to life, but as much like life as possible. If every human being is a unique combination of determined forces he or she cannot totally understand or control, then a character in a play should be, too. If the environment does have a unique shaping role in our lives, then the environment of the stage should have a similar role. If people in life are driven by irrational forces which can never be fully

→ to p. 233

A play ought to be written in which the people should come and go, dine, talk of the weather, or play cards, not because the author wants it but because that is what happens in real life. Life on the stage should be as it really is and the people, too, should be as they are and not stilted.

Anton Chekhov

STYLES OF TWENTIETH-CENTURY THEATRE

T he most striking difference between the modern theatre and that of previous ages is the fact that theatre in the twentieth century is almost always described as a series of constantly changing "isms." Indeed, the rate of change has been so rapid that at times it boggles the mind. Naturalism, expressionism, theatricalism, absurdism—the list seems endless. Moreover, it would appear that no sooner did one "ism" get established as the dominant style of production than another came along and took its place. Nothing underscores the fragmentary and eclectic nature of modern theatre more clearly than the way the many "isms" have come in and gone out of fashion. Essentially, each "ism" is a single angle of vision on the totality of human experience that is either reflected by the playwright in the script or imposed as a style of production by the director. In either case, the result is a production that has a number of well-defined characteristics that set it apart as a particular style. This parade of

NATURALISM

The Moscow Art Theatre's 1902 production of Maxim Gorki's **The Lower Depths.** Gorki's play depicting the fragmented events in the lives of the dregs of society was ideally suited to the naturalistic aesthetic of the truthful presentation of the unpleasant, the ugly, and the everyday. Naturalism was based on the idea that environment and heredity shape the character and fate of individuals, and this belief is reflected in the grubby setting, the tattered costumes, and worn props of the MAT production.

"isms" did not occur in a historical vacuum. Generally, each new "ism" was a violent reaction—both aesthetic and philosophic—to the dominant "ism" that preceded it. Thus it is possible for us to place the emergence and flowering of each new production style historically. But in observing this, two facts must be kept in mind: Once a style of production goes out of fashion it does not disappear for good. Expressionism, for example, flourished in Germany in the first two decades of this century. But the expressionist's way of looking at life and thinking about theatre has been regularly used as a theatrical style by playwrights, directors, and designers ever since. Second, in spite of the great diversity of styles that characterizes the modern theatre, each new style has basically been a reaction against naturalism. Naturalism is the dominant style of twentieth-century theatre and we will best understand the rich variety of our theatre if we see the many changes that the "isms" represent against the backdrop of the naturalistic theatre.

SYMBOLISM

From the early 1890s to 1910 the symbolists led the revolt against naturalism. The symbolists were committed to a theatre of poetry, allusion, soulful spirituality, and evocative images. Many directors saw symbolism as a way of opening up the theatre from the tawdry confines of the naturalist's commitment to realistic settings. Gordon Craig was one of the most important leaders of the symbolist movement and his designs for Henrik Ibsen's **The Crown Pretenders** reveal the nature and spirit of this revolt.

226

EXPRESSIONISM

Believing the naturalist's commitment to externals was false to inner truth, the expressionists sought to express the ecstacy, pathos, and horror that existed on the underside of reality. The movement had its origins in Germany in the decade before World War I and flourished throughout Europe until the early 1920s. The skeleton scene of the 1922 New York production of Georg Kaiser's **From Morn to Midnight** shown here is a good example of the expressionist style of production, which stressed imaginative lighting, symbolic decor on an almost empty stage, and the distortion of natural appearances.

FUTURISM

A movement celebrating irrationality, violence, speed, and the new technology had its origins in Italy. Led by Filippo Tommaso Marinetti, his Theatre Manifestos (First Manifesto, 1913; Second Manifesto, 1915) called for abstract sets, costumes, and properties, rapidly changing lighting and sudden noises, mechanistic movement, and, above all, the constant shocking of the audience's sensibilities. Marinetti's production of **Cocktail** was presented at the Theatre of Futurist Pantomime in Paris in 1926. The sets, costumes, and masks were by the futurist designer Enrico Prampolini.

DADAISM

A nihilistic international art movement dedicated to the destruction of traditional art forms. It first came to prominence in 1916–18 at the Café Voltaire in Zurich, Switzerland, under the leadership of Jean Arp, Richard Huelsenberg, and Tristan Tzara. Tzara's 1920 production in Paris was typical of dadaist theatre. It had no semblance of a logical plot, used grotesque, almost puppetlike costumes, and the dialogue consisted of gibberish and phonetic poems. Dadaism was the primary stimulus of many avant-grade movements and was the forerunner of the "happenings" of the 1950s and 1960s.

CONSTRUCTIVISM

A revolutionary theatre movement which originated in Russia in 1912 and played an important role in the theatre until the late 1920s. In the beginning it was architectural in its emphasis and this is revealed in "constructivist" stage settings. This prompted Vsevolod Meyerhold—its most illustrious practitioner—to develop a complementary nonillusionistic style of acting known as "biomechanics." One of Meyerhold's greatest successes was his influential constructivist production of **The Magnificent Cuckold** (1922) by the Belgian playwright Fernand Crommelynck.

SURREALISM

An extremist movement in literature and painting which evolved from dada. It called for an imaginative evocation of the dream world through the presentation of grotesque images. Since it sought to dissolve the lines between waking and sleeping, the physical and the spiritual, the real and the unreal, it was more successful in painting and poetry than in theatre, where it is impossible to do away with the living physical presence of the actor. Nonetheless, surrealism did have a great impact on the theatre, where its basic impulses were absorbed into other theatrical styles. One of the most successful presentations of surrealism in the theatre was Salvador Dali's production of **Bacchanale** in 1939.

THEATRE OF CRUELTY

The term "theatre of cruelty" was coined by Antonin Artaud in the 1930s. He sought to create a theatre so completely involving the spectators that they suffer with the characters on stage and hence are actually psychologically and physically changed by the performance. Artaud's theories greatly influenced Jean-Louis Barrault, Jean Genet, and Peter Brook. Pictured here is his 1935 production of Percy Bysshe Shelley's rarely performed play, **The Cenci.**

THEATRICALISM

One of the most elusive yet well-defined of the twentieth-century movements. In its broadest sense, it represented a revolt against naturalism by insisting that theatre not create an illusion of life but be openly itself— that is, theatrical. However, in the 1920s, particularly in Russia and France, theatricalism emerged as a specific production style greatly influenced by the cubist painters. Two of its most influential practitioners were the Russian directors Alexander Tairov (1885–1950) and Eugene Vakhtangov (1883–1922). Tairov's production of Jean Racine's **Phèdre** at the Kamerny Theatre in Moscow in 1920 was an outstanding example of theatricalist performance.

EPIC THEATRE

The term "epic theatre" was first used by the German director, Erwin Piscator (1893–1966). It was then used by Piscator's colleague Bertolt Brecht to describe a new form of non-naturalistic drama. Epic style is openly theatrical in its use of placards, film clips and projections, visible lighting instruments, and partial set pieces. It also uses techniques to distance audiences; that is, to make audiences always aware that they are members of an audience watching a play. Today when we use the term "epic theatre," we think of Brecht's plays, but Brecht took many of his ideas from Piscator's productions. One such production was of Jaroslav Hacek's **The Good Soldier Schweik** (1928).

ABSURDISM

"Theatre of the absurd" is a term often applied to the plays of Eugène Ionesco, Samuel Beckett, Arthur Adamov, and others. It derives from surrealism and abandons all the traditional techniques of dramatic construction in its efforts to present the essential absurdity of human existence. As a theatrical style it is imagistic, often grotesque, and depicts a reality verging on three-dimensional nightmare. The production shown here is of Ionesco's **Victims of Duty** presented by the New Orleans Theatrical Company in 1965 under the direction of Richard Schechner.

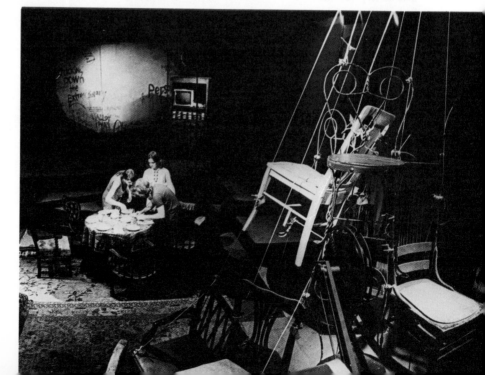

One of the most articulate leaders of environmentalism is Richard Schechner, director of the Performance Group. In **Environmental Theatre** he says: "I call the work I'm discussing environmental theatre because its first scenic principle is to create and use whole spaces—literally spheres of spaces, and spaces within spaces—which contain, or envelop, or relate, or touch all the areas where the audience is and/or the performers perform. All the spaces in a theater are actively involved in all the aspects of the performance. And the theatre itself is part of larger environments outside the theater." Shown here is Schechner's 1973 production of Brecht's **Mother Courage.**

RITUALISM

Throughout the twentieth century there have been numerous attempts to create production styles that reflected the ritualistic origins of theatre. In recent years this kind of production has been accentuated by the growing interest in the relationship of shamanism and theatre. Because Jean Genet conceives of theatre ritualistically, his plays are particularly well suited to this style. Herbert Blau's production of **The Balcony** at the San Francisco Actor's Workshop is a striking example of this production style. In doing this play about the hallucinated ways of the world, Blau says "the hardest task is to preserve its Mystery; that is, to show that life . . . is a sacrament."

NEOREALISM

The "isms" always seem to come full circle and the naturalists' insistence on detailed verisimilitude in production reasserts itself. But there has been a profound change, as the Longwharf Theatre (New Haven) production in 1972 of David Storey's **The Changing Room** indicates. The performance of this play about rugby players in northern England, set in a locker room, was discussed by Stanley Kauffmann in "Notes on Naturalism": "The pleasure in watching **The Changing Room** was a pleasure in abstraction, not in reproduction; in stylistic exercise, not in any of the historical "scientific" aims of naturalism. And thus that pleasure, rather than being dusty with century-old courage, became ultra-contemporary and free: the creation of a paraworld that merely resembles, more than is usual in the theater, the world outside but whose purpose is to reward by not being the world outside, by being created by artists within its own perimeters. . . . Their painstaking, minute reproduction of reality becomes, by their act of reproduction, an abstraction from reality. . . ."

known, then characters in plays should be presented in this way. If the real motivations for what we do are always hidden, disguised, and never really revealed, then action in the theatre should also be hidden and ambiguous. In short, life on the stage should be natural—as much like actual life as possible. Theatre should create the illusion of reality.

In his preface to *Miss Julie*, Strindberg talks about his "characterless characters"; that is, characters whose motivations are so numerous and varied that what happens to them "is the result of a whole series of more or less deep-seated causes" that can never be known. Since we can never be sure why things happen in life, action on stage should also be ambiguous and paradoxical. Ibsen's working notes to *Hedda Gabler* reveal the same thing. Hedda's psychological motivations are so complex that the reasons for her suicide can never be totally known, with the result that the meaning of her death will always be uncertain.[4]

However, there is a contradiction in all this. For all the talk about the theatre being like "life as it is," it was still theatre. The world of an Ibsen or a Chekhov play is as much a fictional "other" world as the world of *Hamlet*. The great naturalistic plays are also composed, coherent, and self-contained. Yet as soon as these plays went into production, the basic contradiction caused problems. If stage characters really are "characterless," then how does the actor present his or her character to an audience so it can be understood? If our motives are hidden in real life, which of the countless possible motives does the actor choose? The reasons for Hedda Gabler's death may be ambiguous in Ibsen's script, but whoever plays Hedda has to have chosen strong and definable reasons for committing suicide. Perhaps by carefully studying the script and searching her own life experience, she will find the right combination to make Hedda's suicide believable both to herself as an actor and also to the audience. But she does not act in a vacuum. What guarantee is there that her "interpretation" (because that is what it is) of the role is compatible with the interpretations created by the actors playing the other characters in the play? In short, if each actor discovers the unique combination that is his or her character, how are these characters integrated into the plot and presented to the audience so the play has coherence and meaning? All the actors/characters must be linked together by some common meaning if the script is to make sense to the audience in performance. The problem looks like this:

$$\text{In play P} \longrightarrow \begin{cases} \text{Actor A becomes Character X} = AX \\ \text{Actor B becomes Character Y} = BY \\ \text{Actor C becomes Character Z} = CZ \end{cases}$$

For this mixture to have meaning (M) for an audience, the following equation must exist:

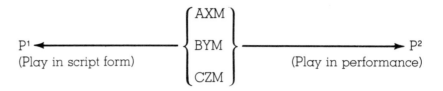

$$P^1 \longleftarrow \text{(Play in script form)} \quad \left\{ \begin{array}{c} \text{AXM} \\ \text{BYM} \\ \text{CZM} \end{array} \right\} \quad \longrightarrow P^2 \text{(Play in performance)}$$

Certainly, the meaning must come from the script, but since that script is filled with ambiguity, a single meaning must be chosen from it by someone. The play needs an interpreter who will find a common meaning uniting the characters and their actions. The director is that interpreter. He is the more or less objective arbiter who insures that the play's numerous ambiguities will be presented in a unified and meaningful way.

What the director must do for the actor's interpretation of the characters, he or she must also do for the staging of the play. Think of the implications of the naturalists' idea that a performance should create an illusion of reality; that is, be as much like life as possible. The idea had profound effects not only on the work of the actor but also on the stage setting, costumes, and decor which we will discuss in the next chapter. In life itself we turn our backs to people during conversation, we whisper and mumble, we scratch our heads or groins, we move about in all sorts of random ways. But this kind of behavior can happen effectively on stage only if it is very carefully planned. If every actor in a given scene did all the things that seemed "natural" to the behavior of the character he or she was playing, no matter how authentic that behavior might be, the result would be chaos. Again, some outside observer is necessary to judge which actions on the stage will serve to communicate the play's meaning to the audience, and which ones will not. That person is the director.

The director emerged, then, with the rise of naturalism as the dominant style of theatre. Naturalism gave way to many other forms by the end of the 1800s, but the realism it emphasized has remained a major style in theatre, and the importance of the director has remained and has even grown.

Our explanation of how and why the director emerged as a dominant and necessary figure in the theatre raises two important questions.

1. If some person functioning as a director became necessary with the advent of naturalism, why not the playwright? Certainly the playwright should know better than anyone else what should or should not go on the stage.

2. Why do we still have directors, since the theatre very quickly passed through its naturalistic period to such other forms as ex-

pressionism, symbolism, etc.? Or, put another way, why does it now appear that a director is essential to the successful production of all plays? Today, the director's role seems as crucial to the performance of plays by Sophocles, Shakespeare, or Molière as it is to those of Ibsen, Strindberg, or Chekhov. The answers to these questions are directly related, and they have to do with the commercialization of theatre. Theatre became big business.

Theatre Becomes Big Business

By the end of the nineteenth century, the industrial revolution had already transformed Western society. The specialization of jobs that developed in all work also affected the theatre. By the end of the last century, a theatrical production required a team of collaborating experts. At the same time, the theatre had openly become a business. To be sure, it had to a certain extent been a business since the end of the sixteenth century; at least there is evidence that some people had made a lot of money from the theatre since Shakespeare's day. But no one thought of it as "show biz" until the heyday of the all-powerful actor-managers of the nineteenth century. By the 1890s, theatre had become production for profit, and the actor-manager arrangement was becoming increasingly unprofitable. A new way of doing things had to be found.

The modern commercial theatre is an expensive business. It requires large numbers of people to get a production on, and all those specialists cost money. It often takes place in expensive locations with high taxes and an even higher overhead. Its huge staffs—from actors to ticket-takers—are unionized and expensive (even though all but the biggest stars are usually underpaid). The business side of theatre has become increasingly complex and demanding. The old adage about the theatre being "three boards, two actors, and a passion" (Spanish playwright Lope de Vega, 1562–1635) might still reflect its underlying spirit, but it is a far cry from the big business theatre had become by the beginning of the twentieth century. (Today, a big musical can cost more than $1 million just to get it ready for opening night.) As theatre became more and more of a business, the old stock companies became too expensive and too unwieldy to maintain. Soon each production became a separate venture that had to be carefully planned, prepared as quickly and efficiently as possible by a staff of artists and technicians hired specifically for it, and presented effectively. Art, yes, but the box office called the tune.

Growing costs and the need to make it at the box office have led to the recent emergence of another person in the theatrical process, the producer. Like the director, the producer has a forerunner in the *choragos* we mentioned earlier, the person responsible for raising money for the Greek festivals. By the end of the First World War, the theatre had become such a vast commercial enterprise that it required an expert to administer the increasingly complex business aspects of a theatrical production. The producer raises the money, negotiates for the use of a theatre building (the ownership of theatre buildings is a separate and big business), hires all the artists and works out arrangements with their unions (actors, stagehands, musicians, technicians, and today even directors), plans the publicity, handles public relations, coordinates the box office, and sees to it that all local, state, and federal regulations are adhered to. Given the massiveness of this responsibility, it is little wonder that the producer in the commercial theatre also picks the plays to be produced. There is too much at stake for the producer not to want to develop a "property" that has a good chance of making a profitable return on the investment. The producer has these responsibilities even in the noncommercial professional theatre. The theatre is big business whether or not it is for profit.

Industrialization and the emergence of the theatre as a business have changed the theatre in many ways. Two major effects on the basic practices of the theatre are:

1. the gradual divorce of the playwright from the production process; and
2. the rise of the director as the specialist who coordinates the production process.

The divorce of the playwright was practically an accomplished fact by the middle of the nineteenth century. The actor-manager called for starring vehicles on demand from playwrights writing in garrets, distant villas, or even the luxurious rooms of a patron. Until his last years, Ibsen wrote in Italy and sent his finished plays to Germany or Norway to be produced. Even Chekhov, who had close ties with the directors and company of the Moscow Art Theatre, wrote his plays away from Moscow, at the most went to an initial reading rehearsal, and seldom attended the opening performance of his plays. The divorce was final as plays were increasingly produced by specialists for the purpose of profit.

It soon became the norm to have actors rehearsing in one place; designers creating the scenery and costumes at another; lighting specialists planning effects with increasingly sophisticated equipment; and the producer taking care of all the business and promotional details. Time was short, and even short time costs money. In the meantime, the playwright was expected to be ready to revise or rewrite a scene or an act if it became necessary. He was the writing specialist. If he participated in the process at all, it was as a silent observer sitting in the back of the darkened theatre, always prepared to rush back to his room "to do his thing"—write and rewrite. So a new specialist was born and grew to maturity: the director, intermediary between the playwright and the other specialists, "author" of what took place on stage, coordinator of that collection of people and skills brought together to "produce" the theatrical event.

Now obviously this commercial process is not the only way theatre is created. Increasingly, talented theatre artists are moving away from this kind of theatre and are working in residential repertory companies, nonprofit professional theatres, and in the countless small experimental groups that have sprung up all over the world. But in spite of these changes, the director is usually still the dominant figure in the production process—whether it be of an established classic or a far-out new play, whether it is on Broadway or in the local college. In many ways the director has been largely responsible for shaping the theatre of the twentieth century. This artist has come to have a powerful role in the theatre, and it is important to understand how he or she goes about fulfilling it.

THE JOB OF THE DIRECTOR

The director's basic task is to transfer the world of the play contained in the script to the concrete reality of the stage. To accomplish this task requires many talents and a wide-ranging imagination and knowledge. Above all, a director must have perception and a capacity for adaptation. If the director's function is to bring unity to all the diverse parts that combine to make the theatrical event, then he must first be able to recognize the governing unity within the work itself. He must have the talents to adapt all the materials with which he has to work—including himself—so that unity is given to all the elements to be present in the production. How does he find that unity? Let us grant that a person has the required talent, nature, and experience to be a director. How does that person go about discovering the world of the play to be directed?

The Play—The Starting Point

Everything begins with the script. Very often it is one the director has always wanted to direct. He may be hired to direct it by a producer. It may have been brought to him by the playwright or by an actor anxious to perform in it. It may be the collective choice of a company. Or it may be a play that the director has done before which he now wants to do in another way. Whatever the case, the script is the starting point for the director.

In approaching the script the director must realize that, unlike the playwright and the actor, he does not find the play within himself. The play is the creation of someone other than himself and can never become his own as it does become the actor's. He doesn't find the play within himself so much as he receives it into himself. It is as if he bids the play to come to him. His first job is to be receptive. How does one prepare oneself to be receptive to the play?

The problem is easier to define when dealing with one of the established plays of history than when working with a brand-new script. In making himself receptive to Chekhov's *The Cherry Orchard*, for example, there are a number of things a person can do. First, he could read the two or three excellent biographies of Chekhov. He does this not because the play is *about* Chekhov's life, but *from* it. The director tries to make the playwright's life as much a part of his own as possible. He looks at photographs and at the paintings of artists the writer mentions; he reads the books Chekhov loved or strongly responded to; he reads his short stories, his marvelous notebooks, his voluminous correspondence, and all his other plays. Then he turns to the memoirs of Chekhov's friends and associates. Finally, the director reads the history of Chekhov's time, especially the social history. Pictures from the period—photographs, paintings, or whatever is available—are also helpful.

What about reading the critics? Not yet! One of the difficult problems facing a director is the question of interpretation. The director's biggest temptation is to move to an interpretation too soon, before the play has totally entered his being. Reading criticism encourages this. Criticism is interpretation, and the better the critic, the more likely it is that his or her interpretation will take over before the director has assimilated the play into himself. The critics should come later, after the director feels his own true sense of the play. Then they can be valuable. Critics are worthy opponents and helpful friends against whom the director can test his own experience of the play. The aim of this whole process is to become steeped in the world of the play by coming to know Chekhov's world, the world in which *The Cherry Orchard* was written.

The problem of working with a new script is more difficult. There is usually not a great body of known and easily available material in which the director can immerse himself. There may be a few other plays the author has written which he can read. The director can carry on a correspondence with the playwright, or possibly even spend time with him, not just to discuss the play but to discover more about the person who wrote it. But this will be of limited value at best, and what if it is not possible to make such direct personal contact? Then what does the director do? He must find the connection between the play and the world outside the theatre. He must find the larger context of the play, one he can enter into. The context may be legend or history; it may be other fiction, a specific historical event, or a figure in history. If the context is contemporary, there will be certain aspects of the contemporary world that will be more relevant to the play than others. Maybe it's the drug culture, racial antagonism, or feminism; perhaps the play deals with the conflicts and ways of a particular locale. Whatever combination it may turn out to be, the director must seek out every kind of information related to the play and playwright and steep himself in it.

This first aspect of the director's job—being receptive to the play—is very easy to describe and nearly impossible to explain. What is involved is reading the play over and over and over again—until finally it enters into the director's imagination and consciousness. The only thing he must resist in this process is the inevitable tendency to begin "to direct" the play in his mind. To interpret the play directorially too soon is a mistake. The director must let the play work on him right up to the beginning of the rehearsal process.

Enter: The Actors

Up to this point the director has worked almost entirely on his own and his work has been preparation for what now begins—the work with the actors, designers, technicians, and all the other people who come together to create the theatrical event. The first step in the rehearsal process is the "casting" or choosing the actors to play the roles. The process of casting takes many forms: the director may ask actors he believes suitable for the roles to be in the cast; sometimes casting is done in consultation with the producer and (if it is a new play) with the playwright; in repertory theatres the company membership largely determines which actors are assigned the roles; in ensemble companies casting is often a collective process; in many commercial and campus productions there is open casting, where anyone can try out for the parts. The director may choose any of these methods—or a combination of them—to cast the play.

Without question, casting decisions are among the most important a director makes in the course of doing a play. Alan Schneider, an American director, once observed that "casting is style." What he meant is that in deciding which actors should play the roles, the director determines the tone and quality of the whole production, no matter what rehearsal techniques he may employ. A decision to cast Laurence Olivier and Judith Anderson instead of George C. Scott and Colleen Dewhurst as Macbeth and Lady Macbeth will set the production in a direction that makes the style and tone of the eventual performance inevitable. Every other casting decision—while not as decisive—will have a similar effect. Clearly, it is just as important for the director to know the actors who will be in the production as it is to know the play itself. They must not be in conflict.

Having selected the cast, the director then begins another crucial phase—helping the actors discover their roles. This is the rehearsal process and there are several possible approaches to it. Some directors begin by having the actors read and discuss the script for an extended period of time; others get them on stage almost immediately. Some give explicit instructions; others let the actors work pretty much on their own. No matter what methods the director uses, he must always be attuned to the actors. He must help them find the characters they are to play. The ability to do this perhaps explains why so many directors have also been actors. While the ability to work and communicate with actors is unquestionably essential to the director's work, experience as an actor does not guarantee that a director will be successful in this. What is essential is that the director know, understand, and be so at home with actors' methods, techniques, and vocabulary that he can not only feel confident and trusting in the ways they work, but that he can also communicate that confidence and trust back to them. Just as playwrights write for actors, directors must work first and foremost with actors. This means being comfortable with them (no

Right, a page of Max Reinhardt's promptbook for his 1940 production of **Everyman** by Hugo von Hofmannsthal. Reinhardt's notes are keyed to text references, left.

And music's voice, and lo! the cup o'erflows!
I love you well, sweet guests, and pray that you
Enjoy the moment fully, holding close
And tenderly your dear ones, Ah! make use
Of this fair hour with all your faculties—
With hands and eyes and hearts and kissing mouths!
Let me not need entreat you more, dear guests!
And you, beloved cousin: sing to us!

FAT COUSIN:
Alack! alas! my skinny brother's called!
Now comes the eternal song about "cold snow!"
(They sing with laughter.)

THIN COUSIN:
(Sings.)
"Dear Mrs. Love, hast thou no concern?
I'm in misery: feel me burn!
Cold, cold snow indeed thou art,
To melt with the fire of my choking heart!
Dear Mrs. Love, come along with me,
And all that heart shall be full of glee!
(All sing. The dull tolling of a bell is heard. Everyman pushes his glass away.)

EVERYMAN:
What bell is that? It can mean nothing good,
Methinks, so loud and fearsome is the sound!
Now terror strikes my heart! Why toll that bell,
And at this hour?

A GUEST:
I hear none, far or near.

[38]

Grumbling cousin: Such a feast is a general exertion to make existence as repelling as possible. When my cousins start singing a climax is reached.

① is so overjoyed, that he trys to find news words over and over a

② General embracing

③ In the embrace

④ Dear Mrs. Love Alack Alas

⑤ Dear Mrs. Love Alack Alas
One laughs at him, throws flowers him

⑥ anxious: Param.: What bell?

⑦ again with his hand on his heart

⑧ cries loudly. The canon is interrupted. Everybody stares at Everyman. The tolling of the bell is to be heard distinctly in the growing silence. Paramour tries to calm him. He wards her off.

⑤a Thin cousin, begins a canon, which is bein taken up by the others, while he swings guitar like a bell:
Oh, how well I feel at nightfall, feel a nightfall, feel at nightfall,
When the bells toll rest and quiet, Bimb Bimbam, Bimbam Bimbam, Bum.
(Everybody finally leans back while sing In the midst of the singing a celestial tolling of bells is heard from a distan sounding from high above, increasing seve and warning. Nobody hears it but Everyma who sets his glass on the table and lis terrified. He gets up, first looking at t others, whether they also hear the sound then he asks Paramour and finally cries piercingly.

matter what differences there may be in temperament or in personal style) so he can guide them on their journey to their roles in the script.

Once the actors begin to rehearse, a new element enters into the dynamics of the theatrical process: what the actors discover as they search for their roles and interact with each other. The director may have begun rehearsals with a pretty clear idea of what the play is about and with well-defined interpretations of each of the characters. For example, he may have decided that *The Cherry Orchard* is essentially a political play about the passing of the Russian aristocracy in the late nineteenth century, and defined the characters in the play according to this interpretation. But as the actors develop their roles in rehearsal, this interpretation may be modified. The director could come to see the political aspects of the play as a theme external to the drama of personal dispossession at the core of Chekhov's play. Or it could be just the reverse: what the director believed to be an essentially personal play could come to have much more social significance. For this reason the director must always be receptive to what each of the actors discovers about the play in rehearsal.

Some people may insist that the director must have completed his preparations by the time rehearsals begin. If this is true, doesn't it mean the director's most important and creative work is done prior to coming to the theatre—in his mind and at his desk—rather than in the dynamic context of the production process itself? Doesn't this idea tend to make rehearsals little more than a time to execute and perfect the director's decisions? Here are the approaches and answers of three great modern directors to these questions.

On the methods of Bertolt Brecht, German playwright and director (1898–1956):

> During rehearsals Bertolt Brecht sits in the auditorium. His work as a director is unobtrusive. When he intervenes it is almost unnoticeable and always in the "direction of flow." He never interrupts, not even with suggestions for improvement. You do not get the impression that he wants to get the actors to "present some of his ideas"; they are not his instruments.
>
> Instead he searches, together with the actors, for the story which the play tells, and helps each actor to his strength. His work with the actors may be compared to the efforts of a child to direct straws with a twig from a puddle into the river itself, so that they may float.
>
> Brecht is not one of those directors who knows everything better than the actors. He adopts towards the play an attitude of "know-nothingism"; he waits. You get the impression that Brecht does not know his own play, not a single sentence. And he does not want to know what is written, but rather how the written text is to be shown by the actor on the stage. If an actor asks: "Should I stand up at this point?" the reply is often typically Brecht: "I don't know." Brecht really does not know; he only discovers during the rehearsal.[5]

Jean Vilar, director of the People's Theatre in France (1912–1970):

> The staging of a play is always the result of compromise. Compromise, at least, between the visual and aural imagination of the director and the living, anarchic reality of the actors. For my part, I never set anything definitely or precisely before the first rehearsals. I have no papers, no notes, no written plans. Nothing in my hands, nothing up my sleeve: *Everything in the minds and bodies of others*. Facing me, the actor.
>
> To compel an actor to integrate voice and body into a predetermined harmony or plastic composition smacks of animal-training. An actor is more than an intelligent animal or robot. Slowly and patiently, I believe, a sort of physical *rapport* grows up between him and me, so that we understand each other without need of many words. It is essential for me to know him well, and to like him even if he isn't very likeable. It is impossible to produce successfully a work dependent on the good will of so many, to direct a play well, *with people one doesn't like*. To love the theatre is nothing. To love those who practice it may be less "artistic," but it gets better results. Nevertheless, though I do not "attempt to mold the various parts" . . . to a concept of *ensemble*, it is still true that after a (variable) number of rehearsals one sometimes has to guide some of the actors (without their being necessarily aware of it) toward *ensemble* play, to bring them into a certain harmony of *tone* with the rest. Not that the director arbitrarily selects this tone; it is born of the polygamous interaction of the voices, bodies, and minds of the other actors and the script. When this point is reached, it must be "set." It is the first, mysterious moment when the fate of the production is decided. The actor is sometimes unaware of it, and so much the better, for he would otherwise freeze what should remain spontaneous. Now, too, the director can see clearly what a particular actor can "give." Often, he will see many other things besides, such as, for example, the contrapuntal importance of a part hitherto seen as purely subsidiary. The indefinite visions of the loving reader of a play are replaced by the physical view and orchestral audition of the work, through the intermediary of the Misses X and Y and Messrs. Z and W. The drama [from Greek *dran* = to act, movement] has just been born. At least, for the director.[6]

To paraphrase Louis Jouvet, French director (1891–1951):

> In point of fact, a play directs itself. One has only to be attentive and relatively detached, to see it come to life and work upon the actors. Acting upon them, in some mysterious way, it tests them, enlarges or diminishes them, embraces or rejects them.[7]

These three influential directors in their different ways point to the importance of the rehearsal process in finally establishing a unity and a meaning for the production. We started this discussion by observing that the director must be receptive to the actors' contributions to the overall meaning of a production. In order to maintain this very necessary atmosphere of openness, he must resist the tendency to impose a fixed interpretation upon them. But at a certain point in the rehearsal process everything begins to jell. Of the many possible approaches and interpretations of *Hamlet* or *The Cherry Orchard*, certain ones will emerge that are right for a particular production. The director must be able to recognize this moment. "When this point is reached," as Jean Vilar said, "it must be 'set.' It is the first, mysterious moment when the fate of the production is decided."

In working with the actors, then, the director must cast the play; "block the action" (assist the actors in developing their movements on stage); help the actors to learn their lines; deal with problems of interpretation and intonation; guide the rhythm and timing of the performance as it gradually comes into being; help the actors as they make the awkward transition to working in the actual set, with the props, and in their costumes; and finally, bring all the actors cooperatively to the proper pitch for the play's opening.

Not only, of course, is the director dealing with the actors, but he is dealing with the producer, set designers, costume designers, lighting technicians, and many, many others. There is lots to do and he is the one who has to see that it all gets done before opening night! It is a huge task and not everyone is successful at it.

THE PERSONAL QUALITIES OF THE DIRECTOR

To succeed at the difficult job of directing a play requires some special personal qualities and skills. How are these developed? There is no tried and true recipe for turning out a fine director. As in the case of actors, there is no clearly established way of preparing to be a director. An actor—with or without talent—will take years to learn his or her craft. The "craft" of directing, insofar as it exists, can be learned in a matter of weeks, if not less. It consists of learning such basic things as how a stage works, certain principles of movement and position on stage, some elementary principles of lighting technique, how to prepare the script for rehearsals (what is known as a "promptbook"), and so on.

But the mastery of this craft, as necessary as it is, doesn't make a director. Certainly most directors never studied directing, and examining the backgrounds of great directors in the theatre reveals no consistent pattern of development. The first modern director, Duke Georg of Saxe-Meiningen, obviously had nothing but his own ideas to guide him. André Antoine, the first important naturalistic director, had no formal training; in fact, during the early years of his career in the theatre he worked during the day for the Paris gas company. But certain characteristics they hold in common do give us a clue as to the nature of the director's art. There may not be clearly defined ways to train a director, but that does not mean that anyone who wants to can do it. For all of the thousands of people directing plays in the world, a good director is hard to find and a great one is rare. It requires a special combination of background, learning, temperament, and instinct to be that servant-master who has become such a vital force in the theatre. Two talents are absolutely essential:

1. the ability to see; and
2. a sensitivity to language.

The Ability to See

The director must be able to think in images. This means being able to see the production in her mind as it develops, picturing how all the elements will combine. This is crucial. It also means being able to evoke images that will help all the people involved in the production—especially the actors—to bring the play to life. There may be mental images, a scene from a well-known movie or novel, or even a reference to a specific painting or photograph. For example, Brecht believed that the paintings of Pieter Brueghel would evoke the tone and quality he wanted in his play *Mother Courage*, and he had the actors study these paintings as they developed their roles. In his production of Georg Buechner's *Danton's Death*, a nineteenth-century play about the French Revolution, Max Reinhardt used the heroic and monumental paintings of Théodore Géricault as visual metaphors for the play. In more recent times, perhaps the best-known instance of a director using visual images as a metaphor for the whole production was Peter Brook's use of Jacques Louis David's painting *The Assassination of Marat* for his production of Peter Weiss's *Marat/Sade (The Persecution and Assassination of Jean-Paul Marat as Performed by the Inmates of the Asylum of Charenton Under the Direction of the Marquis de Sade)*. Many elements of the production were drawn from it and from other of David's works—the setting, the costumes, the groupings and movements of the actors, and, perhaps most important, the visualization of several of the roles. Mediocre directors talk the actors to death. A good director knows the truth of the cliché "a picture is worth a thousand words." Visual images are an important way of communicating with the actor, and the director should know how to incorporate them into the rehearsal process.

Similarly, visual images provide the director with an invaluable means of communicating with the designers. A good director has well-developed instincts about spatial relationships; she knows how to express meaning with space. Designers are necessary collaborators in this aspect of her work. They know what light, color, materials, texture, shape, and space can do to bring the play's environment to life. The successful director never forgets that the designers create the performance every bit as much as she does. Design is the unlisted major actor in the production of every play, and for this reason the designers must be treated with as much

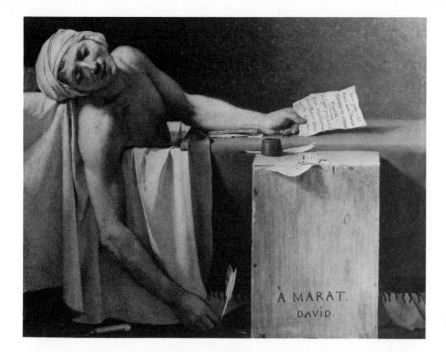

Marat, the 1793 painting by Jacques Louis David.

Max Waldman's photograph of Marat in the bath in Peter Brook's production of Peter Weiss's **Marat/Sade**.

imagination and sensitivity as the actors. They must discover the play as the actors do, and their task is just as difficult. If the designers are expected only to execute the director's wishes—usually presented to them in the form of a ground plan together with rough sketches—the production will be impoverished. The design elements of production must be evoked from the play itself, and the use of visual images is the director's most effective means of helping the designers to achieve this. Again Peter Brook's production of *Marat/Sade* is instructive. Notice how David's painting is the primary source of the production's design elements. (See photographs on p. 245.)

The director should have an extensive knowledge of art—not just as history, but as visual experience. She must learn how to look and, in looking, to see. This involves looking at art books, photography, visual images in the environment; it means going to museums, galleries, and exhibitions. The director knows that the visual artist can open her eyes to the world of the play. This is true of any play, but it is particularly the case when the director is working on a play from the past. Nothing assists a company in getting a concrete sense of an earlier world than the visual images representing that world. The way into the world of Greek tragedy—no matter what form the production may finally take—includes the careful study of ancient vases and entablatures. When preparing one of Corneille's or Racine's plays, a director would want to be familiar with French neoclassic painting, sculpture, and architecture.

A Sensitivity to Language

The director should have an ear for language and know how it works. She must be able to help the actors master language and use their voices effectively, but she must also be able to extract as much meaning as possible from language. If you think about it, the script is what she has to work from. Whatever meaning a play ultimately has must be rooted in the script. And what is a script? Words. Language.

The following dialogue from act 1 of Chekhov's *Uncle Vanya* might seem to hold little meaning when read through quickly. The director must discover, in effect, each speech: What does it mean? How does it relate to the play as a whole? How does it relate to the character speaking it? How does it interact and relate to the speeches that precede and follow it? Yelena (the bored young wife of a retired professor), Astrov (an idealistic but somewhat cynical doctor who is attracted to Yelena), Vanya (the disgruntled and disillusioned caretaker of the family estate), and Sonya (Vanya's niece, who is hopelessly in love with Astrov) are sitting around outside the house and there is the following series of speeches:

YELENA: I have always heard that you were very fond of the woods. Of course you can do a great deal of good by helping to preserve them, but doesn't that work interfere with your real calling? You're a doctor, aren't you?

ASTROV: God alone can know what a man's real work is.

YELENA: And you find it interesting?

ASTROV: Yes, very.

VANYA (*sarcastically*): Oh, extremely.

YELENA: You are still young, I should say certainly not over thirty-six or seven, and I have an idea that the woods do not interest you as much as you claim. I should think that you would find them quite monotonous.

SONYA: Dr. Astrov plants new forests every year, and he has been awarded a bronze medal and a diploma. He does his best to prevent the destruction of the forests. If you listen to him you will agree with him entirely. He claims that forests beautify the earth, and so teach man to understand the beautiful, and instill in him a feeling of respect and awe. Forests temper the severity of the climate. In countries where the climate is warmer, less energy is wasted on the struggle with nature and that is why man there is more gentle and loving; the people there are beautiful, supple, and sensitive, their speech is refined and their movements graceful. Art and learning flourish among them, their philosophy is not so depressing, and they treat women with refinement and nobility.

VANYA (*laughing*): Bravo, bravo! All this is charming, but not convincing, and so, (*To* ASTROV) I hope you'll permit me, my friend, to go on burning logs in my stove and building my barns with wood.[8]

This is the initial confrontation between Yelena and Astrov that eventually leads to their unrealized infatuation. The key speech is Sonya's and it is one of the most difficult in the modern repertoire to get just right. It is a defense of Astrov in response to the queries of her stepmother and the sarcasm of her Uncle Vanya. It is also the first definite evidence that she adores Astrov—something the play subsequently confirms. It is also clear that she doesn't really understand him; it is as if she is parroting the words she has heard him say in many such discussions with Vanya. So the quality of her speech must be somewhat like a rote recitation. Yet the recitation must have the warmth and conviction of a loyal and unquestioning love, not that of a dedicated environmentalist. That her speech is a "performance" is indicated by Vanya's response, which is in the form of an applause. Only if the director can work through dialogue in this way will she be able to discover the rhythms and meaning of the entire play. The meaning in this scene is found in the language. If the director is to discover meaning here, she must be sensitive to the ways people express and reveal themselves with words.

THE DIRECTOR'S SIGNATURE

Every production reveals the individual stamp of its director. The following pairs of photographs clearly illustrate this.

It would be difficult to imagine a director who did not have a love of language. And often directors have had a special love of poetry. The language of poetry is usually more evocative and complex than prose. The images of poetry can be a gateway into the world of the play in the same way that visual images can be helpful. If the director can introduce just the right lines of poetry, she may help the actor discover some aspect of his or her character.

Finally, the director must be sensitive to language because the rhythms of language are totally interrelated to the rhythms of the body itself. The voice is not a separate entity. When the director directs an actor, she directs the working together of the body and the voice. The rhythms of language shape and are shaped by the rhythmic movements of the rest of the body. A good director understands how the complex subtleties of language govern the actor's physical performance. Voice and body work together in a unified presentation. In achieving the unity required by performance, the director must work with the actor in establishing vocal interpretations and developing vocal rhythms—giving vocal form to the drama implicit in the words. (For example, in his production of *Othello*, Olivier recognized that vocal intonation was one of the keys

OEDIPUS THE KING

Left: Laurence Olivier's pageantlike production at London's Old Vic in 1945.

Right: Tyrone Guthrie's ritualistic production at the Stratford (Ontario) Shakespeare Festival in 1955.

to realizing the Moor's character, and that his downfall was dramatized not only by what the words of the script said, but by how they were spoken.) To be successful in her work, the director must know language in all its manifestations.

THE DIRECTOR AS INTERPRETER

We observed earlier in this chapter that the director emerged as a dominant figure in the theatre during the past century primarily because someone was needed to provide coherence and order to the many diverse elements of a theatrical production. This need was compounded by the fact that the naturalistic theatre sought to represent as directly as possible the ambiguity of human experience. It is the director's job to resolve the ambiguity in a play (or at least to present it in a clarified manner) so it can be understood by an audience. The director, then, is the interpreter of the script. She must deal with the contradictions in the text so that the performance has the unity required of a work of art.

Certainly the theatre has gone through many changes since the advent of naturalism at the end of the last century. Indeed, there has been a constant stream of changing avant-garde styles—symbolism, expressionism, futurism, epic theatre, absurdism, guerrilla theatre—but the realistic portrayal of experience that came with naturalism is still the dominant conventional form of theatre.

Today we expect ambiguity in all experience and, in demanding it, find it. Earlier ages took things at their face value. One did not go to the theatre to find out *why* something happened (interpretation) but to experience the reenactment of *what* did happen. For example, to Shakespeare's audiences *Macbeth* was a play of fated ambition and revenge. It wasn't necessary to understand "why" Macbeth and Lady Macbeth acted as they did. This was their fate. The play shows their choosing of it and what happens to them because of what they choose. Today we feel compelled to explain their actions; so much so that for the past fifty years we have been inundated with articles like "How Many Children Had Lady Macbeth?" written in an effort to explain the mystery of this great play.

Interpretation of this kind has probably always taken place to some degree. We need some amount of interpretation to understand

Left: Max Reinhardt's baroque production at Salzburg in 1925.

Right: Peter Brook's stripped down, circuslike production at Stratford-on-Avon in 1970.

the past. Occasionally, however, a director has decided that her primary role is not to translate the text of the play to the stage, but to alter its meanings so they can be better understood by the audience.

This kind of thinking about the director's role has led to what have become known as "concept" productions; that is, productions in which the director imposes on the script a concept that alters the play so it will be "more interesting" or more readily understood. Such an approach often comes at the play from a new angle and can be very exciting and challenging, particularly if the director's imagination is exciting and challenging. But this approach has also led to some abominable and irresponsible productions—*Hamlet* as a rock opera, *Medea* interpreted as a female Charles Manson, *Troilus and Cressida* set in the American Civil War, *Love's Labour's Lost* played in psychedelic drag.

But successful or not, concept productions raise a very important issue. We should ask ourselves once again: "What is the nature of theatre?" If its chief function has always been to present the other world of mystery, then it should not be too concerned with explanation. If its purpose is to allow us to confront the ghosts that haunt us, then those ghosts should not be rationalized. If its aim is to put us in

touch with the naked landscape of feeling, that landscape should
not be tamed and made too comfortable. The theatre reveals mystery; it should not demystify it.

Oedipus, for example, remains a hero of great stature as long
as he is not suffering from an "Oedipus complex." Once a director
attempts to explain him in terms of repressed hopes and fears,
traumatic childhood experiences, or a vitamin deficiency in infancy,
Oedipus loses the dimension of mystery that is the source of his
stature. Which of us can understand Hamlet or Lear? And which of
us can forgive Othello or Macbeth? Because they seem mysteriously
beyond our powers of understanding, they remain heroes for us.

Whenever the director functions primarily as an interpretive
critic of the play, she not only runs the risk of undermining the play
by demystifying it, but in her efforts to make the play accessible she
can very easily block the audience's experience of it. We should not
forget that theatre has its own unique form: the transformation of the
world of the play into the presence of a performance. As David Cole

THE CAUCASIAN
CHALK CIRCLE

Left: Bertolt Brecht's famous
Berliner Ensemble production in
1955. This was Brecht's last
production.

Right: Tyrone Guthrie's 1965
production at the Minnesota
Theatre Company. Note the
stylistic similarities between
Oedipus' mask (p. 249) and the
mask-headdress of the Governor's
wife.

pointed out, if the theatre assumes the critical task of alleviating strangeness, where is the audience to go "for the experience of strangeness itself?"

A certain amount of interpretation is as necessary as it is inevitable. But the director must always realize that her chief function is to *serve* the play—not to *save* it by imposing an interpretation that will make it more interesting, or modern, or accessible, or relevant.

THE DIRECTOR AS CHIEF EXECUTIVE

The director is that expert-specialist who coordinates all the diverse elements that make up the multiplicity of experience that is the stage. He must be a combination of traffic cop, drill sergeant, schoolteacher, labor arbitrator, corporate executive, and group therapist; and through it all he is expected to be an artist, too. Think of the

A director who cannot detach himself from his work during the final rehearsals is only a mediocre craftsman, however much it might seem that this is the very point at which he should be most intensely involved in it. Failing this detachment, the director blinds himself—the worst possible error. Such poor fools forget that the theatre is a play, in which inspiration and child-like wonder are more important than sweat and tantrums. It is true that such detachment is so difficult to achieve at the right time that it is not surprising to find that few directors either desire or achieve it.

Jean Vilar, "Murder of the Director"

many responsibilities! He supervises the whole rehearsal process from casting through the final dress rehearsal. He coordinates and finally judges the appropriateness of the work of the designers and technicians as they create and construct the settings, costumes, lights, properties, music, and sound effects. He makes the whole production fit in with the producer's demands, needs, and time-table.

In working with designers the director is involved with every step in the process of creation, although usually less intimately than with the actors. Design in the theatre is a creative process and the director must permit the designers to be the creators that they, in fact, are. Few things will produce worse results in production than if the designers feel they are simply technicians who carry out a director's concept. Ideally, they should not be cut off from the actors' rehearsal process. A designer has a mastery of space and materials that no one else involved with the production—not even the director—has. The director does not have a designer in order to tell the designer what to do; the production has one because the designer can reveal things about the play that no one else can. In any case, the director as executive must still coordinate the activities of the design staff so they mesh with the rehearsal process and the production schedule—all the while (it is hoped) staying within the budget.

The beginning of technical rehearsals is one of the most traumatic moments in theatre. This is the time at which the actors rehearse with costumes, props, lighting, and so on. It is the time at which all the strands of the production process must start to come together to form a single and coherent whole. Until that moment the director has been closely involved with every element in the process. Now he must begin to rather quickly remove himself; no longer the executive, he assumes his role of "audience of one." Failure to withdraw can undermine the whole process.

In working with the producer, the director must recognize that no matter what the nature or scale of the theatre, it is a business. It costs money, usually a great deal of money. An off-Broadway play can cost up to $100,000 or more to open (and, as we mentioned, a Broadway musical today can cost more than $1 million before it opens). Even a typical university or community theatre production costs several thousand dollars—exclusive of any salaries that are paid. The director must always be conscious of the fact that people, time, and materials are expensive and that while he may not be the "Budget Director," he is responsible for controlling expenses. He will establish most of the priorities and make most of the decisions that determine how the money is spent. So he must always work with the producing staff to insure that all the time and effort of the rehearsal process have at least a fair chance of surviving the play's opening.

Through all of this it should be clear that the director is primarily concerned with handling human problems. His work deals not only with what artists have created, but with the people who have done the creating. The result is inevitably compromise. Ever the diplomat, the director is always conscious of the fact that the theatre is a turbulent world whose artists are creative and often temperamental people. Usually it is the director who must find a way to bring diverse elements into harmony.

One of the theatre's biggest problems as an art form is the necessity to compromise. While few people are more idealistic than those who devote their lives to the theatre, invariably their idealism is undermined by the theatrical process itself. Some people are lazy, others are miscast, still others so pigheaded that nothing gets done. Whatever the reasons, there inevitably comes a time in the rehearsal process (at least in conventional theatre practice) when everyone—usually beginning with the director—realizes that

---

In the notes that Elia Kazan published on his production of **A Streetcar Named Desire**, it seems clear that, in order to direct the play, Kazan had to discover that Stanley Kowalski represented the sensual and vengeful barbarism that was engulfing our culture, while Blanche Du Bois was Western civilization, poetry, delicate apparel, dim lighting, refined feelings and all, though a little the worse for wear to be sure. Tennessee Williams' forceful psychological melodrama now becomes intelligible: it was about something, about the decline of Western civilization. Apparently, were it to go on being a play about a handsome brute named Stanley Kowalski and a faded mangy belle named Blanche Du Bois, it would not be manageable.

Susan Sontag, "Against Interpretation"

"Good Lord, we open in two weeks and we will never be ready!" This is when the "great cover-up" begins. It is no accident that the theatre's word for taking shortcuts is to "cheat," and that is just what begins to happen. The tricks of the trade, which until now had been so carefully avoided or discouraged, are pulled out of the bag. Character relationships are "set" even though they haven't been realized. Things in the setting get faked. Lighting decisions are made that, while not right, will do. And on and on. Everyone's energy and ability are used to "cover up" the inadequacies of the production. This situation presents the director with his biggest temptation. (If the situation has really developed, he's already given in to the temptation.)

Given the limitations of money, schedules, and the innate shortcomings of the people involved, the rehearsal process will always run out of time. Nobody ever feels a show is ready to open. There is no question that deadlines are good for people—even for theatre people—but as the time runs out and the production is not nearly ready to be presented to an audience, the moment inevitably comes when the director feels compelled to impose order on the chaos. Everyone who has ever worked in the theatre has probably experienced that moment: The director rises from his seat in the auditorium, walks with determination up to the stage, and *takes over!* He imposes characterization, interpretation, stage business, line readings, production values, and so on. Thus, in addition to all the creative work he does and stimulates, the director must also be able to take charge. If, by necessity, theatre is an art of compromise, then the director must know what difficult decisions have to be made and when to make them.

THE DIRECTOR AS GUIDE

Finally, perhaps the best way to describe the director is as a dedicated guide. One of the most important personages in the first two parts of Dante's *Divine Comedy* is the Latin poet Virgil. Virgil guides Dante as he journeys down through the Nine Circles of Hell and then up the Mountain of Purgatory. Virgil does not actually participate in Dante's experience as he accompanies him, but he does share in it by observing, warning, and helping him to understand what he is experiencing. Virgil is Dante's loyal and loving companion on his journey through Hell and Purgatory to the gates of Paradise. Once there, Virgil can go no further and he must leave Dante. Human experience is of no help in this final stage of the journey. Ideally, the director should be such a "dedicated Virgil," the one who guides all those involved with creating the theatrical event to the other world of the play.

The idea of the director as a "dedicated guide" will help us understand what the director's function is and what qualities he needs to fulfill his role. Directing is an art of suggestion, of evoking the creative talents of others. A director:

1. helps the actors find their characters by evoking the character from the psyche of each of them;
2. stimulates the imaginations of the designers so their visions can be realized on the stage; and
3. evokes from himself that fullness of response to the performance taking shape so that he can serve as a faithful representative for the audience, whose needs the performance must fulfill.

He must have almost infinite patience and a deeply rooted trust in the artistry of the people with whom he works. He must be willing to discuss and experiment. In guiding the actors to awareness, he must have a keen sense of when to be gentle and permissive and when to be firm and demanding. Most important, he must be able to see and communicate what he sees to everyone, in a form concrete enough to help them discover the play. To see in this way, he must be receptive, attentive, responsive, and discerning. But, like Virgil, he must know that at a certain point he can go no further. Only the actors can be at one with the world of the play once it is realized in performance.

The director, then, is that creator-servant who serves the text of the playwright, guides the actors to the world of the play, provides the unity that makes performance possible, and, finally, represents the audience, whose view he must ultimately share.

NOTES

[1]The exact date of Meyerhold's death is uncertain. He disappeared in 1939.

[2]The Duke's theatre company was known as the Meininger Company.

[3]Similarly, the Greek, medieval, and Japanese theatres were thought of as symbolic models of the cosmos.

[4]To be sure, Ibsen's notebooks resolve much of this ambiguity, but the play itself does not.

[5]Hubert Witt, editor. "Bertolt Brecht the Director" in *Brecht: As They Knew Him.* New York: International Publishers, 1974, p. 126.

[6]From "Theatre Without Pretensions" by Jean Vilar, from *Directors on Directing,* ed. by Toby Cole and Helen Krich Chinoy. Copyright © 1953, 1963 by Toby Cole and Helen Krich Chinoy. Reprinted by permission of The Bobbs-Merrill Company, Inc.

[7]Louis Jouvet. "The Profession of the Producer, II." *Theatre Arts Monthly,* 1937.

[8]Anton Chekhov. *Uncle Vanya* in *Six Plays of Chekhov* edited by Robert W. Corrigan. San Francisco: Rinehart Press, 1962, p. 185.

[9]Cole, *The Theatrical Event,* p. 152.

Chapter 8

EQUUS

A stage designer is, in a very real sense, a jack-of-all-trades.

He can make blueprints and murals and patterns and light-plots.

He can design fireplaces and bodices and bridges and wigs.

He understands architecture, but is not an architect:

can paint a portrait, but is not a painter:

creates costumes, but is not a couturier.

Although he is able to call upon any or all of these varied gifts at will,

he is not concerned with any one of them to the exclusion of the others,

nor is he interested in any one of them for its own sake.

These talents are only the tools of his trade.

His real calling is something quite different.

He is an artist of occasions.

Every play—or rather, every performance of a play—is an occasion,

and this occasion has its own characteristic quality,

its own atmosphere, so to speak.

It is the task of the stage designer to enhance and intensify

this characteristic quality by every means in his power.

Robert Edmond Jones, **The Dramatic Imagination**

The Designer
and Theatrical Space

As the lights dim and the curtain goes up at the opening of a play, you may see an elaborate set composed of platforms, ramps, and columns. The actors may be dressed in stunning costumes—colorful capes, strange masks, elaborate gowns. There might be images projected on a screen at the back of the stage and other areas may be brightly shining with light. Then again, there may be no curtains or even a stage in the traditional sense. Instead, the actors may walk out and occupy a space surrounded by an audience sitting on the floor or on folding chairs. The actors may be wearing leotards and the only scenery may be a chair or a bench, perhaps not even that.

In both cases, the total visual effect did not happen by chance. Someone planned, selected, designed, and implemented what we see. That person is the designer. We will talk about the designer as if he or she were one person when, in fact, there are usually several: a scene designer, a costume designer, a lighting designer. Whether there is one or there are several, the designer has the job of transforming the space of the stage into the place of the play.

Designers are not simply skilled technicians, although they must be that, too. They are artists whose work contributes to the unity of a production. As one of the greatest designers in the history of the American theatre, Robert Edmond Jones (1887-1954), said, they are "artists of occasions." As you look at the photographs in this book, you will see some fine examples of the work of gifted designers, people who know how much the elements of design contribute to the unity of a production. Take, for instance, Santo Loquasto's designs for Chekhov's *The Cherry Orchard* on page 136. By imaginatively combining light and space, he represented the interior—in this case, an old nursery—where the action of the play takes place and also made the cherry orchard a living presence on the stage. Beyond this, Loquasto's design created a sense of lightness and openness that carried out the tone of the production.

THE TRANSFORMATION OF SPACE

As important as costumes, lighting, and sound effects are to the success of a production, they are only part of the larger job of the designer. That job is to transform the stage or playing area into the world of the play. (I will use the term "playing area" in this discussion since the word "stage" is limiting.) The area in which actors perform today varies from the traditional proscenium stage to the thrust stage to theatre-in-the-round to the open space of a gymnasium, loft, or park square. (See p. 291 for a description of thrust and proscenium stages and theatre-in-the-round.) Each kind of playing area presents different problems to the designer. But whether the playing area is a sixty-by-eighty-foot proscenium stage or a small open area in a church hall with the audience seated around it, the designer's task is to transform that space into the world of the play.

And whether it is the impressive stage of a Broadway theatre or the informal performance space of some small experimental group, we in the audience recognize almost immediately that every playing area is a very special place with a very special aura about it. We become particularly conscious of this specialness when we compare an empty stage at the moment a performance is about to begin with an empty room in a home, even if the decor of these two spaces were to appear identical. The difference between them is the difference between an ordinary room and the same room prepared for a party or special event. The environment of the stage radiates a sense of expectancy and excitement. It is a place where something special is going to happen. The space has been transformed: it is where the other world of the play will be made present for us. It is a sacred space in the sense that we consecrate or set aside sacred places where we experience a reality different from our everyday one. In different religions, sacred spaces are designed with the idea that a divine spirit will be revealed to believers there. The spaces are set aside for this purpose. In the everyday world, we see public places set aside on occasion, transformed for the special purpose of an inauguration or a parade or a funeral—Pennsylvania Avenue in Washington, D.C., for a presidential inauguration, for example.

This is close to what we experience when we go to the theatre. We enter into a special place where the mysterious "other" world of the play is going to be made present for us. Good designers think of their job as creating the site where the world of the play can be realized and take place. The designer creates a world of space that is appropriate to the world of the play and at the same time lets the audience experience it as the something "other" that it is. One can

---

Whenever people still come to celebrate their common faith, consecrate their solidarity, activate their dynamism or invent new solutions, sacred settings are clearly marked out.
                    Jean Duvignaud, "The Theatre in Society: Society in the Theatre"

There are ... privileged places, qualitatively different from all others—a man's birthplace, or the scenes of his first love, or certain places in the first foreign city he visited in youth. Even for the most frankly non-religious man, all these places still retain an exceptional, a unique quality; they are the "holy places" of his private universe, as if it were in such spots that he received the revelation of a reality other than that in which he participates through his ordinary daily life.
                    Mircea Eliade, **The Sacred and the Profane**

> T heatre ... is **transformational,** creating or incarnating in a theatre
> place what cannot take place anywhere else. Just as a farm is a
> field where edible foods are grown, so a theatre is a place where trans-
> formations of time, place, and persons (human and non-human) are ac-
> complished.
>
> Richard Schechner, "Towards a Poetics of Performance"

go even further: the designer must transform the space of the stage so the play *can* become present.

The theatre designer is a *master of transformation.* He transforms what British director Peter Brook refers to as the "empty space" of the stage to the "sacred space" of the play. This transformation creates the sense of surprise and expectancy we feel when we confront the accomplishments of a great designer. We discussed earlier the idea that our excitement and pleasure in the theatre are derived from our sense that a form of action is being fulfilled—that the events taking place on the stage come from somewhere and are going somewhere that we know is preordained. The sense of suspense the stage setting creates in us is similar. We anticipate that something special is going to happen in that space. We may not know what it will be, but it is as if the space *does* know. The designer's use of space expresses the destiny of the play; it constantly reveals that destiny to us every bit as much as the actors do.

THE DESIGN PROCESS

In the quotation at the opening of this chapter, Robert Edmond Jones says a theatre designer must be a jack-of-all-trades who can build a set, paint scenery, drape or sew a costume, apply makeup, draw blueprints, work the lights, and so on. Designers may be temperamental or patient but to succeed they all must have a well-developed visual imagination and sure instincts about spatial relationships. By that I mean the designer must know what light, color, materials, texture, shape, and space can do to bring the play's environment to life.

The designer must also have a thorough mastery of technical craft. For years there has been a running debate over whether a designer needs to be a trained technician, that is, whether he should actually be able to paint a set or sew a costume. There are probably many first-rate theatre technicians who cannot and should not design, but it does not follow that the designer need not be a master of stagecraft. Ideally, the designer should have mastered all the tools of the craft because many artistic decisions will be governed by practical concerns. What will happen when all the elements of design—sets, costumes, lights, props—come together? Will they clash or be in harmony? What about the sight lines of the theatre where the production will take place? Can the audience see? What about acoustics? If there is more than one stage set, how will they be changed? If the production is scheduled to tour, are the sets easily adaptable to a variety of stage spaces and will they stand the wear and tear of touring? And always there is the issue of costs. A designer who doesn't know the details of stagecraft can easily bankrupt a production before it opens.

There is no single way the designer masters the tools of the craft. Many designers got their start as technicians in school and college productions. Others were painters or sculptors whose interests turned to theatre. Today, most designers are graduates of theatre departments. No matter what route the designer has taken, there are certain areas he or she must be skilled in to be successful in the theatre. These include two- and three-dimensional design, drafting, color rendering, scene painting, lighting technique, property making, the fundamentals of costume design and construction, and at least the basic principles of acting. But craft, by itself, is not enough. An imaginative designer is also knowledgeable about art history, dramatic literature, and theatre history. This last area is particularly important since mastery of craft requires an understanding of the history of theatre design. Experience in all of these fields is necessary if one wishes to be a professional designer. Professional designers belong to a union and candidates must pass difficult union examinations in many areas. Having passed the exams and joined the union, the professional designer can be approached by a producer or director to design a production.

The designer begins the process of design in much the same way that the director and actors begin their preparation. The designer, like all other artists of the theatre, must take a journey to the play. He must sense its atmosphere, must immerse himself in it, must, as Robert Edmond Jones put it, "be baptized by it." The designer does the same kind of research and preparation as the director—reading the play over and over and, in particular, looking at paintings, pictures, photographs, and visiting actual places relevant to the play. Gradually the design of the world of the play takes form in his visual imagination. Then he can transform those images into the concrete terms of the stage. To succeed in this, he should avoid the inevitable impulse to design "too soon." Even the roughest kind of preliminary sketches can lock his imagination in prematurely. Rather, the designer needs time to absorb the images along with the spirit of the play.

Two areas of work in particular require great sensitivity and creativity if the final production is to be successful. First, discovering the visual world of the play he will create on the stage is as we said, the designer's primary job. The design must serve the play and express its meanings. He can make a tremendous contribution to the production in this area. Second, the designer must create sets, costumes, props, and lighting that serve the actors as well as the script. Let's look at this second idea more closely.

DESIGNING FOR ACTORS

Sets

You may have attended a performance where the audience applauded the set as the curtain first opened. "The audience came out singing the sets" is an expression often applied to lavish musical productions. You might think this would please the designer, but it doesn't—at least not a good one—because it indicates that she may have failed in a fundamental way. We said that the environment of the stage radiates a sense of expectancy and excitement. It anticipates the performance about to take place. But only actors can create the performance. For this reason, the stage should have a quality of incompleteness until it is peopled with actors. It needs the presence of actors to fulfill it, and if the setting strikes us as a fully satisfying creation in its own right, it may well mean that the designer has forgotten or violated one of the theatre's basic axioms: *The stage is first of all a place for actors.*

The environment or setting of the play is an essential part of a production. As in life, "action" on the stage is the interaction of the characters and their environment. The setting is not just a surrounding and it certainly isn't decoration. Far from being a neutral background, it reveals the play's action. It is an extension or, in Aristotelian terms, a "form" of action. Whether simple or complex, the setting is one of the primary means whereby the world of the play is achieved.

One doesn't design and build a set and then stick the actors into it and expect them to fit. On the contrary, the setting must evolve out of the actors. Brecht had this in mind when he said: "The set needs to spring from the rehearsal of groupings, so in effect it must be a fellow actor." ("Groupings" means blocking, patterns of movement and gesture, the visual relationships of movement.) Before the designer can visualize the set, she must see and know what the actors are doing. There are sound psychological and physiological reasons for this.

The spaces in which we live are a form of self-extension. Your room, your apartment, your home is an extension of yourself—a kind of personal stage set. It expresses you, it reveals your image of yourself, it mirrors your taste, it shapes and conditions you, and on some occasions it can even determine how you act. Think of what it means to feel "out of place." In the public realm, one way we have of demonstrating power is by controlling our position in space and

*I*t doesn't make good theatre sense for an audience to applaud a set for its abstract "beauty." A set is a utensil which cannot be judged until its worth is proved in practice by the whole course of the play's development on the stage.

Harold Clurman, **Lies Like Truth**

the setting of events. Picture a king seated on a throne with his subjects kneeling before him. Important events need "the proper setting."

Similarly, stage space is not neutral. It is an extension of the actors. Richard Schechner, who has been exploring this idea in his work with the Performance Group, observes:

> The performer works in a place where all the things he sees and touches are extensions of his body. He uses his actual body in spaces that are extensions of his fantasy body.[1]

By this I think he means that just as a person's life spaces are extensions of his or her body, personality, and self-image, so, too, the space of the playing area in theatre is an extension of all the actor-character relationships.

There are, then, two kinds of space on the stage: the space the actors create with their bodies and the space in which the performance of the other world of the play occurs. A designer is extremely conscious of both spaces and the ways they interact. She recognizes that the play demands its own environment and that the actors will create theirs as well. These must be in harmony. On the practical level of creating an environment for the play, these two spaces will be in harmony only if the designer works within these guidelines:

1. The human body is the source of all design for the theatre; that is, the set, lighting, and costumes must serve the actor.
2. Stage settings are extensions of the actors.
3. The actor should be included as much as possible in every phase of the design process.
4. The environment of a play should evolve out of and together with the rehearsal process.

In designing for actors, the designer is careful to think of the actors as elements of the setting, and of the setting as an actor. Only if there is a constant interaction between the actors/characters and the setting/environment will that necessary marriage between the world of the play and those who create it in performance take place. At an early point, the designer begins to study the actors as they move, knowing that she cannot visualize the setting until she can see what the actors are doing. The actors' movements and gestures, their interpretations of their characters, and the stage groupings give the designer important hints as to what is appropriate for the play's environment. This must be a time of active exchange between actors, director, and designer. At this point, the designer can shape the future of all aspects of the production as much as anyone else. In the early rehearsals of the first production of Arthur Miller's *Death of a Salesman* (1949), Jo Mielziner, the designer, hit upon the skeletal image of the Lomans' house set against the background of the towering city as an image of Willy's mind in which the action of the whole play took place. (See photograph on page 84.) This idea changed everything in the production. Parts of the play were rewritten, Elia Kazan's direction took on a new focus, and the relationships of all the characters were altered. In short, the designer opened up the play for everyone working on the production. Mielziner had been the first to discover the world of the play, and because things weren't locked in too soon, that world was fully realized in one of the most memorable productions of the twentieth-century theatre.

Only after a good deal of interaction is the designer ready to start the process of actual design. Director Richard Schechner describes well what the designer's attitude should be at this point: "Start with all the space there is and then decide what to use, what not to use, and how to use what you use." The designer isn't an interior decorator; together with the actors she is creating an environment in which the characters of the play can be realized. By following the principle of "less is more," the designer will never be tempted to give the actors more than they need to fulfill their function, and in so doing the designer will have fulfilled hers.

One of the questions the designer faces fairly early is how realistic or nonrealistic the stage setting will be. The question is not asked in just this way, of course. The real question is, What style extends and enriches the meaning of the play? In the preceding chapter we discussed some of the movements that have developed in the theatre beginning in the last century, and if you look again at those illustrations of stage settings, you will see a great range of styles. They vary from the very realistic setting of *The Changing Room* (p. 232) to the abstract setting of *A Midsummer Night's Dream* (p. 246). Every stage set is the product of a number of design decisions made by the designer in collaboration with the director. But no matter what style is finally chosen, it must be developed from the script if it is to be effective.

The designer often must deal with the problem of working with a play that has been conceived for one kind of theatre space but must be produced in another kind of theatre space. The dynamic of Greek tragedy, for instance, depends on the movement and chanting of the chorus, and the structure of the fifth-century B.C. theatre reflects that dynamic. The main acting area is a place for dancers. It is difficult to imagine *Oedipus the King* performed on the thrust stage at Shakespeare's Globe. The designer must deal with this problem all the time: Shakespeare on a proscenium stage, Chekhov on a thrust stage, Euripides in a garage, Congreve in a tent. In each case, the space of the performance is essentially incompatible with the design of the play. Still the designer cannot throw up her hands in despair and say, "I can't do it!" More than anyone else, she must discover solutions that keep the heritage of theatre alive. (Some plays are almost impossible to do except in the performance space for which they were written. For instance, *A Sleep of Prisoners* by British playwright Christopher Fry is about four prisoners of war who are being kept in a church. It is written to be performed in a church. The plot of the play is built around a series of dreams based on biblical texts, and the action is clearly designed so the space of the whole church is to be used—chancel, aisles, organ, loft, narthex, etc. When the play is produced on a proscenium stage—usually loaded with religious decor—it is so two-dimensional that it loses its energy and becomes boring and pretentious.

Many designers believe the key to the design process is finding the right "design metaphor" for the play. This metaphor, they feel, opens up the play, defines it, and provides a governing image that will unite the many diverse production elements the designer is responsible for creating. For example, Mordecai Gorelik, who designed the first production of Arthur Miller's *All My Sons*, used a New England church as his design metaphor for that play. *All My Sons* certainly contains that image, but it also contains many more. And here is the problem with a single design metaphor: it narrows rather than expands the meaning of a play. The designer's task is to express all of the play's marvelous fullness and not to reduce its scope. Unquestionably, all kinds of images can guide the designer in her journey to the play—and she should use them—but finally the image of the play is itself. A play *is*. It is not something else. The world of the play is its own metaphor. Failure to understand this can lead to gimmicks, imposed styles, irrelevant symbolism, and abstract concepts that distort the world of the play rather than reveal it to us.

We have focused our attention almost entirely on the stage settings up to this point. Obviously, the environment of the stage is composed of many elements other than the setting, and the designer is responsible for creating all of them. These elements include the costumes (and sometimes makeup), stage properties, actors' properties, lighting, and sound (and when necessary, music). In some instances one designer is responsible for all these things—certainly this was true in earlier days. Today the production staff of a play may be composed of a number of design specialists: a set designer, costume designer, lighting designer, sound specialist and/or music director, and all the other technicians—people to cut and sew costumes, carpenters, painters, and so on.

COSTUMES

David Atkinson in the armor of Don Quixote in the musical **Man of La Mancha** (1965), based on Miguel de Cervantes's life and novel.

The elaborate, colorful costumes of **Jesus Christ Superstar** were inspired by the rock/drug culture of the 1960s.

The costumes of the English Restoration theatre are vividly represented in John Gielgud's revival of William Congreve's **Love for Love** in 1947.

Cecil Beaton's lavish rendering of Edwardian costume in a production of Oscar Wilde's **Lady Windermere's Fan** (1946).

The simplest of costumes served effectively in **For Colored Girls Who Have Considered Suicide When the Rainbow Is Enuf**, a dramatic presentation of the poems of Ntozake Shange (1976).

Skin as costume. Nudity has been theatricalized with increasing frequency during the last decade, principally in experimental theatres such as the Living Theatre's production of **Paradise Now** shown here. In recent years, the idea of skin as costume has been used in commercial productions such as Peter Shaffer's **Equus**.

The character of the General in Jean Genet's **The Blacks** is a good example of how costume can create the illusion of multiple reality by the use of masks. (English Stage Company production, 1966.)

Above: Alwin Nikolais's multimedia productions have been among the most innovative in the contemporary theatre. In **Sanctum**, he combined costume, light, and music to create a new form of theatre-dance.

Left: Since the time of Richard Wagner, some of the most striking costume and set designs have been done for opera. This is evident in a recent revival of the Jean Cocteau/Igor Stravinsky opera, **Oedipus Rex.**

Costumes

If the spaces in which we live and move are extensions of ourselves, so, too, are the clothes we wear. Each of us is a costumer. Not only do "clothes make the man," but we create an image of ourselves every day as we decide on the "costumes" we will wear. We have come to think that there are "suitable" clothes for lawyers, executive secretaries, movie stars, college professors. A dress code in schools defines how a student looks. Clothes establish rank, reveal social class and condition, and express relationship. In short, every time we put on clothes, we reveal, project, extend, and define ourselves. Clothes help create and reveal our identity.

Small wonder, then, that costumes are so vital to the life of the theatre. Costumes can be as elaborate as a queen's coronation garb or as simple as a naked human body (skin is a costume, of a sort). There is an inseparable relationship between clothing and identity in the theatre. This is true of every play, but we can see the function of costume especially well in one of the masterpieces of the twentieth-century theatre, Jean Genet's *The Balcony*. In this play, Genet is exploring the many levels at which appearance and reality interact. The action is set in a brothel where the patrons act out their fantasy lives. The opening scene shows a bishop dressed in full regalia. In the stage directions, Genet describes him as

> *obviously larger than life. The role is played by an actor wearing tragedian's cothurni* [the platform-soled boots of the ancient Greek theatre] *about twenty inches high. His shoulders, on which the cope* [a bishop's cape] *lies, are inordinately broadened so that when the curtain rises he looks huge.*[2]

As the scene proceeds, the character is undressed. By the end of the scene, the grand ecclesiastical lord has been revealed as only a little man who works for the gas company, shivering in his underwear.

Shakespeare used costumes as a way of developing character and charting a play's action. King Lear moves from royal trappings in the opening scene to "wretched rags" in the mad scenes on the heath to "fresh garments" for his final reconciliation and death with Cordelia. Similarly, Hamlet's growth in character is revealed by the progression of his costumes. He moves from the black of mourning to the princely robes in which he dies.

In the modern theatre, practically every major playwright since Ibsen and Strindberg has used costume as a way of presenting character. There is a wonderful anecdote that Stanislavski relates in *My Life in Art* that illustrates this. In the initial production of Chekhov's *The Cherry Orchard* at the Moscow Art Theatre, Stanislavski played Lopahin, the former serf who has become a successful landowner and who buys from the now impoverished Madam Ranevsky and her brother Gaev the estate (the cherry orchard) where he was raised. After one of the early performances of the play, Stanislavski asked Chekhov, who had been in the audience, how he liked his performance. Chekhov replied: "It was fine, fine! Only Lopahin wears brown shoes." Stanislavski couldn't figure out what Chekhov meant for the longest time, when suddenly he realized what the playwright was getting at. In the play, Lopahin comes dressed in the proper formal "morning clothes" to pay his respects to Madame Ranevsky. Stanislavski had disregarded Chekhov's notes that Lopahin wear brown shoes because he felt no one could ever have such bad taste as to wear brown shoes with formal black and gray attire. But that was just Chekhov's point: Lopahin might be successful and rich, he might socialize with the members of the household and finally buy the estate from them, but he wears the wrong shoes. At heart, he is still a scruffy little peasant.

Costumes, then, reveal and define both the play's characters and the meanings of its action. Costumes also have a direct and interesting relationship to the language the actor speaks. We pointed out in Chapter 6 that language is an important means by which we define ourselves and the occasion. Since clothes do the same thing, the two tend to be interrelated, especially when we present ourselves publicly. (A speech in the locker room at halftime will be quite different from a speech at a formal dinner.) The relationship between language and costume can be of great help to the actor in mastering and then speaking the lines from the other world of the play. Stark Young, one of America's most influential drama critics, said: "Costume is a kind of decor that can give to speeches their right placement and scale."

Many actors today have difficulty handling the stately formality of the verse in Greek tragedy. But if they were to put on the platform boots (*cothurni*), the megaphoned masks, and the long, flowing costumes the actors wore when those plays were written, the costumes themselves would assist the actors in achieving the right approach to the lines. Try to imagine speaking and moving in such a costume. Your delivery would automatically become more measured, formal, and stately. Similarly, the magnificent Elizabethan language of Shakespeare's plays in many ways corresponds to the rich and elaborate costumes the actors wore in Shakespeare's time. (It is interesting to notice the effect that Shakespeare's language has on audiences when his plays are performed in costumes more or less inappropriate to the period depicted in the play. Productions done in leotards, for instance, tend to give the language a spare and lean quality. The performance moves toward abstraction. This can be very interesting as it focuses our attention on the poetry itself, but inevitably some of the richness of the Shakespearean world is lost. To attempt to do *Hamlet* in tweed suits would be a nearly impossible task.)

The relationship of costume to language exists in contemporary plays as well. In a Noel Coward comedy there is a direct correspondence between the sophisticated dialogue the actors speak and the sophisticated clothing they wear. Clearly, costume can be a great help to the actor in discovering the world of the play. Early ideas from the costume designer may help the actors to become the characters. This underscores again the importance of the designer's involvement in the rehearsal process. The costumes are a part of the actor's working self; in fact, they are a part of the character.

In approaching the job of costume design, the designer is careful to keep in mind the following:

1. The designer must discover the world of the play and reveal it in the costumes. Costumes communicate ideas, information, and feelings. Under ideal conditions, each production should have its own costumes designed for it, not rented or borrowed. Costumes should express the designer's own discovery of the play, not the discoveries of someone else. Secondhand costumes, no matter how beautiful and apparently appropriate, have come from another play—even if it is another production of the same play.

2. The costumes must be designed for the actors who will wear them. The effectiveness of a costume in performance depends totally on the actor's ability to make it a functioning part of his or her character. A costume for a large, heavy actor such as the late Zero Mostel will have to be quite different from a costume for Woody Allen. The costume must present the character of the play and, at the same time, must permit the actor to play the role. For this reason the designer must know and work with the actors who will embody the roles. The designer must be an active participant in the rehearsal process, and the actors should be able to work with at least elements of the costumes as they develop.

3. Each costume should be derived from the character it will serve. The brown shoes for Lopahin were what that character would choose. In this way the costumes in a production will have the unity of tone, style, and expressiveness that has been determined by the play.

4. Costumes of a period play present a problem. The designer must bring into harmony a number of often conflicting demands: the period in which the play is set, the period in which it was written, and the audience's expectations and frame of reference. Take *Hamlet*, for example. The play is set in eleventh-century Denmark, but medieval Danish costumes would be wrong for Shakespeare's play and probably unidentifiable for most audiences. Costumes which are exact replicas of the clothing worn in Shakespeare's time (the early 1600s) would also be wrong for the actors and for the audience. Elizabethan dress was extremely bulky, heavy, and cumbersome; it had to serve many nontheatrical functions; and it was unlike the costumes Shakespeare's actors generally wore. So the designer must come up with costumes that are expressive of the play, comfortable to work in for the actors, and appropriate to the audience's preconceived ideas—based on other plays, movies, paintings, and drawings—of what Elizabethan costumes looked like.

Finally, a word should be said about makeup. For most plays, makeup is the actor's responsibility. In realistic drama, it serves a function very similar to that of makeup outside the theatre. It highlights facial features so they are not bleached out by the bright lights of the stage. But in some kinds of theatre—the Japanese Kabuki, commedia dell' arte, Restoration comedy, or Greek tragedy—makeup is carefully designed. It is like a facial mask. When makeup is used this way it must be in harmony with the actor's costume—it is part of the costume.

Properties

Stage properties or "props" play an equally important, if not so obvious, role as the costumes in creating the world of the play. There are two types of stage properties: set properties and actors' properties. A set property is any movable object that functions as part of the stage setting, ranging from a chair or picture to fireplace tools or a lamp. Actors' properties are those objects used by the actor that can be disposed of, set down, or removed. (Parts of costumes are not thought of as props. A sword worn as part of a costume is not a prop, but one hanging in a rack is.) Properties can be created, found, begged, borrowed, or stolen (in most productions it is a combination of these), but as with the other elements of design, the cardinal rule pertaining to them is that every property should express the play. Nothing should be used just to fill up the set or to make it look pretty, more natural, or whatever.

Properties have always served an important function in the theatre, but they have played a particularly significant role during the past century since the development and influence of naturalism. In earlier periods, many of the current functions of properties could be achieved with language. Shakespeare, for example, could "dress" the set with poetry while Ibsen, using the nineteenth-century conventions of "natural" language, could not. Ibsen used properties as symbols to provide metaphoric meaning that a predominantly naturalistic theatre denied him. He also used properties as a way of defining and extending both character and action. In *Hedda Gabler*, many stage properties are used in this way. For example, we have already mentioned that the picture of Hedda's father, which dominates the Tesmans' living room, reveals how powerfully Hedda's father governs her psychic and emotional life. Indeed, the whole set—drawn draperies, cut flowers, heavy furniture—is used in this way. The same is true of the actors' properties. Hedda's use of her father's pistols reveals her link to her father. They play an important role in the plot, and finally they are the means of her suicide. Stage properties, then, can be used as symbols that deepen and enhance the play's meaning. They can reveal character, suggest

A hand prop: Macbeth's dagger. The Old Vic production with Laurence Olivier and Judith Anderson (1937).

A shaman's ceremonial charm, representing a sea monster devouring a man.

mood, define the situation, and create irony and contrast. Modern drama has grown increasingly dependent on the symbolism and imagery of props to achieve emotional depth.

Properties have a special significance for actors as they develop their roles. If you ever visit a theatrical museum or even a room in which stage props are stored, you may have a strange experience. The properties have a kind of aura about them, like the radiant afterglow of a magical dust. It is as if the play still shines through them. This is both real and imagined. Certain cultures believe that the objects used in religious rituals retain their sacred quality. David Cole, quoting anthropologist Jacqueline Monfouga-Nicolas, tells us:

> Once an object has been used in the Bori possession ritual, it is believed to retain certain properties ever after (for example, the power to cause impotence or repel witches) and "becomes invested with a halo of fear and respect."[3]

Museums all over the world attest to the fact that objects can take on special powers when used on special occasions or by special people. These objects can be anything from religious relics to the baseball that Henry Aaron hit to break the home-run record. Part of the "magic" of the theatre is that stage properties have much the same function and a similar kind of power. Ordinary objects are transformed by the world of the play. The sword used by Laurence Olivier in playing Hamlet is just a sword, but it is also Hamlet's sword.

The fact that stage properties can be transformed in this way has a very practical use for the actor. Props can be of invaluable assistance to actors as they discover and develop their roles. Certain props become "security blankets" for them during the rehearsal process. Often, scenes that have not been working in rehearsal suddenly come to life when the actors are given props to use. Properties, in other words, are a means whereby actors can discover and be possessed by their roles. John Gielgud confirms this:

> There are many actors who say, "Oh, I can't rehearse without a particular property in this scene, I must have my book," or "I must have a handkerchief in that scene," or "I wanted to have a bag—or something." You suddenly begin to feel these things will help you to become part of the character.[4]

There is probably a good reason for this—one that a shaman would understand and accept. The actor's journey to the world of the play to find his or her character is a journey into the depths of his or her own being. This can be difficult, even painful, and the actor may encounter inner conflict or resistance in the process. A property, being inanimate, seems to help the actor overcome these resistances. An actor playing Richard II or Macbeth may be having a terrible time achieving the spirit of kingliness required by the role; put a crown on his head or in his hands and the crown begins the process of transformation. Indeed, historically that is the meaning of the ceremony of coronation. Queen Elizabeth II of England actually became a queen in the political sense the moment her father died. But at her coronation she was given a sacred charge and she took a sacred oath, and when the crown was put on her head it was believed she became a more powerful, a more special, a sacred person. The ritual involves a process of transformation and the crown is the medium of that transformation. Stage properties can have similar powers to transform.

Stage properties serve another important purpose: they make the world of the play real for the audience during performance. This is most obvious in naturalistic theatre, where the environment plays a significant role. For example, Victorian-style furniture establishes the period so important to an understanding of Ibsen's plays. Stage properties serve the same function in all plays. How is the audience to experience Volpone's lust for "infinite riches in a little room"? Certainly Ben Jonson's poetry will help, but the "infinite riches" have to be there, too. Nothing manifests the mysterious reality of Madame Pace's shop in Pirandello's *Six Characters in Search of an Author* more powerfully than the scraggly properties that are hurriedly erected to suggest it while the audience watches. Try to imagine *Macbeth* without a dagger! Props serve as a link between actor and play and audience, and if the right link is chosen (or made), the connection will allow the experience of theatre to be more fully realized.

The Designer

The prime mission of the scenic artist is to establish style (always in conjunction with the director). What is the manner of presentation we are about to witness? The designer must create signposts and symbols, clues and innuendoes, that will communicate instantly to the audience and provide a key to the personalities on the stage. Sometimes this must be achieved in a split second between the rise of the curtain and the first word spoken by the actor. Mood, light, form, color, and even subliminal sound may be the means at the scenic artist's hand.

Jo Mielziner, *Designing for the Theatre*

The classic themes of love and death are reassessed by the Swiss playwright Max Frisch in his **Don Juan; or, The Love of Geometry**. Together with his countryman Friedrich Duerrenmatt, he brought a bizarre new theatricality to the post–World War II theatre. This production at Carnegie-Mellon University was directed by Laurence Carra.

Left: Charles Autry's costume sketch for the character of Dionysus in Euripides' **The Bacchae**.

Below: Dionysus in Robert Benedetti's production of **The Bacchae** at the University of Wisconsin—Milwaukee in 1968.

Left: The excitement and color of Brechtian theatre is captured in Al Tucci's costume sketch for the Governor in **The Caucasian Chalk Circle**.

Below: The fully realized design of the costume for the Governor (right) in the University of Wisconsin—Milwaukee production of **The Caucasian Chalk Circle**, directed by Corliss Phillabaum in 1976.

Above: E. J. Dennis's lighting for **One Flew over the Cuckoo's Nest** shows how projections, scrim backdrops, and area lighting can project mood and meaning in a performance. (University of Wisconsin—Milwaukee, 1972)

Below, left: The designer's finished sketch for a stage setting. Maura Smolover's design for Eugene O'Neill's **A Moon for the Misbegotten.**

Below, right: Maura Smolover's set for the production of **A Moon for the Misbegotten** at the Cleveland Playhouse in 1976.

While artificial lighting—first candles and then gas—had been regularly used on the stage since the seventeenth century, the invention of the electric light in 1879 transformed the nature of the theatrical event. Its vast range of intensity, complete controllability, ready flexibility, and almost infinite capacity for varying nuances made it a significant new resource for the theatre artist.

The first person who really understood the role of light in the theatre was the Swiss designer Adolphe Appia (1862–1928). For many years Appia worked as a designer with Richard Wagner at Bayreuth. In the 1890s he published a number of books and monographs defining an aesthetic of the theatre based on light. The most important of these works was *Music and the Art of the Theatre*, published in 1899. (One should not be misled by the word "music" in the title. Forty percent of the book is devoted to the aesthetics and practical applications of light on the stage.) Appia's underlying premise was that light should be the guiding principle of all design. He believed that light alone could be the unifying force among the many contradictory elements of production. These include:

1. the inanimate, vertical, and (at that time) two-dimensionally painted settings;
2. the horizontal and apparently neutral stage floor;
3. the materials, colors, and shapes of the costumes;
4. the lighted stage space;
5. the combination of two-dimensional and three-dimensional stage properties; and
6. the living, moving presence of the actor.

Appia observed that the two-dimensional/three-dimensional and the living/inanimate were inevitably in conflict. Light, he believed, could unify them.

His greatest contribution was the idea that light could do much more than just illuminate the stage space. Light, with its capacity to create shadow, can create space within space. (See photographs on pp. 286 and 287.) It can both define and reveal; it is, in fact, a "living" element. "Living light" creates on the stage a completely unified, three-dimensional world in which the two-dimensional and three-dimensional, the animate and inanimate are brought into harmony.

Finally, Appia recognized something else of great significance. He understood that light can communicate meaning and feelings to an audience directly and almost instantaneously, that it can "say" things to an audience as no other element of production can. American scene designer Lee Simonson, who was largely responsible for making people in this country aware of the importance of Appia's work, comments on this point in *The Stage Is Set:*

> Appia's supreme intuition was his recognition that light can play as directly upon our emotions as music does. We are more immediately affected by our sensitiveness to variations of light in the theatre than we are by our sensations of colour, shape, or sound. Our emotional reaction to light is more rapid than to any other theatrical means of expression, possibly because no other sensory stimulus moves with the speed of light, possibly because, our earliest inherited fear being a fear of the dark, we inherit with it a primitive worship of the sun. The association between light and joy, between sorrow and darkness, is deeply rooted and tinges the imagery of almost every literature and every religion. It shows itself in such common couplings as "merry and bright," "sad and gloomy." How much less lonely we feel walking along a country road in a pitch-black night when the distant yellow patch of a farm-house window punctures the darkness! The flare of a campfire in a black pine forest at night cheers us even though we are not near enough to warm our hands at it. The warmth of the sun or of a flame does of course play a large share in provoking the feeling of elation that light gives us. But the quality of light itself can suggest this warmth effectively enough to arouse almost the same mood of comfort and release, as when, after a dingy day of rain and mist, sunlight strikes our window-curtains and dapples the floor of our room.
>
> Between these two extremes of flaming sun and darkness an immense range of emotion fluctuates almost instantly in response to variations in the intensity of light. The key of our emotions can be set, the quality of our response dictated, almost at the rise of the curtain by the degree and quality of light that pervades a scene. It requires many more moments for the words of the players or their actions to accumulate momentum and to gather enough import for them to awaken as intense and direct an emotional response. And as the action progresses our emotions can be similarly played upon.[5]

To think of light in these ways is to think of it as an actor in the performance. And this was Adolphe Appia's contribution.

Imagine a stage lighted by gas or candles and you can understand the vast changes that came with the electric light. Candles and gas lit the stage in front, from the sides, and from above. Obviously one could not achieve any of the lighting effects we take for granted today. No spotlights followed an actor's movements. No quick changes or subtle changes in color or brightness were possible. Part of the stage could not be in darkness while another part was lighted. These and other effects were not possible before the electric light.

One could argue with good reason that lighting has played a governing role in all production styles that have developed since the introduction of electric lighting. It is next to impossible to imagine the twentieth-century theatre without the electric light. Yet the basic theatrical event has not changed that much. The wildest expressionist play that depends totally on the magic of electricity and a medieval mystery play are recognizable blood brothers. Thus the question: If electric light was such a revolutionary force creating a new means of expression and having profound effects on the nature, quality, and techniques of theatrical production, why hasn't it changed the essential nature of theatre? The answer: Because light was always there as a dramatic element in every script. It was present in the language. Aeschylus' *Oresteia* was originally produced in an open-air theatre in ancient Greece in the middle of the day, but *Agamemnon* (the first play of the trilogy) opens in the darkness of the early morning hours as signal fires announce to the waiting watchman the fall of Troy.

> I've prayed God to release me from sentry duty
> All through this long year's vigil, like a dog
> Couched on the roof of Atreus, where I study
> Night after night the pageantry of this vast
> Concourse of stars, and moving among them like
> Noblemen the constellations that bring
> Summer and winter as they rise and fall.
> . . . . .
> But now at last may the good news in a flash
> Scatter the darkness and deliver us! *(The beacon flashes.)*
> O light of joy, whose gleam turns night to day,
> O radiant signal for innumerable
> Dances of victory![6]

Hamlet was produced at the Globe Theatre in the afternoon daylight, but the play's opening scene is set at midnight on the battlements of Elsinore.

> Last night of all,
> When yon same star that's westward from the pole
> Had made his course t' illume that part of heaven
> Where now it burns, Marcellus and myself,
> The bell then beating one, —

The lighting or sense of light and darkness was in the language, in the poetry of the play. Even today, with all our technological wizardry, lighting designers still return to that poetry for the cues for their designs.

Most cultures have identified light with discovery or enlightenment and darkness with mystery or evil. Lighting in the theatre (both the electrical lighting and the lighting of the language) usually works to reinforce this idea. Light does more than illumine the stage, suggest mood and atmosphere, give emphasis to stage relationships, and create space. It actually completes the whole environment by bringing all the elements within it into harmony.

LIGHTING

Perhaps the most imaginative artist of light in the twentieth-century theatre is the Czech designer Josef Svoboda. Here are photographs from some of his most memorable productions.

Owners of the Keys,
Tyl Theatre, Prague (1962)

The Insect Comedy,
National Theatre, Prague (1965)

Tristan, act 1,
Festspiele Bayreuth
(1976)

Tristan, act 2
Festspiele Bayreuth
(1976)

Sound and Music

The ultimate combination of music and theatre occurs in opera, but since the music is so clearly dominant in this form of performance, a discussion of opera is not part of this book. Music is equally dominant in the musical theatre, which we will discuss in the next chapter. But there are times when music does serve the theatre in a supportive capacity. We earlier discussed the role of music in melodrama, and we know that music played an important role in the Greek, Oriental, and Elizabethan theatres. In more recent times it has figured in the work of playwrights such as Yeats, Brecht, and Lorca. But in each of these instances, music and song provide a lyrical extension to the action. They serve as an ironic counterpoint to it. They comment upon it. They deepen or redirect it. They are more language than music. This is the case with Feste's songs in Shakespeare's *Twelfth Night:*

> What is love? 'Tis not hereafter.
> Present mirth hath present laughter;
> What's to come is still unsure.
> In delay there lies no plenty;
> Then come kiss me sweet and twenty,
> Youth's a stuff will not endure.

Or the Fool's song in *King Lear:*

> He that has and a little tiny wit,—
> With heigh-ho, the wind and the rain,—
> Must make content with his fortunes fit,
> For the rain it raineth every day.

Music used in this way is a means of verbal expression (like the sounds of words themselves), and this is different from the music of opera or the Broadway musical in which it carries the meaning.

When we speak of sound as a design element of production, we are referring to sound effects used to reveal the play. The most obvious purpose of using sound in production is to create an illusion of reality. Today, records and tapes of just about any sound effect one could possibly imagine are available. Many theatres have such advanced sound systems that a technical director can create realistic sounds for just about everything: gunshots, doors slamming, bells, crowds, automobiles, noises, thunder. This kind of sound is most appropriate for the realistic theatre, but it is a means of expression available to any production and it is an important means of creating the world of the play.

In recent years directors have used sounds in increasingly subtle and interesting ways. Some have used sound effects to break the stage illusion; others have used random sounds as a comment on spoken language; still others have produced plays with a total sound environment. In his remarkable production of Peter Weiss's *Marat/Sade*, Peter Brook had the inmates of the insane asylum at Charenton make sounds, both on and off the set, as a contrapuntal rhythm to the dialogue. There were long stretches of time when the audience would experience nothing but the eerie combination of strange, almost inhuman, vocal noises and weird rapping and knocking in parts of the set. The effect enhanced the logic of madness which made the production disturbing yet fascinating.

Sometimes sound effects are built right into the text of the play and have a symbolic meaning. A good example of this can be found in Chekhov's *Uncle Vanya*, where the rapping of a watchman's rattle is woven throughout the play's second act. In nineteenth-century Russia, a watchman would go about an estate clacking his sticks—much as our present-day guards make rounds with clock and key. The purpose of this noise was both to frighten prowlers and to let the members of the household know that they were being protected. Chekhov did not include this effect only to achieve realism. He also used it as a thematic symbol. This becomes very apparent at the end of the act. Yelena and Sonya have just had an honest talk with each other and because of it their feelings are exposed. The windows are open, it has been raining, and everything is clean and refreshed. Yelena thinks she can play the piano again. But as Sonya goes to get permission, the watchman's rattle is heard. Yelena has to shut the window—the source of refreshment—and Serebryakov says no to the piano-playing. Their lives have been so protected by "watchmen" that they have no feelings left.

Finally, sound's greatest contribution to the theatre resides in its evocative power. It is still customary in most theatres in France to begin each performance with three knocks. These knocks announce to the audience that the performance is about to begin. They also call forth the play just as shamans call forth the spirits of the other world using sound. *Death of a Salesman* ends with the haunting siren call of the flute: we may not know exactly what it means, but the sound evokes for us the beckoning freedom that Willy Loman could find only in death.

No matter how it is used, sound, like all design elements, must always express the play. Sometimes it creates illusion, sometimes it shatters it. It can evoke mood, serve as counterpoint to language, and at times even become a form of language itself. But it must never be added on; it must never be used to create an effect for its own sake.

The role of the stage designer has changed and grown through history. In the past century in particular the designer has emerged as a person of special importance, who must be able to perform a wide range of activities, all of them essential to the success of a production.

DEVELOPMENT OF THE STAGE OR PLAYING SPACE

The designer works within certain bounds. Usually he is given a script and a particular group of actors to work with, but we have not talked about one of the most important influences on his work, the actual physical stage or playing space. Today the designer must be able not only to perform a wide range of activities but to design for a variety of stages or playing spaces. Looking at the diagrams on this page, you will notice that each playing space creates different spatial relationships, imposes certain restrictions, and makes special demands.

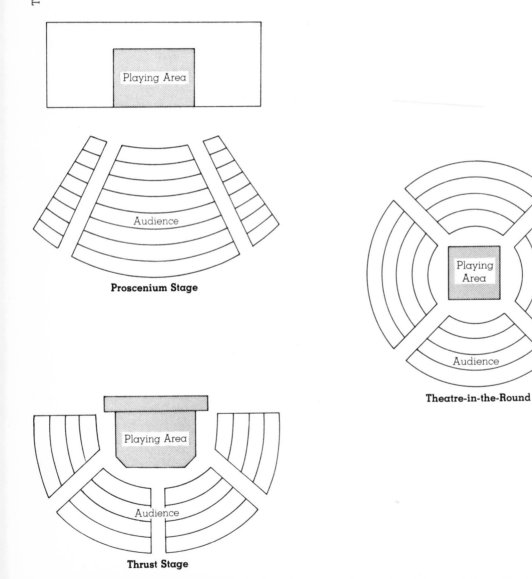

Proscenium Stage

Theatre-in-the-Round

Thrust Stage

The proscenium or picture-frame stage establishes a marked separation between the playing area and the audience. Everything on the stage tends to have a two-dimensional quality because of the frame of the proscenium arch. The designer must create depth and find ways to heighten the three-dimensional presence of the actors. Theatre-in-the-round resolves these problems but creates new ones for the designer. The single perspective on the playing area of the proscenium theatre now has the multiple perspectives of the circle. The fixed stage setting is replaced by movable stage pieces. Care must be taken to arrange things so members of the audience are not distracted by other audience members sitting on the other side of the circle. Stage properties must be placed so the actors can play in all directions. The thrust stage combines elements of the proscenium stage and of theatre-in-the-round. When actors move out onto the thrust area, they have the immediacy made possible by theatre-in-the-round, but the back platform is suitable for a permanent set. The designer must make it possible for the performance to move easily between these two quite different playing spaces. In recent years, more unconventional playing spaces have been developed: converted gymnasiums and lofts, environmental stages (see photograph on p. 231), square or rectangular spaces with the audience seated in a semicircle within them, streets and parking lots, even parks and lobbies of office buildings. As the pictures throughout this chapter show, many of these types of playing areas have long histories. Variations of the proscenium can be traced back through the Renaissance to the ancient Roman theatres. The thrust stage is clearly related to the stage of the Elizabethan playhouse. Theatre-in-the-round is as old as theatre itself, having its origins in primitive tribal dramas. And there have been versions of environmental theatres throughout history.

Beginnings: The Playing Space as Symbol

For people living in preindustrial cultures there were only two kinds of space: "the world" and "chaos." The world was territory inhabited by humanity and was believed to be an extension or copy of the world of the gods. Chaos was everything that existed beyond the frontiers of the world, "a sort of 'other world,' a foreign, chaotic space, peopled by ghosts, demons, 'foreigners' (who are assimilated to demons and the souls of the dead)."[7] The inhabited world was a consecrated space; that is, its design corresponded to what people living in these cultures believed was the design of the world of their gods. It was a model of the universe as their gods created it. This was particularly true of its ritual spaces—places of worship and healing—where the mysteries of the gods were revealed to the people.

Until the middle of the Renaissance (fifteenth century), theatres

THEATRICAL SPACE

Right: A primitive ritual space. Nuba ritual dance, the Sudan.

Below: The ancient Greek theatre at Epidaurus. In this contemporary production of Euripides' **Hecuba** we see the amphitheatre, orchestra floor, and skene.

Above: The illusion of space is created by this early sixteenth-century stage backdrop rendered in perspective by Baldassare Peruzzi.

Left: The highly polished dance floor of the Japanese Nōh theatre. The piece of scenery on the right is the Nōh representation of a mountain covered with autumn foliage. The play is **Momiji-gari.**

Above: A model of the interior of the Globe Theatre, the best known London theatre in Elizabethan times. It was octagonal in shape and open to the sky in the center. All of the levels were used as performing spaces.

Right: Moving out of the theatre altogether. Street theatre, exploiting the idea of the theatricality of everyday life, moved out of theatre buildings and performed in public places such as parks, city streets, and plazas. Shown here is the Bread and Puppet Theatre involved in an anti-war protest in New York City in the 1960s.

A picture-frame stage. Boris Aronson's set for Archibald MacLeish's allegorical **J.B.** (1958) successfully overcame the tendency of the proscenium arch to flatten all theatrical space and to create a two-dimensional effect.

and theatre spaces were thought of in a similar way. Theatre space was consciously designed as a place to reveal mystery. The stage was thought of symbolically. The place of performance represented an actual ritual place, a model of the world, or some combination of the two. The space, shape, and nature of the classical Greek theatre were derived from "the sacred ground" or ritual place of the god Dionysus. The stage space of the Japanese Nōh theatre, with its narrow bridge and tree representing the axis of the world, expresses symbolically the Buddhist cosmic myth. In the Middle Ages, theatre was first performed in churches in the form of "mystery" plays (plays dealing with the birth, death, and resurrection of Christ); but even when the theatre eventually moved outside and the plays were performed on pageant wagons and later on mansion stages, the structure and symbolism of performances were modeled on those that had existed within the churches. The Elizabethan theatre was conceived as a model of the world in which the drama of life took place.

In a theatre in which the space was conceived and constructed as a model of the world, a designer in the modern sense was unnecessary. The playing space did not change from play to play. Every play was performed within the context of an unchanged stage world. When place and setting were defined in a play—and Shakespeare did this best—it was in the language of the poetry:

Knew you not Pompey? Many a time and oft
Have you climbed up to walls and battlements,
To towers and windows, yea, to chimney tops,
Your infants in your arms, and there have sat
The livelong day with patient expectation
To see great Pompey pass the streets of Rome.
Julius Caesar (act 1, scene 1)

In his time Shakespeare was almost unique in this. Certainly none of his contemporaries incorporated so much detail about setting and place into the texts of their plays.

If you look at the stage directions in Elizabethan plays, you will find they are minimal. "Enter," "exeunt," "alarum," "he dies," etc.; little or nothing about the place or time. Compare these to the detailed descriptions of the stage setting in the plays of Ibsen and in

The Globe Theatre was a magical theatre, a cosmic theatre, a religious theatre, an actor's theatre, designed to give fullest support to the voices and gestures of the players as they enacted the drama of the life of man within the Theatre of the World.

Frances Yates, **Theatre of the World**

plays written since. The contrast is instructive. For instance, here are stage directions for the opening scene of Ibsen's *The Wild Duck:*

> *(An expensive-looking and comfortable study in* WERLE's *house; book-cases and upholstered furniture; in the middle of the room a desk with papers and ledgers; lamps with green shades give the room a soft, subdued light. In the rear, open double doors with portieres pulled apart reveal a large, elegant drawing room, brightly illuminated by lamps and candles. Front right, a small door to the office wing. Front left, a fireplace with glowing coals in it. Farther back on the left wall, double doors to the dining room.)*[8]

Contrast this with Shakespeare's directions for the opening of *Hamlet:*

> *Elsinore. A platform before the castle.*

In Elizabethan theatre, while there were certain technical things to accomplish, such as moving from one stage level to another, nothing had to be designed. Insofar as space was defined within this world, it was defined by the actors and the language of the script. By and large, until the end of the sixteenth century stage space was modeled on an image of a divine cosmos.

The Move to Realism

Then things began to change. The idea that there is a single reality revealed to us by divine forces gave way to the Renaissance belief that reality is whatever we perceive with our senses. Since each person perceives things differently, reality is a different and unique thing for each person. The world is no longer what *we experience* in common, but what *I perceive.* The world of the theatre was no longer one world, but many worlds. The history of the theatre since the latter part of the sixteenth century is a history of fragmentation. This shift in thinking affected every aspect of theatrical production in profound ways. It changed the audience's relationship to the stage and hence the design of the theatre building itself. It made the point of view of the individual more important than the collective point of view of society, leading eventually to the emergence of the director as the force who would impose a unified point of view on the performance. It transformed the idea of an actor as a presenter of reality to a person in whom reality must be perceived (in earlier theatre the audience did not identify with the actor as an actual person like themselves). It led to new scenic techniques—especially painted perspective—which, in turn, led to a need for a scene designer.

The painted perspective settings of the Italian Renaissance theatre were related to the growing realism in painting at that time. As painters moved to a more natural representation of the human

figure and its environment, they, too, used perspective. The development of perspective marks the transition from the concept of
the stage as a symbol of the divine world to the idea of depicting our
natural environment as we actually see it. (See photograph on p.
293.) Although the early painted perspective settings look artificial to
us now, they were the beginning of realism (in the sense of a literal
depiction of reality) in the theatre. It was also the beginning of design in the theatre as we have come to know it.

The designer is first recognized as a dominant figure in two
forms of entertainment that might be called spectacles rather than
theatre: the court masques in England and France and the "intermezzi" of the Italian courts. These royal entertainments, popular in
the sixteenth and seventeenth centuries, were elaborate spectacles
with little dramatic content (they were like giant pageants) in which
mythological events and figures of fantasy were presented as
realistically as possible for the pleasure of the nobility. While the
subject of these spectacles was nonrealistic, the designer worked to
achieve realistic effects. The designer, in effect, turned the stage into
a picture. This was first done in Italy by Palladio (1508–1580). In
England the great designer of masques was Inigo Jones, who in 1605
consciously used the proscenium arch as a picture frame to enclose
his production of "The Masque of Blackness." The masques and
intermezzi combined poetry, music, ballet, and choral singing. They
were produced with elaborate settings and extravagant costumes.
At the peak of their popularity, they included fireworks, processions,
and fantastic stage effects. By the middle of the seventeenth century,
there were numerous treatises and handbooks on how to achieve
these fantastic effects.

Now for us there are four things to note about these develop-
ments:

1. The theatre was still presenting mystery, but through realistic
   means. The audience was persuaded that it was experiencing
   mystery as a natural event.
2. The idea developed that theatrical production should create an
   illusion of reality—what appears on the stage must appear real.
   (Of course, there is a contradiction in this. The illusion can never
   be more than illusion. Just as we know the actor is not *really* the
   character he or she is playing, so, too, do we know that the place

represented on the stage is not really the place it depicts. So the designer "tricks" us into thinking it's real, and we willingly cooperate—"the willing suspension of disbelief.")

3. Once the idea is accepted that the environment on stage must show the world as we actually see it, the responsibility for creating the stage environment shifts from the script and the actor to the scene designer. In Shakespeare's theatre, stage sets were minimal by today's standards; space was evoked from one moment to the next by the lines the actor spoke. In *The Merchant of Venice*, for example, the Rialto, Shylock's house, Portia's country estate, and the courtroom were all set in what might be thought of as "neutral" or "fixed" space. It was Shakespeare speaking through the actors who transformed the Rialto into the courtroom and the audience had to actually participate imaginatively in this transformation. With the new convention, place could not be created in this way; it could be accomplished only by a change of scene and this usually meant a change of scenery. This need to design each scene separately led to the development of machinery and techniques to change scenes as rapidly and efficiently as possible.

4. As the conventions of the picture-frame stage became firmly established, the relationship between the audience and the stage began to change. The audience was looking at a "picture" of events taking place within and behind a frame, the proscenium arch. There was a clear-cut demarcation between the two and this was to be enhanced by the development of lighting as an element of production. (The stage is lit, the audience in the auditorium is in darkness, passively looking in.)

The implications of these changes became fully apparent in the second half of the nineteenth century when naturalism became the dominant theatrical style. In naturalist philosophy, life's mysteries could be explained by forces of environment, heredity, economics, and the psyche. This being the case, if the theatre was to present mystery, these forces had to be presented as accurately and as effectively as possible. If the environment really did govern people's lives, then it needed to be shown as it actually was. So each stage setting had to be a unique environment. In the Moscow Art Theatre's production of Gorki's *The Lower Depths*, the set revealed the squalid conditions in which the dregs of society lived. (See photograph on p. 224.) This demand for realism, coupled with the nineteenth-century belief that experience should be viewed with detached objectivity, led to the convention of the "fourth wall" which characterizes the naturalistic theatre.

The fourth-wall convention assumes that what is taking place on stage is actually taking place, as if in another room, and that the audience is looking at it through an invisible fourth wall. The audience must behave as secret watchers (hiding in the darkened auditorium) who must not let the actors know they are watching.

At the end of the last century, this became a dominant convention in theatre. While such a direct representation of reality can be effective, it presented immense problems and three in particular. First, the nature of the settings was increasingly determined more by extratheatrical values and norms—economic, social, political, and psychological conditions—than by the personal vision of the playwright. That is, the designer made decisions based on standards that existed outside the theatre rather than on those inherent in the play. Second, the proscenium stage seemed to encourage the audience to become more and more passive, with the result that the driving energy of all performance—the dynamic interaction between actors and audience—was greatly diminished. Third, no matter how one tries to work within the convention of the fourth wall, it cannot be done. In the end, fourth-wall naturalism isn't natural. Who ever saw a living room with all the furniture facing the same wall (the one that isn't there), with no pictures or electrical outlets on that wall, and with all the big pieces of furniture jammed up against the other three walls? Everything must be arranged so that the actors "living" in that room must usually face the unseen audience sitting outside that invisible fourth wall. Naturalism, for all its desire to create an illusion of reality, is as unreal as any other form of theatre.

The Twentieth Century

People working in the theatre were quick to recognize this. The conventions of staging and setting which have dominated the twentieth-century theatre are a rejection of the naturalists' point of view. For all their differences, one thing that links theatre people as diverse as Gordon Craig, Vsevolod Meyerhold, Max Reinhardt, Bertolt Brecht, Antonin Artaud, Peter Brook, and Richard Schechner has been their insistence that the theatre is a theatre and that its purpose is to make present the world of the play and not some copy of life as it exists outside the theatre.

Nothing could have been more liberating for the designer than this present point of view. Living as we do in a time when there is no single governing metaphysical view of the world, there is no way we can have a symbolic theatre similar to those of earlier times. And theatre has freed itself of the need to be totally realistic. This means the stage is, in effect, an empty and neutral space and each production requires the creation of a new theatrical world, one that will manifest the world of the play. Every production begins at "ground zero." Designers are now free to become a major creative force in the theatre. They have responded with wonderfully imaginative and inventive designs.

The design of all that exists as part of the theatrical setting is crucial. That setting affects the actors' performances, expresses the play's meanings, and shapes the audience's perception of the experience. Every theatrical performance should, to borrow words from *Hamlet:*

amaze indeed
The very faculties of eyes and ears.

NOTES

[1]Richard Schechner. *Environmental Theater.* New York: Hawthorn Books, Inc., 1973, p. 213.

[2]Jean Genet. *The Balcony.* New York: Grove Press, Inc., 1958, p. 1.

[3]David Cole. *The Theatrical Event.* Middletown: Wesleyan University Press, 1975.

[4]Hal Buron, editor. Interview with John Gielgud by Derek Hart in *Great Acting.* New York: Hill & Wang by arrangement with the British Broadcasting Corporation, 1967, p. 143.

[5]Lee Simonson. *The Stage Is Set.* New York: Harcourt, Brace Jovanovich, Inc., 1932, pp. 365–66.

[6]Aeschylus. *Agamemnon,* trans. by George Thomson, as it appeared in *The Oresteia Trilogy,* ed. by Robert W. Corrigan. New York: Dell Publishing Co., Inc., 1965, p. 29.

[7]Mircea Eliade. *The Sacred and the Profane.* New York: Harcourt, Brace Jovanovich, Inc., 1959, p. 29. This book is a rich source of material on the nature of sacred spaces.

[8]Henrik Ibsen. *The Wild Duck,* trans. by Otto Reinert, as it appeared in *The Modern Theatre,* ed. by Robert W. Corrigan. New York: Macmillan Company, 1964, p. 342.

Chapter 9

AH!
LA PÉ...LA PÉ...
LA PÉPINIÈRE !!!
REVUE
en deux actes et quatre tableaux de M.M.
ALBERT PAJOL et ADOLPHE COUTURET
AIRS NOUVEAUX MUSIQUE ARRANGÉE et BALLET de M. JACOUTOT
Costumes dessinés par JAPHET exécutés par Mme Louise CAFFARD, décors de M. MÉNESSIER
DISTRIBUTION
Tous les Soirs à 9½ h. DIMANCHES et FÊTES MATINÉES à 2 HEURES
CONCERT de la PÉPINIÈRE (près la gare St Lazare.)
PAJOL & Cie EDITEURS 27, Rue Bergère

The theatre is a place of entertainment.

    But how puny we have made the term!

Entertainment, as we now commonly view it, is merely pastime.

    Is our leisure more dreary to us than our working hours presumably are?

I am entertained when my interest has been aroused,

    when my detached capacity for feeling, thought,

    sentiment, laughter, and passion are brought into play.

I am entertained when my senses are quickened,

    my soul touched, my mind alerted.

Being healthy, I cannot be fed adulterated stimulants or strong sedatives;

    nor am I gratified by timid stabs at my sensibilities.

I want my entertainment to exercise my faculties as vigorously

    and as completely as possible.

    The tired businessman's place is not in the theatre, but in bed.

Harold Clurman, **Lies Like Truth**

The Audience
and the Theatrical Event

I n the opening chapter we described going to the theatre—the air of excitement in the lobby, the sense of anticipation as we settle into our seats. As we wait for a performance to begin, there is always an atmosphere of expectancy and excitement. We know this is a special occasion and we are conscious of the fact that the people sitting around us feel the same way. We are not just part of a crowd, we are members of a special group. We are an audience, and our presence, together with the actors' presence, creates the theatrical event. While it is true there can be no performance without an actor, the theatrical event does not occur until a group of spectators gathers together in a theatre to experience and participate in the performance which the actors make present for them. The audience is the final essential participant in theatre.

We have observed several times that the origins of theatre can be traced back to the ritual performances of the shamans of primitive cultures. The shaman is the envoy of the tribe, who by means of trance gets to the other world of the gods and/or the dead. The shaman is sent by the tribe to fulfill its need to be in touch with the mysterious realm of both the eternally living and the dead. His journey has meaning and power only because the members of the tribe grant it those qualities. Their belief that his journey will satisfy their needs gives the shaman's performance both its power and its credibility. Without that credibility, which only the tribe can provide, the shaman's performance could not exist.

The same thing is true of the theatrical performance. It is a reciprocating event in which the audience is an indispensable partner. Both performers and audience are necessary sources of energy, and if the flow of that energy between them does not exist or is broken for any reason, the performance will cease to exist. Whether it be at the Festival of Dionysus in ancient Greece, a performance of Shakespeare in Central Park in New York City, or a show at the local dinner theatre, the community of performers and audience accomplishes the magic that we call theatre. Theatre exists because we, the audience, need it to exist and agree to let it exist. Because each one of us has a deep need to be in touch with the mysterious, we agree to the kind of activity that makes those mysteries present for us in the theatrical event.

THE AUDIENCE'S EXPECTATIONS

Since going to the theatre is such a special occasion, we come to it with certain well-defined expectations which we hope will be satisfied by the performance. First, we expect the play to be related in some way to our own life experience. This does not mean that we expect to have actually experienced the events taking place on stage—it is unlikely that we will have—but rather that we expect

The art of theatre attracts and seduces to the extent that it pictures to man and woman a momentary vitality from which the imagination derives a pleasure often more durable than that of sex.

Vitality and pleasure, and . . . an all-embracing, constant, daily need for untruth. . . . Yes, the deception of ourselves by others and of others by ourselves is that natural demon in us which leads to theatre. . . . For creatures and things deceive us constantly, even the most faithful and sure. Few, if any, of our admirations and loves are free of illusion; that is, of errors of judgment, if not of outright lies. Everything in the realm of the senses and imagination . . . is subject to vagaries, hesitations, instability. There is no human work or creature which, in the light of some revealing happening, is not finally seen in its true contradictions. And there is no art which more necessarily unites illusions and reality than theatre. . . .

Truth and lies. Secrets and exposure. Theatre, in its essence, is made of our essence. It will never die.

Jean Vilar, "Secrets"

---

them to be authentic in terms of our feelings and experience. For example, none of us has actually experienced what happens to Macbeth, but we know what it is to be driven by an overpowering ambition, to be visited by the ghosts of a guilty conscience, to be undone by unexpected circumstances. We are moved by Shakespeare's play because it rings true in terms of what we know about ourselves. Similarly, Tennessee Williams's *The Glass Menagerie* deals with characters and situations that may not be a part of the lives of most audiences, yet we all recognize that the need for daydreams and self-delusion has something in common with ourselves and people we know. In short, we go to the theatre expecting the performance to be an authentic representation of some aspect of life as we know or can imagine it.

Perhaps more important, we go to the theatre expecting the performance to be presented in a manner and form we are used to. These expectations are largely based on plays we have already seen. We enjoy having what pleases us repeated. For this reason, we may have difficulty understanding and enjoying a play by Shakespeare or some other work of the classic repertoire the first time we see one, especially if this is our initial theatre experience. The expectations of most people going to the theatre for the first time today are based on their experience of television or the movies. The language, the complexities of plot, and the breaks into scenes and acts in *Hamlet* and *As You Like It* are a far cry from a typical Hollywood movie or the latest popular TV detective series. Yet our experience of television can be instructive. We enjoy the detective series on TV partly because its patterns of sameness are satisfying to us. We know what the form will be; we are "hip" to its special gimmicks and devices; we look forward to the variations, but we count on the fixed structure and the recurring theme. The popularity of a television series is in large part the result of its meeting the expectations that it initially created in us.

Much the same thing happens in theatre. If our experience of it has been limited to summer-stock comedies and musicals, we will probably find a production of Chekhov, Brecht, or Genet a jarring and/or boring experience. Similarly, as Joseph Papp discovered at the Repertory Theatre of Lincoln Center in New York City, so-called "sophisticated" audiences who are used to the classics and expect the theatre to be a museum of masterpieces are disappointed by productions of experimental new plays. Even audiences of avant-garde productions come to the theatre with certain expectations that have been shaped by their previous theatregoing experience. No matter what our previous experience, we come wanting what we have known and enjoy having it repeated.

This expectation can have some interesting variations. Children who have had no experience of theatre (and hence have no expec-tations) can often respond enthusiastically to productions that bore or mystify the parents who take them. Or to take a striking example of another kind: When first performed in the 1950s, Beckett's *Waiting for Godot* was found by many audiences to be little more than an incomprehensible clown show. They saw little or nothing in the performance of the play that related either to what they thought theatre should be or how they experienced their own lives. That is, it didn't appear to relate to their own self-dramas or the life-dramas they saw taking place around them. They tended to reject the play. In 1957, the Actor's Workshop of San Francisco presented *Waiting for Godot* for the inmates of San Quentin prison. Most of the mem-bers of this very special audience had never seen a play and they certainly were not sophisticated theatregoers. Yet they responded to the performance with enthusiasm. Everything about the play was very clear to them. They found the bitterness and hopelessness, the anguish and frustration, and the meaninglessness of waiting im-mediately and powerfully recognizable.[1] Today, more than twenty years later, there have been so many productions of *Waiting for Godot* and similar plays that audiences no longer are baffled by it. They have grown used to experimental drama of this kind and feel comfortable with Beckett's play because it meets their expectations of what a serious experimental play is supposed to be. By now, of course, *Waiting for Godot* is no longer experimental—if it ever was. It has become a classic of the modern repertoire.

The fact that a play like *Waiting for Godot* is now accepted by most people who go to the theatre tells us something else significant about the expectations of audiences. We may want the performances to be like what we are accustomed to, but we also want to be surprised. We want going to the theatre to be a moving, joyful, and exhilarating experience. The theatre gives us a heightened sense of life and self-awareness, and also a sense of new possibilities. It is like a prism which captures the sun's diffuse rays and gives them a burning focus. Life experience—whether it be of joy or sorrow, aspiration or despair, accomplishment or frustration— when re-created on stage has a sharpness and clarity that it does not normally have outside the theatre. We go to plays hoping we will have a fuller and deeper understanding of the real and imagined dramas of our own lives. When this understanding happens, the satisfaction overpowers our need to have what we are used to.

We are also attracted to theatre because we expect that all of the issues raised by the play will be resolved. Resolution is satisfying. We want evil punished and virtue rewarded; we like it when true love triumphs and seemingly impossible obstacles are overcome; we need to feel there is a cause-and-effect relationship between error and suffering. We like clear-cut resolutions and we expect the theatre to provide them, even though we know our problems are seldom so neatly resolved in real life.

Thus far in discussing the audience's expectations we have been concerned with the interaction of the audience with the production itself. But our expectations are also governed by another powerful force: the presence of other people in the audience. The audience comes to the theatre to be precisely that—an audience. This explains why various forms of participatory theatre usually fail—except as a novelty—in their attempts to get the audience more involved. We come to the theatre precisely because an "other" world is being made present in our presence. It is all well and good to insist that the world of the play is related to the world we normally live in outside the theatre, and it is probably true that we present ourselves in theatrical ways in much of our everyday behavior. However, we go to the theatre not because it is like life but because it is "other." Since it is, we can, while there, cast off our social roles and remain *unpresented*. We actually want to become a member of an audience, which is a very special state.[2]

T heatrical dichotomy is the double experience that is at the heart of
all theatre-going. The audience knows they are in a theatre watching a play that is make-believe, it's not really happening. They see before them actors on a stage who pretend to be certain people and pretend
to be in a particular, developing situation; the actors invite the audience
to join in this make-believe. And, given a good theatrical experience, the
audience does indeed enter into the play, it allows itself to be carried
away, but for most of the time the audience is well aware of reality. It
doesn't lose itself entirely in the fantasy world. A double experience is
taking place: the audience is caught up in the play and yet it's also
aware that it's part of an audience sitting in a theatre. The audience
plays at make-believe and knows that it is playing. . . . The audience
connives with the actors and with each other. They play together and in
playing they enter into a particular relationship with the others in the
theatre.

Ann Jellicoe, "Some Unconscious Influences in the Theatre"

Being in an audience satisfies a deeply felt human need: participating in a collective response. We look forward to sharing our
responses with the people sitting next to and around us. (When we
say "laughter is contagious," we mean that we are infected by the
joyous response of those sitting around us.) We become very aware
of the dynamics of an audience at the conclusion of a production of a
powerful and moving play. Frequently, there is silence. This doesn't
indicate disapproval, but rather that everyone has been so deeply
moved that applause seems inappropriate because it would break
the mood everyone shares. (In large audiences some people will
feel embarrassed by this and will begin to clap because they believe it is expected. This is understandable because there are audience conventions as well as the conventions of performance which
we discussed earlier. Applause is such a convention. It is the audience's way of communicating back to the actors. It acknowledges
the entrance of a star, our satisfaction with the set, our approval of
the performance.)
    The fact that the audience responds to itself as much as to the
performance becomes apparent when we observe audiences clap-
ping at the end of a movie. Clearly, the members of the audience
are expressing their pleasure at what they have just seen. They are
probably also reacting to the reinforcing effect of liking something *as
a group*. Similarly, with television: We miss the sensations of viewing as a member of an audience, so producers often provide us with
one—a sound track of audience responses. Our reaction to TV pro-

ductions of plays or reruns of movies is totally different from our reaction to live theatre because we are not sharing the experience with an audience. The audience needs feedback from itself and this need is one of the major elements in our experience of theatre.

THE THEATRE'S RESPONSE

As members of an audience, we go to the theatre with certain expectations and we count on their being fulfilled. But the playwright has an equally legitimate right to fulfill the truth of his or her vision as it is re-created in theatrical form, even if it means violating the audience's expectations. This condition is always a source of potential conflict. In fact, one could write an interesting history of the theatre based upon the interaction of these two legitimate and potentially conflicting rights. On the one hand, the playwright gives the audience what it wants. On the other, the playwright must be true to his or her own vision of reality.

This has always been an issue. For example, Sophocles was extremely popular at the Festivals of Dionysus because he wrote his plays in an accustomed form and presented the tragic nature of humanity in terms that were accepted by the majority of the community. Euripides, on the other hand, while an equally accomplished playwright, was relatively unsuccessful because he rejected those terms and used new and (to the audience) alien forms. In Elizabethan times Ben Jonson was the favorite of the educated intellectuals because he used the classic themes and forms of the Renaissance tradition. Shakespeare was not highly regarded by this group because he violated the then-accepted rules of the theatre and wrote for the popular audience. By the second half of the nineteenth century, when the theatre had become firmly established as a commercial enterprise, this conflict became especially clear. Theatre was marked then by the continual struggle between what audiences wanted and what playwrights believed to be the truth. Ibsen, Strindberg, Chekhov, and Shaw were not only rebelling against the full-blown romantic plays and popular melodramas that dominated the nineteenth-century stage, they were determined

The audience ... isn't really responding at all to the ideas of the dramatist but to a magical, an almost ritual occasion which he has envisaged and realized.

Lionel Trilling, "All Aboard the Seesaw"

to dramatize what they believed were the central issues and conflicts of the time, even if their work was unpopular and unrecognized. And audiences, indeed, found their plays disturbing and unpleasant.

Box office and art are even more at odds today. Broadway is openly commercial. So are summer theatres, musical tent theatres, and dinner theatres. Art, yes, but making money is the name of the game. And to make money you give the consumer public what it wants or what you think it wants. This does not mean productions in these commercial theatres are not well done. For the most part, they are produced with considerable professionalism by very talented artists. But they are clearly intended to satisfy the audience's expectations, not challenge them. We are in New York City on vacation and we want an evening of fun in the theatre with glitter and glamour. It is a hot summer night and we go to the theatre to laugh and relax. Friends come for a visit and we take them to a dinner theatre for good food, pleasant conversation, and entertainment. We pay our money and enjoy ourselves. This is theatre as a pastime where we can forget the cares of our daily routine, and as such it serves an important and valid function. But it is not a theatre that seeks to surprise us, make us more aware, test our ideas and attitudes, expand our consciousness, jar our preconceptions, or reveal to us the truth of our natures—including its own limitations and paradoxes.

The conflict between the audience's expectations and the artist's aims is clearly defined when you look closely at two types of twentieth-century theatre: the musical theatre and the theatre of the avant-garde.

Musical Theatre

The musical is probably the most popular form of theatre in the world today and has certainly been America's greatest contribution to the history of the theatre. Its origins can be traced to the operettas so popular in Europe during the nineteenth and early twentieth centuries. The musical is neither a watered-down opera nor a souped-up play. It is a hybrid form which in recent decades has incorporated into itself jazz, cabaret, burlesque, dance, the musical revue, and elaborate spectacle. The musical is not a dramatic form in the sense that tragedy and comedy are, since it is not governed by a dominant way of looking at life. But like all the dramatic forms, it draws upon many possible sources: nonmusical plays, stories, novels, old movies, and even comic strips.

It is easy to like musicals. They have something to please everyone. They are not threatening and seldom make demands on us. This is due in part to the fact that they usually present an upbeat view of life, have relatively simple character types that are easy to

Above: **Oklahoma!** (1943). The first of many great successes by the team of Richard Rodgers and Oscar Hammerstein II. Often referred to as the first "modern" musical, it was highlighted by the choreography of Agnes De Mille.

Below: **My Fair Lady** (1956). Alan Jay Lerner and Frederick Loewe's musical version of George Bernard Shaw's **Pygmalion.** Starring Rex Harrison as Professor Higgins and Julie Andrews as Eliza Doolittle, it reintroduced the "patter" song which had been so popular in the comic operettas of Gilbert and Sullivan.

Left: **West Side Story** (1957). Leonard Bernstein's celebration of New York City. Full of beauty and violence, the play dealt with the conflicts and aspirations of ghetto youth. Marked by a serious theme (racial prejudice) and sophisticated music, it showed the musical theatre's ever-widening range.

Below: **Cabaret** (1966). Based on Christopher Isherwood's stories of decadence and despair in Berlin in the 1920s, **Cabaret** was one of the most popular musicals of its decade. Joel Grey starred in the original production, which borrowed some of its most dazzling effects from Bertolt Brecht's **The Three-Penny Opera.**

Right: **The Wiz** (1975). A musical based on L. Frank Baum's **The Wizard of Oz**. Directed and choreographed by Donald Mac-Kayle, the success of **The Wiz** was clear evidence that black theatre had entered the mainstream of the commercial theatre.

Below: **A Chorus Line** (1975). In the 1970s the director-choreographer became as important to the musical as the composer and lyricist. Richard Bennett's play about the struggles and inner tensions of Broadway dancers also confirmed the old truth that audiences are fascinated by plays based on the theatre itself.

identify with, have plot lines that are not difficult to follow, and end happily. We are also attracted by the magnificent stage settings and costumes which are so lovely to look at, and by the often dazzling choreography of the dance numbers which are so exciting to watch. But the chief reason for musicals' popularity is the music itself.

The musical is ideally suited to themes of romance, idealism, and aspiration. (Even when the subject matter of the lyrics is sad—such as in a blues song—the music itself is affirming.) In its climactic moments, the musical presents drama through the medium of song. Any dissonance in the conflicts of the plot is resolved by the harmonies of the score. The world as presented in the musical is often the way we wish life would be, even if we know that it seldom is.

Perhaps it is this essentially optimistic view of life that accounts for the phenomenal growth of the musical theatre in the 1930s and 1940s. Our theatre has had musicals in some form since the middle of the nineteenth century (the first big American musical was *The Black Crook* in 1866), but it was Jerome Kern's *Showboat* (1927) that first began to combine several of the elements which we now associate with this form. Shortly thereafter, the combination of the Great Depression and World War II made American audiences receptive to the romantic sentiments, upbeat themes, and the bright production numbers that characterized the musicals of that era. George S. Kaufman and Moss Hart's *Of Thee I Sing* (1930) was a delightful spoof of American election campaigns. George Gershwin's *Porgy and Bess* (1935) was a hauntingly beautiful version of DuBose and Dorothy Heyward's novel of the Gullah blacks. *Pins and Needles* (1937), produced by the International Ladies Garment Workers Union, was so popular it was performed at the White House. The 1940s were the decade of the blockbusters. To a nation exhausted by a global war, Rodgers and Hammerstein's *Oklahoma!* (1943), *Carousel* (1945), and *South Pacific* (1949), Irving Berlin's *Annie Get Your Gun* (1946), Leonard Bernstein's *On the Town* (1944), and the delightful fantasies *Brigadoon* (1947) and *Finian's Rainbow* (1947) were much needed tonics. *Oklahoma!* and *South Pacific* were particularly noteworthy: the first introduced ballet (the choreography of Agnes De Mille) into the musical; the second introduced the shadows of serious themes into the form. Since the 1950 production of Frank Loesser's *Guys and Dolls*, the musical theatre has been wonderfully wide-ranging and eclectic (and increasingly expensive to produce). Mention of just a few of the biggest hits—*My Fair Lady* (1956), *West Side Story* (1957), *Fiddler on the Roof* (1964), *Man of La Mancha* (1965), *Jesus Christ Superstar* (1971), *A Chorus Line* (1975), *The Wiz* (1975), *Ain't Misbehavin'* (1978)—suggests how all-embracing the form has become.

The musical theatre has great staying power. The music and lyrics of some of its best songs live on long after the production has closed. The works of George Gershwin, Cole Porter, Richard Rodgers, Lorenz Hart, Oscar Hammerstein II, Leonard Bernstein, and

Stephen Sondheim have entered the mainstream of our popular culture. We all know their songs, which are recorded by nearly every pop vocalist and instrumental group. We look forward to revivals of the musicals in which they originally appeared. It is like seeing an old friend. The music of musical theatre is not ephemeral, but has a life of its own. This prompts regular new productions in high schools, colleges, and community theatres, professional revivals, and movie and TV versions. All of these productions create new audiences who, in turn, have expectations that the musical has created.

The musical is the ultimate form of consumer theatre today. It appeals to a mass audience and it is capable of generating new audiences. While expensive to produce, it generates a great deal of money; it can continually perpetuate itself. Most important, it has shaped and continues to shape people's expectations of theatre and at the same time it gives them what they want in return. When audiences buy tickets to a musical, they generally believe they are getting full value for their money.

The Avant-Garde Theatre

While the musical frankly attempts to satisfy audience expectations, the avant-garde just as strongly tries to jar or upset them. "Avant-garde" is a Napoleonic military term referring to the first wave of soldiers who enter into battle, and it was first used in reference to the arts in 1825. It is related to the ideas of revolution and progress and its origins can be traced to the emergence of the romantic movement in the last quarter of the eighteenth century. Avant-garde artists are the makers of change, the revolutionaries who storm the frontiers of the new.

Given the fact that every work of art is the product of an individual artist's personal vision of the world, change in art is inevitable. Historically, these changes have occurred so gradually as to be hardly noticeable at the time. While we can look back and discover periods of profound—even revolutionary—change in the arts, these periods were usually not experienced as revolutionary. Rather, change was a part of a slow, ongoing evolutionary process. There is no question that such change did provoke some kind of antagonistic response from audiences. For example, as noted earlier, when Euripides introduced new themes and stylistic devices into the classical Greek theatre, he was probably reflecting the tensions and social upheavals of the fifth-century world more accurately—and more disturbingly—than his older colleague Sophocles. Euripides was seldom awarded the first prize at the festivals; Sophocles often was. For all of that, Euripides was not thought of as a revolutionary by his contemporaries, and later Aristotle considered his innovations as part of the evolution of classical dramatic form.

For the last one hundred years, change in the arts has been thought of more in terms of revolution than evolution, and the pace of change has become increasingly rapid. The plays of Ibsen, Strindberg, and Chekhov are quite conventional to us today, but at the end of the last century they seemed radically new and angered most audiences. The same thing was true of the expressionists, symbolists, and dadaists of the first decades of this century. Playwrights like Frank Wedekind (1864–1918), Ernst Toller (1893–1939), and Luigi Pirandello (1867–1936) believed the plays of their nineteenth-century predecessors were outmoded and they sought to create revolutionary new forms. The "theatre of the absurd," which dominated the theatre in the 1950s, consciously rejected the mechanical plots, stereotyped characters, and carefully hewn dialogue of the Naturalist theatre.

During the past decade numerous groups have been experimenting with new modes of performance. The Living Theatre was determined to obliterate the distinctions between theatre and life and eventually moved out of the theatre altogether. The Open Theatre developed works that had no conventional dialogue. Andre Gregory, Richard Schechner, and Andrei Serban reworked old plays in startling new ways. Charles Ludlam and Richard Foreman dealt with themes of sex, death, and violence in terms that had been taboo. Robert Wilson created lengthy productions with non-actors that were meant to stretch the audience's attention (and nerves) to the breaking point. Peter Brook and Herbert Blau have been experimenting with performance spaces, poetic texts, and abstract patterns of movement in an effort to make the theatre more expressive.

The point is, the work of each of these innovators has tended to provoke a violent and usually negative audience reaction when first produced. This was so because they were consciously—to use Ibsen's phrase again—"fighting a war to the knife" with the theatre of the past.

The dominant characteristic of the avant-garde has always been this antagonistic spirit. And the antagonism of avant-garde art always induces uneasiness in audiences. In fact, uneasiness may be a key word in what critic Harold Rosenberg has referred to as the "tradition of the new." For avant-garde artists, a work of art is expected to throw the audience off balance; it *should* violate the audience's expectations. Now in a way all art has always done this, but avant-garde artists are antagonistic in a profoundly different way. Because they are committed to originality, the new and the novel are the hallmarks of their creativity. Genuineness of vision requires avoiding anything that has been done before; and genuineness of craftsmanship means refusing to repeat old techniques. But this creates the artists' biggest problem: they are always struggling with the burden of history. It is difficult and probably impossible to create anything that is totally new and uninfluenced by the past.

Right: One of the most powerful American experimental groups in the 1970s is Herbert Blau's Kraken Company. Its production of **Seeds of Atreus,** based on the **Oresteia** of Aeschylus, explored the ancient play's haunting themes by combining vocal, verbal, and visual metaphors into ritualistic patterns.

Below: Victor Garcia has been one of the theatre's daring directors in recent years. His setting for Jean Genet's **The Balcony** was a sixty-five foot funnel with a parabolic mirror at its base. Perhaps his most striking production was of Federico Garcia Lorca's tragedy **Yerma,** which was performed on a gigantic trampoline.

THE AVANT-GARDE THEATRE

Richard Foreman founded the Ontological-Hysteric Theatre in 1968. **Sophia = (Wisdom), Part 3: The Cliffs** was first produced in 1973. In his **Manifesto** (1972), Foreman proclaims his confrontational aims: "Only one theatrical problem exists now: How to create a stage performance in which the spectator experiences the danger of art not as involvement or risk or excitement, not something that reaches out to vulnerable areas of his person, but rather the danger as a possible **decision** he (spectator) may make upon the occasion of confronting the work of art."

THE AVANT-GARDE THEATRE

Peter Brook has been one of the twentieth century's excitingly eclectic directors. In recent years he has been primarily concerned with developing new kinds of theatrical environments. Shown here are theatrical exercises performed in an African village in 1973.

One of the dominant characteristics of the avant-garde is its tendency to break down the distinctions among traditional art forms. Stephanie Evanitsky's Multigravitational Aerodance Group has been exploring the boundary zones between theatre and dance. **Carry** was choreographed in 1973. Like all of Evanitsky's work, it is performed on a large scaffold in midair.

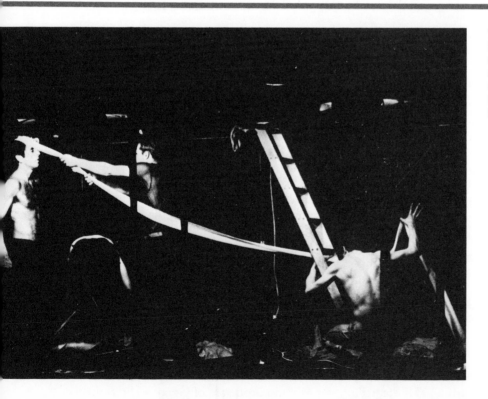

The Living Theatre, an innovative group active in the 1950s and 1960s, frequently aroused controversy because of its actor-audience confrontations. Here is its production of **Frankenstein** in the late 60s.

Furthermore, because avant-garde artists create for the future they must create not only the work, but the audience as well. And audiences willing to be jolted as avant-garde artists wish to jolt them are not easily come by. This explains why avant-garde artists tend to feel alienated and isolated, and why the rest of us very often think of them as self-serving and even subversive. The very success of an avant-garde movement creates the opposition that will eventually put it out of fashion.

The avant-garde, by taking the innate tendency of all art to be antagonistic toward its audience and making that antagonism the conscious and central premise of the artist-audience relationship, is always drastically changing both the audience's expectations and responses to works of art. This has been particularly true in the theatre, where every significant new development in dramatic structure, performance, technique, and style of production that has occurred in the twentieth century has had its origins in some form of assault on the audience's conventional expectations. The result has been that those audiences have tended to have an initial hostile response to all "new" theatre. The antagonism of audiences is a response in great part to the antagonism they sense in avant-garde theatre. It is important to see at the same time that change is rarely comfortable and that many of the theatre conventions we now take for granted were met angrily by earlier audiences.

THE AUDIENCE'S REACTION
Shock and Beguilement

The presence in most societies of some form of the avant-garde is the best evidence of the antagonism that always exists between the playwright and the audience. In the avant-garde theatre, expectations which the audience wants fulfilled by the performance are usually at odds with the world of the play that the playwright has discovered. Yet we in the audience unconsciously know this and we keep coming to the theatre in spite of ourselves in the hopes that an authentic representation of the wonders of humankind will be made present for us. We want to be beguiled, as we are with musicals. Sometimes we need to be shocked. Shock and beguilement. These are the principal means whereby the artists of the theatre transform the audience's conventional responses into a new awareness.

We are beguiled by the magic of the performance itself and by the glamour of the occasion. Not just the glamour of "stars," openings and bright lights, dressing up, feasting and drinks—few of us will ever experience all this although one should never underestimate the attractiveness of the idea—but the glamour of "forbidden fruit." The disturbing yet exciting eroticism of Genet's *The Balcony*. The suave urbanity of Noel Coward or Maggie Smith. The overwhelming and commanding presence of Laurence Olivier or Paul Scofield, Irene Worth or Helene Weigel as they embody our darkest ambitions, deepest greed, aspirations to integrity, yearnings for happiness. The theatre is a sexy, violent, energetic, visceral, menacing, fun, and thought-provoking place that has beguiling power.

But it shocks us, too. Jean-Paul Sartre, writing about the plays of Beckett, Ionesco, and Genet, makes just this point:

> Far from being in any way afraid of shocking audiences, all the authors I have mentioned deliberately try to shock them, since the result of shock should be some sort of relaxation of inhibitions. I believe that Beckett was speaking for all of them when he exclaimed as he heard the whole audience frantically applauding the first night of *Waiting for Godot*, "My God, there must be something wrong, it isn't possible, they're applauding it!" Because in fact all these playwrights . . . maintain that, strictly speaking, audiences ought not to accept a play until after they have been shocked to the core.[3]

An incident that I experienced will illustrate what Sartre means. In 1966, a modern version of a medieval mystery play was performed instead of a sermon on Easter Sunday at the Church of St. Mark's in the Bowery in New York City. This seemed a strange choice since at the time the church—the home of Theatre Genesis—was one of the nation's centers for avant-garde performance. People came to the church wondering, "Why would St. Mark's be putting on something as old-fashioned as this?" The service began using the traditional liturgy and proceeded uneventfully to the point where the performance would occur.

The minister was in the pulpit making the weekly announcements when suddenly "all hell" broke loose. Grotesquely dressed actors stormed up the aisle. Some grabbed hold of the minister and brutally dragged him out of the church; others went to the sanctuary and broke the candles, threw the crucifix and communion vessels out of the chancel, and jumped up on the altar. They literally ravaged the place. The congregation—including the many people who had come to see the play rather than to worship—was numb with shock. Suddenly, the main actors who were to perform the Gospel story of Christ's death and resurrection entered the chancel. King Herod was chewing on a raw bone of meat, blood slobbering down his chin and over his clothes; soldiers were making an ear-shattering din; other actors were performing in the most bestial ways. Into the midst of this was led a hippie-looking Christ, dressed only in a loincloth, writhing in pain and dripping blood because of the "crown of thorns" made of spikes and nails that had been placed with great force upon his head. He was scourged, tried, condemned, and led to the now-desecrated altar. Laid out upon the altar, he was then lowered behind it, as if into a tomb, to a chorus of raucous shouts and laughter. Soon the chancel cleared of actors.

The people in the congregation were stunned. They felt violated, and the sudden empty silence only increased these feelings. One sensed that they were about to respond in rebellious outrage. Suddenly, in the midst of this tense and intense silence, a hand appeared from behind the altar and gradually the nude body of the figure of Christ appeared. He had risen! Now everyone in the congregation—no matter what their religious beliefs, including the lack of them—had *experienced* the mystery of the resurrection.

This was not some Sunday School pageant, but a violent and brutal reenactment of the central drama of the Christian church. Believers and nonbelievers alike had been brought to a powerful new awareness of one of the central experiences of Western culture. And this awareness was achieved by our shattering experience of the whole production.

Now obviously most theatre does not shock our sensibilities in such an extreme way. But if you think of the theatre's great plays—Oedipus' bleeding, empty eye sockets, Medea's murders, Gloucester's eyes being stamped into jelly, the sudden appearance of Pirandello's six characters, the vicious anger of George and Martha's arguments in Albee's *Who's Afraid of Virginia Woolf?* the frightening and grotesque masochism of *Marat/Sade*—you will discover that shock has always been one of the theatre's most powerful means of transforming the audience's normal expectations into new perceptions.

But do we want to be shocked? Do we want to come to a new awareness? Do we want our normal expectations transformed into new perceptions? On a conscious level, probably not. One of the reasons we have such ambivalent responses to theatre is that each performance forces us to face certain difficult questions that each of us must face; questions that come out of our repressed and secret lives. The questions Orestes asks his sister Electra over the tomb of their murdered father in the second part of Aeschylus' *Oresteia:* "Are you alive?" "Where are you living?" "What is your life?" The questions Hamlet asks at Ophelia's grave as he contemplates the skull of Yorick. The distraught Masha's question to Dr. Dorn in Chekhov's *The Sea Gull:* "Why am I in mourning for my life?" Gogo's and Didi's questions as they wait for Godot.

These are first and last questions. The performance of any play poses questions having to do with the purposes of being, the direction of our lives, the way we live our lives, the fact of our mortality, and it poses them in such a way—the direct and living confrontation of the actors/characters who embody them—that we in the audience must ask ourselves, as Hamlet asks imploringly of the ghost of his father: "Say, why is this?" "What should we do?" Of all of the arts, only theatre forces us to confront these kinds of questions every time we experience it. It is little wonder, then, that the theatre evokes such mixed responses within us. These may be questions we need to deal with, but who wants to face them at the end of a hard day? This

W e are quite willing to be made sad and to weep at a show; we
refuse to be troubled by any difference or difficulty in the
dramatist's sense of life.

   We do not say that we cannot abide the pessimism in Williams's
Camino Real (it is not pessimistic but romantic); we say it is incomprehensible. We do not confront the core of Godot's bitterness; we say it
is unintelligible. We do not object to the brutality in Shakespeare because we do not actually relate to Shakespeare: he represents
"poetry"—which may be translated as high-minded entertainment. . . .

   Our inability to see theatre as real communication through the
mask of fable makes us increasingly customers for the confection of
slick expression and tidy craftsmanship—a form of fancy packaging—
qualities which need not be disdained but which the majority of the
most important plays do not possess.

Harold Clurman, Lies Like Truth

reaction cannot be dismissed as unworthy or unserious. It raises
central issues about our experience of theatre: Why do we go to the
theatre?

   It is undeniable that at times we go to escape the daily routine.
Most of us occasionally want the arts to be diverting, to turn us away
from the limitations of reality, to distract us from the complexity of
our lives. In fact, many people argue that this should be the chief
function of the arts. Theatre is neither exempt from nor immune to
this attitude. Much of theatre (not to mention movies, television, and
novels) serves this need for evasion and diversion. A large number
of plays and other forms of performance evade the tough answers
implicit in the very questions they raise, soften harshness, and blur
crucial distinctions. In the end, however, plays of this sort are un-
satisfactory. While we may be temporarily overcome by sweet sen-
timent or sadness or other vague good feelings, before long an
awareness of the play's unreality (moral, not aesthetic) comes over
us. There has been something unsatisfying, empty, or false about
the experience. More often than not, we pass this awareness off or
just forget about the whole thing. Whatever our reaction, if the play
lets us do this, the theatre has failed to fulfill its primary function.

Responses, True and False

Two well-known modern plays are an interesting contrast in what
they tell us about playwrights' treatment of issues and audiences'
reactions. One play does not look contrived yet clearly is, and one
appears to be contrived but, in fact, is not.

Robert Anderson's *Tea and Sympathy* (1949) was a very successful play when it was first produced. It is an example of an apparently serious but morally evasive play. Its three main characters are a "jock"-type preparatory schoolteacher whose aggressive, overt masculinity disguises uncertainty about his sexual identity; his attractive, patient, and unfulfilled wife; and a sensitive young teenage boy who is more interested in poetry and music than he is in athletics and the "rah-rah" attitudes of the teacher. Continually challenged by the older man, the boy comes to doubt his own identity and fears that he may be "the queer." The woman, observing this process, tries without success to persuade her husband to change his attitude and behavior toward the boy. Finally, she determines that the only way the boy can be assured of his masculinity is to have a heterosexual experience and the play ends with the lights gradually dimming as she joins the boy in bed.

Audiences were very moved by the play and particularly by its last scene. But that scene is a cheap and easy way out of the issues that the play raised. In fact, it unintentionally raises even more difficult issues. What reason have we to believe that being gently seduced by an older woman is going to solve the boy's problem? Are identity crises so easily solved? What about the guilts—Oedipal or other—that the boy will feel? And what about the moral implications of the woman's decision? Given the value system built into the play, can she commit adultery without deep personal consequence? All of these questions are blurred by those dimming lights. The play's resolution is right out of sentimental, romantic "pulp" fiction.

In contrast to this, let us consider Brecht's *The Caucasian Chalk Circle*, a play based on the old fable of King Solomon's decision concerning who was the "true" mother of a child—its actual blood mother or the woman who loved and cared for it. The play is written in two parts. Part I shows the servant woman Grusha picking up the infant prince who has been "forgotten" by his mother the queen as she escapes to safety in the midst of a palace revolution. Grusha's only motivation is a natural instinct for goodness. She flees with the child, knowing that the revolutionaries want to kill him, shares what little she has with him, uses her last pennies to buy him milk, tries to abandon him herself but finds she cannot, gives up her fiancé and marries a horrible man—all to protect the child. As she says, her life and the child's have "become one." Then we learn that a counter-revolution has been successful and that the queen has been restored to power. This section of the play ends with the capture of Grusha and the child. Now a young boy, the prince is to be returned to his real mother, who wants him not out of love but because he is the rightful inheritor of the kingdom's property and wealth.

Part II tells a totally different and seemingly unrelated story. It deals with the boisterous and earthy peasant Azdak—how he inadvertently saves the emperor during the revolution, how he becomes a judge by accident, and how he makes unconventional but humanly just decisions in this capacity. With the counterrevolution completed, he is about to be deposed from his position just as the "motherhood" of the prince is to be decided. When enters a messenger! The emperor, remembering how Azdak saved his life, reappoints him judge. Azdak handles the case, awards the child to Grusha, divorces her from her horrible husband so she can marry her true love, and the play ends with a celebration during which Azdak quietly disappears. Presumably everyone lives happily ever after. As the curtain falls, the storyteller says:

> And after that evening Azdak vanished and was never seen again.
> The people of Grusinia did not forget him but long remembered
> The period of his judging as a brief golden age,
> Almost an age of justice.[4]

Brecht's point is that in life we don't have golden ages of justice; messengers don't come in at the last minute; goodness isn't rewarded; true love doesn't triumph. The play's "happy" ending, far from neatly resolving the play's issues (except in a dramaturgic sense), makes us morally aware of issues we really don't like to face.

Anderson's play is sentimental because it evokes an excessive, simplistic response from us that is not warranted by the situation he created. Whether consciously or not, he played on our all-too-human tendency to accept easy answers, our willingness to turn away from difficult questions. Brecht's play, in contrast, confronts us with real issues about the truth of our nature, the workings of justice, and the uses and misuses of power.

Masterpieces

Our comparison of these two plays raises another interesting point about audiences. *Tea and Sympathy* was the top box-office hit for a serious play during the 1949–50 Broadway season. (This is astounding when one considers that Miller's *Death of a Salesman* was running at the same time.) The production was followed by an equally successful film version of the play. Then it dropped out of sight. It has never had a major revival and today is seldom, if ever, produced. For all but theatre historians, it has been long forgotten. *The Caucasian Chalk Circle*, on the other hand, is considered one of the masterpieces of the modern theatre. It is performed throughout the world; it is a staple in the programs of professional repertory and university theatres; it is taught in our colleges; and it is published in countless anthologies of plays.

What makes a masterpiece a masterpiece? Why do certain plays endure? What qualities do they have in common? In answering these questions we must remember that artists don't sit down to create masterpieces; they make what they can and what they must. It is the audience that creates masterpieces. This happens when generation after generation, century after century, people find a poem, a piece of music, a painting, or a play satisfying and meaningfully related to life as they experience it. Sentimental art, no matter how popular it may be in its own time, does not last. Masterpieces always confront us with the truth about ourselves. This is why great theatre artists finally always trust audiences. It is not that the box office doesn't lie; it often does. But for all of our tendencies to retreat from the world of the play, our need for genuine primal dialogue (which of all the arts only theatre can provide) is so great that ultimately we embrace the masterpieces of the theatre—old and new—even at the risk of being discomforted. It is the very presence of the truth about ourselves—and the directness with which performance can reveal it to us—that continually attracts us to the theatre.

Our feelings as we come to the theatre are a combination of embrace and retreat, excited anticipation and fearful expectancy. On a deep level of our being we know we need to confront truth in imaginative ways, no matter how hard a day we may have had. One of the old sayings about the theatre is that "it is always dying, yet is very much alive." The source of that cliché is the audience. Audiences invariably retreat from the theatre's truth—"it is always dying"—yet they never succeed in actually doing so; they have an overpowering need to embrace that truth—"it is very much alive."

THEATRE AND SOCIETY

As members of the audience, we have a strong influence on the performance of the actors. Our laughter, our applause, our response is felt by them. However, there is another dimension to the audience's involvement in the theatrical event and that is the impact of the audience in its larger sense, the impact of society as a whole on theatre. Theatre is a public art.

The expectations and responses of an audience do not exist in a vacuum. We come to the theatre as individuals but we are also members of a community, and social values play a significant role in our experience of the theatrical event. Indeed, because theatre is such a public art it is inextricably linked to the world in which it exists. The theatre—like all of the arts—reflects the society in which it takes place. It mirrors not only our individual natures, but also the nature of our world.

Like so much about the theatre, its relationship to the larger society of which it is a part presents us with a welter of seeming contradictions. Unquestionably, there is a constant interaction between the conventions of performance and the values, attitudes, and conventions of behavior of the society in which the performance takes place. Every time we go to the theatre, not only do we bring certain preconceptions about what a play is and what our experience of it should be, but we also bring certain values and norms of socially acceptable behavior against which we test everything that happens on the stage. We have already noted how the angry reaction in England in the 1950s to John Osborne's *Look Back in Anger* reflected the relation between theatre and society. In our own country, the production of *Hair* is an instructive example. It is inconceivable that the sexual explicitness of its theme and language, the nudity of the performers, and the style of production would have been acceptable to audiences in the 1940s or 1950s. By the end of the 1960s, social attitudes had changed so drastically that productions of *Hair* drew large and enthusiastic audiences wherever they played. In short, our attitudes shape our response to the theatrical event and if the performance is to "make sense" to us, it must appear authentic in terms of the values, attitudes, and behavioral patterns that exist in the social world outside the theatre.

More often than not, great playwrights choose to violate these preconceptions which the audience brings to the theatre. But if the playwright is to be successful in this, he or she must overcome our resistances and beguile and persuade us into accepting—at least while we are experiencing it—the truth of the "alien" vision of the world presented in the play. The theatre does not transform the world. Rather, *it is capable of transforming how we see the world.* It can encourage change by showing in understandable ways social changes that have already taken place which much of the audience may not have recognized or publicly acknowledged. Its power is prophetic. It makes change public; it gives the unnameable a name. Through performance, the theatre can penetrate an audience's subconscious life and force a society into a recognition of its real condition. This is what Martin Esslin meant when he wrote in *An Anatomy of Drama:*

> The theatre is the place where a nation thinks in public in front of itself. . . .
>
> Is the fact that it has become possible to speak certain words in public merely an indication of a change which has already happened, or does it actually initiate the change? My guess is that there is a more complex link between these two alternatives. The change has happened in the minds of a few people, an elite, an avant-garde. But the fact that it is brought into the open and seen to be accepted without overt indignation or sanctions against those who have dared to breach the taboo then becomes a further powerful factor in dissolving the taboo in the minds of those who were still afraid to breach it.[5]

Changes in modes of art are some of the first symptoms of a social instability that will eventually make itself felt in more material and political ways. Theatre does not change society so much as it reflects the changes that occur within it. The arts are incapable of providing the models that will transform society. Rather, they pro-

THE AUDIENCE AND THEATRICAL SPACE

The character of any theatrical occasion is reinforced by the physical surroundings in which the audience experiences the play. This physical environment determines, to a significant extent, the formality of the occasion and the accessibility, both physical and aesthetic, of the actors to the audience. Throughout history, the use of theatrical space has reflected the way society viewed the role of the audience in the theatrical event.

Left: A contemporary photograph of the ancient Roman theatre at Orange in southern France. The theatre, built for the provincial Roman legions, was derived from the Greek amphitheatres.

Below: A performance of Molière's **Le Malade Imaginaire** at Versailles in 1674. The grand spectacle of the occasion was typical of court festivities of the period.

Left: A disgruntled member of the audience shows disfavor with the performance by pelting an actor with fruit and vegetables at Baldwin's Theatre in San Francisco in the 1870s.

Below: Ariane Mnouchkine's **1789** at Le Théàtre du Soleil in 1970. The theatre is a converted munitions factory on the outskirts of Paris. The production, based on the events of the French Revolution, depended on a constantly changing relationship between the performers and the audience.

Above: The politically activist Teatro Campesino (Farm Workers' Theatre), directed by Luis Valdez, regularly performed for Chicano workers on the huge farms and grape ranches in California in the 1960s. Note the proximity of the audience to the playing space.

Right: An audience at the Metropolitan Opera, Lincoln Center for the Performing Arts, New York City.

vide us with a true picture of life as it is and in doing so they renew our belief in the power of the imagination to transform our condition.[6]

This explains why changes in theatrical style are so significant in the study of theatre. They reflect a change in what is shown. When Ibsen or Strindberg, Beckett or Brecht developed a radically new theatrical form, it was not because he was consciously trying to be a theatrical rebel (although he was often forced into that position), so much as it was that he had discovered a truth about the world that could not be expressed in the established dramatic forms. So he had to discover a form that would express the nature of the world as he had come to see it. He created a new kind of mirror.

Changes of interpretation that take place in the productions of the great plays of the past also show the close relationship of theatre and society. One of the characteristic qualities of masterpieces is that they never become dated. This does not mean that they remain fixed or static. Every age sees the great plays of the past through its own eyes. This is yet another way that the theatre mirrors not only ourselves but the world in which we live.

When Shakespeare's *The Merchant of Venice* was first produced in 1598, for example, presumably under Shakespeare's supervision, it is clear that it was a serious romantic play with a number of interwoven comic subplots. The central character was Antonio—the merchant of Venice—and the role was played by James Burbage, the leading tragic actor in Shakespeare's company. The character of Shylock, the Jew, was conceived as a comic figure and was played in a red wig by the leading comic actor of the time, Will Kemp. As the comic butt, Shylock's role reveals not only Shakespeare's dramatic design but also a great deal about the generally held social attitudes toward the Jews in Elizabethan England. Over the years these attitudes changed. As they did, so did the interpretation of Shylock's character and his function in the dynamic of the play. In the eighteenth and nineteenth centuries he was played first as a melodramatic villain and then gradually more sympathetically as the character became humanized. By the end of the nineteenth century in Henry Irving's production of the play, Shylock had become the play's central figure, although he was still portrayed as evil. By the mid-twentieth century, the interpretation of Shylock had swung almost 180 degrees. In Morris Carnovsky's famous production of the 1950s—the first major production in which Shylock was played by a Jewish actor—Shylock was not only the central character in the play, he was played almost as a tragic hero.

The history of the changing interpretation of Shylock's character corresponds directly to the changes in society's attitudes toward the Jews. Indeed, the productions of this play reveal those changes. This does not mean that through the centuries Shakespeare's play was altered or added to; the text remained the same. While it is true that Shakespeare may have written more than he consciously in-

tended—this is quite a common thing for great artists to do—the fact
is that each succeeding age discovered something about itself in the
play and it is that which was shown in the theatre. The production of
every play—old or new, major or minor—is an act of discovery that
also reveals. It is a mirror that reflects not only each member of the
audience to his or her self, but also the values, attitudes, and standards of behavior in the society of which the audience is a part.

As our discussion of the interpretation of Shylock indicates, the
relationship beween the theatre and society is always changing. As
public attitudes and social conventions shift, there are corresponding changes in the theatre. These changes are reflected in any
number of ways: the introduction of new subject matter, the development of new character types (dramatic heroes invariably reflect the moral values and spiritual aspirations of their age) and the
emergence of new conventions of language, production, and performance style. This can be seen, for example, in the contemporary
theatre's increasing preoccupation with illness and age, with senil-
ity and death. It is probably no accident that as we have become
more conscious of the problems and concerns of the aged, these are
reflected in the theatre. In the period of 1976 to 1978, Peter Nichols'
The National Health, Michael Cristofer's *The Shadow Box*, David
Storey's *Home*, Ronald Ribman's *Cold Storage*, Hugh Leonard's
Da, D. L. Colburn's *The Gin Game*, Bernard Slade's *Tribute*, and
Arthur Kopit's *Wings* were all successful in New York. In fact, the
New York Drama Critics voted Cristofer's play as the best of the
1976–77 season and Leonard's as the best in 1977–78. All of these
plays deal with some aspect of growing old.

The fact that these changes in the theatre are probably an accurate reflection of what is taking place in society does not mean that

audiences respond to them enthusiastically. Quite the contrary. We have implied that the artist is the seismograph of his age; that is, he perceives the changing currents of what is happening in the present moment long before the rest of society does, and he incorporates these perceptions into his work. But for the very reason that these perceptions are new, most members of the audience will not understand them, will resist them, or will be shocked by them. When Ibsen had Nora walk out on her husband at the end of *A Doll's House*, nineteenth-century audiences were horrified; a few years later when he introduced the subject of syphilis in *Ghosts*, they were outraged. Looking back, we can see that Ibsen was accurately reflecting changes in sensibility and attitude that had already occurred or were in the process of taking place. But this didn't in any way alter the violence of the audience's reaction.

Change in the arts always creates tension in the audience. When a work is presented in terms they are not accustomed to, the initial response of most people is usually to reject the work altogether. Genuine works of art, however, have a tremendous staying power. If the artist's vision of reality is authentic, it will not remain rejected; somehow the audience will come to terms with it. To accomplish this we may turn to the critics, those professional "discerners" (the word *critic* is derived from the Greek *kritein*, meaning "to discern"), in the hope that they will help us understand a new and alien vision or form.

The Critic's Role

We should make a distinction at the outset between the critic and the reviewer who reports on theatre for the newspapers or television. Both are called "critics" and some critics function in both ways, but there is a crucial distinction between the two. While reviewers do have a tremendous influence on the financial success or failure of a production, their primary function is to give a report on it for their readers or viewers. In this capacity they are part of the theatre's economic structure. They function as part of the marketing process. They tell their hypothetical "average" reader/viewer what the play is about, how the actors performed, and whether the reader/viewer should spend money and time to go to it. This is not unimportant and we all depend on reviewers for this kind of information, just as we depend on other kinds of buying guides and consumer reports. But the majority of play reviews are just that: reports for the record, immediate reactions written in haste to meet a deadline, or evaluations made by a person sometimes only slightly more knowledgeable about the theatre than most of the audience. Finally, reviewers tend to be more interested in the audience's taste and probable reaction than in the nature and meaning of the performance itself. This kind of criticism has to do with journalism, not theatre. As we said, we may check the review in the newspaper before we buy play tickets, but it is not the kind of criticism that concerns us here.

Critics are not writing for publication in tomorrow's newspaper. Their work is more reflective and usually makes an effort to deal with the subject within the whole tradition of theatre. The critic of the theatre is more than a member of the audience. He serves the whole of theatre in a very special way. He is a mediator between the performance and the audience. We have said that the audience's expectations and the playwright's aims are often, and necessarily, at odds with each other and that this fact is an inevitable source of tension in theatre. It often creates a gulf between the spectator and the performance which good criticism can bridge. The critic can be a kind of knowledgeable umpire who makes sure that the rules of the theatrical game are followed. If they are changed or broken, he records the fact and explains why. We noted earlier how Ibsen's plays were violently rejected by both the audience and journalistic critics when they were first performed. *Ghosts* was referred to as "an abomination," an "unbandaged sore," a "cesspool," "garbage." Today these responses strike us as ridiculous. It was only through the efforts of George Bernard Shaw, William Archer, and other critics that people came to understand what Ibsen was attempting and why his plays were of such enormous significance. This has always been one of the critic's most important functions.

The history of theatrical criticism is one of the key records of the history of the changing relationship between society and the theatre. Criticism codifies and interprets theatrical conventions; it influences their acceptance; it judges their effectiveness. The critic is always most powerful and visible in periods of radical innovation. Shaw certainly helped win understanding of naturalism. We have a special need for critics in the twentieth century, when change has been so rapid and so great. We need the critics to explain to us what is going on.

A good example of this is the modernist movement that has come to be known as the "theatre of the absurd." When the early plays of Beckett, Ionesco, and Adamov were first being performed in the 1950s and early 1960s, audiences found them so different from what they were used to that they could not understand them. They did not have well-knit plots, logically motivated heroes, or understandable language. Yet they had a compelling power and a vitality the theatre had been lacking. People found themselves going to them, being moved and amused by them, and applauding them, fully aware that they did not always know what they meant or what their authors intended. It was through the efforts of critics—first in articles and then in books—that theatregoers gradually came to know what to expect. Actually the process is more complicated than this. Today, not only do we look to the critics for guidance and instruction, we also turn to the playwrights themselves. The most influential critics of the twentieth century have been playwrights—

Shaw, Brecht, Pirandello, Eliot, Duerrenmatt, Frisch, Ionesco, Sartre—and their writings on the theatre have become the basis for most other critical writing. The theatre of the absurd is a good example of this. Most essays on the subject cite Ionesco, Adamov, Pinter, and Sartre—all playwrights—as the authoritative voices.

The great critics in history have always known that every artist is attempting the impossible, and that the critic has as much responsibility to the playwright as to the audience. Critics stand ready to receive the other world of the play. They are capable of being touched by it; they can feel deeply into the nature of every performance and have the intelligence, learning, and sensibility to perceive the reasons for its nature. All theatrical performances have an element of strangeness and mystery that we can never fully comprehend. Intelligent and sensitive criticism, criticism that captures and expresses the sensual experience of performance, can help the audience to find a common ground with that other world. Being more interested in revealing than judging, critics have the capacity to reveal the dynamics of performance and, when necessary, what performance means. In thus serving the play and the performance, critics also serve the members of the audience by guiding them and enlarging their capacity for response. For finally, the purpose of all criticism is to enhance our perception.

THE THEATRE AS A MODE OF PERCEPTION

The audience's participation in theatre involves observing, listening, *receiving* the play. We need not act on what we see and hear. We need only perceive what is being presented as fully as we can. We need not identify with the characters or the action. In fact, we never really can. We always know that the people and events of a theatrical performance are imaginary and that our responses to them are to things unreal. Macbeth's murderous career arouses strong feelings in us, but it does not make us feel like a murderer or a district attorney. We may be moved to tears as King Lear's "heart bursts smilingly," but we never directly identify with the blindness that caused his downfall. Nineteenth-century Southern audiences are reported to have cried copiously at productions of *Uncle Tom's Cabin*, but there is no evidence that they went home after the theatre and freed their slaves. Brecht's *The Mother* and *The Measures Taken* are propagandist "learning" plays, but people did not rush out and join the Communist party after seeing them. Even the famous first performance of Odets' *Waiting for Lefty*, following which the audience was induced to leave the theatre shouting "Strike!" had no affective results. As members of the audience, we do not "believe" what is going on; we perceive all of the meanings expressed by the performance.

This is an important distinction because it brings the true nature of the theatrical experience to the surface. Our experience of theatre is an experience of awareness, and our perceptions are necessary to complete, as it were, the electrical current of the theatrical event. For the performance of any play to be successful, it must enhance, enlarge, and sharpen our awareness. In fact, that is its primary purpose. This is accomplished by the many elements of the production working simultaneously and often in opposition. Our emotions are awakened by ambiguities of text and action; by contradictions, juxtapositions, and ironies; by surprises and shocks; by multiple and often contradictory images; and by conscious and unconscious techniques of distancing. These are characteristics of all great plays in performance, and the most noble aim of theatre is to provoke wonder by making the familiar unfamiliar.

The presence of others in the audience who will share in the event encourages us to be open and receptive to the other world of the play that will be made present for us on the stage. Our unspoken, but nonetheless acknowledged, communion with our fellow audience members makes heightened perception possible. English theorist-director-designer Gordon Craig (1872–1966) commented on this in his book on actor-manager Henry Irving. Irving was the most famous actor in England during the last quarter of the nineteenth century and one of his most popular roles was Mathias in Leopold Lewis's now long-forgotten play *The Bells*. Craig describes the audience's tumultuous response when Irving first appeared on stage:

> The hurricane of applause at Irving's entrance was no interruption. . . . It was a torrent while it lasted. Power responded to power . . . he [Irving] deliberately called it out of the spectators. It was necessary *to them*—not to him; it was something they had to experience, or to be rid of, or rather released from, before they could exactly take in what he was going to give them.[7]

"It was necessary *to them* . . . something they had to experience . . . before they could exactly take in what he was going to give them." The basic theatre act is transformational: life experience is transformed into a play, the play is transformed into a performance, the actors into characters, stage space into play space, real time into dramatic time, clothes into costumes, a group of people into an audience.

The theatre is often referred to as a "temple of change." Everything about it involves change. It is a place where we can acknowledge our limitations because while there we can entertain the possibility of other realities. From its earliest beginnings, the theatre has provided a guarantee that we need not be trapped by our life roles, that indeed we can transcend them. It has guaranteed that at least imaginatively, we can move into new roles, new relations, situations, milieus, even into other periods of history. In theatre, above all, we can have other realities. The illusion of the stage is the reality

D rama is about the **changes** that happen to the characters. Take any drama and compare who, where, and what any character is at the beginning and at the end, and also see what the scenes are about: always they are about changes, from life to death, from not in love to in love (or out again), from rich to poor or vice-versa, etc.

Richard Schechner, "Towards a Poetics of Performance"

of our dreams. What could be more attractive? Every generation has shown just how attractive it is. The paradoxes of the theatre challenge our souls to take giant steps and we come to it because we want and need to take those steps.

This is as true today as it ever was. In fact, I see many signs heralding a theatrical renaissance. While the number of productions in the commercial theatre has decreased (due largely to the exorbitant cost of mounting them), attendance and profits are higher than they have ever been in history. The burgeoning regional theatre in this country is an even more reliable measure of the theatre's vitality. From New Haven to Seattle, Louisville to San Diego, resident companies are performing for most of the year to near-capacity audiences. The repertoires of these companies are significant. The plays of Shakespeare, Molière, and other classics are regularly performed. The masterpieces of the modern theatre are now a part of most theatregoers' experience. The rich heritage of American drama is being rediscovered. And perhaps most important, new plays are increasingly being given their initial productions in regional theatres rather than in New York City. These theatres have made the wide and varied spectrum of drama available to audiences everywhere.

At the same time, there are probably more successful experimental theatre groups than ever before. These groups are exploring the frontiers of performance. They test new modes and techniques. They experiment with new variations on the actor/audience relationship. They develop new forms of drama and give aspiring playwrights an opportunity to grow in their vision and craft. Significantly, these companies are not only located in New York (Off-Off-Broadway) but thrive in cities large and small all over the nation.

Finally, colleges and universities are presenting thousands of performances each year. Our schools are not only training the theatre artists of the future; more important, they are developing an educated and responsive audience. Going to the theatre is rapidly becoming a part of the life experience of many college students, and we can be hopeful that this will create an abiding appetite that only

I n all drama, even the most frivolous, I think that there is some attempt, rarely conscious, to relate the participants to God, or at least to
some aspect of God, albeit such aspects are often those represented in
Greece by such figures as Dionysus or Aphrodite, where God is seen not
in his capacity of all-wise, all-powerful Father but as the personification
of Sex, of Mirth, or as the glorification of youth.

The theatre is the direct descendant of fertility rites, war dances
and all the corporate ritual expressions by means of which our primitive
ancestors, often wiser than we, sought to relate themselves to God, or the
gods, the great abstract forces which cannot be apprehended by reason,
but in whose existence reason compels us to have faith.

Tyrone Guthrie, **A Life in the Theatre**

a lifetime of theatregoing will satisfy. It is my hope that this book will
enhance your participation in this experience and thereby help to
insure that this renaissance will realize its full potential.

The major theme of this exploration has been that the primary
purpose of the theatre throughout all of history and in every culture
has been to make present the mysteries of being by manifesting
them in the other world of the play. Audiences have always gone to
the theatre because the experience of performance fulfills their
deeply felt need to be in touch with mystery. We cannot be at one
with mystery, and mystery can never be fully identified with; but we
can perceive it, participate in it, and have a more heightened
awareness of it. In all performance of theatre, persons appearing to
come from a world beyond this world materialize to meet an audience. By participating in the theatrical event, we in the audience
enter into relations with that world and in so doing come to a new
and renewed, profound and joyful, deeper and expanded consciousness of ourselves and of our world.

NOTES

[1]It is interesting to note that a number of the prisoners who saw the performance then founded their own theatre group and later produced *Waiting for
Godot* themselves. The members of this group eventually served their time and
were released, but the group stayed together. Today the San Quentin Company is
one of the country's more important experimental companies.

[2]We might add that another reason audience participation is so unsatisfying is
that most participatory performances have such a poorly conceived idea of the
audience's role as a theatrical participant. Audience members are asked to give
up their traditional role and become props for the actors. They are, as Elizabeth
Burns put it in her book *Theatricality*, "neither themselves nor 'characters,' involved wholly neither in a theatrical nor in a real life situation."

[3]Jean-Paul Sartre, *Sartre on Theatre*, New York: Pantheon Books, Inc., 1976, p. 156.

[4]Bertolt Brecht. *The Caucasian Chalk Circle*, trans. by Eric Bentley, as it appeared in *The Modern Theatre*, ed. by Robert W. Corrigan. New York: The Macmillan Company, 1964, p. 238.

[5]Martin Esslin. *An Anatomy of Drama*. London: Maurice Temple Smith Ltd., 1976, p. 102.

[6]Theatre does this in a very special way. French theatre theorist Jean Duvignaud develops the idea in his *Sociologie du Théâtre* that only that which is in opposition or contradiction to the commonly held social consciousness of a culture becomes (or is capable of becoming) the subject matter of theatre. He argues persuasively—and most of the plays ever written support his thesis—that theatre never shows the average, but the criminal, forbidden, or that which society as a whole does not consider acceptable—or at least it is outside the boundaries of what most people think of as normal. Asocial emotions and acts are made desirable or attractive by actors; the feelings and responses provoked by difficult situations (sex, violence, death) are channeled into acceptable and bearable forms. It is the theatre's capacity to open up audiences to unknown or socially unacceptable experiences that enables it to alter consciousness and thereby have the power to modify the codes of social experience.

[7]Gordon Craig. *Henry Irving*. New York: Longmans, Green and Co., 1930, p. 52.

Bibliography

Appia, Adolphe. *Music and the Art of the Theatre*. Translated by Robert W. Corrigan and Mary D. Dirks. Miami: University of Miami Press, 1963.

A pioneering work in the theory of modern theatre. Although much of the book is devoted to the problems of staging Wagner's operas, its primary value today is Appia's discussion of the aesthetic role of light in theatrical production.

Aristotle. *Aristotle's Poetics*. Translated by S. H. Butcher, introduction by Francis Fergusson. New York: Hill and Wang, 1961.

A readily available and inexpensive edition of Aristotle's *Poetics* in S. H. Butcher's famous translation. Fergusson's introduction is a helpful guide to understanding Aristotle's ideas.

Artaud, Antonin. *The Theatre and Its Double*. Translated by M. C. Richards. New York: Grove Press, 1958.

The avant-garde manifestos which developed the idea of the "theatre of cruelty." Artaud's efforts to discover the basic dynamics of primitive theatre led to a redefinition of the nature of the theatrical event which has influenced most of the major theatre artists of the past two decades.

Atkinson, Brooks. *Broadway*. Rev. ed. New York: Macmillan, 1974.

A fact-filled, anecdotal, and amiable history of the New York commercial theatre. Atkinson, long-time drama critic of the *New York Times*, traces the development of Broadway from its beginnings to the present by focusing on the principal plays and players of American theatre history.

Barrault, Jean-Louis. *The Theatre of Jean-Louis Barrault*. Translated by Joseph Chiari. New York: Hill and Wang, 1961.

A selection of essays and reflections by one of the great actor-directors of the twentieth-century French theatre. They range from analyses of some of his memorable productions to penetrating discussions of the art of acting.

Bay, Howard. *Stage Design*. New York: Drama Book Specialists, 1974.

A practical discussion of all the elements of scene design by one of America's well-known stage designers. The book, lavishly illustrated, deals not only with technical aspects of design, but with aesthetic principles as well.

Bentley, Eric. *The Life of the Drama*. New York: Atheneum, 1964.

A brilliant study of the basic elements that are combined to make a play and an examination of the forms of drama that have been dominant in Western theatre. This book, while difficult because it assumes a wide knowledge of drama and literature, is one of the major studies of how theatre works and is highly recommended to anyone seriously interested in drama.

_____, ed. *The Theory of the Modern Stage*. Baltimore: Penguin Books, 1976.

An anthology of the writings of the major theatre practitioners and theorists of the nineteenth and twentieth centuries. This valuable collection includes essays dealing with both the aesthetic principles and the ideological bases of the modern theatre.

Blau, Herbert. *The Impossible Theatre: A Manifesto*. New York: Macmillan, 1966.

In telling the story of the San Francisco Actor's Workshop, the Workshop's co-founder examines the relationship of theatre to society, analyzes in detail many of the Workshop's major productions, and discusses the nature of dramatic form and the art of theatre based on its practice. While often negative in its assessment of contemporary theatre practice, the book aims at discovering new possibilities for the American theatre and as such has been an inspiration to many theatre artists.

Brecht, Bertolt. *Brecht on Theatre*. Translated by John Willett. New York: Hill and Wang, 1964.

The basic collection of the theoretical writings of one of the most important theatre artists of the twentieth century. Arranged chronologically, these essays are particularly helpful in showing the development of Brecht's theory of "epic" or nonillusionistic theatre. It also includes several documents relating to his major plays.

Brockett, Oscar G. *History of the Theatre*. 3d ed. Boston: Allyn and Bacon, 1977.

Probably the most inclusive recent history of world theatre. Profusely illustrated, Brockett's book covers theatre architecture, major dramatic movements, and the major figures in theatre history. Written for students.

Brook, Peter. *The Empty Space*. New York: Avon Books, 1969.

An analysis of contemporary theatre practice by one of today's most influential and experimental directors. Brook has gone back to ground zero—the empty space—to reexamine the essential elements of every theatrical event.

Burns, Elizabeth. *Theatricality*. New York: Harper and Row, 1973.

A study of convention in the theatre and in social life. Using numerous examples from British and American drama, the author discusses in great detail the sociology of performance in terms of the many kinds of convention that govern our experience of theatre.

Burns, Tom, and Elizabeth Burns. *Sociology of Literature and Drama*. Baltimore: Penguin Books, 1973.

An anthology of thirty-three essays on the relationship of sociology to literature and drama. This rich collection is particularly valuable in making available several important essays on the sociology of theatre that have heretofore not been translated into English.

Burton, Hal, ed. *Great Acting*. New York: Hill and Wang, 1968.

A collection of penetrating and revealing interviews with some of the great British actors of the twentieth century, including Edith Evans, Laurence Olivier, Sybil Thorndike, Peggy Ashcroft, Ralph Richardson, Michael Redgrave, John Gielgud, and Noel Coward.

Chaikin, Joseph. *The Presence of the Actor*. New York: Atheneum, 1972.

Provocative essays on the nature and craft of acting by the founder of the Open Theatre. Chaikin has been associated with many of the most significant experimental companies of the last two decades, and writes authoritatively about the role of the actor in the new theatre.

Clark, Barrett H. *European Theories of the Drama*. 3d ed. Revised by Henry Popkin. New York: Crown, 1965.

The most recent edition of the standard collection of writings on dramatic theory from the Greeks to the present. In addition to its broad coverage of dramatic theory, it includes biographical and bibliographic materials. It is an important theatre reference book.

Clurman, Harold. *Lies Like Truth*. New York: Macmillan, 1958.

A lively collection of Clurman's reviews and occasional essays. Being both a critic and a director, he writes about performance both in this country and in Europe from the point of view of the theatre practitioner. Clurman's discussions of individual performances in great plays are particularly illuminating.

_____. *On Directing*. New York: Macmillan, 1972.

One of the best books on the art of directing currently available. Clurman includes the working notes, preparatory analysis, and sections of his promptbooks for some of his most significant productions. This book is particularly helpful in showing how a director goes about his job.

Cole, David. *The Theatrical Event*. Middletown, Conn.: Wesleyan University Press, 1975.

An analysis of all the elements of theatre, this book attempts to redefine the nature of the theatrical event in terms of myth and ritual. Its basic argument rests on Cole's belief that the performances of the shamans of primitive societies can enlarge our understanding of what happens in theatre.

Cole, Toby, ed. *Playwrights on Playwriting*. New York: Hill and Wang, 1961.

This volume is one of the best collections of writings on the art of theatre by playwrights themselves. While its focus is largely on the twentieth century, the book includes a number of valuable documents from the past. A good bibliography.

Cole, Toby, and Helen Krich Chinoy, eds. *Actors on Acting*. Rev. ed. New York: Crown, 1970.

The theories, techniques, and practices of the world's great actors told in their own words. This comprehensive collection of actors' views on acting is the most important reference book on the subject. In addition to helpful introductory notes, it also has an extensive bibliography.

_____. *Directors on Directing*. Rev. ed. Indianapolis: Bobbs-Merrill, 1963.

A large collection on the theory and practice of directing by the great directors of the nineteenth- and twentieth-century theatre. The long introductory essay on "The Emergence of the Director" is particularly helpful and the book includes a large bibliography.

Corrigan, Robert W. *Comedy: Meaning and Form*. Rev. ed. New York: Harper and Row, 1979.

A new and enlarged edition of the major writings on comedy in the twentieth century. Also includes excerpts from some of the classics of comic theory and a selected bibliography.

_____. *The Modern Theatre*. New York: Macmillan, 1964.

An anthology of forty modern plays from Buechner to Beckett. The volume also includes writings on the theatre by each of the playwrights represented and a listing of their plays.

_____. *The Theatre in Search of a Fix*. New York: Delacorte Press, 1973.

A collection of essays on the theatre, ranging from Greek and

Roman times to the present. The essays concern themselves with the forms, themes, and social and cultural context of the theatre in evolution.

————. *Tragedy: Vision and Form.* Rev. ed. New York: Harper and Row, 1979.

A new and enlarged edition of the major writings on tragedy in the twentieth century. Also includes excerpts from some of the classics of tragic theory and a selected bibliography.

Craig, Gordon. *On the Art of the Theatre.* New York: Theatre Arts Books, 1925.

Probably the most important book of this influential twentieth-century theorist. It includes writings on playwriting, directing, scene design, and Craig's revolutionary essay on the actor as a marionette.

Dukore, Bernard. *Dramatic Theory and Criticism: Greeks to Grotowski.* New York: Holt, Rinehart and Winston, 1974.

The most recent large anthology of dramatic theory and criticism. While not as comprehensive as the Clark collection (see above), it has a more readable format, fuller coverage of the twentieth century, and a more up-to-date bibliography. A standard reference volume.

Eliade, Mircea. *The Sacred and the Profane.* Translated by Willard R. Trask. New York: Harcourt Brace Jovanovich, 1968.

A discussion of the significance of religious myth, symbolism, and ritual within life and culture. This noted historian of religion traces manifestations of the sacred and the otherworldly from primitive to modern times in terms of space, time, nature, and life itself.

————. *Shamanism: Archaic Techniques of Ecstasy.* Translated by Willard R. Trask. New York: Harvest Books, 1970.

The best and probably most influential book on the history and nature of shamanism. A landmark study in the field of religious anthropology, this book is a major source for those historians and theorists interested in the origins of theatre.

Esslin, Martin. *An Anatomy of Drama.* New York: Hill and Wang, 1977.

A brief, informal discussion of the nature of theatre. Because of his long tenure as director of radio drama at the BBC, Esslin is particularly good when he writes on the differences between theatre, film, radio, and TV.

————, ed. *The Encyclopedia of World Theatre.* New York: Scribner's, 1977.

The most recently published theatre encyclopedia. With more than 400 photographs, extensive index, and more than 2,000 entries, this book is especially wide-ranging in its coverage of theatre theory, dramatic literature, and stage design. A valuable reference work.

_____. *The Theatre of the Absurd*. Rev. ed. New York: Overlook Press, 1973.

The standard work on one of the twentieth century's most important theatrical movements. Filled with detail, Esslin traces the development of the theatre of the absurd and relates it to the history of the nineteenth- and twentieth-century theatres.

Fergusson, Francis. *The Idea of a Theater*. Princeton: Princeton University Press, 1968.

A study of a number of the great plays in terms of Aristotelian theory. This very important book reexamines the basic concepts in Aristotle's *Poetics* in light of modern scholarship. It is especially brilliant in its discussion of the nature of dramatic action.

Freud, Sigmund. "The Uncanny," in *Collected Papers*. Vol. 4. New York: Basic Books, 1959.

Freud's most succinct discussions of the psychology of otherness. Since Freud's theories are so relevant to many of the ideas put forth in the opening chapters of this book, his essay will be particularly useful to students wishing to explore these ideas further.

Funke, Lewis, and John E. Booth, eds. *Actors Talk About Acting*. New York: Avon Books, 1973.

A two-volume collection of interviews with some of the leading actors of the twentieth century. Included are: John Gielgud, Helen Hayes, Vivien Leigh, Morris Carnovsky, Shelley Winters, Bert Lahr, Sidney Poitier, Alfred Lunt, Lynn Fontanne, Jose Ferrer, Maureen Stapleton, Katharine Cornell, Paul Muni, and Anne Bancroft.

Gassner, John, and Edward Quinn. *The Reader's Encyclopedia of World Drama*. New York: T. Y. Crowell, 1969.

A standard encyclopedia of world drama. It has many illustrations and a helpful index.

Goffman, Erving. *Presentation of Self in Everyday Life*. New York: Overlook Press, 1973.

A probing investigation of the theatricality of everyday life. The book is particularly good in its discussion of the relationship of role-playing in life and roles in theatre.

Goldman, Michael. *The Actor's Freedom: Toward a Theory of Drama.* New York: Viking Press, 1975.

An important book which discusses the theatre as "a means by which man attempts to complete his relation to the world, especially to everything in the world that strikes him as dangerous and strange." Goldman's views on the relationship of the actor to the script are particularly interesting.

Gorelik, Mordecai. *New Theatres for Old.* New York: Octagon Books, 1975.

Contains interesting and lively discussions of the various styles and movements of the modern theatre.

Grotowski, Jerzy. *Towards a Poor Theatre.* New York: Simon and Schuster, 1970.

One of the most influential theatre books of the twentieth century. It has become a bible-guidebook for most contemporary experimental groups. As Peter Brook put it, "No one since Stanislavski has investigated the nature of acting . . . as deeply and completely as Grotowski."

Guthrie, Tyrone. *A Life in the Theatre.* New York: McGraw-Hill, 1959.

An autobiographical account of a major director's many successful efforts to create theatres. The passages describing Guthrie's philosophy of the stage are particularly rich.

Heilman, Robert B. *Tragedy and Melodrama: Versions of Experience.* Seattle: University of Washington Press, 1968.

One of the best books distinguishing between tragedy and melodrama. It is full of detailed examples, is carefully annotated, and has a large and helpful bibliography.

_____. *The Ways of the World: Comedy and Society.* Seattle: University of Washington Press, 1978.

A companion volume to the author's earlier books on tragedy, melodrama, and modern tragicomedy. Structured in much the same ways, it too is rich in example and has an extensive bibliography.

Huizinga, Johan. *Homo Ludens: A Study of the Play Element in Culture.* Boston: Beacon Press, 1955.

A pioneering study of the nature of play and its role in both life and theatre.

Ionesco, Eugène. *Notes and Counternotes.* Translated by Donald Watson. New York: Grove Press, 1964.

A valuable collection of the Roumanian-French playwright's theatre essays. His discussions of the role of language in theatre are particularly insightful.

Jellicoe, Ann. *Some Unconscious Influences in the Theatre.* Cambridge University Press, 1967.

A fascinating lecture on the nature of theatre audiences and the playwright's relationship to them, published as a booklet.

Jones, Robert Edmond. *The Dramatic Imagination.* New York: Theatre Arts Books, 1941.

Still one of the wisest volumes on the art of the theatre by one of this century's greatest scene designers.

Kirby, E. T. *Ur-Drama: The Origins of Theatre.* New York: New York University Press, 1975.

A valuable and persuasive study of the shamanistic origins of theatre in India, China, Japan, and Greece. Has a detailed bibliography.

Lahr, John, and Jonathan Price. *Life-Show.* New York: Viking Press, 1973.

A richly and imaginatively illustrated book on "how to see theater in life and life in theater." The authors discuss all of the elements of the theatrical event and show how we re-create them in our everyday lives.

Langer, Susanne K. *Feeling and Form.* New York: Scribner's, 1953.

One of the landmark books on aesthetic theory. Langer's analysis of the nature of dramatic form and her discussions of the major forms of theatre are still some of the best available.

Lommel, Andreas. *Masks: Their Meaning and Function.* New York: McGraw-Hill, 1972.

An encyclopedic anthropological study of masks. Richly illustrated.

Meyerhold, Vsevolod. *Meyerhold on Theatre.* Edited by Edward Braun. New York: Hill and Wang, 1969.

A collection of the great Russian director's theatre writings. An invaluable book for those interested in the experimental theatre of the first half of this century.

Mielziner, Jo. *Designing for the Theatre.* New York: Clarkson N. Potter, 1965.

A memoir of the stage designer's career and a portfolio of his most important designs. His chronicle of the designing process for the opening production of Arthur Miller's *Death of a Salesman* is particularly valuable.

Miller, Arthur. *The Theatre Essays of Arthur Miller.* Edited by Robert Martin. New York: Viking Press, 1978.

A collection of all the famous playwright's writings on theatre. The playwright's relationship to the society outside the theatre is stressed.

Piaget, Jean. *Play, Dreams, and Imitation in Childhood.* Translated by C. Gattegno and F. M. Hodgson. New York: W. W. Norton, 1962.

One of the great and influential books on child development. The French child psychologist points to the many ways childhood play is related to theatrical behavior.

Rosenberg, Harold. *The Tradition of the New.* New York: McGraw-Hill, 1965.

While this book is largely devoted to the visual arts, it is an important study of the nature of avant-garde movements. It includes a valuable essay on the nature of dramatic characters.

Saint-Denis, Michel. *Theatre: The Rediscovery of Style.* New York: Theatre Arts Books, 1969.

A wise little book on classical style in the modern theatre by the founder of the Young Vic and Juilliard theatre schools. It is especially good on the subject of actor training.

Sartre, Jean-Paul. *Sartre on Theatre.* Translated by Frank Jellinek. New York: Pantheon Books, 1976.

A collection of the French playwright-philosopher's theatre writings. Part One includes documents, lectures, and conversations on the theatre. Part Two includes documents and interviews on his plays. The essays reveal the existential basis of his theatrical theory and practice.

Schechner, Richard. *Environmental Theatre.* New York: Hawthorn Books, 1973.

Probably the major study of environmental theatre. It encompasses the theories and techniques of Schechner's Performance Group as it has evolved over the past decade. It has an extremely useful bibliography.

Schechner, Richard, and Mady Schuman, eds. *Ritual, Play and Performance.* New York: Seabury Press, 1977.

A collection of essays on the sociology of theatre. Contributors include: Johan Huizinga, Gregory Bateson, Claude Lévi-Strauss, Ray Birdwhistell, Erving Goffman, Victor Turner, and Jerzy Grotowski.

Schevill, James. *Break Out!* Chicago: Swallow Press, 1972.

A collection of creative and critical pieces documenting the theatre's search for new environments. It includes plays, manifestos, interviews, and essays by the author and by many of the major figures of the contemporary theatre.

Simonson, Lee. *The Stage Is Set*. New York: Theatre Arts Books, 1962 (1932).

The famous American stage designer's account of the New Theatre movement, with special emphasis on the revolutionary new techniques introduced by Appia, Craig, and Reinhardt. Includes many classic illustrations.

Sontag, Susan. *Against Interpretation and Other Essays*. New York: Dell, 1967.

A collection of essays and reviews on drama, film, and literature. Sontag is particularly brilliant (and controversial) in her essay on the tendency to impose interpretations on works of art rather than let them speak for themselves.

Southern, Richard. *The Seven Ages of the Theatre*. New York: Hill and Wang, 1961.

An imaginative history of theatre focusing on those periods when performers used new kinds of playing spaces to create new forms of theatre. Southern's study is very helpful for an understanding of how and why the physical theatre has evolved as it has.

Stanislavski, Konstantin. *Building a Character*. Translated by E. R. Hapgood. New York: Theatre Arts Books, 1948.

One of several of the Russian master's books on the methods used by actors to create a role.

_____. *My Life in Art*. Translated by J. J. Robbins. Boston: Meridian Books, 1956.

The autobiography of one of the most important figures in the modern theatre. It tells of Stanislavski's career at the Moscow Art Theatre and how he later developed his system of actor training.

Styan, John L. *Drama, Stage and Audience*. Cambridge University Press, 1975.

A study of how a play "works" in the theatre. Styan discusses the details of performance and how they generate life, meaning, and excitement on the stage for an audience.

_____. *The Elements of Drama*. Cambridge University Press, 1960.

A book of dramatic theory that analyzes the elements of a play, how they are organized, and how a play's structure shapes the audience's responses.

Vilar, Jean. *The Tradition of the Theatre*. Unpublished translation by Christopher Kotschnig.

A collection of theatre writings by the director of the Théâtre National Populaire. While Vilar's book has not been published in its entirety in English, several of the most important essays have been. The following essays are still available:

"Murder of the Director." *Tulane Drama Review* 3 (December 1958).
"Secrets." *Tulane Drama Review* 3 (March 1959).
"The Director and the Play." *Yale French Studies* 3 (1949).
"Theatre Without Pretensions," in *Directors on Directing*, edited by Toby Cole and Helen Krich Chinoy (see above).

Wilder, Thornton. "Some Thoughts on Playwriting" in *The Intent of the Artist*, A. Centeno, ed. Princeton: Princeton University Press, 1941.

An important document on the art of playwriting. Wilder discusses the four fundamental conditions that separate the drama from the other arts.

Young, Stark. *The Theatre*. New York: Hill and Wang, 1963.

A selection of Young's reviews in the *New Republic* from the period of 1921–1947. The writings reveal Young's philosophy of dramatic art.

Periodicals

The Drama Review (formerly the *Tulane Drama Review)*
Modern Drama
New York Theatre Review
Performing Arts Journal
Theater (formerly *Yale/Theatre)*
Theatre Journal (formerly *Educational Theatre Journal)*
Theatre Quarterly

ILLUSTRATION CREDITS

Cover—*King Lear* performed at the Delacorte Theatre in Central Park, New York City. Photo by Fredda Slavin

POSTERS

iii *Don Quixote* produced by Henry Irving at the Lyceum, 1896. Poster by the Beggarstaff Brothers. Philips Ltd., London

2 *The Country Wife*. Reproduced by courtesy of the National Theatre of Great Britain. Design by Richard Bird and Michael Mayhew

32 *Rosencrantz and Guildenstern Are Dead*, a Young Vic production. Poster designed by Nick Jenkins. Reproduced by the courtesy of the Young Vic Theatre, London

54 *Streamers*, a 1976 production at the Goodman Theatre, Chicago, directed by Gregory Mosher. Designed by Sandford. Reproduced by courtesy of the Goodman Theatre

88 *The Cherry Orchard*. Poster, Paul Davis. Art director, Reinhold and Schwenk

148 *Hamlet*. Reproduced by courtesy of the National Theatre of Great Britain. Design by Richard Bird and Michael Mayhew

186 *Waiting for Godot* produced by Edgar Lansbury and Joseph Beruh. Reproduced by permission of Edgar Lansbury.

216 *On the 20th Century*. The Producer Circle Co., NY

258 *Equus* presented by Kermit Bloomgarden and Doris Cole Abrahams. Poster designed by Gil Lesser.

302 Félix-Édouard Vallotton. *Ah! la Pé . . . la Pé . . . la Pépinière* at the café-concert La Pépinière (Paris, Pajol & Cie); (M.A. 119, issue 30, May 1898)

PHOTOGRAPHS

11 Queen Elizabeth II. Fox Photos
11 Nixon in Rome. U.P.I.
12 Prisoners. Danny Lyon/Magnum Photos
12 Montgomery, 1965. © James Karales/D.P.I.
13 Hockey violence. Wide World Photos
13 Kent State University. Photo by Douglas Moore
14 Kiss. Photo copyright © 1977 Bob Gruen
14 Kids dressed like Kiss. Los Angeles Times photo
19 Initiation rites, Upper Volta. Folco Quilici, Rome
19 *Macbeth*. T. F. Holte
20 Punch-and-Judy. Benjamin R. Haydon. *Punch on May Day* (detail). 1829. The Tate Gallery, London. Photo by John Webb

20 *Jesus Christ Superstar*. Joseph Abeles Studio
21 Mardi Gras. Scott, Foresman Staff
21 *Momiji-gari*. Photo by Tatsuo Yoshikoshi
22 *Tribe*. Nikolais Dance Theatre. Chimera Foundation for Dance, Inc. Photo by Tom Caravaglia
35 Sri Lanka mask. Yvonne Hannemann
36 Greek mask. Louvre Museum, Paris
37 Brakebill Mound mask. Peabody Museum, Harvard University. Photograph by Hillel Burger
38 Children with masks. Photo by Ralph Eugene Meatyard
41 Marceau. Max Waldman/Magnum Photos
44 *The Dybbuk*. Ansky's *The Dybbuk*, Vakhtangov production, Moscow, 1922. Programme du Théâtre Habima from the collection of the Centre Nationale de la Recherche Scientifique, Paris
45 *Oresteia*. Photo: Pic
49 Tlingit helmet. Courtesy American Museum of Natural History
50 Milkmaids, France. The Bettmann Archive, Inc.
51 *Oedipus Rex*. Stratford Festival, Ontario
53 False Face mask. Cranbrook Institute of Science, Bloomfield Hills, Michigan
57 *Miss Julie*. Angus McBean photograph, Harvard Theatre Collection
59 *Antigone*. Photo by Jaromir Svoboda
60 *A Streetcar Named Desire*. Culver Pictures
62 *Othello*. Angus McBean photograph, Harvard Theatre Collection
64 *Richard III*. Theatre Collection, The New York Public Library at Lincoln Center. Astor, Lenox and Tilden Foundations
65 *Volpone*. Walter Sanders *Life* Magazine © 1945 Time Inc.
69 *Look Back in Anger*. Joseph Abeles Studio
71 *Dionysus in 69*. Photograph by Max Waldman © 1969
77 *Waiting for Godot*. French Cultural Services
81 *Hedda Gabler*. Virginia Museum Theatre
82 *King Lear*. Photo by Luigi Ciminaghi
84 *Death of a Salesman*. Photo by Eileen Darby
93 *Macbeth*. Gjon Mili *Life* Magazine © 1946 Time Inc.
97 *Bérénice*. Photo by Nicolas Treatt
99 *Long Day's Journey into Night*. Culver Pictures
100 *Oedipus*. Photo by Jaromir Svoboda
105 *The Trojan Women*. Courtesy of La Mama, NY. Photo by Amnon Ben Nomis
106 *The Duchess of Malfi*. Photo by Eileen Darby
112 *Dracula*. Photo by Martha Swope
114 *Riders to the Sea*. Photograph by Dermot Barry
116 *The Frogs*. Willy Saeger

Index

Ribman, Ronald, 332
Richard III, 64, **64**
Richardson, Ralph, 167*, **178**
Riders to the Sea, 113–15, **114**
Ritchard, Cyril, **120**
Ritual, **19,** 44–53
  as distinct from theatre, 49–51
  and myth, 47–50
  as similar to theatre, 47, 158
  and theatrical space, **292**
Ritualism, **232**
Ritz Brothers, 123
Robards, Jason, Jr., **99**
Rodgers, Richard, **311,** 314–15
Roman theatre (ancient), **329**
Rome, classical, 192, **194,** 220
Rosenberg, Harold, 87, 316
Rousseau, Jean Jacques, 104–5

Sacred and the Profane, The, 261*
Sanctum, **271**
San Quentin Company, 338
Santayana, George, 91*, 115
Santo Loquasto, 260
Sarcey, Francisque, 133
Sartre, Jean-Paul, 205*, **210,** 321,
  334–35
Sartre on Theatre, 205*
Scapin, *see Tricks of Scapin, The*
Schechner, Richard, 23*, **71, 230,**
  231, 262*, 265, 266, 300, 316,
  337*
Schiller, Friedrich, **200**
Schneider, Alan, 239
School for Scandal, The, **122**
School for Wives, 52, 117
Scofield, Paul, **19, 171,** 321
Scott, George C., 239
Sea Gull, The, 142, 322
"Secrets," 305*
Seeds of Atreus, **317**
Sendak, Maurice, 39*
Serban, Andrei, 30*, **105, 136,** 203,
  316
Serreau, Jean-Marie, **77**
Servant of Two Masters, The, **130**
1789, **330**
Seven-Year Itch, The, 129
Shade, The, 106
Shadow Box, The, 332
Shaffer, Peter, 196*, 270
Shakespeare, William
  and acting, 154, 176–77, 181, 185,
    194
  and audiences, 8, 209–10, 250,
    305, 309, 323*, 328, 337

and comedy, 117, 119, 123–24
and costume, 273, 274, 279, 280
Globe Theatre, 221, 267, 296
language of, 79, 194, 202–4,
  209–10, 273, 279, 296
and playwriting, 61–62, 66–67,
  76, 192, **197,** 223, 272, 296–97
and tragedy, 91, 92, 98, 110,
  111
typical performance described,
  5–6
As You Like It, 16
Hamlet, 6, 8, 24, 67, 92, 111,
  151–53, 176, 181, 183, 223, 274
Julius Caesar, 27, 177
King Lear, **82,** 98, 139, 288
Macbeth, **19, 93,** 111, 139, 203,
  250, **281**
Merchant of Venice, The, 328
Midsummer Night's Dream, A,
  120, 250, 251
Othello, 61–62, **62,** 64, 111, 150,
  153, 202, 204
Richard III, **64,** 64
Romeo and Juliet, 194
Taming of the Shrew, The, 117
Tempest, The, **135**
Twelfth Night, 123–24, 288
Shamanism, 36, 158
Shamanism, and acting, 158–161,
  160, 281
Shange, Ntozake, **269**
Shaw, George Bernard, 118, **206,**
  223, 309, 311, 334–35
Shelley, Percy Bysshe, **229**
Sheridan, Richard Brinsley, **122,**
  199
Showboat, 314
Shylock, 328, 332
Simon, Neil, 7, 52, 76, 90, 117
Simonson, Lee, 283–84
*Six Characters in Search of an
  Author*, 64, 282
Slade, Bernard, 332
Sleep of Prisoners, A, 267
Smith, Maggie, **132**
Smolover, Maura, **282**
Socrates, 116
Soliloquy, 26, 67, 68
"Some Thoughts on
  Playwrighting," 25*
"Some Unconscious Influences in
  the Theatre," 308*
Sondheim, Stephen, 315
Sontag, Susan, 255*
*Sophia = (Wisdom), Part 3: The
  Cliffs*, **318**

Sophocles, 7, 8, 17, **59,** 59–60, 92,
  99–103, **100, 192,** 235, 309, 315
Sound effects, 288–89, *see also*
  Musical theatre
South Pacific, 314
Space, Time and Architecture,
  298*
Spain, seventeenth-century, 191
Spitz, René, 43*
Stage Is Set, The, 284
Stages, *see* Playing spaces
Stage settings, 58–59, 80, 260–267
Stanislavski, Konstantin, 143, 161,
  168, 173–74, 194, 208, 218, 223,
  272–73
*Stanislavsky on the Art of the
  Stage*, 67*
Stephens, Robert, **135**
Stevenson, Robert Louis, 104*
Storey, David, **232,** 332
Strange Interlude, 117
Strasberg, Lee, 174, 177
Stravinsky, Igor, **271**
Streetcar Named Desire, A, **60,** 61,
  78, 177, 255*
Street theatre, 8, **294**
Strehler, Giorgio, **82, 130**
Strindberg, August, 57–58, **57,** 117,
  140, 193, **203,** 209, 223, 233,
  235, 309, 316, 328
Styles of twentieth-century theatre,
  (photo essay) **224–32**
Surrealism, **228**
Svoboda, Josef, **59, 100, 286–87**
Sweden, nineteenth-century, *see*
  Strindberg, August
Sweeney Agonistes, 211*
Symbolism, **225,** 316
Symposium, 116
Synge, John Millington, 110,
  113–15, **114,** 117, 123, **207**

Tairov, Alexander, 218, **229**
Tale of Mystery, The, 106
Taming of the Shrew, The, 117
Tandy, Jessica, **60**
Tartuffe, 117
Tea and Sympathy, 324–25
Teatro Campesino, 8
Television, 15, 28–30, 113, 210
Tempest, The, **135**
Terence, **194**
Theatre and Its Double, The, 206
Théâtre du Vieux Colombier, 174
*Theatre in Society: Society in the
  Theatre, The*, 261*